New Brighton

New Brighton

A Complete Record
of the Rakers in
the Football League

GARTH DYKES

BREEDON
BOOKS
SPORT

First published in Great Britain by
The Breedon Books Publishing Company Limited
44 Friar Gate, Derby DE1 1DA
1990

ISBN 0 907969 65 8

Printed by Butler and Tanner Limited, Frome, Somerset.
Jacket designed by Graham Hales and printed by Arkle Print Ltd,
Northampton.

Contents

Acknowledgements

IT is a great pleasure to thank my many footballing friends who have given readily from their experience to help in the compilation of this book, but my largest debt of gratitude is to Ann for her help and encouragement and for managing to ignore the fact that two rooms seem permanently knee-deep in football-related material.

Sadly, one whose contribution was immeasurable did not live to see the finished work. I refer to my late friend, Alex Wilson, whose encyclopaedic knowledge of football's history has enriched this book.

I would particularly like to thank Michael Braham, Jim Creasy, Douglas Lamming, Peter Windle and Ian Garland for their invaluable assistance during the two years which I have spent on this project.

From the Wallasey district, Michael Swaffield has been generous in his help and interest, befitting his role as player-manager of New Brighton Rakers, a five-a-side Manchester University-based soccer team, who keep alive the name of the 11-a-side originals. Also from the Wirral district I owe a debt of gratitude to Paul Gee and to former players Harry Gee, Ted Redfern and Beau Ratcliffe, who kindly loaned treasured photographs and related material.

My gratitude also to the staffs of the Football League offices at Lytham St Annes and the British Newspaper Library at Colindale. Many correspondents and friends from the Association of Football Statisticians have supplied valuable details. In alphabetical order they are: Tommy Barnes, Bill Donnachie, Brian J.Hobbs, David A.Howgate, Mike Jay, Wade Martin, Tony Matthews, Dr Steven Phillips, Dr John Rowlands, Roy Shoesmith, Mike Simpson, Ray Spiller and Roger J.Triggs.

Finally, my thanks to Michael Bennett for his excellent photographic work.

Note: The Publishers and Author are grateful to Dave Twydell for use of material on New Brighton Tower FC and the New Brighton grounds. This originally appeared in his book *Rejected FC*. Volumes 1 and 2 of this book contain details of many former League clubs and more information may be obtained from the author at 12 The Furrows, Harefield, Middlesex.

Photographic Credits

Photographs have been supplied by Colorsport, Illustrated News Picture Library, Liverpool Daily Post & Echo and from private collections.

TO MY MOTHER,
whose love of sport I inherited.

Foreword

AS a schoolboy in the North-West in the immediate post-war years, my lifelong love of the Association game was forged in the relatively modest theatre of the Third Division, Northern Section.

It is 40 years since New Brighton embarked on what was to be their final Football League campaign but, in memory's flickering picture-show, my clearest impressions are of a stalwart defensive trio comprising Corbett, Topping and Richardson. Don Carter's midfield machinations also remain an indelible memory.

Given my early esteem for the Rakers, it is indeed a privilege to be afforded the opportunity to record their history in a more permanent form than the ephemeral pages of Saturday evening *Sport Finals* and the like.

Tracing the history of the club has been a fascinating task and amongst the 279 players who have qualified for inclusion in the 'Who's Who' section, one has been aware of the number of fine centre-forwards who have worn the Rakers' colours. Jimmy Dunne and Dennis Westcott spring immediately to mind, both launched into League football by New Brighton. Other outstanding forwards include 'Joe' Wilcox, Horace Williams, Leo Stevens and Jack Stamps. The fact that such talent departed New Brighton to 'balance the books' must be the main reason for the club's lack of success and eventual demise.

The Rakers have provided a fair share of occupational hazards for the researcher, not least in the number of players — not always related — with identical surnames playing at the same time. Some relief was felt, however, when season 1935-6 was tackled. Noting that players registered for this season included Hoggan and Hogg and Torrance and Lawrence, I was happy to learn that only Hoggan and Lawrence appeared in the first team. The possibilites for error in the hurriedly 'phoned-in match reports, if all four had been playing, did not bear thinking about.

Garth Dykes
Leicester
June 1990

Notes on the text

Scope: The qualification for inclusion in the 'Who's Who' section is an appearance in a peacetime Football League match, but not including the unfinished 1939-40 season. The seasons covered therefore are: 1923-4 to 1938-9 and 1946-7 to 1950-51.

Abbreviations: cs — close season; FA — Football Association; FL — Football League.

Debuts: The debut date relates to a player's first appearance in a Football League match for New Brighton.

Physiques: The heights and weights recorded are figures obtained from the period when the player was on New Brighton's books.

Transfer Fees: Many of the fees quoted are from contemporary Press reports. Clubs have traditionally been reluctant to disclose transfer fees, but the figures quoted are thought to be reasonably accurate.

Honours: Basically covers international caps and representative (ie inter-League) appearances. Club honours include League championships and domestic Cup Final appearances.

The New Brighton Story

N EW Brighton Association Football & Athletic Club came into being some two months after a meeting held at Egerton Street School on Tuesday evening, 28 June 1921, when it was agreed that the new club should take over the interests and fixture list of South Liverpool AFC.

In a matter of six weeks, a new ground had been fashioned from a rough, unturfed, forested slope. On that site was created a stadium to accommodate 10,000 spectators, with a grandstand to seat 1,000. Before the prospectus for the new limited company had been issued, the new team had played their first-ever fixture, away at Hurst, and won by 3-1. It was a remarkable achievement and fully reflected the enthusiasm for a professional club in the borough.

Dr Tom Martlew, chairman of the committee, had earlier explained to the packed meeting at Egerton Street School that the idea of a professional club in Wallasey had first arisen some 18 months earlier, when the South Liverpool club were seeking a ground on the New Brighton side of the Mersey. The project had been in abeyance, since no suitable ground had been found, but the matter had gained momentum and the meeting sought £10,000 to float the new company, which would enable the club to get into first-class football almost immediately. It was proposed that the South Liverpool club be taken over, renamed New Brighton, and that the new club would take over South Liverpool's fixture list in the Lancashire Combination for season 1921-2.

The meeting heard that much preliminary work had already been put into the question of housing the new club. The Tower Athletic Ground was the first one considered, but this had already been let to Harrowby FC. Any question of ground-sharing had been frowned upon by the amateurs, who appeared less than enthusiastic at the thought of a professional club operating in the vicinity. A week or so later, the Tower Company suggested that it might be possible for Harrowby to be compensated and the ground purchased for a sum of £50,000. That had 'put the lid' on that idea. A three-acre site at Oakside Farm, where football had been played, was offered for £10,000, but the committee thought it was over-priced.

The Rake Lane site was considered the best. It enjoyed a central position and, although in need of much work, was large enough for the purpose and capable of improvement. Estimates had been obtained for the levelling of the ground and making it fit for play by September.

On the question of a team, Mr Bob Alty, chairman of the South Liverpool club and soon to become manager of New Brighton FC, assured the meeting that applications had been received from a dozen first-class players and, to applause from the meeting, he promised that they 'would not spoil the ship for a ha'porth of tar'.

A long discussion took place regarding the name to be given to the new club, many feeling that Wallasey should form part of the title. All the discussions were in the event pointless, as the committee, who had been involved in negotiations in advance of the meeting, had committed themselves to the name 'New Brighton'. A Mr Kingham suggested that the demand for a club was so great that it would pay even if it was called the 'Salmon Tin Dribblers'.

Mr W.Hardy moved that the New Brighton Association Football and Athletic Club be formed. Mr H.Smith seconded it and the resolution was carried unanimously, and with some applause. The Rakers, as they were soon to be known, had embarked on their great adventure.

The *Wallasey & Wirral Chronicle* for Saturday, 27 August 1921, announced the teams selected to represent New Brighton in their opening fixtures. For the record, these were:

First team (v Hurst at Hurst): Carpenter; Shepherd, Finney, Jagger, Hulme, Paterson, Pickup, Beattie, Lyon, McQuarrie, Millward.

Second team (v Garston Gasworks at Garston): Carrell; Littleton, Glover, Humphries, Kelly, White, Waine, O'Neill, Newman, Ashcroft, Boycott.

The club's colours were to be blue and white hooped jerseys. Admission charges were fixed at one shilling (5p) and two shillings (10p) and the club's first board of directors comprised Dr Tom Martlew (chairman), Mr T.I.Overington (vice-chairman), Dr Robert Martlew, Messrs F.Crawford, P.R.Collins, J.Finerty, Earl Goodwin, A.Kingham, W.Ridge, T.Sampson, A.Stockdale, H.Smith, J.Storey and C.Thorburn.

After their encouraging opening at Hurst, New Brighton suffered their first defeat on Atherton's quaintly-named Flapper Fold enclosure. Atherton's outside-right, Peter Cowper, joined New Brighton seven years later and was club leading goalscorer in his first season.

Wallaseyans had their first look at their new team, and the rapidly transformed Sandheys Park, on 10 September 1921. Whiston Parish were the visitors in an extra-preliminary round of the FA Cup competition. With both Harrowby and Poulton Rovers playing away, the Wallasey sporting public had something of a 'fete day', all roads seeming to lead to Rake Lane. It proved, however, to be the day of the underdog. The little colliery village team, in the same league as New Brighton Reserves, spoilt the celebrations by winning 5-3. Starring in the visitors' team were the brothers Alan and John Leadbetter, both of whom were later to join New Brighton.

To commemorate the first home match, a Saturday evening dinner had been arranged at the Marine Hotel. Despite the club's defeat, there was an optimistic atmosphere prevailing, although team manager Bob Alty was reported to be 'looking glum'.

One down at half-time and facing a stiff breeze, New Brighton appeared to be in trouble at Rochdale, but second-half goals by Beattie and Jack Lyon brought a deserved away victory. It proved to be the start of a run of seven consecutive wins.

Jack Lyon netted the first hat-trick by a New Brighton player, in their first home league match, against Rochdale Reserves, who they beat 5-2. George Bryson, having earlier knocked himself out against the Rochdale upright, recovered to score twice. Gene Carney, later to have three spells with New Brighton, scored one of Rochdale's goals.

A 3-1 win at Morecambe marked the debut of Peck, the former Glentoran and Irish Amateur international goalkeeper. When Hurst were well beaten by 5-0 at Sandheys on 5 November, New Brighton sat proudly at the head of the Lancashire Combination.

After Lyon's third hat-trick of the season had earned a 3-2 win at Dick Kerr's, Stockport County Reserves proved too good for New Brighton, inflicting their first home league defeat by 3-1.

December proved unrewarding, with only one point and no goals from three Combination matches, but excellent progress was made in the Lancashire Junior Cup. Yet another Lyon hat-trick accounted for Bacup Borough, and a fine 2-0 victory over Lancaster Town sent the 7,000 crowd home to celebrate the New Year and their team's entry into the Lancashire Junior Cup Final.

The team hit a rich vein of form in January, four league wins resulting with a goal-average of 14-2. Alan Leadbetter, formerly of Whiston Parish, made a scoring debut at Leyland on 7 January.

The highest point of the season came on 4 February. The Lancashire Junior Cup Final at Preston's Deepdale was contested in atrocious conditions, snow falling throughout the game in ever-increasing quantities. Despite the conditions, the crowd of 14,000 saw a fine match, although it ended goalless. The replay was fixed for Burden Park, Bolton, on 11 March.

In what was proving to be an eventful first season for New Brighton, another highlight came on 18 February when table-topping Lancaster Town, undefeated at home since New Year's Day 1921, were beaten by the only goal of the game on their own ground. This result put New Brighton into third place, one point behind Lancaster Town and Chorley, with a game in hand. Even the Reserves, occupying bottom place in the Liverpool County Combination, managed to beat Sutton Commercial by 5-1 at Sandheys that day.

A 1-0 defeat at Bacup was followed by such a hostile reception after the match that New Brighton protested to the Lancashire FA. Stones and wood were thrown at the New Brighton players, all the way from the ground to the railway station.

The following Saturday proved to be far more rewarding. New Brighton's captain, Billy Hulme, received the Lancashire Junior Cup before being carried shoulder-high off Burden Park amid cheers of the wildest enthusiasm.

The team came down to earth with a bump one week later, when Fleetwood ran up five goals without reply. It was the heaviest defeat so far for New Brighton. With a stiff Easter programme looming, every point was becoming vital. The team rose magnificently to the challenge by taking nine points from the five matches preceding the Easter fixtures. New inside-forward signing Wright from Huddersfield Town proved a fine short-term capture, scoring seven goals in his first four matches.

A break from the exacting League programme came in the shape of the Liverpool Senior Cup semi-final against Tranmere Rovers on Wednesday 5 April. A crowd of over 7,000 at Sandheys saw New Brighton lead twice on a muddy, waterlogged surface, only to lose 4-2.

Over Easter, Combination games saw Darwen win 3-2 at Sandheys on Good Friday, New Brighton gaining their revenge at Darwen on the following day by winning 2-1. A superb defensive display by Lancaster Town enabled them to take both points from the Monday encounter at Sandheys and, with the victory, Lancaster virtually assured themselves of the championship.

The final league match of the season was won with nine men against Rossendale United. Jack Reid was carried off and Jack Lyon sent off, a sad end to the centre-forward's otherwise successful season which had seen him score 40 goals in all matches. Third position in the Lancashire Combination table was an excellent performance in New Brighton's initial season, which ended with the following record:

Played 34 Won 22 Drawn 3 Lost 9 Goals For 72 Against 38 Points 47.

This eventful first season was wound-up at the Tower Grounds in the semi-final of the Victoria Hospital Cup, against Harrowby. A crowd of over 9,000 saw the Pinks unexpectedly topple their professional neighbours in an ill-tempered encounter by 1-0.

The 1922-3 season dawned amidst a welter of ground improvements and the usual optimism associated with new football seasons everywhere. Notable additions to the playing strength included Kenny Campbell, the Scottish international goalkeeper from Partick Thistle; Billy Crooks, an Irish international inside-forward from Manchester United; Eugene Carney, an outside-left from Rochdale; and Jimmy Jones, an experienced full-back from Bolton Wanderers. The most notable departure was that of Alec Finney to Bolton Wanderers. On the administration side, Mr Bert

11

Two new faces joined New Brighton for the 1922-3 season. Bert Pelham (left), was appointed secretary whilst Scottish international goalkeeper Kenny Campbell (right) was transferred from Partick Thistle.

Pelham, a well-known member of the Liverpool County Football Association and local secretary, was appointed club secretary.

There was a large crowd of Wallaseyans present at Fleetwood on the opening Saturday of the season. Fleetwood had drubbed the Rakers 5-0 the previous season, but this time New Brighton came out with flying colours by winning 2-0.

Jack Lyon began his season, after suspension, against Atherton on 9 September. He scored twice in a 6-0 win, which put the Rakers on top of the table after four matches. A visit to Leyland brought the season's first defeat by 1-0 as Rakers' inside-left Dai Williams was sent off and later suspended for four weeks.

New Brighton then successfully overcame the first preliminary hurdle of the FA Cup at the expense of Chester, who were beaten 4-2 in front of 7,000 spectators.

The two leaders of the Combination, New Brighton and Darwen, met at Darwen and shared the points in a 1-1 draw, Jack Reid becoming the second New Brighton player to be sent off this season, for arguing with the referee.

In a scrappy game, New Brighton lived to fight another round of the FA Cup by beating Northwich Victoria by the only goal of the game at Northwich. Back in the League a goalless draw at Chorley attracted record gate receipts, over £117 being taken.

Special excursion trains ran from Liverpool Lime Street to Witton, fare five shillings (25p), for the second qualifying round of the FA Cup. Albert Leadbetter, who returned after injury, scored both New Brighton goals in a 2-1 win. On the same Saturday, George Bryson completed his third hat-trick in succession for the Rakers' Reserves, who enjoyed an unbeaten record so far.

After beating Horwich RMI, 3-2 at Rake Lane in a Combination fixture, the Rakers resumed their FA Cup campaign by beating Sandbach Ramblers 5-0. New Brighton were first out of the hat for the next round — and this time they drew League opposition — Crewe Alexandra, at home. Rakers warmed up with a 7-1 win over Prescot in the Lancashire Junior Cup, and then came the big match.

Eight thousand spectators packed into Sandheys Park and saw a fine Cup tie. Crewe scored first and, despite some fine goalkeeping by Scott, Billy Crooks scored the equalizer after intense pressure on the Crewe goal. There was no further addition to the score, and the replay was set for the following Wednesday. A goal by Pickup was sufficient to see the Rakers home, but they were indebted to Kenny Campbell, who was unbeatable in goal.

League fare was becoming something of an anticlimax after the excitement of the Cup, but two late goals accounted for Eccles United at Sandheys.

12

The surprise of the next round of the FA Cup was the Rakers' 3-0 victory against Second Division Coventry City. When Jack Lyon scored the first goal of his hat-trick, the cheering was heard all over Wallasey. It was also said that a local man at Birkenhead Park Station heard it — and threw his hat into the air.

Isthmian League side, Clapton, were the next hurdle and the amateurs were not expected to be an easy touch. Traditional Cup fighters, they numbered the FA Amateur Cup and the London Cup amongst their achievements.

In a rush of Cup-tie enthusiasm, a Rakers' supporter penned the following, which appeared in the local *Chronicle*:

> *"There's a goalie in (New) Brighton named Campbell,*
> *Most difficult shots he can handle,*
> *He fists them out from near and far,*
> *Round the posts and over the bar.*
> *And at every possible angle."*

The sixth-qualifying round kicked-off ten minutes early in bad light, which gradually worsened until about 25 minutes from time when the fog lifted. It was a poor game and the Rakers only managed to score after Mason, the Clapton goalkeeper, had been injured. His deputy, Bryant, fumbled a Dai Williams shot after 51 minutes, giving New Brighton victory by the only goal of the game.

Rakers' followers could not have wished for a better Christmas present than to see their team in the hat alongside all the star teams of football. For a minor club, and one so young, it was considered a great honour to have reached the first-round proper. The draw paired them with The Wednesday (the 'Sheffield' tag had still not been officially adopted), seventh club in the Second Division. The game was to be played at Hillsborough on 13 January 1923.

All the Cup activity had left the Rakers with League matches in hand and they proceeded to enjoy the Christmas programme. Three home games were won, 13 goals being scored without reply. On New Year's Day 1923, Hurst were beaten 2-0 and the Rakers moved to the head of the Combination table.

It was estimated that 2,000 New Brighton supporters journeyed to Hillsborough for the first-round proper of the FA Cup. On a heavy ground, The Wednesday swung the ball about to great advantage and the 36,000 spectators witnessed a rousing struggle. Only one goal in arrears right up to the last quarter of an hour, the Rakers finally went down 3-0. Some consolation for the New Brighton directorate was their share of the 'gate' of £2,470. This game proved to be Jack Pickup's last in the Rakers' colours, as he left to take up a coaching post in Central Europe, a week after the Cup tie.

On a ground said to resemble 'a derelict marsh', New Brighton went down 3-1 at Rossendale United. Back at home, Jack Lyon scored all four goals in the 4-0 win against Morecambe and then a long-overdue away victory (only the second of the season) came at Hurst, watched by a record crowd for the Hurst Cross enclosure.

News reached Wallasey that Jack Lyon's brother, Jimmy, a Derby County stalwart, had played a big part in the downfall of The Wednesday in the second round of the FA Cup — brotherly love, indeed, gaining revenge for the Rakers.

On the wettest Saturday of the season, the Rakers were beaten 2-0 at New Cross on 3 March, but the Reserves beat Rainford 14-0, seven New Brighton players getting on the score-sheet. On 10 March, a 6-1 win against Rochdale Reserves gave the Rakers their tenth consecutive home win, but there were problems in store. On the following Wednesday it was announced that the Rakers' skipper, Scottish international goalkeeper Kenny Campbell, was to be transferred to Stoke. Very shortly afterwards it was revealed that manager Bob Alty had resigned, following differences with the club's directors.

Meanwhile, members of the Football League Management Committee met the Northern Section clubs in Leeds. The clubs requested that the section be increased to 22 clubs. The Management Committee agreed that, if two suitable clubs could be found, they would propose the increase at the annual meeting of the League. New Brighton's directors took little time to decide that they would make an early application to fill one of those two vacancies.

At the onset of Easter, Combination leaders Chorley took both points and also ended New Brighton's undefeated home record, by the only goal of the match. Hulme, the former Rakers' captain, and Peter Kelly, who was later to assist New Brighton, were outstanding for the visitors. Further set-backs over Easter effectively ended the Rakers' chances of winning the Combination championship. Then more home defeats, by Fleetwood and Lancaster Town, left supporters to reflect on how the loss of Kenny Campbell and team manager Bob Alty, had demoralized the side.

Meanwhile, the Rakers' Reserves put the first silverware on to the sideboard by winning the Liverpool County Challenge Cup, 2-1 against North Liverpool at Anfield on Easter Monday morning. In the afternoon, the trophy was paraded around Sandheys Park before the kick-off in the Lancaster Town fixture.

The Rakers at last recaptured their form in beating Dick Kerr's 5-1 and Chorley 4-1 in the semi-final of the Lancashire Combination Cup. Heroics by Voas in the Rakers' goal, which included the saving of a penalty-kick, could not prevent defeat by Atherton, who won 2-1, but two wins redressed the balance. The 4-1 victory against Darwen was notable for the gallant display by Darwen goalkeeper Robinson, a famous Blackburn Rovers player of old.

A Monday visit to Bacup was marked by similar events as the previous season, when a huge lump of wood, amongst other missiles, was hurled at the New Brighton team. This time a penalty award to New Brighton resulted in a pitch invasion and the referee receiving a nasty gash on his leg. Later, Max Reid was sent off, in company with Hall of Bacup. The Bacup chairman, a local minister, later stated that Reid's dismissal was one of the gravest injustices he had ever seen. The Rakers departed with the points from a 2-0 victory and their now customary police escort to the railway station.

A fortnight later, a Commission ruled that Bacup's ground should be closed for the first four weeks of 1923-4. Max Reid was suspended for 14 days and fined £1, whilst Hall, the Bacup player, was suspended to the end of the season and for 14 days the following season, as well as being fined £1.

By defeating Everton 'A' by 3-0 at Sandheys Park, the Rakers' Reserves made certain of winning the Liverpool County Combination title. Unfortunately, the seniors, who could only draw at Lancaster Town, were now virtually out of the race for the Combination championship.

On 23 April, over 9,000 spectators paid almost £500 at the gate when the Rakers drew 2-2 against Tranmere Rovers in the semi-final of the Liverpool Senior Cup. The replay at Prenton, three days later, saw Tranmere the winners by 2-0 before a crowd in the region of 10,000 spectators.

The League programme wound up with a visit from Bacup Borough, the Rakers winning 3-2 in what was, thankfully, a sporting contest. To end the season, only a comparatively weak side was sent to the Giant Axe ground, Lancaster, to contest the Lancashire Combination Cup Final. A penalty converted by Jimmy Niven after 25 minutes of the second half proved to be the only goal of the game, thus ending the season on a high note.

At the annual meeting of the Football League, held on Monday 28 May 1923, the voting for the election of four clubs to the Northern Section resulted: New Brighton 45, Doncaster Rovers 45, Ashington 45, Durham City 45, Wallasey United 0, Nuneaton Town 0.

The Rakers were in and many congratulations came the way of the Sandheys Park management on bringing League football to Wallasey after a period of over

20 years. The only sour note was the domestic squabble which had arisen between the newly-formed Wallasey United and New Brighton AFC. Wallasey United, in the charge of Bob Alty, the former Rakers' manager, had applied for associate membership of the League, with little hope of success. There was obviously no room for two League clubs in New Brighton and their application could, at best, only detract a few votes from New Brighton. In the event, Wallasey United proved to be short lived. They resigned from the Cheshire County League after only one season, vacating the Tower Grounds, which were taken over by the famous amateur team, Northern Nomads.

In early June, the Rakers announced their retained list which comprised: Backs: Niven, Jones, Critchlow and Glover. Halves: Max Reid and Jack Reid. Forwards: Crooks, Edge, Lyon, Goodacre, Gemmell and Bryson.

Amongst the new recruits were Peter Quinn, an FA Cup Finalist with Preston North End in 1920; Billy Kirsopp the former Everton inside-forward; Allan Mathieson the Irish international inside-forward from Exeter City; Harry Gee from Burnley, Sam Challinor from Accrington Stanley and goalkeeper Bert Mehaffy, the Irish international from Belfast Celtic. Of the players who departed Rake Lane in the close season, Brophy signed for Aberdare, Gene Carney for Reading, Graham for Ashton, Gault for Mold, Dai Williams signed for Morecambe and Stanley Royle, the amateur winger, transferred locally to Wallasey United.

Gross proceeds from the pre-season trial matches at Sandheys amounted to £127 4s, all of which was donated to various charities and good causes. An item of £5 was paid to Hartlepools United AFC Air Raid Appeal. This was towards the rebuilding of the Hartlepools grandstand which was wrecked by air raids during World War One.

New Brighton FC in 1923-4, the Rakers' first season in the Football League. Back row (left to right, players only): Jones, M.Reid, J.W.Mehaffy, Glover, Gee. Front row: J.Reid, Whitter, Crooks, Lyon, Mathieson, Burton.

15

New Brighton opened their League programme at Park Avenue, Bradford, with the following team:
Mehaffy; Niven, Jones (captain), Max Reid, Jack Reid, Challinor, Edge, Crooks, Lyon, Thompson, Quinn.
A goal down within 60 seconds, the Rakers rallied magnificently to draw 1-1. They actually put the ball past Scattergood, the Bradford goalkeeper, twice, but Harry Thompson's effort was disallowed.

The first home match in the Third Division was a Wednesday evening game against Chesterfield which ended goalless. It proved to be the first of many matches in which the Rakers' forwards failed to find the net, 18 of their 42 League matches ending without a goal.

An early season injury to full-back Jimmy Niven proved more serious than had first been thought, but Ted Glover proved an excellent deputy, Everton signing him at the close of the season.

In September a new trainer 'Sandy' Watson, the former Clyde and Bradford full-back, joined the Sandheys staff. He enjoyed a distinguished playing career and had 11 years experience with the Park Avenue club, which had included training duties in recent years.

After a month's League football the Rakers, with seven points from eight matches and a goal-average of 6-6, stood in 12th place. Other League newcomers, Doncaster Rovers, were having a hard struggle and occupied bottom place.

Max Reid became the season's first sending-off in an ill-tempered Lancashire Senior Cup replay against Southport. He was suspended for one month from 10 October.

The high spot of the season came in the October meetings against Tranmere Rovers, League leaders and local rivals. The sides had met on various occasions in Cup matches, but the first Football League meetings were to provide the Rakers' first win against the Rovers. A goalless draw at Sandheys attracted an attendance of over 13,000 and, one week later, 15,500 packed into Prenton Park when Jack

Another New Brighton staff line-up for 1923-4. Back row (left to right): J.Jones, Wilson, Spencer, Voas, Mehaffy, Niven, Glover, Critchlow, Kirsopp. Middle row: Newman (trainer), M.Reid, J.Reid, Challinor, Gee, Thompson. Front row: Burton, Jordan, Crooks, Bryson, Lyon, Mathieson, Quinn, Edge.

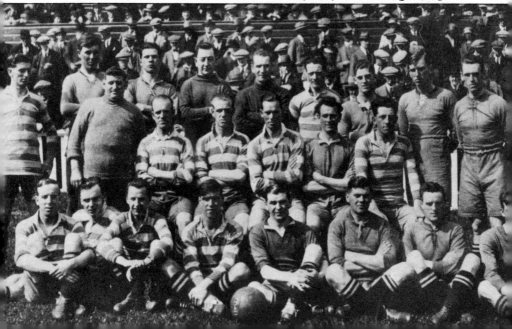

Lyon's first goal of the season proved to be the winner in a rousing encounter which ended 2-1 in New Brighton's favour.

The following six matches yielded only two goals, one of which was a wind-assisted 50-yarder by full-back Jimmy Jones at Hartlepools. In the FA Cup, after drawing 1-1 at Southport, the Rakers went down by the only goal at Sandheys, Jack Lyon putting a penalty-kick straight into the hands of Halsall, the Southport goalkeeper.

The heaviest defeat of the season to date came at League leaders, Wolverhampton Wanderers, on 24 November, when a seriously depleted New Brighton team were outclassed in a 5-1 defeat. It proved a bad day for Merseyside all round, with an almost unique record of losses. Liverpool, Everton, New Brighton and Tranmere Rovers were all defeated — as were Harrowby, Thorndale and New Brighton Baptists in the local amateur leagues.

The Rakers' first visit to Ashington saw them beaten 5-0 in a game played in slush and snow. Seventeen-year-old 'Duke' Hamilton, a local Wallasey boy, made his Football League debut for the Rakers. Later in his career, Hamilton won championship medals with both Chesterfield and Tranmere Rovers.

One week later the Rakers' forward line, so often 'slated' for its lack of punch, surprised everyone. Wigan Borough were beaten 5-1, every New Brighton forward getting on the score-sheet. The same team failed to reproduce their form on New Year's Day at Southport, however, losing 3-0. After 23 matches, New Brighton stood in seventh place in the table with a goal-difference of 21-23.

John Mehaffy, younger brother of Bert, made his debut at Walsall. Twice an Irish League representative, he was a fine goalkeeper but he found few opportunities at Rake Lane, due to his elder brother's consistency.

New Brighton Reserves 1923-4. Back row (left to right): Critchlow, Gee, J.Mehaffy, Gutteridge, Spencer, Leadbetter. Front row: Whitter, Mathieson, Wade, Jones, Burton.

January proved an unrewarding month for New Brighton, with five consecutive defeats, and February's only victory came thanks to two goals by new signing 'Panty' Howard, the former Manchester City centre-forward. At League leaders Rochdale, Bert Mehaffy was badly injured, a kick beneath the eye and a dislocated finger causing his retirement from the match. Five of Rochdale's six goals came after Howard had taken his place in goal. The season's second 5-0 victory over lowly-placed Barrow provided New Brighton's only hat-trick of the campaign. It was scored by Jack Lyon, but it provided more than half of the centre-forward's modest 'bag' of five goals for the season.

Three away defeats over Easter left the Rakers in 18th position and this was their placing when the season closed. With ten points in hand of the bottom two teams, there was never any serious threat of having to apply for re-election, but it was a disappointing placing after the team's good start. The Rakers' Reserves ended on a bright note by winning the championship of the Liverpool County Combination for the second season in succession. They also won the Cheshire Senior Cup, after a replay, against Tranmere Rovers.

Quite a number of the previous season's players were released prior to the start of 1924-5 but the defence, with the exception of Ted Glover and Sam Challinor, remained intact. Popular full-back Jimmy Niven had recovered from the cartilage trouble which sidelined him for practically the whole of 1923-4. Bob Walker, a new full-back from Bradford, and Legh Collins, a half-back from Nelson, were expected to provide stiff competition for places. It was the forward line that was expected to cause the most problems. Edge, Lyon, Quinn, Kirsopp, Thompson and Howard had all departed. To take their places, new recruits included Bill Lacey, the Irish international from Liverpool, 'Gene Carney, returning after a season with Reading, Jonah Wilcox, a centre-forward from Bradford, Peter Kelly, an inside-forward from Chorley, and Harry Hird, an experienced inside-forward whose previous clubs included Bury and Blackpool.

As in the previous season, Bradford were the first League opponents. On a bright and sunny afternoon, more suitable for cricket than football, a splendid attendance of 9,000 had to be content with a goalless draw. Injuries to Jimmy Jones and Jack Reid saw the Rakers reduced to nine men in the second half. Making their initial appearance in the new Midland Combination at Hull City, Rakers' Reserves gained an encouraging success in a high-scoring match, gaining the points in a 4-3 win.

After three games and only one goal scored, team changes saw Allan Mathieson introduced in place of Hird, whilst Harry Gee took over from Collins in the half-back line. The changes brought an immediate improvement and the season's first victory, 3-1 against Rotherham County. Three days later, in a display of brilliant marksmanship, Rochdale were beaten 5-0. Joe Wilcox, who had started the season quietly, gave his best display to date in recording a hat-trick. From late September, an excellent run of results brought consecutive home victories of 4-0, 4-1, 3-2 and 5-0. In away matches, one win and two draws put the Rakers into second place in the table.

In October, Bill Lacey was selected to play for Ireland against England at Goodison Park. Alas, he sustained a knee injury in the match and did not appear again for the Rakers, who were later compensated by the Irish FA. Commenting on Lacey's selection, the *Wallasey & Wirral Chronicle* recalled that the last New Brighton player to be capped for his country was goalkeeper J.W.Robinson, who played against Ireland, Scotland and Wales, whilst on New Brighton Tower's books.

Whilst the Rakers were surmounting the first hurdle of the FA Cup, against Stalybridge Celtic at Sandheys on 15 November, all the football headlines concerned

Opposite: New Brighton players in training, August 1924. From left: Peter Kelly, Joe Wilcox (partly hidden), Max Reid, Bert Mehaffy and Harry Gee.

19

Sam Chedgzoy's unique corner-kick for Everton against Arsenal at Goodison. Chedgzoy startled the football world by dribbling the ball several yards from the corner-flag before shooting at goal. It was a unique move which caused the FA to amend the rules governing the taking of corner-kicks. Chedgzoy's son, Sidney, played for the Rakers, without getting into the first team, three seasons later.

In the fifth qualifying round of the FA Cup, a goalless home draw against Accrington Stanley proved a sad disappointment and in the replay Accrington won 3-2.

The best away performance of the season came on New Year's Day, when neighbours Tranmere Rovers were beaten 3-1. In heavy conditions the Rakers got off to a flying start with a Wilcox penalty in the first minute. Tranmere's only goal was a Dixie Dean shot which deflected off Jack Reid and into the net. At the mid-point of the season, the Rakers occupied third place in the table, level on points with Southport, and six points behind the leaders, Darlington.

In mid-March Joe Wilcox scored hat-tricks in successive home matches, bringing his total for the season to 30. But the team's proud home record was finally upset by Doncaster Rovers, a shaky defensive display resulting in a 2-0 defeat. The absence of Jack Reid — recently hospitalized — was proving a difficult problem for the selectors, McCrae, Collins, Spencer and Gutteridge all having deputized for the senior pivot. It was not until the signing of Peter Gaffney that the situation was resolved, as the newcomer marshalled the defence in a good run-in to the season.

League champions Darlington were the final opponents of the season and only fine goalkeeping by the Darlington custodian, Crumley, kept the score down to a single goal by Joe Wilcox. This win put the Rakers level on points with second-placed Nelson, but with an inferior goal-average. The top five teams in the table,

New Brighton, 1924-5. Back row (left to right, players only): M.Reid, Niven, Mehaffy, Jones, Gee. Front row: Whitter, Mathieson, Wilcox, Kelly, Carney, J.Reid.

20

viewed today, constitutes a register of ex-League clubs: Darlington, Nelson, New Brighton, Southport and Bradford.

An end-of-season meeting of the New Brighton Supporters' Club revealed that over £1,000 had been raised for the club. It was a wonderful effort, but the Rakers were labouring with an overdraft of over £10,000 and a shortage of working capital to pay summer wages. This after what had been the club's most successful season. It was a problem which was to hinder the club throughout its history.

As the players reported for duty on 11 August they saw the results of a busy close season, in the new banking carried out at the river end of the ground, which had increased the holding capacity by a further 2,000 spectators.

Thirteen of the players retained were those mainly responsible for the previous season's success, whilst those who departed included Wilcox, Niven, Lacey, Carney, Walker, Spencer and Collins. The greatest loss was Wilcox, who had scored 35 goals in 1924-5. The centre-forward's move to Bristol Rovers was as much for domestic, as any other reasons. His replacement was Stan Sayer from Tranmere Rovers, an experienced, ball-playing centre-forward. The new leader caused a flutter by scoring six goals in the final public trial. The 'Whites' beat the 'Stripes' 10-1, as some defenders tried in vain to come to grips with the new offside law which had come into force this season.

The season opened well with a 3-2 win at Barrow, Sayer (two) and Whitter scoring for New Brighton. The local derby against Tranmere Rovers at Sandheys brought a good 3-2 win, but heavy rain spoiled both the football and the attendance. The first home defeat came on 26 September when Crewe Alexandra won 3-2. The Rakers were without Bert Mehaffy and Gaffney, but contributed to their own downfall when Alf Duggins missed from the penalty-spot.

For the first time in their history, the Rakers beat Southport on 10 October, but the main news of the week concerned the dancing ban imposed upon New Brighton's players. The club's directors had concluded that too much dancing was bad for the team and a new club rule came into force which stated that 'the directors

New Brighton pictured on 2 May 1925, before the final League match of the season, against Darlington at Rake Lane. New Brighton beat the Third Division North champions 1-0 with a goal from Wilcox. Back row (left to right): Carney, Niven, Heyes (assistant trainer), Max Reid, Critchlow, Watson (trainer), A.L.Davies, R.Jones, Hird, Lacey, Spencer, Leadbetter, Gutteridge. Seated: Gemmell, Whitter, Wade, Wilcox, J.Jones, J.Mehaffy, Mathieson, Gee, Denwood. Front: Kelly, J.Reid, Gaffney, Walker, Waine.

consider it misconduct for the players to dance until the early hours of the morning, and such conduct is not conducive to physical fitness'. The next three matches were lost with a goal-difference of 3-11!

In early November, Stan Sayer requested his release and Jimmy Dunne took over at centre-forward. Just over 2,000 spectators saw the young Irishman's debut in appalling weather conditions. The newcomer showed some pretty footwork and scored once in a fine 3-0 victory against second-placed Rochdale.

League form was proving inconsistent but the first and second rounds of the FA Cup were safely negotiated, home wins against Barrow and Darlington yielding a plum tie against the Wednesday at home. At the same time, it was announced that the Rakers had signed Jimmy Broad, Everton's widely-travelled centre-forward.

In the week before the Cup tie, the Raker's preparations included a visit to the Nantwich brine baths. The Wednesday party arrived at New Brighton on Friday afternoon and stayed overnight at the Victoria Hotel. Alderman Blanchard, a Wednesday director, said that they had every reason to be hopeful of a good result, whilst accepting that there were no certainties in the FA Cup. In a rousing struggle, the Rakers avenged their previous defeat by the Wednesday in 1922-3, winning 2-1 thanks to an Arthur Gee penalty and a fine winner by the new centre-forward, Jimmy Broad. A crowd of just over 10,000 — the lowest of all the third-round matches — netted receipts of £707.

The 'luck of the draw' deserted the Rakers after three home ties, when First Division Notts County were drawn at Meadow Lane. New Brighton put up a plucky fight, but failed to beat 41-year-old Albert Iremonger in the Notts County goal, and went down 2-0. The match drew 18,944 spectators, who paid £1,249. On the

New Brighton, 1925-6. Back row (left to right): M.Reid, J.Watson (trainer), Worrall, Mehaffy, Jones, E.W.Davies, Booth. Front row: Whitter, Sayer, E.Wade, Mathieson, Hannah, J.Reid.

22

same day, the meeting of Manchester City and Huddersfield Town attracted the biggest fourth-round crowd, 74,799 spectators paying £4,688 in gate receipts.

Shortly after the Cup tie, 'Ginger' Kelly, one of New Brighton's best players, was transferred to Notts County for a fee of £1,500. Before the Rakers' supporters had recovered from their disappointment, Jimmy Dunne was on his way to Sheffield United and, subsequently, international fame. 'Gene Carney, the outside-left who had assisted the club two seasons earlier, was signed from Aberdare, but it was the signing of another outside-left which caught the imagination. William Aguire, a recruit from the Bilbao Athletic Club, 11 times Spanish champions, made his debut for the Rakers' Reserves against Bootle Borough at Sandheys. Sadly, the Spaniard did not measure up to Third Division requirements and soon moved on to assist Harrowby. A month or so later, a trial was given to D.B.Mackie, an American newcomer. He scored on his debut for the Reserves, but departed without making his League bow.

The brothers Mehaffy faced one another when Rotherham United visited Sandheys on 27 March, and John, in the visitors' goal had a busy afternoon as the Rakers ran out comfortable winners by 5-1. The Good Friday visit of Coventry City brought a repeat performance, two 5-1 victories within a week being good going, but the next three fixtures yielded only two points, as the team began to feel the strain of four matches within five days.

A good 4-1 win against Accrington Stanley was followed by an even better result — a 1-0 win at Prenton Park against Tranmere. An Arthur Gee penalty was the clincher in what was New Brighton's fifth win in six League meetings with Tranmere Rovers.

The final game of the campaign was at Grimsby Town and there was no 'end-of-season' feeling at Blundell Park. A crowd of over 14,500 assembled to watch the game which Grimsby needed to win to ensure the Third Division championship. Inspired goalkeeping by Bert Mehaffy kept Grimsby at bay until ten minutes from time when Carmichael scored the only goal of the match. Grimsby won the title with a point to spare over Bradford.

John Mehaffy, who was overshadowed by his elder brother, Bert, at Rake Lane. John, who once scored a penalty for New Brighton Reserves, faced his brother following his transfer to Rotherham United in January 1925 and when the Rakers entertained Rotherham in March 1926, John conceded five goals. He later played for Dundalk and Coleraine in Irish football.

The Rakers finished in mid-table with 42 points from the same number of matches. Despite the new offside law, their goal tally had reduced from the previous season. The new rule which stipulated that only two defenders should be between the attacking player and the goal — instead of the previously required three — had the general effect of increasing the number of goals scored throughout the League.

Despite the conflicting claims of cricket, bowls and tennis, a crowd in the region of 4,000 made their way to Sandheys Park in fine weather and brilliant sunshine for the Rakers' first public trial match of 1926-7. Horace Williams, the new centre-forward from Mold, caught the eye with two fine goals, and when, a week later, he scored four in the final trial, he gave every indication of solving the club's centre-forward problem.

New Brighton began their fourth season of League football with a home match against Ashington. In brilliant sunshine and torrid heat, Williams netted a fine hat-trick to give the Rakers a 4-0 victory. In the early part of the season the new centre-forward's striking rate was outstanding by any standards. He scored in each of his first five matches and, by the end of November, had scored 22 goals in 17 appearances.

For the local derby at Prenton Park, record receipts of £864 were taken at the gate. It was Tranmere's first home game of the season and they swept the Rakers aside in a 4-1 win. Four days later the Rakers redeemed themselves with a sensational win against Bradford at Sandheys. After trailing 1-0 for 80 minutes, three goals were scored in the final ten minutes, bringing a victory which was hardly deserved on the previous run of the play. Continuing their habit of snatching things out of the fire, a draw at Wrexham came thanks to Jack Reid's equalizer two minutes from time.

Horace Williams' second hat-trick of the season accounted for Wigan Borough at Sandheys on 18 October and it proved to be the start of a run of 12 undefeated

New Brighton Reserves 1926-7. The goalkeeper is J.Foulkes, father of the Manchester United and England defender Billy Foulkes.

matches, which included a 5-0 demolition of the eventual champions, Stoke, whilst the 4-1 win against rival seasiders, Southport, included Williams' third hat-trick of the season.

Three goals in nine minutes accounted for Accrington Stanley and brought the season's first away win on 6 November. John Mathieson, brother of Allan, made his debut in this match and Ernie Hawksworth, the former Blackburn Rovers player, scored a goal on his second appearance. Horace Williams scored two, despite missing a penalty. Lincoln City became the first visitors to take a point from the Rakers at Sandheys. In strong winds and lashing rain, 6ft 4ins Albert Iremonger in Lincoln's goal, again proved a formidable barrier.

A draw at Wrexham in the first round of the FA Cup raised hopes of a good run in the competition, but the Rakers failed to capitalize in the replay despite the fact that Wrexham were reduced to ten men when Longmuir was injured after 55 minutes. A second replay, in dense fog at Anfield, saw Wrexham win in convincing fashion by 3-1. The 300-minute Cup duel had netted total receipts in excess of £1,500 and an aggregate attendance of 28,623 spectators.

Two goals in the last three minutes at Crewe proved too little too late as the Rakers went down 3-2. At this point they occupied sixth place in the League with 21 points from 17 games.

In the Christmas Day defeat at Chesterfield, Bert Mehaffy was badly concussed after 20 minutes play. He had to stay in Chesterfield over the weekend and returned to New Brighton with the Chesterfield team on the following Monday. He was, however, not fit to play and his place in goal was taken by Jim Foulkes, who did well to keep a clean sheet in one of his infrequent senior appearances.

Rakers' Reserves celebrated Christmas by beating Poulton Rovers 7-1 at Clayton Lane on Christmas Day. They were 6-0 up at half-time, George Shelton scoring a hat-trick within 15 minutes. Without exerting themselves in the second half, they ran out comfortable winners.

Ashington's first home defeat of the season provided the Rakers with their second away success on 15 January. The local derby against Tranmere Rovers was played in treacherous conditions of ice and mud at Sandheys. There was little to choose between the teams and a goalless draw resulted. By beating Wrexham, New Brighton retained their unbeaten home record and, after 25 matches, they stood in seventh place with 32 points. They were seven points behind the leaders, Stoke, and four points behind Rochdale, in second place.

For the second time in three seasons, Doncaster Rovers broke New Brighton's unbeaten home record. A much rearranged side did well to bring a point away from Stoke, the Third Division North leaders and eventual champions. A 3-0 home win against Rotherham United at the end of February was followed by a crushing 7-2 defeat at Southport. It proved to be the start of a six-match run which included three home defeats and yielded only one point. After losing 3-0 at home against Halifax, the Rakers had dropped to tenth in the table with 36 points from 35 matches.

The Liverpool Senior Cup Final at Anfield on Monday 11 April saw the Rakers outclassed in all departments by a strong Liverpool side, who won 8-2. Then an Easter double over Walsall was followed by a 3-0 win against Crewe, but the Rakers' best display of the season came in their third game within the space of five days. Every New Brighton forward scored as Nelson were beaten 7-2.

The season wound up with a 4-0 defeat at Hartlepools, a 3-0 victory at bottom-placed Barrow and a 2-1 home defeat by Stockport County.

The season's close saw New Brighton in tenth place, equal on points with Tranmere Rovers. Horace Williams' goal tally for the season was 34 and, with more support in the second half of the season, he could have done even better. George Camsell created a new record with 59 goals for the Second Division champions, Middlesbrough.

Under the headline 'Football World Astir', the *Wallasey & Wirral Chronicle* for 6 August 1927 revealed that Bert Pelham's duties had been extended from secretary to secretary-manager. 'Sandy' Watson was continuing as trainer, and would be joined by Ernie Gault, the former Everton player, who took over duties as assistant trainer and groundsman. Further ground improvements undertaken during the close season had increased the ground capacity to approximately 20,000.

The retained players were: Mehaffy, Reaney, Higgins, J.Reid, Beattie, Whitter, Williams and Wade. Amongst the new recruits were Hoddinott, a Welsh international from Rhyl, Dickie from St Johnstone, Howson from Bath City, Carr from Barnsley, Smedley from Nottingham junior football, Sanderson from Stockport County, Harley from Caernarfon Town and Laycock from Mansfield Town.

The opening fixture was at Darlington and the New Brighton party arrived late after being held up on their train journey. The team had to change on the train, were a goal down shortly after the kick-off and lost 3-0 to the former Second Division side.

The first home match was against Doncaster Rovers, who had won on their last two visits to Rake Lane. When they opened the scoring it looked as though they were in for yet another triumph, but a sound defensive display by Jock McDonald, making his first appearance in the Rakers' colours, was a big factor in the 3-1 victory. A Horace Williams hat-trick provided half of New Brighton's six goals against Ashington, who put up a plucky fight, but were overrun after the interval. Despite an inspired display by Bert Mehaffy — who was given an ovation by the sporting Doncaster crowd — New Brighton went down 5-1 to the team they had beaten at home five days earlier. All the early signs indicated that this was to be another season of fortnightly fete days at home, interspersed with unrewarding away trips.

Horace Williams played his last game for the Rakers at Crewe before moving on to Blackpool. The stocky little centre-forward's loss was greatly regretted, but, as usual, the money was welcome. A dashing leader and superb opportunist, he left behind the memory of some stunning goals. Some of his teammates also no doubt recalled the day when his usually-favoured dress of 'plus-fours' vanished from the dressing-rooms. They were later found, flapping from the top of the flag-pole at Sandheys Park!

Williams' departure let in Alex Harley, who had scored four goals against Welshpool for the Reserves just before his first-team debut. Later in the season he was to score four again, this time for the first team in the FA Cup second-round tie against Rhyl Athletic at Sandheys. Despite a loss of form, and first-team place, during February and March, Harley's final total of 20 League and Cup goals was a commendable effort in 31 appearances.

Bert Mehaffy produced another splendid display of goalkeeping at Bradford City. The previous season's Second Division wooden-spoonists bombarded the New Brighton goal and it was only the Irish international's masterly display which prevented a much heavier defeat than the eventual 3-1 scoreline. After seven matches, the Rakers had seven points and stood in tenth place. Halifax Town were the early pace setters at the head of the table.

In a change from the usual pattern of results, two successive home matches — against Tranmere Rovers and Lincoln City — were lost. A draw at Hartlepools was followed by a win at Nelson — the season's first away success — and a goalless draw against Stockport County.

In late October the 80mph winds which swept the country had its effect on Sandheys Park. The grandstand roof was blown off and the hoardings on the Rake Lane side of the ground were destroyed. The Barrow home match, scheduled to take place on 29 October had to be postponed, and the lost gate money, plus reconstruction costs, were estimated to be in the region of £1,000. A reconstruction fund was immediately launched, but the first collection, taken at the Rochdale match on 12 November, raised only £21 and included a large percentage of half pennies and a huge amount of foreign coins!

In their first FA Cup encounter, the Rakers visited non-League Shildon. The ground was in an appalling state and both sides had difficulty in keeping their feet, but New Brighton won comfortably by 3-1. In the second round the Rakers again drew non-League opponents. Rhyl were much the better side in the first half, being two up within 25 minutes. They failed to stay the course, however, the Rakers scoring six times without response after the interval, Alex Harley getting four of them.

The luck of the draw continued to favour New Brighton when the third round was pulled out of the hat. The famous amateur team, the Corinthians, were to be the visitors on 14 January.

Four games within eight days over the Christmas holiday period yielded only three points. The Darlington match at Sandheys on New Year's Eve, which ended goalless, was played in heavy snow. The attendance of 1,829 was, at the time, the smallest ever for a home New Brighton League game.

Two weeks later, the best attendance of the season saw the Rakers progress into the fourth round of the FA Cup, at the expense of the Corinthians. The amateurs played the more cultured football, managing to combine effectively on a pitch which resembled a mud-heap. It was a dour contest in which Third Division strength finally overcame the amateur stylists.

On the following Saturday, Crewe were visitors to Sandheys. Both teams had despatched premier amateurs from the FA Cup — Crewe having beaten London Caledonians 3-2. Crewe were reduced to ten men for three-quarters of the game and were beaten 5-1.

Dismissal from the FA Cup came in the fourth round at Hanley. New Brighton defended resolutely but went down 3-0, Port Vale scoring twice in the last five minutes.

In the second half of the season, W.D.Roberts took over at centre-forward. Both Harley and Hoddinott had lost form, and whilst Harley did regain his place, Hoddinott played only once after mid February.

The arrival of 16-year-old Sidney Chedgzoy junior in February suggested a change of direction with the encouragement of youngsters, rather than a reliance on old stagers, who invariably failed to last the season.

In early March it was revealed that Horace Williams had been placed on Blackpool's transfer list at £250. He failed to find his form at Bloomfield Road, providing an expensive misfit for the Second Division club.

The Rakers occupied 13th position in the League at the end of March, with 31 points from 32 matches. In the Easter games, three points were taken from Wigan Borough and Wrexham were beaten at the Racecourse. The season's last victory — 4-0 against lowly Durham City — featured a fine hat-trick by Roberts.

The final match of the season was at Park Avenue, where a crowd of 9,538 saw the Rakers give the champions a good run for their money. Fred Laycock put New Brighton in front but McLean equalized. Bradford's winner came courtesy of Jock McDonald, who put through his own goal.

The Rakers finished the season in tenth place for the second season running. They had 42 points from 42 matches and, strangely enough, won 14 games, lost 14 and drew 14. Seventy-two goals were scored and 62 conceded. In League matches, four forwards scored a double-figure total of goals — Harley and Laycock 14, Dickie 11 and Roberts 10.

At the annual general shareholder's meeting held at Princess Road schoolrooms in late July, the financial statement showed a loss on the season's workings of approximately £500. Bad weather was given as part of the explanation — 14 Saturdays

Welsh international forward Frank Hoddinott was released by the Rakers in 1928 and joined non-League Newark Town. He finished his career with Grantham Town.

had seen heavy rain, which had affected attendance figures. It was warned that a degree of pruning of expenses would have to be made and the now customary plea for adequate support from the public was made. Season ticket prices for 1928-9 were: Stand £2 2s, Ladies 30s, Paddock 25s.

The review of prospects for the new season in the *Athletic News* revealed that few of the previous season's players had been retained. Three newcomers were Whewell, who had scored 36 goals for Poole the previous season, R.Iddon, a forward whose previous clubs included Preston North End and Manchester United and R.Chambers, a centre-half from Exeter City. Amongst the players not re-signed were Wade, Jack Reid, Whitter, Harley, Laycock, Hoddinott, Sanderson and Howson. Eve-of-season signings included four new forwards, Parker from Stalybridge Celtic, T.Reid from Clapton Orient, 'Jazzo' Kirk from Bath City and Peter Cowper, the former West Ham and Grimsby Town outside-right.

There were five debutants in the side for the opening Saturday. For the first time the Rakers appeared in all-white shirts, the blue collars and cuffs having been abandoned. Barrow were the visitors and they caused a nasty surprise by winning 3-1.

It took some time for the new team to settle. By the end of September three out of four home matches had been lost, whilst two away wins had been gained out of three matches. The team had six points from seven matches and occupied 20th position.

Three wins during October included a surprise 3-1 home victory against Southport, New Brighton scoring twice in the last five minutes. The prophets were again confounded when victory over Tranmere at Prenton Park was secured by 3-1. It was Tranmere's first home defeat of the season. A hat-trick by Bill Whewell accounted for high-scoring Stockport County, one of the Third Division North's early pace-setters with a record of 33 goals in 11 matches. A rather fortunate draw at Halifax owed much to the brilliance of Bert Mehaffy. This was followed by the season's best win. Lincoln City went to to Sandheys with a big reputation, but they were hard pressed throughout. New Brighton led within a minute of the kick-off and ran out 6-1 winners, Parker, Kirk and Cowper each scoring two goals.

New Brighton's visit to Park Avenue on 17 November resulted in a 5-2 defeat. They lost their kit on the rail journey — it was shunted off to Manchester — and ten minutes prior to kick-off the skips had not turned up, but were recovered just in time for a prompt start to be made. Misfortune followed the Rakers on to the field as both Tommy Lewis and Jock McDonald scored own-goals, Peter Cowper was injured and, ten minutes from time, Len Carr was sent off.

FA Cup hopes were dashed at Darlington, where the Rakers went down 3-0. There were 5,023 spectators and the 'gate' amounted to £283. It was New Brighton's fifth visit to Darlington and on each occasion they had been defeated, conceding three goals in each match.

On the Thursday following the Cup tie, Jimmy Dickie was transferred to Bristol City. The popular Scottish outside-left had appeared in 61 consecutive League and FA Cup matches since joining the Rakers in August 1927.

The second consecutive League defeat, by 5-2, provided Hartlepools with their first win for ten weeks. Rakers' goalkeeper, Bert Mehaffy, was seriously injured in the first few minutes. The ten men were level at the interval, Len Carr acquitting himself well in goal. Mehaffy was to be absent from the first team for three and a half months, but the local amateur, Les Flood, was to prove a sterling deputy.

December was an unrewarding month, both Christmas fixtures against Crewe Alexandra being lost, and only four points were secured from seven fixtures.

The New Year began well, however, with two wins and two draws in January. At Chesterfield on New Year's Day, Les Flood received an ovation from the sporting Saltergate crowd, who saw their team dominate the play but fail to get a single shot past the amateur goalkeeper. This 2-0 win gave the Rakers 21 points from 22 matches and 14th place in the table. Their four away wins was equalled only by Bradford City — lying second in the table, but their home form, usually a strong point, was second worst in the division.

Walter Wadsworth, the former Liverpool centre-half and Bristol City captain, made his first appearance for New Brighton at Doncaster Rovers. He was the sixth centre-half used in 23 matches, but the 38-year-old pivot quickly removed all doubts about the position.

A goalless draw at Southport in mid-February ended a sequence of League defeats at Haigh Avenue, the Rakers gaining their first point in six visits. The second 6-1 win of the season followed. Wadsworth and Cowper both scored two for New Brighton as Rochdale finished with only nine men, after goalkeeper Mittell received a broken nose and Silverwood a knee injury.

Harry Lewis, the former Hull City and Liverpool inside-forward, made his debut for New Brighton Reserves on 9 March. He had assisted Liverpool to the League Championship in season 1920-21, but he did not manage to get into the Rakers' first team.

Bert Mehaffy, who was making his way back to full fitness in the Reserves, was awarded a benefit. Tranmere Rovers provided the opposition at the end of April, when a crowd of about 2,000 saw an enjoyable match which Tranmere won 4-2.

Home games wound up with a goalless draw against Rotherham United. Len Carr, usually a left-back, being unsuccessfully tried at centre-forward. A 1-1 draw concluded the season at Wigan Borough. The Rakers finished in 14th place with 39 points from 42 games, of which 15 were won, nine drawn and 18 lost. Sixty-four goals were scored and 71 conceded. Peter Cowper led the goalscoring list with 16 from 40 matches. Jock McDonald and Bobby Morrison were the season's only ever-presents.

Some familiar faces were missing when the curtain was rung up at Sandheys Park in August 1929, the most notable being Bert Mehaffy, who had returned to

Ireland to assist Belfast Celtic. The defence, one of the soundest in its class last season, was otherwise retained in its entirety. The greatest changes were seen in the forwards, which had lacked blend. A new left-wing pair of George Pither, recently with Liverpool, and Alf Oakes, who had scored 47 goals for Rhyl in 1928-9, were expected to start as first choice. Centre-forward Tom Reid's knee was reported to be sound after his cartilage operation the previous season, whilst the vastly experienced Tommy Page was expected to supply the necessary craft to the front line. Joe Taylor, a recommendation of Peter Kelly's, proved a fast and fearless leader in the trials.

All the early season optimism received a severe jolt when two defeats in quick succession and four goals conceded without a reply made doleful reading. A 2-1 home win against Wrexham proved to be only a brief respite as three consecutive away games were lost with a goal-difference of 1-13.

The arrival of Dick Johnson, the former Liverpool and Stoke inside-forward, was to prove a smart move by the Rakers' management. His debut brought the season's second win and, three weeks later, his hat-trick at Crewe helped achieve the first away success.

The return of 'Ginger' Kelly at the end of October caused keen interest. Always a trier who never spared himself in the team's interest, Kelly had been a prime favourite with the Rakers' supporters before his move to Notts County in February 1926. A knee injury ended his Meadow Lane career, but an operation was thought to have cured his problems. Sadly, Kelly could not retain his place in the Rakers' first team after appearing in eight League matches, which produced only five points.

On 16 November, Kenny Campbell returned to Rake Lane. He had not played any football after leaving Leicester City in the close season. The Scottish international, a non-smoker and teetotaller, proved perfectly fit in his 37th year and his return proved to be the turning point in the hitherto disasterous season. His mere presence had a psychological effect on his co-defenders, and the gathering confidence linking the defensive lines gradually hauled the Rakers away from the foot of the table.

The first round of the FA Cup was played at top speed on a muddy ground with a heavy ball. The visitors were Lancaster Town and they were under pressure throughout as the Rakers ran out 4-1 winners before a crowd of 4,500. In the second round, New Brighton went down fighting at Doncaster to the only goal of the game after 63 minutes. The Rakers' veterans, McDonald, Wadsworth and Campbell, marshalled a magnificent defence but the forwards were ragged and easily contained by the Doncaster defenders.

The Christmas holiday matches began badly, Lincoln City winning 4-1 at Sandheys and Tranmere Rovers by 3-1 in the Christmas Day meeeting at Prenton Park. Rakers avenged themselves in the Boxing Day return with Tranmere with a 3-0 win, and followed up with a 5-0 win against Barrow, Dick Johnson getting a hat-trick. On New Year's Day, and with the Rakers playing their fifth match in ten days, York City took a point in a 1-1 draw. At this stage, New Brighton had 16 points from 22 matches with a goal-average of 29-54 and stood in 20th place. Their defensive record was the worst in the division, led at this point by Port Vale.

The Rakers' first win in the 1930s was even more convincing than the 5-0 scoreline suggested. Wigan Borough's goalkeeper, Mittell, made many fine saves but Joe Taylor scored two and Dick Johnson three — his second hat-trick of the season. The win heralded the start of a good run of results and an end to the constant team changes which had not had the desired effect. From 11 January to 29 March, during which time 13 League matches were played, the Rakers' record was eight wins, four draws and one defeat, goals-for 31, against 11. The usual team at this time was — Campbell; McDonald, Carr, Lewis, Wadsworth, Smedley, Cowper (or Roscoe), Johnson, Taylor, Oakes, Pither.

During this period of new-born confidence, the club attracted the attention of

First Division club scouts. The names of Smedley and Carr were foremost in the rumours but, as the Rakers' supporters held their breath, no firm news was forthcoming about their promotion to a higher sphere.

The run of success was ended at Saltergate on 7 April, Chesterfield's 1-0 win being their 17th successive home victory. A good point from Doncaster Rovers, where the Rakers had earlier lost in the FA Cup, preceded the Easter fixtures. League leaders Stockport County were beaten 3-2 on Good Friday. It was the first time since Christmas that the Rakers had conceded two goals at Sandheys but their three first-half goals, whilst kicking down the slope, put the game beyond Stockport's reach.

Easter Monday's visitors, Chesterfield, lying third in the table, took a point in a 1-1 draw. This was New Brighton's last home game of the season.

An end of season listlessness was apparent at Lincoln. The team had an off-day and found themselves 5-1 down with only a few minutes to play. At this point, Joe Taylor scored two fine opportunist goals to give a little respectability to the scoreline. The season ended at Edgeley Park, where runners-up Stockport County won 2-0.

The Rakers finished 13th in the table with the following record: P 42 W 16 D 8 L 18 F 69 A 79 Pts 40. Port Vale were the champions, whilst Barrow and Halifax Town occupied the bottom two places. Both were re-elected, Halifax with 40 votes, but Barrow polled only 22 and were pressed hard by Mansfield Town (15) and Manchester Central (13). Prescot Cables also applied, but did not receive a single vote.

A tuneful start to the 1930-31 season was promised when Jack Taylor, of Seacombe, volunteered to broadcast music through a series of amplifiers around the ground before matches and at half-time.

As 25 out of the previous season's 40 points had been obtained in the second half of the season, few changes in personnel were deemed necessary. Nevertheless, missing faces included Walter Wadsworth and the two Peters, Cowper and Kelly. Two centre-halves — Jack Reid, returning from Ireland after an absence of three seasons, and Matthew Dixon, formerly of Preston North End and Everton, were candidates to replace Wadsworth. For the outside-right berth, Sid Waites was signed after appearing in the pre-season trials. His previous clubs included Lincoln City, Halifax Town and Stockport County. A new reserve goalkeeper, Ken Greatrex, was signed from Wrexham to replace Ted Maher as Kenny Campbell's understudy.

Just short of 5,000 spectators were present on the opening Saturday of the season to see Jock McDonald lead out the Rakers for their game against Lincoln City at Sandheys. The game was lacking finesse, but nothing in speed and incident. Goals by Oakes and Johnson saw the Rakers home, but there were sighs of relief from the home supporters when the final whistle sounded with the score at 2-1.

During September and October, the team's form seemed too bad to be true. More robust than scientific and lacking cohesion, they sank like a stone to the bottom of the table. On 1 November, after losing 2-0 at Rotherham, New Brighton's record was P 13 W 1 D 3 L 9 F 8 A 29 Pts 5. Strangely enough, at the same time, the Reserves led the Football Combination League.

The signing of Billy Matthews, the veteran centre-half of many clubs and two Welsh caps, proved to be a good move. A dominating personality, Matthews played a big part in settling the Rakers' defence, whilst finding the time to assist the attack from free-kicks and dead-ball situations.

November brought four defeats and only one victory and there was no progress made in the FA Cup, Carlisle being comfortable 3-1 winners at Brunton Park. The attendance was 9,300 and the gate receipts totalled £515.

Whilst the seniors were losing at Carlisle, the Reserves won 4-1 against Llandudno. Alf Oakes registered a hat-trick — all headers — and Leo Stevens scored the other.

31

Apart from his goal, Stevens had done little of note, so his selection to lead the first-team attack against Rochdale the following week was something of a surprise. Nevertheless, on his debut, Stevens was not slow to capitalize on an unsteady Rochdale defence and scored both goals in New Brighton's welcome 2-1 victory. Fortune smiled on the Rakers on their visit to Crewe. An injury-weakened side enjoyed the run of the ball and triumphed 3-1 to provide the first away win of the season.

A 5-3 win against York City preceded the Christmas meetings with Doncaster Rovers, from which a highly creditable three points were gained. League leaders Lincoln City took revenge for their early season defeat at Rake Lane. The breezy Imps' forward line gave the Rakers' defence a hectic afternoon and Ken Greatrex, New Brighton's reserve goalkeeper, enhanced his reputation, despite being beaten four times.

Whilst the seniors were going down 3-0 at Peel Park, Accrington, on a pitch which resembled a skating rink, the Reserves had a field day, beating Ellesmere Port Town 9-1. Wally Curr scored four, Joe Templeman three, F.Baker and N.Baker one each. It could have been double figures, but Templeman missed a penalty.

Leo Stevens, rewarded with a professional contract, was improving all the time, but, as the season drew to its close, the future was looking uncertain. Attendances of less than 3,000 were becoming a frequent experience and this was obviously insufficient to run a first-class team, let alone strengthen it.

A disappointing Easter produced only two points and two home attendances which totalled only 6,847. After losing 2-0 at Rochdale on 11 April, the final home game against Crewe Alexandra — who were also in need of points — proved a 'nervy' affair. A headed goal by Leo Stevens gave the Rakers an interval lead. In the second half, New Brighton showed more 'snap' and two further goals by Stevens gave the home team a deserved victory. More important, it meant that the Rakers had escaped the necessity of applying for re-election.

Rochdale and Nelson were the applicants, and the Seedhill club were unlucky. In the first vote Rochdale were re-elected with 40 votes, Nelson and Chester each polled 27. On a second vote, Chester (28) were elected, Nelson (20), Manchester Central (4) and Merthyr Town (0) were not.

The Rakers finished the season in 19th place with 33 points from 42 matches. They had recorded 13 wins, seven draws and 22 defeats, 49 goals were scored and 76 conceded. Only Nelson had scored fewer goals (43) and it was this lack of fire-power which had been the main cause of the Rakers' poor showing. Leo Stevens was leading goalscorer with 13, despite having played in only 19 matches.

A meeting of shareholders at the end of April revealed an overdraft of £6,450, whilst the players were owed £180 — more than one week's wage. There were other pressing creditors and the situation was not eased by the seven per cent bank interest on the overdraft. Various schemes were discussed and means were found to pay the players and the groundsman's wages during the summer. It was a bleak prospect, bad trade was having its effects everywhere.

On 1 August 1931 the Rakers had signed only three players and were without a manager, secretary or trainer. Bert Pelham had departed to become secretary-manager of Southport FC in April 1931 and was not replaced. Mr George Peers took over duties as honorary secretary and, just before the season began, Angus McKinnon was appointed as trainer.

Despite their financial troubles, a slimmed-down Rakers faced the new season bravely. A late flurry on the transfer market saw the following team open the season at Sandheys on 29 August: Walker (from Wolves); Clement (Watford), Carr, Pollock, Matthew, Smedley, Parle (Walsall), McCosh (Exeter City), Stevens, Miller (Watford), Henderson (Burnley).

Had Ben Twell been fit — he had taken a knock in the trials — the former Southport leader would most probably have been selected in preference to Stevens,

New Brighton
programme
for the visit
of Barrow
in January
1932.

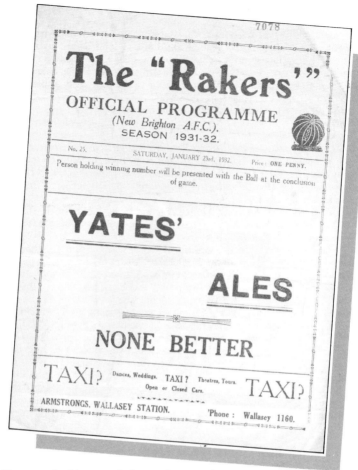

7078

The "Rakers'"

OFFICIAL PROGRAMME
(New Brighton A.F.C.).
SEASON 1931-32.

No. 25.   SATURDAY, JANUARY 23rd, 1932.   Price: ONE PENNY.

Person holding winning number will be presented with the Ball at the conclusion of game.

YATES'

ALES

NONE BETTER

TAXI?   Dances, Weddings. TAXI? Theatres, Tours.   TAXI?
                    Open or Closed Cars.

ARMSTRONGS, WALLASEY STATION.   'Phone: Wallasey 1160.

which would have resulted in an entirely new forward line from the previous season. The new combination were well beaten by Gateshead, who scored twice in the first half, during an almost incessant bombardment on the New Brighton goal. A lack of understanding and weakness on the wings was evident in the Rakers' ranks, for whom McCosh opened the season's scoring account. Walker, the new goalkeeper, was the outstanding man in the New Brighton team.

Rakers' supporters were becoming accustomed to their team's indifferent starts to the season but the opening to 1931-2 was by far the worst to date. A point from the second match, at Halifax, was obtained despite the absence of Carr and Stevens through injury. A big disappointment, however, was Peter Miller's failure to convert a penalty-kick.

The next ten matches were all lost and it was not until 31 October that the long-suffering Rakers supporters saw their team win, against Doncaster Rovers, a penalty by Jimmy Smedley being the game's only goal.

In September it was announced that New Brighton had lost £336 on the year ended May 1930, against a loss of £1,467 the previous year. Such a reduction had not been achieved without considerable effort and sacrifice. There was a reduction of £500 in the amount debited to players' and trainers' wages and secretarial salary, in comparison with the previous season.

33

Negotiations had been in progress for some considerable time for the transfer of the club's headquarters from Rake Lane to land owned by the Corporation in Gorsey Lane. It was hoped that a new municipally-owned sports centre could be built in time for next season. Sadly, the idea had to be abandoned in January 1933, mainly because of objections from ratepayers, who disliked the idea of the Council subsidizing their local club, which was, of course, a private company.

On 10 October Beau Ratcliffe made his debut at Hartlepools and was soon to replace Billy Matthews at centre-half. He proved to be one of the club's best-ever defenders.

At about this time, the Rakers Reserves included a newcomer in F.Soo at centre-half against Liverpool Cables. The trialist was not registered with the Football League and vanished after that one appearance. Given the unusual surname, it seems a fair assumption that this was Frank Soo, nine times capped by England in wartime internationals.

Thirteenth time lucky at Doncaster, the Rakers had finally broken their long spell of ill luck and defeats, but it was to be two months before the next League success.

When news came of the demise of the Wigan Borough club — who resigned from the Football League on 26 October — doubts were expressed as to whether the Third Division North could continue as a whole, in view of dwindling receipts at all grounds. To underline the point, the Rochdale v New Brighton match at Spotland on 7 November (which, incidentally, proved to be Rochdale's last League win of the season — the next 26 matches producing but a single point), was witnessed by only 1,888 spectators and the receipts were a little over £60. Directors of most Third Division clubs were having to dip down, rather deeply, into their own pockets to meet current expenses and help their clubs over what was a most difficult time.

An unexpected point from a goalless draw at Carlisle United was a heartening fillip for the team's first-round FA Cup tie against York City at Sandheys.

Showing form far in advance of their League record, the Rakers were three goals up within 34 minutes. York pulled one back and missed a penalty, but a rousing tie ended in the Rakers' favour. The attendance was 3,367 and the receipts £165.

Hull City were New Brighton's second-round opponents. They were steadily climbing the League after a poor start and had won each of their last three games, which included a 4-1 home victory against Mansfield Town in the first round of the Cup. A crowd of 4,500 assembled at Sandheys for the 2.15pm kick-off, and before 2.30pm they were stunned into silence as Hull led 3-0 and went on to finish comfortable 4-0 winners. Hull's new centre-half, England international Jack Hill, was outstanding for the visitors.

The smallest Boxing Day crowd in the country (2,661) saw the goalless draw against Darlington at Sandheys. Just across the river, 52,991 saw Everton beat Blackburn Rovers 5-0, Dixie Dean, the former Tranmere Rovers player, scoring a hat-trick.

When Stockport County were beaten 2-1 on 30 December to provide the second League win of the season, thoughts returned to 1929-30, when the Rakers' season, 'took off' after Christmas. There was to be no repeat performance, however, as the next win was not obtained until 6 February and, almost a month later, came win number four, against Southport on 5 March. At this point, some improvement coincided with the return of Tommy Lewis and the advent of amateur winger, Alf Liggins. Leo Stevens scored 13 goals in the final ten League matches, including four against Carlisle United on 4 April. In what constituted a 'mini-revival', five wins came in this ten-match spell. But the season ended without a single away victory, the Rakers' travelling record being: P 20 W 0 D 3 L 17 F 13 A 53 Pts 3.

A total of 24 points from 40 fixtures was the team's worst performance to date. Fortunately, only one place was to be filled at the League's annual meeting, due to Wigan Borough's resignation. Rochdale were re-elected with 47 votes, despite having totalled only 11 points (goal-difference 48-135).

Leo Stevens scored more than half of the team's 38 League goals with 20, the next highest being Jimmy Smedley with four. Stevens was tenth in the list of goalscorers for the division which was headed by A.Hall (Lincoln City), who scored 41 for the Third Division North champions.

With the exit of football, baseball made its debut at Rake Lane on 14 May, New Brighton being represented for the first time in the English Baseball Association's First Division competition. Louis Page, the Manchester United footballer, captained New Brighton in their first match, against Oakfield Social. Only about 500 spectators turned up to see New Brighton win by 27 runs. Amongst the footballers taking part were Ken Greatrex, J.N.Stevens (brother of Leo) and Charlie Quayle.

During the 1932 close season the Rakers transferred Leo Stevens, the ex-Wallasey tram conductor, to Everton. He scored a hat-trick in the Goodison pre-season trials but, as Dixie Dean's understudy, was destined to make only two First Division appearances.

In the Rakers' trials, encouraging form was shown by some of the junior signings, notably George Bradshaw (an amateur goalkeeper from High Park Villa, Southport) and Bill Major, a local centre-half from Poulton.

The new season opened at Rotherham and new Rakers on view at Millmoor included Robb (formerly of Chesterfield), Barley (Hull City), Kitching (Tranmere Rovers), Jimmy Parle (Walsall) and Charlie Quayle, an amateur from Bootle who led the attack. The only forward remaining from the previous season, Peter Miller, was at outside-left. New Brighton lost by the only goal, Rotherham forward Parkin charging both Ken Greatrex and the ball into the net.

The first home match was against Mansfield Town, who had been transferred from the Southern Section. A single goal by Quayle after 19 minutes secured the points for New Brighton. A 2-2 draw with Accrington Stanley marked the promising debut of C.S.Amery, who deputized for Parle, an early injury victim with a dislocated shoulder. Mansfield took their revenge at Field Mill, Johnson scoring four of their goals in a 5-0 win, the Rakers being out-manœuvred at almost every point.

At Prenton Park, New Brighton stunned local rivals Tranmere. Amateur outside-right Alf Liggins' trickiness and speed laid on first-half goals for Miller (two) and Amery. A second-half onslaught by the home side saw Bell and Fishwick reduce the arears, but the Rakers hung on to clinch a famous victory.

Jimmy Dickie, the Scottish outside-left and a former Rake Lane favourite, returned to New Brighton from Chester. He was a newcomer, along with amateur goalkeeper George Bradshaw, for the home match against Barrow on 24 September. It proved an eventful match. Kitching scored for New Brighton after five minutes and they should have increased their lead, but Smedley failed from the penalty-spot. In the second half, a blunder by Bradshaw, saw him throw the ball into his own goal after he had been knocked down and harassed by a posse of Barrow attackers. Another freak goal decided the contest. A 40-yard lob by Tinnion, the Barrow right-half, found the net with Bradshaw well off his line after clearing a previous shot.

At the annual shareholders' meeting, held at the end of September, the report and financial statement revealed that a loss of £558 had been sustained. There were some interesting comparisons. In season 1930-31, the expenditure on players' and trainers' wages was £2,915. A reduction in receipts from League matches of over £1,000 had led to numerous cuts in expenditure. Amongst these, travelling and match expenses had been reduced from £758 to £371. Very much the difference between a profit and loss was the £672 paid in bank interest charges.

Continuing to show unpredictable form, the Rakers surprised Carlisle United by winning 3-1 at Brunton Park, thanks to an inspired display of goalkeeping from

Bradshaw and goals by Dickie, Amery and Liggins. After eight matches, New Brighton had seven points. They had already won more away games than in 1930-31, but their home form was letting them down.

By failing to take a single point from the next six matches, the Rakers found themselves in the unhappy position of wooden spoonists on 26 November, when the FA Cup draw produced a Merseyside clash between the Rakers and Tranmere Rovers at Prenton Park. Without the funds to treat themselves to trips to fashionable spas or brine baths, the Rakers found themselves a goal down within two minutes of the kick-off. The first FA Cup meeting of the local rivals proved to be an instantly forgettable match. The ball was repeatedly booted out of the ground, so much so that at one point there were three balls on the pitch. Tranmere won 3-0 and eventually progressed to the fourth round before losing to Leeds United, after a replay.

December was a busy month, which began with a draw of 1-1 with Stockport County at Sandheys. The visit to Barnsley on 10 December brought a quite unexpected victory, as the Yorkshire side had already beaten New Brighton 5-3 at Rake Lane. On this occasion, however, goals from amateur centre-forward R.E.Shaw and Miller gave New Brighton a well-deserved 2-1 win.

Walsall were the next visitors, and local enthusiasts were interested to have a look at the side that was scheduled to meet Arsenal in the FA Cup on 14 January. The Rakers were two down after 48 minutes, but rallied to draw 2-2. The local correspondent did not give much for Walsall's chances against the Arsenal! When the game did come around, however, the League Champions and 1932 FA Cup runners-up were unable to match the Rakers' result and went down 2-0 in one of the biggest FA Cup upsets of all time.

Three ducks, all of the wrong variety, constituted New Brighton's Christmas fare. A 5-0 defeat at Wrexham on Christmas Eve was followed by a 3-0 defeat by Rochdale at home on Boxing Day. At Rochdale, one day later, the home side won 1-0. Some relief was expected from the New Year's Eve visit of Rotherham United, who had concluded their holiday programme with a 9-2 defeat at the hands of Mansfield Town in which, incidentally, three of the Stags' forwards scored hat-tricks. Only 1,855 spectators turned up, but they were rewarded with a 5-2 win against the Millers. It was the first home win for the Rakers since 31 August.

Earlier in the same week, 4,520 had attended a charity match at Rake Lane between Wallasey Police and Wallasey Unemployed. Dixie Dean was the referee and Kenny Campbell kept goal for the unemployed. The proceeds were in aid of the Chief Constable's Children's Clothing and Distress Fund. In a goalless draw, former international goalkeeper Campbell showed that he had lost none of his old skill and agility.

A bad start to the New Year was made, a visit to Gateshead on 2 January resulting in a 2-0 defeat. It was a holiday on the North-East coast but the game attracted only 3,001 spectators — another blow to the Rakers' finances, made even worse when their coach broke down and the team had to stay overnight at Darlington.

A rousing game at Accrington Stanley saw John N.Stevens (brother of Leo) score twice on his Football League debut. Unfortunately, he finished on the losing side, Accrington winning by the odd goal in nine.

After scoring first at Darlington, New Brighton went down 2-1. There were only 1,642 spectators, which constituted the lowest attendance for any League match involving the Rakers during the season.

On 21 January in the home 'derby' against Tranmere Rovers, Albert Gray, Tranmere's Welsh international goalkeeper was in constant action and did well to keep the score down to 1-0 at half-time. An injury to Jimmy Smedley, who was temporarily blinded when his eye was cut by the lace on the ball, caused him to retire. The Rovers gradually wore down New Brighton's depleted defence and drew level after 71 minutes. The sharing of the points left New Brighton at the foot of the table. Their record at this point was: P 26 W 5 D 5 L 16 F 35 A 66 Pts 15.

After New Brighton were beaten 2-1 at Barrow on 4 February, League leaders Chester visited Rake Lane on the following Wednesday. The gate receipts were £172 — 3,384 spectators constituting a good midweek attendance. With only 90 seconds of the game remaining the score was 1-1 and many spectators had left the ground when a penalty by Dickie and a splendid goal by Liggins ended the most exciting game of the season, 3-1 in the Rakers' favour. In their third game in seven days, a 2-0 win against Carlisle United brought the season's first 'double', and it was also the first time since last August that the defence had kept a 'clean sheet'. A midweek Welsh Cup tie at Bangor gave the Rakers a share of a gate of 3,284, a figure far in excess of some League attendances.

Whilst the seniors were going down 3-0 at York, the Reserves were scoring ten against Liverpool Trams — W.Lowndes, the Egremont United goalgetter, scoring four in succession in his first game in New Brighton's colours.

No time was lost in pitching the amateur centre-forward into League action and his response was electrifying. He scored ten goals in 12 outings, including a hat-trick on his third appearance, against Hartlepools United, and four against Darlington on 8 April. The new leader's arrival coincided with a much needed improvement in results, only two defeats being sustained in the final 11 matches. Amongst the wins, League leaders Hull City went down to a Lowndes' goal at Sandheys and Darlington were beaten 7-0 and exchanged places with the Rakers, at the bottom of the table.

The Liverpool Senior Cup came to Rake Lane for the first time in the club's history, Southport being beaten in most decisive fashion by 6-1 at Goodison Park on 25 April. The victory only confirmed the League form of the Easter games between the two clubs, when New Brighton took three points from the two games.

In their final away match, the Rakers took an invaluable point at Walsall — managing to do what Arsenal had failed to achieve a few weeks earlier.

The team were left needing only a point from their final game of the season, at home against Wrexham, to avoid having to seek re-election. They strove desperately to get it, but a slip by Ken Greatrex in the Rakers' goal presented Wrexham with their first goal. After Billy Lowndes had a goal disallowed for offside, Bamford scored again for Wrexham. During a heavy rainstorm in the second half the Rakers went near on several occasions, but the final whistle sounded with the score at 0-2.

The season's record was: P 42 W 11 D 10 L 21 F 63 A 88 Pts 32. New Brighton were level on points with York City, but their goal-average was inferior. Darlington were bottom of the League with 28 points.

At the annual meeting of the League on 29 May, both Rakers and Darlington were re-elected with 47 votes each. Amongst the items discussed at the meeting, a motion by Tottenham Hotspur to introduce the numbering of players in League matches was defeated.

After a long spell in the doldrums, the Rakers appeared to have gathered together a squad of players which would enable the club to face the coming season with every confidence.

Amongst manager Sawyer's new recruits were Lachlan McPherson, the former Swansea Town and Everton half-back; Jasper Kerr, a full-back whose previous clubs included Everton and Preston North End, and Charlie Butler, a young wing-half from Blackburn Rovers. Of the seven new forward recruits, Tommy Davis, who netted 68 goals for Torquay United Reserves the previous season, scored four goals in the two pre-season trials and was expected to add punch to the attack. Frank Pegg, the former Norwich City winger, and Frank Allen, an experienced utility player, also showed up well in the trials.

The season opened at Doncaster and the Rakers contained the home side well in heatwave conditions, finally going down to the only goal of the game, a penalty which was parried by George Bradshaw, but was converted on the rebound by Emery, the Doncaster captain.

Walsall opened the season at Sandheys and the previous season's giantkillers proved robust opponents. The crowd of 4,658 witnessed a great struggle before goals by Liggins and McPherson saw the Rakers home by 2-0.

Three days later, Barrow were the visitors. After 32 minutes the Rakers were two goals up and appeared well in control. Two minutes after the interval came sensations. Wassell, the Barrow full-back, handled in the penalty area, but McPherson, the Rakers' captain, drove his spot-kick wide of the left upright. Within a minute, Wassell — again — brought down Liggins and New Brighton were awarded another penalty. Frank Pegg stepped forward but his shot passed outside the right-hand upright. Barrow then proceded to wipe out the two-goal deficit, their last-minute equalizer being scored by ex-Raker, Bill Murray.

At Walsall, the Rakers were defeated by the odd goal in three. The Saddlers' win was largely due to the opportunism of their centre-forward, Gilbert Alsop, who ended the season with 40 goals.

A good run of results followed. The season's first away win came at Carlisle, then Stockport County and Crewe Alexandra were beaten at Rake Lane. Attendances were improving as supporters rallied in encouraging numbers. The benefit game for Len Carr and Jimmy Smedley was attended by 4,311 spectators, when Everton brought the FA Cup and eight of their Cup-winning team, to Sandheys Park. An entertaining game ended in a 2-2 draw.

New Brighton 1932-3. Back row (left to right): Bill Sawyer (manager), Smedley, Clement, Greatrex, Carr, Ratcliffe, A.McKinnon (trainer). Front row: Liggins, Parle, Lowndes, Miller, Dickie, Amery.

38

On the eve of the 'derby' game against Tranmere Rovers at Prenton Park, both sides had virtually identical records, each having ten points from eight fixtures. It was not one of the best meetings between the local rivals, the Rovers winning by the only goal of the game.

New Brighton's best performance in October was their 3-1 defeat of Liverpool in the Liverpool Senior Cup semi-final. Davis, Miller and Barley (penalty) were the Rakers' scorers. Barley's spot-kick was the first successful one of the season, three previous awards having been missed.

Alas, League form evaporated after a 2-2 draw at Rotherham on 14 October, four successive defeats being sustained in which 15 goals were conceded and none scored. Six changes for the visit to Gateshead had anything but the desired effect as the new formation went down 6-0. Billy Lowndes, last season's goalscoring hero, made his final League appearance in this match. He had been injured in the pre-season trials and tragically never fully recovered his form and fitness.

Finally breaking their long run of poor results by beating Darlington at home, attention focussed on the FA Cup. Mansfield Town, whose new trainer-coach was Harry Martin, the former Sunderland and Nottingham Forest winger and English international, were the first visitors and a crowd of 4,289 attended the goalless draw. New Brighton had fully three-quarters of the play, but poor finishing left them unable to turn their territorial superiority to advantage.

For the replay at Field Mill, Davis and Miller were reintroduced into the Rakers' forward line, in what proved to be a remarkable Cup tie. New Brighton were two goals down after only 12 minutes. Jasper Kerr received a knee injury within two minutes of the start and was unable to resume after the interval, when Mansfield led 2-0. Against all the odds, the Rakers made a remarkable comeback. Within five minutes Harry Barley scored from a penalty and then from a free-kick which rocketed into the net through a wall of defenders. Barley was having a field day and it was his centre which Frank Pegg headed home to put New Brighton in front. Barley scored his third, and the Rakers' fourth, which was made possible by a brilliant dribble by Tommy Davis. He ran half the length of the field before passing to Barley, who completed his hat-trick. Johnson reduced Mansfield's arrears late in the game, which ended 4-3 in New Brighton's favour. The receipts totalled £320 and 6,300 spectators attended.

The second-round draw booked New Brighton for a trip to Loftus Road, Shepherd's Bush, to meet QPR, lying second in the Third Division South. They had defeated Kettering Town 6-0 in the first round. It proved an exciting Cup tie. A sensational opening saw QPR's centre-forward, Blackman, head home within three minutes. After 17 minutes the Rakers were level through a penalty from Harry Barley. In the closing stages Barley was knocked out in a collision with a QPR defender but, although reeling like a drunk, he insisted on carrying on to the final whistle. It was an example of the never-say-die spirit which had earned New Brighton the right to a replay. Sadly, they were unable to reproduce the form which had earned the replay and Rakers' supporters who saw their team beaten 4-0 must have wondered how ever they managed to draw at Shepherd's Bush. There was some consolation in the gate receipts from the two Cup ties, which totalled £1,329.

On the ever-present subject of finances, the annual meeting of shareholders, held on Monday 18 December, revealed that income had increased, expenses had decreased and there was actually a surplus of £62 17s 8d on the income and expenditure account for the year.

As a prelude to the Christmas holiday programme, Mansfield Town were beaten 5-1 on 16 December, Tommy Davis scoring a first-half hat-trick. Three holiday games within the space of four days yielded only one point, however, and at this point the Rakers stood fifth from the bottom of the table with 16 points from

20 matches. The 'goals-for' column illustrated the team's problems, 22 goals being the lowest in the division.

The Liverpool Senior Cup Final at Rake Lane on New Year's Day was a hard-fought 'derby' against Tranmere Rovers. The Rakers were holders of the trophy but, despite scoring first, they were well beaten 4-1. Ten minutes from time, Jimmy Smedley was sent off the field, for the only time in his career.

Worse was to follow, however, when the Rakers were routed 11-1 by Wrexham at the Racecourse in the first round of the new Northern Section Cup. It was New Brighton's sixth game in 11 days and the defence cracked up so badly that a big score was inevitable. Bamford scored six of Wrexham's goals and Bryant three. Only 2,600 spectators attended, the receipts being £124.

The first League match of 1934 saw the Rakers take a point from Holker Street, Barrow. Three times in the lead, New Brighton had to settle for a draw in a six-goal thriller. Elsewhere in the Northern Section, Stockport County won a sensational match against Halifax Town by 13-0.

At this point the team hovered dangerously near to the foot of the table, with 18 points from 22 matches and a goal-average of 27-40. Their attack was again proving to be the main problem, 27 goals being the lowest in the Division. Barnsley, the eventual champions, had at this point conceded five more goals than the Rakers, but had scored 60.

January and February settled into much the usual pattern, and of the nine matches played there were four home wins, four away defeats and one away draw. In early February the Rakers lost the services of Harry Barley, their talented young winger, who was transferred to Second Division Notts County.

In the Welsh Cup, sixth-round opponents Troedyrhaw, a South Wales mining village of 3,000 people, made house-to-house collections to raise funds to pay their railway fare to New Brighton. Seven of the Troedyrhaw team were said to be unemployed and three others were only in part-time employment. But they gave the Rakers a good fight before going down 3-2. Sadly, there were only about 1,000 spectators and gate receipts totalled only £44. After paying their visitors' travelling and hotel expenses, New Brighton were left with £1 10s out of which to find a total of £12 in bonuses for the winning team!

Defeat in the Welsh Cup came in round seven — the round before the semi-finals — when Bristol City won 2-1, thanks to a goal in the last-minute of the replay at Ashton Gate. There were 1,793 spectators with receipts of about £100, whilst at Rake Lane 1,906 spectators paid £87 to see the first match which ended 2-2.

A good defensive display earned a welcome point in the game at Sandheys against League leaders Chesterfield. One week later, however, in a blinding hailstorm, the same defence was unable to stem Accrington Stanley's goal rush and went under by 8-0. The result could have been even worse, but George Bradshaw made many brilliant saves — including one from a penalty. As it was, the 17 March fixture remains on the record books as New Brighton's worst-ever Football League defeat.

Only two points were gained from three Easter holiday matches. A north-eastern tour to York and Hartlepools resulted in two defeats, whilst the return game against York was won 2-1. One of the best victories of the season followed, when Southport were defeated 5-2 at Rake Lane. New Brighton were five up after 25 minutes and when, shortly afterwards, the visitors lost their goalkeeper, Pitt, following a collision with Alf Liggins, they faced disaster. Full-back Seagrove donned the goalkeeper's jersey and proved unbeatable. A string of magnificent saves encouraged his teammates to fight back and they responded by reducing the deficit by two second-half goals.

The Rakers must have travelled to Wrexham with some trepidation, having lost earlier in the season by 11-1 in the Northern Section Cup. Wrexham were 4-2 up at the interval but New Brighton fought back and were unfortunate not to force a draw, finally losing 5-4. Tommy Davis scored all of New Brighton's goals in a 4-1 win against Hartlepools United, but the season's final away match saw Mansfield win 5-2 to take ample revenge for their previous defeats, in League and Cup, at the hands of the Rakers.

Rake Lane housed a thrilling finale to the season when Barnsley's one-goal victory gave them promotion to the Second Division by a single point. Their nearest rivals, Stockport County, had only managed to make a goalless draw in their final fixture and when news of the result was announced, about 20 minutes after the end of the game, Rake Lane erupted as the Barnsley followers celebrated their team's success.

It had been a remarkable season of football with 1,800 goals being scored in the division's 462 fixtures. There had been five games in which a double-figure total of goals were scored, and, on 24 March, 70 goals were recorded from 11 matches.

New Brighton finished 15th in the table in 1933-4 with this record: P 42 W 14 D 8 L 20 F 62 A 87 Pts 36. Tommy Davis was club leading scorer with 24 goals in 35 appearances. Len Carr and Lachlan McPherson were ever present in League matches.

The new season opened with a visit to Accrington, where the team had met with disaster the previous season. Of the eight newcomers, only two were selected for the game at Peel Park. David McCrae, for ten seasons St Mirren's centre-forward, and holder of a Scottish Cup Final medal, and Wilf Brown, the former Boston United winger, were the Rakers' debutants.

Having only won once away from home in the League in 1933-4, New Brighton's fine 3-1 victory at Accrington was a heartening start to the new campaign.

New Brighton 1934-5. Back row (left to right): Mr Bebbington (assistant secretary), Smedley, Ratcliffe, Bird, Carr, Butler, unknown. Front: Kenyon, McPherson, Davis, Allen, Miller, Amery.

As the season progressed, the Rakers were proving more 'at home' in away matches. For instance, when Crewe were defeated 3-2 at Gresty Road, four of the season's five points to date had been won away from home.

On 27 October, New Brighton turned out in new colours of red and white quartered shirts and navy-blue shorts. The new strip had been presented to the club by an anonymous, but obviously enthusiastic, supporter in the hope that the new colours might bring a change of fortune. At this point, the Rakers held the unenviable distinction of being the only League club without a home victory. Alas, the new strip failed to change the team's luck and a goalless draw was the best that could be managed against visitors, Halifax Town.

David McCrae, who had arrived at New Brighton with a big reputation at the start of the season, departed early in November, having scored only once in 11 appearances.

A win at Rotherham on 3 November was the surprise result of the day, New Brighton being the first team to win at Millmoor that season. A home draw against Walsall preceded the FA Cup first-round tie at Southport. As New Brighton had not won in 18 previous visits to Haigh Avenue, their 1-1 draw was probably as much as could reasonably have been expected. Unfortunately, home 'advantage' was non-existent this season and, after extra-time at Rake Lane, another 1-1 draw

Cartoon from the Liverpool Echo *of 29 October 1934, commenting on New Brighton's new colours. The strip was donated to the club by an anonymous supporter.*

42

resulted. Perhaps it was the visit to the Nantwich brine baths that finally did the trick, as the Rakers won the second replay at Goodison Park by 2-1 and so qualified to meet York City, away, in the second round.

On 26 November, the Rakers lost their brilliant young goalkeeper, George Bradshaw, to Everton. His replacement was Tony Carr, an aviation pilot whose previous clubs included Preston North End and Newport County.

In a robust game, with an excess of Cup-tie spirit, the Rakers' interest in the FA Cup ended at Bootham Crescent, where they went down 1-0.

A heavy holiday programme opened on 15 December with a visit from Lincoln City. It was New Brighton's first home League match for six weeks and they introduced Fred Tarrant, a 21-year-old local amateur at centre-forward. Tarrant, though, failed to solve the team's goalscoring problem and Lincoln took the points with a 2-0 win. On Christmas Day, New Brighton's visit to Redheugh Park provided Gateshead with their first victory since 27 October, by the odd goal in three. Boxing Day finally provided some relief for the long-suffering Rakers' supporters when their team won 3-0, at last winning a home game.

Three days later, home win number-two was recorded — and the season's first 'double' — against Accrington Stanley, 2-1. It was a happy ending to the holiday games, but it had been a terribly disappointing time financially. There were only 4,047 spectators for Gateshead's visit on Boxing Day, whilst 2,815 attended the Saturday game against Accrington Stanley and only 1,225 saw the Northern Section Cup tie at Rake Lane against Crewe Alexandra on New Year's Day. Under £400 was been taken, when a figure of £1,000 had been expected.

At the mid-point of the season, the Rakers stood in 16th place with 17 points from 21 matches. Tranmere Rovers were leaders with 34 points, whilst Southport were at the foot of the table with 14 points.

Tommy Lawrence, the former Hoylake amateur, made his debut at outside-right against Darlington on 5 January. His inclusion did much to strengthen the forward line, which also featured another young winger, Billy Beckett.

Pre-war New Brighton line-up which formed part of a set of cigarette cards. Back row (left to right): A.McKinnon (trainer), Gaskell, Hogg, Temple, Bird, Beedles, Salmon, Hayes (assistant trainer). Middle row: Wilde, Brock, Milligan, Baxter, Hoggan, Lawrence, Amery. Front row: Scully, Torrance, Johnson, Beckett, Lewis, Elliott, Griffiths, Burke, Kitchen.

Alf Ainsworth, newly-signed from Manchester United, was outstanding on his debut which resulted in a 2-0 win over Stockport County.

The Tranmere 'derby' at Prenton on 26 January threw open the promotion race, when the Rakers inflicted Rovers' first home defeat of the season. Frank Allen scored the only goal of the game. Urmston, Tranmere's usually successful spot-kicker, drove a penalty against the woodwork after Beau Ratcliffe had handled on the goal-line. The attendance was 12,316 and receipts of over £600 were taken.

A number of the New Brighton team and directors crossed the Mersey on 30 January to witness the classic fourth-round FA Cup replay at Goodison, when Everton beat Sunderland 6-4, after extra-time. It was a game which even caused hardened sports critics to launch into rhapsodies. On all sides, it was described as one of the greatest games of football ever seen. Some of the atmosphere must have rubbed off on the Rakers, who visited Sealand Road three days later. Second-placed Chester were 4-1 in front after 52 minutes, but enterprising forward play by New Brighton saw them level at 4-4 before Chester secured the winner, six minutes from time.

Southport, 21st in the table, took a point from Rake Lane in a goalless draw which marked the debut of Charlie Bird, the young Hoylake goalkeeper, in New Brighton's team.

The next seven fixtures were all high-scoring affairs. Doncaster Rovers outpaced and outplayed the Rakers to win 7-1 and move to within four points of leaders, Tranmere, with two games in hand. Hartlepools United won 4-1 at Rake Lane on 23 February, and, four days later, New Brighton beat bottom-of-the-table Carlisle United 5-1, Tommy Davis scoring four. The attendance for this match was only 852 (receipts £35), but it included representatives from Aston Villa and Portsmouth and no doubt left the New Brighton directorate hoping for the windfall of a fat transfer fee before the 16 March 'deadline'.

Former Rakers in the news on Merseyside on 2 March were George Bradshaw and Alex Finney, opposed in the Everton-Bolton Wanderers sixth-round FA Cup tie which Bolton won 2-1 before a record attendance of 67,096, who paid £5,961.

New Brighton finally managed to break the Southport bogey. On their 20th visit they recorded their first victory, by 2-0, to progress to the final of the Liverpool Senior Cup competition. A week later, the Rakers visited Haigh Avenue again — this time for a Welsh Cup tie — and won 4-1. It was the eighth meeting of the rival seasiders this season.

At the Shay, the home centre-forward, Alf Valentine, scored five of Halifax Town's six goals. Miller and Davis replied for New Brighton. The second 'double' of the season came against Rotherham, who were a goal up within four minutes, but the Rakers rallied to win 3-2.

Against Walsall, a breakdown on the road — a replacement coach was sent to meet the team in Staffordshire — was followed by a breakdown on the field. In the lead and then level 1-1 at half-time, the Rakers finally lost 5-1, the division's leading goalscorer, Gilbert Alsop, scoring three of Walsall's goals.

Non-League Shrewsbury Town finally ended New Brighton's interest in the Welsh Cup in the seventh round, which needed two replays.

Charlie Bird, Rakers' young goalkeeper, gave an excellent display when New Brighton beat Chesterfield 3-1 at Rake Lane. Amongst many outstanding saves, Bird even managed to keep out a penalty taken by 'Duke' Hamilton — a former New Brighton player.

In the 2-1 reverse at Field Mill, Johnson, the Mansfield Town centre-forward, recorded his 300th League goal and received a tremendous ovation from the crowd and congratulations from the whole of the Stags' team.

The season's third 'double' accounted for Barrow at Rake Lane by 3-1, but the three Easter fixtures yielded only one point. An own-goal gifted the Rakers two points from their final home game against Rochdale and League fixtures were completed with a vist to Lincoln. The Imps had taken 20 points out of a possible 24 in their preceding matches and the Rakers did well to contain the home side to a single goal, which proved sufficient to win the game.

Two extra-time goals by Joe Milligan gave New Brighton a 2-0 victory over Tranmere Rovers in the replayed Liverpool Senior Cup Final at Rake Lane on 10 May. The first meeting, on Jubilee Day, Monday 6 May, had been drawn 1-1 at Prenton Park.

The Rakers' record for 1934-5 was identical to the previous season (14 wins, 8 draws and 20 defeats) but they finished one place lower in the League, in 16th place, with a goal-average of 59-76. Tommy Davis was leading goalscorer with 26 League goals, boosting his aggregate to 50 goals in two seasons.

Doncaster Rovers were champions of the Third Division North with 57 points, two points ahead of Halifax Town. Southport and Carlisle United were the successful re-election candidates, each polling 46 votes. The Northern Section Cup was won by Stockport County, who beat Walsall 2-0 at Maine Road, Manchester.

On Wednesday 22 May, a town meeting of New Brighton AFC at Wallasey Town Hall was attended by 1,000 supporters. The Rakers were again having to appeal for help to keep the club in existence. The bank overdraft was stated to be £12,500 and an immediate sum of £2,500 was required to relieve the present financial position. Total 'gate' receipts had amounted to only £3,510 and amongst the pressing liabilities was a sum of £250 for players' wages. Given that the population of Wallasey was about 100,000, attendances of 3,000 were disappointing in the extreme and the directors were having to subsidise the club to an unlimited degree to keep it going. There were about £2,000 worth of shares still not taken up and the meeting closed with a strong plea for support and a unanimous vote that the club should continue. It was agreed that a committee should be formed to co-operate with the directors to consider a means of financial reconstruction.

In view of the stringent financial situation, it was not surprising that the Rakers were obliged to part company with several of the previous season's best men. Davis, Ratcliffe and Butler were all transferred to Oldham Athletic, whilst long-serving stalwarts, Len Carr and Jimmy Smedley, were given free transfers. Of last season's professionals, only seven were re-signed.

Under the patronage of Lt-Col Moore-Brabazon MP, the 'Rakers SOS League', launched after the May meeting at Wallasey Town Hall, sought donations. Large and small sums were duly acknowledged in the columns of the *Wallasey News*.

Six newcomers were in the New Brighton team which met Tranmere Rovers at Sandheys on the opening Saturday of the season and a crowd of 11,603 saw a clean and thrilling 'derby' which ended goalless. The *Daily Express* volunteered the opinion that 'brighter days appear to be in store for New Brighton', but their optimism proved unfounded as the season progressed.

On the Monday following, the Rakers gave a disappointing display at Barrow. Two down within the first quarter of an hour, they were beaten 3-0.

An early goal — the season's first — by Tommy Lawrence gave the team a bright start at Chesterfield, but their pace slackened and the home side ran out comfortable 3-1 winners. Bird, the Rakers' goalkeeper, was injured at Chesterfield, and his place for the return fixture with Barrow was taken by McMullan, the Irish League 'cap'. Barrow proved a forceful combination and deservedly recorded their first 'double' at New Brighton's expense by 3-2.

The season's first victory coincided with the debut of 'Alf' Ainsworth, newly-signed from Manchester United. In the 2-0 win against Stockport County he was outstanding, as was Ernest Temple, the third goalkeeper to be used by the Rakers in only five fixtures.

The next four games were all lost. At York, the City won their first game of the season, beating the Rakers 2-0. A 5-1 defeat at Crewe proved a personal triumph for Waring, Alexandra's outside-right, who scored a hat-trick. Accrington Stanley took both points from Rake Lane, winning 3-2, but Charlie Amery missed a penalty for New Brighton. After losing 2-1 at Southport on 5 October — the game marking the debut of Norman Greenhalgh — the Rakers had sunk to the bottom of the table with a return of only three points from nine matches.

Third-placed Chester provided stiff opposition at Rake Lane on 12 October and after 70 minutes were leading 3-1. A Norman Beedles penalty and a late equalizer from amateur centre-forward John Search rescued a point. Search was on the mark again with a back-header which proved to be the only goal of the game against Gateshead. Only 2,173 spectators attended this match, which was played in almost gale-force winds. A visit to Darlington proved unrewarding, as the Quakers scored three goals in 20 minutes after half-time and won 4-1.

November opened with a visit from Halifax Town. Matt Hoggan, the Rakers' captain and centre-half, sustained an ankle injury soon after the interval when the score was 1-1. After he went off, Halifax scored three more goals against the disorganized defence to record their first away win of the season.

The absence of Hoggan and its effect on the team can best be illustrated by a list of the results during his absence (New Brighton scores first): Oldham Athletic (a) 0-6; Southport (a) 0-2; Wrexham (h) 0-4; Rotherham United (a) 0-5; Workington (h) 1-3; Hartlepools (a) 1-4.

The Southport match was a Northern Section Cup tie and the Workington game an FA Cup first-round match.

As this dismal period also included defeat in the Liverpool Senior Cup, 3-2 by Southport at Rake Lane, the captain's return, for the home game against Carlisle United, was warmly welcomed. Fortunately, his presence seemed to restore confidence and Johnson, the centre-forward signed from Nantwich, had his most successful day in League football, scoring a hat-trick in New Brighton's 3-0 win.

The Christmas holiday fixtures promised a severe test, with three away fixtures. Walsall, with 17 points from nine home games were nevertheless beaten 2-1 on an ice-bound Fellows Park. One of the Rakers' goals was scored by J.W.Lawton, a local product, playing in only his second League match.

On Boxing Day, whilst the Rakers were going down 2-0 at Lincoln, neighbours Tranmere Rovers were making history by beating Oldham Athletic 13-4 at Prenton Park. Nine of their goals were scored by 'Bunny' Bell, who, incidentally, lived in Sherlock Lane, Wallasey. With half a century of goals against them already, the Rakers could not have relished having to visit Tranmere just two days later. Recovering from early 'stage fright', New Brighton rallied in the second half, reducing their arrears to 2-1 by virtue of a stunning 35-yard free-kick from George Brock. Just before the end, Tranmere scored again to seal their victory. The 'top v bottom' clash attracted 13,529 spectators, which, when added to the 11,603 who attended the opening fixture of the season, gives some idea of the interest generated by these local 'derbies'.

At the mid-point of the season, the Rakers had only ten points from 21 matches and were very firmly anchored at the bottom of the table.

The new year began in much the same way as the old one had ended, Lincoln City winning 5-0 at Sandheys before 4,319 spectators. When Chesterfield were visitors on the first Saturday of the new year, only 3,216 turned up to see New Brighton lose 2-1, and, one week later, 2,208 witnessed a 1-0 home win against Mansfield Town. The winner in this match was scored by Dennis Westcott, who celebrated his League debut in the best possible way. A member of a well-known Wallasey footballing family, he had made his reserve-team debut a month earlier and scored twice against Northern Nomads.

At Stockport County, an icy surface made ball control difficult but the Rakers adapted themselves well to take an unexpected point. Westcott was again on the mark in the 1-1 draw. When Crewe were beaten 3-1 at Rake Lane on 25 January, five points had been gained from a possible six.

An inevitable outgoing transfer occurred when Charlie Amery left for Tranmere

Rovers. His going coincided with a heavy 5-2 defeat at Accrington Stanley. Dennis Westcott, now a professional, scored both of New Brighton's goals.

The visit of Southport matched two clubs struggling to avoid having to seek re-election. The Rakers' confidence was at a low ebb following their inept display in the Welsh Cup at Shrewsbury on 6 February. The non-League side were 3-0 up within seven minutes, four goals ahead at the interval, and ran out winners by 8-1. Thankfully, it was a different display altogether which enabled the Rakers to take the points from Southport. Westcott brought his goal tally to six in five games and only six points now separated the last eight clubs in the table.

A visit to Chester coincided with the first outing held by the newly-formed Rakers' Development and Improvement Association. The timing proved unfortunate, as Chester won 8-2. They had actually won their previous home game, against York City, by 12-0, and their win against the Rakers gave them a total of 24 goals in three consecutive League matches.

A much reshuffled side visited Gateshead, where New Brighton included the newly-signed 20-year-old Norman Richardson at left-back. Richardson was to prove a wonderful servant to the Rakers, totalling over 200 League appearances in a 15-year association which spanned the war and two 'home' grounds — Sandheys Park and the Tower Grounds. Another new signing was Billy Wright, a right-half, who came with Richardson from Bolton Wanderers. Their signing was a brave effort by the New Brighton board to give the team a chance to climb away from the foot of the table. There were 13 matches left and many of them were against clubs in the lower reaches of the table, so it promised to be quite a dog-fight.

Gateshead's unbeaten home record looked in danger when New Brighton led 1-0 at the interval, but it was not to be and three good goals gave the North-Eastern club a deserved victory.

As part of the 'Pools War' which had been simmering for some time, the Football League adopted 'secrecy' tactics by not releasing their fixture lists until the 11th hour, to prevent the pools companies from printing their coupons. The first instance of this policy caused a slump in attendances at Rake Lane, when only 1,490 spectators turned up to see Oldham Athletic take the points in a 3-1 win.

When Halifax Town obtained their first 'double' of the season by beating the Rakers 3-0 at the Shay, it was becoming obvious that only a total reversal of form would give New Brighton a chance to avoid having to seek re-election.

A home draw against Darlington, who had arrived at Rake Lane with the reputation of being very poor travellers, was followed by a 3-0 defeat at Wrexham. The first victory for six weeks came in the home game against Rotherham United by 3-0, Westcott (2) and Brown being the Rakers' scorers.

A trip to Mansfield, who were lying in 21st position, resulted in a 2-0 win for the Stags, and when the Easter fixtures yielded only three points from as many games, any hopes of avoiding the necessity of seeking re-election were finally dashed.

One of the most enjoyable events in this otherwise miserable season came on Monday 19 April when a Rakers' 'Past XI' met the 'Present XI' at Sandheys. Some 2,500 spectators enjoyed another glimpse of their old favourites, whose movements were not so brisk, but many retained a nimbleness of footwork which revived memories of their heyday.

The 'Past XI' was: Bert Mehaffy; Collins, Shepherd, Morrison, Jack Reid, Gee, Spencer, Kelly (sub Lewis), Williams, Whalley, Carney. The referee was Jack Lyon and the linesmen were George Bryson and 'Sandy' Watson, the former trainer.

A light-hearted contest ended in a draw of seven goals each and after the game all the players were guests of the Rakers' Development Association at a hot-pot supper at the New Brighton Ferry Hotel.

When the serious business resumed, the least successful season in the club's history wound up with only one point from the remaining three fixtures and a final record of 24 points from 42 matches. There were only nine wins and six draws and the goal-average was 43-102. The team's record was the worst, in every aspect, in the division. They had recorded the least number of wins, the most defeats, scored the least and conceded the most goals. The Reserves, by comparison, had enjoyed a good season, finishing 11th in the Lancashire Combination, scoring 111 goals in their 40 matches. They were also runners-up in the Combination Cup.

Chesterfield were the champions of the Northern Section, whilst Chester were runners-up. Chester also won the Northern Section Cup.

On 8 June, New Brighton were re-elected along with Southport. The voting resulted — Southport (47), New Brighton (38), Shrewsbury Town (7), Wigan Athletic (6).

It came as no great surprise in the 1936 close season when Dennis Westcott, who was New Brighton's leading goalscorer the previous season, despite playing in only 18 matches, was snapped-up by Wolverhampton Wanderers.

After such a poor showing in 1935-6, the Rakers were busy in the summer months and their team building reflected the need for men of experience to blend with the younger players.

There were six debutants in the side which ran out at Boundary Park, Oldham, on the first Saturday of the new season. The team was: Hawthorn (from Airdrie); Greenhalgh, Richardson, Wright, Vaughton (Boston United), Brock, Mustard (Wrexham), Ainsworth, Watters (Ayr United), Shiels (Belfast Celtic), Watkins (Bolton Wanderers).

Amongst other signings, Billy Fogg (Clapton Orient) and Hugh Bulloch (Newcastle United) soon became first-team regulars. Leslie Roberts, an inside-forward with extensive experience, did not establish himself until later in the season.

A goal from ex-Raker Tommy Davis helped Oldham to a 3-1 win in the first game, but the introduction of Fogg at outside-right and four other positional changes in attack helped account for Port Vale, the former Second Division club, by 2-0 at Sandheys.

The season's first 'derby' against Tranmere Rovers drew 9,579 spectators to Rake Lane. In a dramatic finish, Tranmere won 2-1, Eden's winner coming so late in the game that there was not even time to kick the ball upfield for a restart before the final whistle sounded.

The Rakers were already having their usual problems in attack. Their approach work was often good but, once in front of goal, they frittered away their chances. Even the club's official programme stated: 'Everyone interested in the Rakers is crying out for a centre-forward and an outside-left'.

The new centre-forward was not long in arriving and Paddy Shiels was switched to outside-left. The new leader, Jack Leonard, a Scottish recruit who had played for Hibernian, scored on his debut but, after a five-match run, lost his place, having failed to supply the necessary fire-power to a weak attack.

The introduction of Hugh Bulloch at centre-half and the switching of Willis Vaughton to right-back, proved to be an inspired move. Bulloch, who took over the captaincy from Mustard, proved a fine, wholehearted pivot. In October the team were unbeaten in five games and conceded only one goal. The two wins and three draws lifted them to 11th in the table, their record at this stage being 13 points from 13 matches with a goal-difference of 13-12.

For the first time, the Rakers cleared the first hurdle of the Northern Section Cup by beating Wrexham 1-0 at the Racecourse, the scene of their 11-1 drubbing three years earlier. In the Liverpool Senior Cup, however, New Brighton made the mistake of underestimating their opponents, South Liverpool. With Bulloch the only absentee from the side which had gone six games without defeat, they took matters far too easily and were beaten 1-0.

A 'gate' of 8,435 saw League leaders Chester defeated 1-0 at Rake Lane. It was Chester's first away defeat of the season and Willie Hawthorn's fifth consecutive 'clean sheet' in the Rakers' goal. A week later, the team fell from grace by losing 4-0 at Rochdale, who displayed form very much above what could have been expected from a team lying 22nd in the table.

New Brighton visited Sincil Bank for the first round of the FA Cup, and did extremely well to hold Lincoln City to a 1-1 draw. The replay at Sandheys saw the Rakers in front after 42 minutes through a penalty by Mustard. Lincoln equalized after 57 minutes and in the 78th minute, Watters restored New Brighton's lead. Callender, however, headed a fine equalizer to take the tie into extra-time. The tired, mud-spattered teams battled on through a heavy rainstorm and, seven minutes from the end, Lincoln went ahead for the first time in the game, through Horne, his goal proving the decider. The receipts for the two games were £377 at Lincoln and £228 at New Brighton.

Welsh amateur international W.D.Foulkes joined the Rakers in December and scored three of the team's six goals that month, but only three points were taken from five matches. On Christmas Day, the first-ever morning kick-off (11am) at Sandheys saw 5,618 pass through the turnstiles to witness the Rakers' sixth home draw of the season, against Stockport County. Boxing Day visitors, Oldham Athletic, drew a crowd of 7,036 and they took both points thanks to two goals from ex-Raker Tommy Davis — who had become an Irish international since leaving Rake Lane. This defeat proved to be the first of seven consecutive reverses which left New Brighton third from the bottom of the table.

The return of Hugh Bulloch, who had been absent due to a leg injury and influenza, sparked a revival, the 2-1 win at Darlington being the team's first in almost two months. Both New Brighton's goals were scored by Bill Hullett, a young opportunist centre-forward who had been recruited from Everton in January.

As the 'deadline' for transfers approached, New Brighton inevitably were sellers when George Brock, who had first joined the Rakers on a month's trial as a 19-year-old in August 1935, left for Wolverhampton Wanderers.

With the return of Bulloch, a good run of results followed. In February, two games were won and two drawn, which lifted the Rakers to 16th place in the League.

In March, three home games were won and three away matches lost. Of the home wins, Rochdale were beaten 5-1 and Rotherham United 4-0. The Rochdale game featured a hat-trick by Alf Ainsworth and an unusual goal by Bill Hullett. The centre-forward restarted the game after the interval by passing to Ainsworth, who dribbled past three opponents. There was a quick interchange of passes between Hullett and the inside-right before the centre-forward drove the ball into the net. From the time of the restart until Fawcett picked the ball out of the back of the net, Hullett and Ainsworth were the only players to have touched it.

At the end of March the Rakers had edged up to 15th with 32 points from 36 matches. The month had seen the side dismissed from the Northern Section Cup, the eventual winners of the trophy, Chester, thrashing New Brighton 9-2, five goals coming from outside-left, Sargeant.

April began off the field at the Town Hall, where a rally of supporters and friends of the club met to enlist support for the Rakers' '50,000 Shillings Fund', a scheme devised by the Rakers' Improvement and Development Association. Over 400 subscription lists were issued and 50 helpers carried out house-to-house canvassing. The weekly progress of the fund was faithfully recorded in the columns of the *Wallasey News*, and it included such diverse items as a £10 donation from Lt-Col Moore-Brabazon MP, to 1s 3½d, proceeds of a house-to-house collection, 'per Mr Hughes'.

On the field, the six remaining League fixtures contained only two at home and with the Rakers only six points above Darlington in 22nd place, a good start to the month was imperative. Bill Hullett was unfortunately sidelined due to an injury sustained in New Brighton's 3-0 defeat by Rhyl in the Welsh Cup semi-final. To fill Hullett's place, Norman Greenhalgh, recently recovered from an operation for appendicitis, was selected to lead the attack. His normal position was half-back or full-back, but as temporary leader he did a fine job, scoring six goals in four games. York City were beaten 4-1 and Hartlepools United 4-0 at Rake Lane, whilst a point was gained at Carlisle United in a 1-1 draw. Well clear of danger at this point the team relaxed and in an inglorious finish lost their last three matches, all away, by 2-1, 3-0 and 5-0.

The team finished in 14th place, their best showing since season 1929-30, with 37 points from 42 matches. There were 13 wins, 11 draws and 18 defeats. Stockport County were the champions with 60 points, Lincoln City runners-up with 57. Two North-Eastern clubs, Gateshead and Darlington, occupied 21st and 22nd places respectively. Both were re-elected, Darlington with 47 votes, Gateshead with 34. Unsuccessful applicants were — Shrewsbury Town (12), South Liverpool (4) and Wigan Athletic (1).

Leading goalscorer in the division was Harston with a remarkable 55 goals in 41 matches for Mansfield Town. The Rakers, who had managed to score only 55 goals between them, had Alf Ainsworth as their leading scorer with 11 goals.

Thanks to the help of the supporters' organization, which raised £370, New Brighton were able to retain their team almost in its entirety. Financial resources had been strained to do so, but it was felt that the club was better placed in regard to the known capabilities of the playing staff, than had been the case in many past seasons.

Barrow were the first visitors of 1937-8 and it was a familiar looking New Brighton side which took the points, the only newcomer being Jack Montgomery, formerly of Manchester United. The new centre-forward's first goal in Third Division football gave the Rakers the lead after 33 minutes and they went on to win 2-1. They enjoyed an early distinction, being the only Merseyside club to start the season with a win.

In the midweek visit to Crewe on 1 September, a first-minute goal by Foster proved sufficient to give the home side the points and meant that the Rakers had got off to a bad start in their new colours, which were worn for the first time. Maroon and white vertical stripes had replaced the old red and white quartered jerseys.

A Norman Greenhalgh penalty after 15 minutes, and a strong defensive display thereafter, accounted for Wrexham at the Racecourse. A 4-0 win at home against Crewe Alexandra followed and was unusual for the fact that New Brighton scored four times in an inspired spell of 14 minutes in the second half. After beating Hartlepools United 4-1 at Rake Lane on 11 September, the Rakers enjoyed the novel position of League leaders for the 48 hours between Saturday and Monday night.

However, a 3-2 defeat at Port Vale knocked New Brighton off their lofty perch and it was the fifth time that the leadership had changed hands within the space of a fortnight. For the next match, at Lincoln, Montgomery was dropped and reserve full-back, Norman Richardson, was chosen to lead the attack. It was a strange selection and Lincoln won easily by 4-1. Montgomery replied in the best possible way by scoring the two goals which knocked Wrexham out of the Northern Section Cup, and was promptly reinstated into the first team.

In a hard, testing game against Hull City, the Rakers failed to maintain their 100 per cent home record. Hull's defence, one of the soundest in the Third Division, proved impregnable and the crowd of 5,792 had to be content with a goalless draw.

The season's first 'derby' at Tranmere proved a remarkable game. Contrary to general expectations, New Brighton were vastly superior in the first half. If only they had finished better, they would have enjoyed a more commanding lead than 1-0. In the second half, a sensational period of six minutes saw Tranmere score four times. Later, Waring added another to complete the rout, Leslie Roberts netting for New Brighton almost on full-time. A crowd of almost 13,000 saw the game.

A visit to the surprise leaders, Gateshead — who had been re-elected at the end

51

of the previous season — proved unrewarding. Gateshead were two up within four minutes of the kick-off and ran out 3-1 winners. At this point, after ten matches, the Rakers had nine points and stood 12th in the table.

A run of better results followed. Home wins against Halifax Town and Accrington Stanley were interspersed with a draw at Carlisle and a fine victory at Chester. It was New Brighton's first success at The Stadium since Chester joined the League. In the 2-1 win, Leslie Roberts had a fine game against one of his former clubs.

Another visit to Prenton Park, this time for the first round of the Liverpool Senior Cup, had many similarities to the League meeting. New Brighton scored first and then lost by a margin of three goals.

Twice in front against Rotherham United — a team which had been beaten at Sandheys in seven successive seasons — the Rakers contrived to lose their unbeaten home record, 3-2. A 2-1 defeat at Rochdale left New Brighton supporters hoping that League form would count for little in cup ties as Workington were the visitors for the first round of the FA Cup. The same visitors had, two years earlier, beaten New Brighton at Rake Lane in the same competition. Only two players remained in the New Brighton side from the team beaten in 1935 — Alf Ainsworth and Norman Greenhalgh. On this occasion, New Brighton proved far superior and won, in some style, by 5-0. Montgomery had his best game since joining the club, scoring four of the Rakers' goals. The attendance was 5,287 and the receipts were £275.

A goalless draw at Southport preceded the second round of the FA Cup at Crewe. The Railwaymen had been FA Cup opponents as far back as the 1922-3 season, when the Rakers won 1-0 at Crewe after drawing at Sandheys. New Brighton managed to win again, but it took a hard struggle and a slice of luck.

In the game at Gresty Road on 11 December, Crewe were leading 1-0 when the referee ordered the game to be abandoned after 84 minutes. Although the local correspondent had considered the whole of the second half to be a 'midnight matinee', it did not prevent many Crewe supporters swarming on to the pitch to remonstrate with the referee, Mr Snape of Swinton. An FA enquiry later closed Crewe's ground for 14 days from 3 January, and the club was ordered to post warning notices and pay the cost of the commission.

A replay was arranged for the following Wednesday. When New Brighton left Liverpool at noon the sun was shining, but almost as soon as the game started, hail and sleet started to fall. It turned into a snowstorm and the Rakers played against the full force of the blizzard, practically throughout the first half and had a hard fight to keep on level terms. At half-time the score was 1-1 and referee Snape dispensed with the interval. Immediately the second half started, Foster scored for Crewe. Montgomery equalized for New Brighton and there was no further scoring.

The replay was fixed to take place at Rake Lane on 20 December and in the third game, New Brighton were on top right from the start. They kept the ball on the move and made good use of their wingers, progressing into the third round for the first time for ten years.

Much of December had been taken up by the FA Cup matches, but a visit to York provided the City with their fourth consecutive win, by a 3-1 margin. On Christmas morning a crowd of 5,565 gathered at Sandheys, despite the dense fog. The start was delayed and the game had to be abandoned at half-time, neither side having scored. Similar conditions at Oldham on Boxing Day made a start impossible and the only consoling feature was that the players had been given a rest at a critical stage in their heavy programme.

January was a busy month, and the team seemed to reserve their best form for the Cup ties, only one point being taken from four League games and home defeats being sustained against Lincoln City and Doncaster Rovers. Bottom-of-the-table Barrow obtained their first win for three months at the Rakers' expense, 3-0 at

Holker Street, and a home draw with Wrexham represented New Brighton's only League success that month.

Second Division Plymouth Argyle were third-round visitors to Rake Lane. New Brighton had the biggest share of the game and deserved their 1-0 victory, but special credit was also due to Rakers' goalkeeper, Willie Hawthorn, who was 'chaired' to the dressing-room after the game. Jack Mustard was New Brighton's scorer, from the penalty-spot after 70 minutes. The attendance was 10,757 and the receipts £717. The best third-round figures were 64,244 (£6,121) for the Arsenal-Bolton Wanderers tie at Highbury.

The fourth-round draw favoured New Brighton with a home tie against Tottenham Hotspur, twice FA Cup winners. Rakers' secretary-manager, Bill Sawyer, commented: "Wallasey should have the biggest football treat in its history".

Listed at 100-1, along with Bradford City and York City, by one of the biggest London bookmakers, the Rakers were desperately unlucky not to progress into the fifth round. A crowd of 13,029 packed into Sandheys and 90 per cent of the spectators were unanimous that Ainsworth's 'goal', just before half-time, was a legitimate one. Referee Seale thought otherwise, however, and the game ended goalless.

The replay, at White Hart Lane, took place on the following Wednesday. London journalists all agreed that New Brighton had had their confidence badly shaken by the referee's allowing of two 'offside' goals — especially as one was in the opening minutes of the game. The Rakers were 4-1 down at half-time and, despite a fine goal from Hugh Bulloch after 63 minutes, lost 5-2. So ended the most profitable and eventful Cup run in New Brighton's history, seven games in four rounds having been watched by 78,327 spectators, who paid a total of £5,292.

League business resumed, but two familiar faces were missing. Bulloch had departed to take up the position of manager of Portadown, the Irish League club, whilst Norman Greenhalgh, who had been watched by a large number of clubs, was transferred to Everton.

Arthur Buxton stepped into the centre-half spot and the vacant left-back role was contested by Richardson and Morris. Albert Wood, an experienced inside-forward from Tranmere Rovers, was signed and proceeded to occupy four different positions in his first four League matches.

The somewhat unfamiliar looking side had a difficult February programme. A visit to Hartlepools resulted in a 1-0 defeat and a 'crowd' of 1,911. A 1-1 draw at Hull City dealt a blow to the Tigers' promotion hopes and did New Brighton's Birkenhead neighbours a good turn. Just over 12,000 spectators were present when Tranmere went to Rake Lane and retained their hold on the leadership by winning 1-0. A visit from Gateshead, lying third in the table, provided the Rakers with their first League win since 6 November, by 4-1. From this point, the corner was turned and the side remained undefeated at home for the remainder of the season.

March saw the return of Paddy Shiels after his cartilage operation. His return was celebrated with a fine 5-1 win against Carlisle United, all the Rakers' goals coming in the second half. Three consecutive wins against Chester (4-0), Rotherham United (2-1) and Rochdale (2-0) set up the side for a hectic holiday programme and a month which contained no less than nine League games.

A benefit match for Rakers' secretary-manager Bill Sawyer, between New Brighton and Everton on 2 May, proved an enjoyable distraction as Norman Greenhalgh had some friendly duels with his former club-mates. Everton won 5-4 in a match which deserved a bigger attendance than 1,387. Two League games in May produced a 1-0 win over Oldham Athletic and a final 1-1 draw against Port Vale was completed by a leg-weary side, who had concluded their programme with four matches in eight days.

New Brighton finished one point better off than the previous season and one place

Harry Topping, a full-back from Exeter City, was signed in time for the 1938-9 season but after establishing himself as first choice, lost his place to Arthur Buxton.

higher in the table. Their record was: P 42 W 15 D 9 L 18 F 60 A 61 Pts 39, position 13th.

Tranmere Rovers were champions with 56 points and Doncaster Rovers finished runners-up. Barrow and Accrington Stanley were re-elected, Accrington with 41 votes, Barrow with 35. Southport won the Northern Section Cup, beating Bradford City 4-1 the Final.

In the Third Division North as a whole, only 1,401 goals were scored, 201 fewer than in 1936-7. It was also the lowest figure recorded since 1925-6, when the new offside law had first come into force. Jack Montgomery, with 24 League goals, was joint second in the Division's scoring list, which was headed by Roberts (Port Vale) with 28.

Huge Bulloch, whose registration had been retained by New Brighton when he left to join Portadown in January, was reported to be returning to the Rakers. Happy news, indeed, on which to close the season.

The most profitable Cup run in the history of the New Brighton club, apart from helping the directors to reduce the overdraft, enabled them to retain most of the team for the 1938-9 season. Two new wingers were signed in Stein (Burnley) and Allmark (Manchester City). Other newcomers included Harry Topping, a full-back from Exeter City, Leslie Turner, a wing-half with three year's experience with Doncaster Rovers, Jack Stamps, an inside-forward from Mansfield Town, and Arthur Frost, who had played centre-forward for the Army.

The customary two trial games were well attended and the season kicked off with a Football League Jubilee Fund friendly against Tranmere Rovers at Prenton Park. The game lacked the usual fireworks associated with these 'derby' games, but Tranmere — now a Second Division team — won at a canter by 6-1.

For the opening of the League season, Small replaced Allmark for the visit of Stockport County, who had just been relegated from the Second Division. The Rakers' line-up had a familiar look: Hawthorn; Vaughton, Topping, Wright, Bulloch, Turner, Small Ainsworth, Montgomery, Wood, Stein. A crowd of 5,782 witnessed a goalless draw — the only one of the day's 44 League games in which a goal was not scored. Ten minutes after the interval, Stockport were awarded a penalty. Hawthorn made a brilliant save from Reid's shot, but was injured when the Stockport player followed up. As the local reporter put it: 'Tempers were not always urbane afterwards'.

Hawthorn, who had not missed a match since August 1936, was unfit to take his place in goal at Chester on the following Wednesday and 22-year-old George Gale, a six-footer from Northwich Victoria, was given an early League debut. He had a relatively quiet time as New Brighton shocked Chester with a display of high-quality football and thoroughly earned their 3-1 victory. Jimmy Stein, the former Everton winger, was in brilliant form and laid on two of New Brighton's goals.

A visit to Accrington resulted in away victory number-two, Montgomery scoring both of the Rakers' goals in the 2-1 win. When Lincoln City were beaten 3-2, the Rakers' third consecutive win lifted them to second place in the table, sharing with the leaders, Oldham Athletic, the distinction of being the only undefeated teams in the division.

Barnsley were the first team to lower the Rakers' colours. New Brighton held the balance of play but made a present of both goals to the visitors. Deputy goalkeeper Gale had an unhappy afternoon. The disappointing 2-1 reverse was witnessed by 7,574 spectators.

With Hawthorn back in goal and Buxton introduced at left-back in place of Topping, the defence was much strengthened and a goalless draw at Lincoln brought the Rakers' points return to eight from six matches. A visit to Boundary Park, to meet unbeaten Oldham Athletic, provided a fine game for the crowd of over

10,000 spectators. Oldham won by the only goal of the game, scored eight minutes from time.

At this time, two young players were actively pressing their claims for promotion from the Rakers' Reserves, who were having a wonderful time in the Lancashire Combination, having scored 29 goals in seven games and suffering only one defeat. Arthur Frost was the first to be promoted, Jack Stamps had a little longer to wait, but both were destined to make big impressions.

Frost's League debut was against Halifax Town at Sandheys. It was a tight match and the Raker's best chance appeared to have gone when a penalty by Jimmy Stein was brilliantly saved by Briggs. The new centre-forward, however, marked his debut with a fine winner, rounding the goalkeeper and scoring from a narrow angle.

It had been a busy month with six fixtures but, at the end of September, the Rakers were handily placed, only three points behind the leaders, Oldham Athletic.

An unchanged team played throughout October. An away victory, 2-1 at Wrexham, was followed by a 3-0 defeat at Barrow. York City, who on the previous Wednesday had visited Rotterdam and were beaten 8-2 by the Dutch national side (as a preliminary to their international match against Denmark on 23 October) were also beaten by the Rakers, but only by 3-2.

A 3-0 home win against Rotherham United ended the month and after 13 matches the team had 16 points and were lying in eighth place in the table, within four points of the leaders, Barnsley.

Doncaster Rovers, the previous season's runners-up, were in top form when the Rakers visited Belle Vue on 5 November. All the fireworks were supplied by the Rovers, whose power in the goal-area was the deciding factor in their 4-1 win. New Brighton's only goal was scored by Wood, who had been injured earlier and was hobbling at outside-left. Wood's injury was to give Jack Stamps his opportunity and he accepted it with both feet. His debut was against the Third Division North leaders, Southport, who had suffered only one defeat in 13 matches and whose defence was one of the best in the division. The game was a credit to the Third Division. Stamps opened his account within seven minutes with a powerful left-foot shot and seven minutes from time, and in failing light, Scott equalized for the visitors. There was a good attendance of 7,755.

The FA Cup draw paired the Rakers with Doncaster, in a repeat of the League game at the beginning of the month. A week before the tie, the Rakers were at their worst, going down 7-1 at Crewe after losing goalkeeper Gale, who was injured in trying to save goal number-five.

Heavy rain on the morning of the Cup tie had an adverse effect on the 'gate' at Belle Vue, just over 11,000 watching the game, whereas there had been over 15,000 present for a League match the week before. Allmark replaced Small at outside-right for New Brighton, who battled hard but went down 4-2. Doncaster progressed to the fourth round where they were beaten 8-0 by Everton at Goodison Park.

The December fixtures were estimated to contain a 1,000-mile 'tour', with visits to Darlington, Gateshead, Stockport County and Hull City. Darlington, who had the worst defensive record in the entire Football League, nevertheless managed to keep the Rakers at bay whilst scoring three themselves. Visitors Carlisle, without an away win since 30 August, obtained the points at Rake Lane, despite playing with ten men for most of the second half. It was the first time that Carlisle had won a match at New Brighton.

Against all expectations, the Rakers' visit to Gateshead resulted in a 3-0 victory, but the game attracted only 2,469 spectators. A stiff five-match programme occupied the Rakers over the Christmas period and they finished 1938 in fine style. A Christmas Eve draw at Stockport County was a good start, but at Hull the home side scored after two minutes and finished 3-0 winners. Considering the conditions — the surface was a mixture of ice and water — there was some good football played. A day later, New Brighton fully avenged their defeat by beating Hull 6-1 at Rake Lane. A hat-trick by Arthur Frost in this match took his tally to 11 in 14 matches.

On New Year's Eve, the Rakers celebrated by gaining their first 'double' of the season against bottom club, Accrington Stanley, by 4-1. At this point, 24 points had come from 23 matches and New Brighton occupied 11th place. Barnsley were the leaders by seven points and the Rakers opened the 1939 fixtures at Oakwell. They succeded in taking a point with one of the best performances of the day. Steve Hughes, the amateur centre-half, made his debut in this match, replacing the injured Hugh Bulloch, and dominated the centre of the field.

Against Hartlepools United on the following Wednesday, only 1,453 spectators turned up, but the faithful few were rewarded with a scintillating display of attacking football, during which New Brighton scored four in a 12-minute spell in the first half. The 5-2 win proved to be Jack Stamps' farewell appearance. Derby County's George Jobey, amongst other First Division managers, had been watching him and, a few days later, Stamps left for the Baseball Ground and greater glories.

An unfamiliar looking forward line of C.Haydon, Ainsworth, Frost, Smith and Stein faced Oldham Athletic at Rake Lane. It was a bad-tempered match and, at one point, the referee found it necessary to call together all the Oldham players (apart from the goalkeeper) to lecture them. Rakers' winger Jimmy Stein was sent off after 75 minutes and Oldham won 1-0, but it was a game best forgotten.

At The Shay, Widdowfield, the Halifax Town centre-forward scored within 30 seconds of the kick-off and the home team won 3-1. New Brighton's goal came from Allmark, making one of his infrequent senior appearances.

Considering that February contained three home games out of four engagements, a return of four points was disappointing. Already severely hit by injuries, the Rakers suffered a further blow when Willis Vaughton fractured both tibia and fibula on 4 February, when Wrexham won 3-2 at Sandheys. It was a win in keeping with tradition, for Wrexham had lost only once in eight previous visits.

Willie Hawthorn was outstanding on his return to the side against Barrow, having been absent since early November with a fractured wrist. Frost and Ainsworth were New Brighton's scorers in the 2-0 win.

A trip to York resulted in New Brighton's tenth successive failure at Bootham Crescent, by 2-0. Then visitors Rochdale were beaten 3-1, Arthur Frost led the line well and scored two of New Brighton' goals, laying on another for Wood. It proved to be the popular centre-forward's farewell performance, as he left for Newcastle United shortly afterwards. The usual howls of criticism were once again directed at New Brighton's management for selling the club's leading scorer. The facts were, of course, that they had no option but to realize on players in order to keep the flag flying.

Supporters' tempers were not improved when the team gained only three points from the next six League matches. A victory, after a replay, in the first round of the Northern Section Cup, caused little enthusiasm, the gate receipts at Wrexham amounting to only £18.

On 18 March, Doncaster visited Rake Lane and won 6-3, their third victory over New Brighton this season. On the same Saturday, Rakers' Reserves were also 'hit for six' at Droylsden, completing an unhappy weekend all round.

April's fixtures opened at Carlisle, where a goal from Alf Ainsworth helped in a share of the points. Carlisle's goal was hotly disputed on the grounds that Hunt (the Northern Section's leading goalscorer) had fisted the ball into the net when jumping to head the ball.

A good start to the holiday programme was made when Bradford City — who were second in the table — were beaten 2-1 on Good Friday. On the Saturday,

Darlington were defeated 3-0, Smith, deputizing for Ainsworth, played well and scored one of New Brighton's goals.

On Easter Monday at Valley Parade, the Rakers were twice in arrears but in the end were deprived of victory only in the last few minutes. The game finished 3-3, Smith, Montgomery and Stein being the Rakers' marksmen. Horace Small hit the crossbar with a penalty for New Brighton, but a draw was a fair result in a rousing encounter.

A visit to Hartlepools resulted in a 3-2 defeat in a game played in a stiff north-easterly wind. Just before the interval, Steve Hughes was injured and was a passenger in the second half.

Gateshead, led by the famous veteran, Hughie Gallacher, won 1-0 in a game with an end-of-season flavour and Chester also took the points, winning 3-1 as New Brighton concluded their season with successive home defeats.

Within the space of a week, hopes of reaching two cup finals were dashed. The first team were knocked out of the Northern Section Cup semi-final by Accrington Stanley, 2-0, whilst the Reserves went down 1-0 in the semi-final of the Lancashire Combination Cup.

Rakers finished 16th in the Third Division North with 39 points from 42 games and a goal-average of 68-73. Barnsley were the runaway champions, with an 11-point margin over Doncaster Rovers. Hartlepools United (21st) and Accrington Stanley (22) were re-elected, but Accrington only narrowly. The voting was: Hartlepools United (38), Accrington Stanley (29), Shrewsbury Town (22), South Liverpool (5), Scunthorpe & Lindsay United (4). Burton Town and Wigan Athletic both failed to obtain a vote.

Ten newcomers, five of whom were Scots, were included in the list of 23 professionals signed for the 1939-40 season. Amongst the new men, Scottish international outside-right Bobby Main was considered a fine acquisition. Thanks to incoming transfer fees, Cup-tie successes and bigger attendances, a profit of nearly £5,000 over the past two years had reduced the bank overdraft from £14,000 to £9,000.

Just under 4,500 spectators attended the curtain-raiser Jubilee Fund match against Tranmere Rovers at Rake Lane, which resulted in a 2-1 win for New Brighton. But the outbreak of war and the subsequent cancellation of League football after three matches ended all hopes for the season. The team finished on a rousing note, however, three first-half goals within the space of nine minutes paving the way for a fine victory against Doncaster Rovers. The Yorkshire side had beaten New Brighton three times in 1938-9 and had not lost at Rake Lane in six seasons.

Prior to the wartime Western Division Regional League beginning, a number of friendly fixtures were undertaken. The first of these, at Crewe Alexandra, resulted in a 5-2 defeat. Former Rakers' leader, Leo Stevens, scored twice against his old club, whilst 16-year-old Ronald Newstead, a Wallasey Grammar School boy, scored the Rakers' first goal.

Despite the return of Beau Ratcliffe and Arthur Frost, and the presence of 'Pongo' Waring and Alan Steen (Wolverhampton Wanderers), Rakers' attractive opener to the new regional competition resulted in a 6-4 defeat at the hands of Wrexham, who included six guest players, including Peter McKennan (Partick Thistle) who scored twice and laid on two other goals.

On 27 October, New Brighton's ranks were further strengthened by the addition of 'Alf' Hanson, the Chelsea and former Liverpool outside-left. Almost 6,000 spectators provided the biggest crowd of any Western Region match when Everton — the 1939 League Champions — visited New Brighton at the end of October. The Rakers were able to field only six of the players who had been registered with them at the beginning of the season, but the mixed team gave their illustrious visitors a good run for their money before going down to the only goal of the game.

The introduction of Malam, the Doncaster Rovers' forward, resulted in New Brighton gaining their first regional league victory over Stockport County, 4-2. Malam proved a wonderfully consistent performer, as he was never absent from his debut on 18 November 1939 until the Rakers' last wartime match on 4 April 1942.

The visit of Manchester City resulted in the biggest Western League attendance of the day but, even so, less than 3,000 spectators passed through the Sandheys' turnstiles. Alex Herd and Peter Doherty (two) were the scorers for the star-studded visitors, who won 3-1.

Crewe Alexandra's visit saw Wallasey brothers opposed, Leo Stevens for Crewe and John N.Stevens for New Brighton. The Rakers won 6-1 to record their best victory to date in wartime football. The team's first visit to Anfield since March 1933 — when they played in the Liverpool Cup semi-final — resulted in a 6-2 defeat, Hanson scoring both of New Brigton's goals against his old club.

A series of friendlies over the Christmas holidays concluded with a win against Accrington Stanley on New Year's Day. A second-half rush by the Rakers saw them score all their goals in the 6-0 win, before 1,070 spectators. On Saturday, 10 January, Liverpool visited Rake Lane for a Lancashire Senior Cup tie. Although first to score, New Brighton were beaten 4-1 before a 'gate' of 2,729 who paid £130.

Five points from the next three games included a good 4-1 win against Wrexham, Arthur Frost netting the season's first hat-trick in the regional league. One month later, New Brighton's best display to date saw them beat the leaders, Stoke City, 3-1. 'Pongo' Waring scored the season's second hat-trick.

After a very successful Easter, during which three matches were won in four days, the Rakers rounded of the month by beating Chester 4-2. The holiday programme had opened with a Good Friday meeting against Tranmere Rovers. An excellent attendance of 5,430 saw New Brighton's comfortable 5-2 win. Arthur Frost was the star of Saturday's fine 3-2 victory against Manchester City at Maine Road. Each goal of Frost's hat-trick was supplied by Bobby Main, making one of his infrequent appearances. On Easter Monday, a sixth-round Welsh Cup tie against Southport was won 1-0, putting the Rakers into the semi-final of the competition.

Crewe Alexandra were opponents in successive weeks. At Gresty Road in the league, New Brighton won 4-0, but one week later they struggled hard to emerge 2-1 winners at home in the League War Cup. In the next round, leaders Stoke City proved a more formidable hurdle and over two matches were far too strong for the Rakers. Stanley Matthews and Freddie Steele played brilliantly in the first leg at Rake Lane, which Stoke won 4-1. At the Victoria Ground, Stoke won 2-1 in an excellent cup tie, the Rakers playing with more method than they had done in the first leg.

Interest in the Welsh Cup ended, after a replay, when Wellington Town beat the Rakers 4-2 at Shrewsbury to qualify to meet Swansea Town in the Final. Birmingham League winners and Shropshire Cup holders, Wellington, with several Football League players in their ranks, were deserved winners over New Brighton. Price, the Huddersfield Town centre-forward scored two of their goals.

In May, the results of two games against Manchester United went in accordance with ground advantage. At Old Trafford, United's 6-0 win put them at the head of the table with 28 points from 18 games. In the return game at New Brighton, the Rakers were able to field a stronger side and, in their best display of the season, won 6-0 — the same score by which they had been beaten a fortnight earlier.

The season wound up at Rake Lane with a visit from Liverpool. The game ended goalless but Rakers were indebted to Willie Hawthorn, who saved a Billy Liddell penalty in the last minute. In the final table, New Brighton finished seventh out of 12 clubs with 23 points from 22 matches. Stoke City headed the table and Liverpool finished in second place.

As the first mention of football fixtures appeared in the local Press at the beginning of August 1940, so it was announced that New Brighton's manager, Bill Sawyer, had died after a short illness, at the age of 69. He had spent a lifetime in the game and served the Rakers since March 1933. Despite all his difficulties in operating on a shoe-string budget, he had retained a cheery disposition and his motto, 'Keep Smiling,' had remained in place on his office wall throughout good times and bad.

Jack Bebbington, who had been assistant to Sawyer, took over and the second season of wartime football opened with a home 'derby' against Tranmere Rovers. There were changes in the structure of league football for this season. The teams played varying numbers of matches and the usual points system was discarded. Goal-average was now to be used and football fans were expected to be statistically minded in order to work out their team's position in the table.

New Brighton's average was given a nasty jolt in September, when five goals were conceded on three consecutive Saturdays. In fact, there were only three matches all season in which the Rakers did not concede a goal but their attack was as potent as any in the league and high-scoring games were commonplace.

After opening the season with a 4-4 draw at home to Tranmere, the Rakers lost the return 5-1 at Prenton Park. At Maine Road, Manchester City scored three in four minutes and ran out 5-2 winners. And when a visit to the Racecourse resulted in another 5-0 defeat, the Rakers' supporters had little to enthuse about thus far.

The season's first victory, 5-3 against Southport, changed the pattern and in the next seven matches, six were won with a goal-difference of 36-15. The most remarkable match in this spell saw Tranmere Rovers defeated by 10-1 at Rake Lane, bringing the total number of goals scored in three 'derby' matches to 25.

Hat-tricks were quite common, but Arthur Frost's three against Crewe on 19 October were unusual in that each goal was 'nodded in' from centres provided by Alf Hanson.

After 11 matches, New Brighton's total of 44 goals was the highest of any club in the League North, but 35 goals against spoilt their average and they occupied 12th spot in the table.

Amongst all the high-scoring games, a 2-1 defeat at Goodison proved to be one of the best matches of the season. Keenly fought between two well-matched sides, two attacks which had been putting up big scores were well contained. The Rakers' hopes were dashed, however, by two goals in a minute by Wally Boyes and Harry Catterick. Malam reduced the arrears, but Everton's win enabled them to take over at the top of the table.

December's programme began at Chester and the Rakers lost 6-2. They were 5-1 down at the interval and, just before half-time, lost Dellow, who was sent off — in company with Cole, the Chester left-half. Three of Chester's goals were scored by Dick Yates and one by Bill Pendergast, two players who joined New Brighton after the war.

After being in the lead for over an hour at Anfield, the Rakers finally lost 6-4. One reporter commented: "I do not think that we have enjoyed a match so much at Anfield this season. For cut-rate football; that is to say football at 30 shillings per head, it was as satisfying as anything seen in normal times." (It should be pointed out that the 30 shillings (£1.50) was the amount paid to each player, not the admission charge).

Snap goals by Waring and Frost in the last two minutes of play gave New Brighton their third win over Southport, in the Christmas Day game at Haigh Avenue, by 4-2.

The January fixtures opened with away and home meetings against Wrexham, the games also counting as Lancashire Cup-ties. By becoming the first visiting side to win at the Racecourse this season, the Rakers began the second leg with a two-goal advantage. Winning at Rake Lane 6-1, the tie was won by the aggregate score of 11-4 and the Rakers' total of goals was boosted to 70 in 18 matches, which put them into eighth place in the league.

Chester were the next Lancashire Cup opponents and their 7-1 victory at The Stadium left the Rakers a virtually impossible task in the second leg. New Brighton won 2-0, but never looked likely to wipe out Chester's big lead.

The League War Cup was also played on the home and away principle and Wrexham were first-round opponents at Rake Lane. There was very little between the teams and New Brighton won 2-1. At half-time in the second leg, Wrexham led 4-1 and 5-3 on aggregate, but in a sensational second-half, New Brighton scored seven times and won 8-5.

The second round began at Tranmere and the biggest crowd of the season (3,800) saw the Rakers win 3-0. Reduced to ten men after a quarter of an hour of the second leg at Rake Lane, New Brighton were always struggling and Tranmere did very well to overcome a three-goal deficit and put New Brighton out of the competition by winning 4-0.

The league fixtures were wound up in typical style, four wins and two defeats producing a goal-difference of 24-18. It was unfortunate that the season's final league game also heralded the campaign's first home defeat, the Rakers being unable to add to their tally of 97 goals as Everton won 4-0.

From a playing point of view, it had been a successful season and New Brighton's 97 goals was the highest in the league. But 82 in the 'against' column reduced the goal-average to 1.18. The Rakers occupied 14th position in the table of 36 clubs but their record was really quite remarkable, considering that only ten of their 26 fixtures had been played at home.

During the course of the season, Alf Hanson, the Rakers' 'guest' outside-left, played twice for the Football League and also appeared for England against Scotland at Newcastle on 8 February 1941.

The goal-average system of determining League placings was discarded for the 1941-2 season and considering that the Rakers went down 13-1 at Manchester United in the season's first game, it was just as well!

Unfortunately, last season's full-backs and half-backs were no longer available and only the forward line had a familiar look. With only one change and ground advantage, the Rakers to some extent re-established their reputation by drawing 3-3 with Manchester United in the return fixture. The point was only narrowly gained, however, as New Brighton scored twice in the last three minutes to draw level.

Fixtures in this season paired opponents on successive Saturdays and the first 'derby' games against Tranmere Rovers ended with New Brighton taking three points, winning 2-1 at home and drawing 1-1 at Prenton Park.

A visit to Anfield with a young RAF goalkeeper, J.R.Bennett, making his debut, resulted in a 7-2 defeat, Cyril Done scoring four of Liverpool's goals. In the return, another new goalkeeper — Colin Campbell, on leave from the Navy, faced Liverpool's attack. It was an exciting match, Liverpool's equalizer coming a few minutes before the end of a 5-5 draw.

New Brighton lost one of their keenest supporters when Mr George Dobson, a 79-year-old Wallasey resident, died on 16 October. Mr Dobson had played for Bolton Wanderers and Everton and in his prime stood 6ft 1in tall and weighed 14st. He had always packed a hefty kick and had once scored a goal direct from a goal-kick, helped somewhat by a following wind and a misjudgement by the opposing goalkeeper.

Two draws with Wrexham were followed by a win and a draw against Manchester City, but the first home defeat of the season came on 8 November when Stoke City — without Stanley Matthews — won 5-3. Debutant goalkeeper Ted Adams, the Rakers' fourth custodian this season, had a fine match, despite being beaten

New Brighton's Visit To Anfield

*Cartoonist's view of a wartime
visit to Liverpool by New
Brighton.*

five times. At the Victoria Ground, Stoke completed a comfortable double by winning 4-0.

Special interest was centred on the appearance of Steve Hughes — on leave from the RAF — for the first time for over a year. He had a good game in the Rakers' 6-3 win against Stockport County. Unfortunately, he was unavailable for the return at Edgeley Park, which the County won 7-1.

Just over 2,500 spectators at Goodison Park saw the Rakers defeated 4-0 — the previous week Everton had beaten Manchester City 9-0. In the return fixture, Everton's superior all-round team work saw them home by 5-1, their ninth successive win.

The season's first competition wound up with two high-scoring games against Chester, 4-3 at home and 1-6 at the Stadium on Christmas Day. The Rakers had taken 14 points from 18 matches with a remarkable goal-difference of 39-74 — an average of over four goals per game conceded.

In the first leg of the War Cup, Southport won 2-1 at Haigh Avenue. In the return, a burst of three goals in 15 minutes paved the way for what looked like being an easy victory. But a spirited Southport fight-back, plus the loss of Leyfield — New Brighton's outside-left — after the interval saw the Rakers only narrowly home by 4-3.

On New Year's Day, Mr John Hayes died aged 61. A joiner employed by the LMS Railway Company, 'Nibs' Hayes, as he had been popularly known, had served the Rakers for many years as assistant trainer. An authority on physical training and a skilled masseur, Mr Hayes at one time had trained the English cycling team, when the World Cycling Championships were held at the Tower Grounds.

Bury proved much too good for New Brighton at Gigg Lane, in a game which produced the remarkable scoreline of 10-5. Bury's fifth goal was scored direct from a corner-kick taken by Don Carter, who joined New Brighton in 1948. It was a day of high-scoring, Ted Drake scoring five times in 20 minutes against the Free French Air Force.

When Bury won the return fixture at Rake Lane by 6-0, the Rakers' chances of achieving a qualifying place in the League War Cup received a severe set-back. They added to their troubles at Blackburn, when a shaky defence conceded another five goals. To round off a miserable afternoon, Waring, New Brighton's inside-right, was ordered off the field just before the final whistle.

A youthful Tranmere Rovers side — unable to secure the release of their many Army players — battled hard, but with little method or balance, and goals from Dellow and Frost decided the issue in New Brighton's favour, 2-0. In the return, veteran inside-forward Waring won the game for New Brighton. He revealed wonderful control of a lively ball and was rarely at fault in his use of it. He had a hand in all three of New Brighton's goals, scoring two of them himself, Rakers winning 3-1.

Waring was again the man who put New Brighton on the road to victory against Chester at Sandheys, scoring both goals in the 2-1 win. At this point the team had won four and lost four of their Cup engagements, but two heavy defeats, at Chester and Blackburn Rovers, ended any chance of the Rakers qualifying.

What proved to be the final wartime match was a 5-0 win at Prenton Park on 8 April 1942. It was gained without the assistance of Waring, who had been suspended for his earlier sending-off at Blackburn. Two of New Brighton's goals in this match were scored by J.Caffrey, a player on loan from Tranmere Rovers.

On 11 July, the *Wallasey News* announced that the Rakers 'were retiring' and would not be taking part in League activities next season. War conditions had made it impossible for the club to carry on as not a single pre-war player of their own was available and the system of guest players was obviously unsatisfactory when all the players had to be recruited in this manner.

Although it was not known at the time, Rake Lane had already housed its final game — the Chester match on 21 February 1942. Bomb damage in the summer of 1942 and the Council's subsequent requisition of the ground for rehousing purposes had rung down the final curtain at Sandheys Park.

In company with Hull City, New Brighton were unable to resume football in the transitional 1945-6 season and their efforts to be ready for 1946-7 were being closely observed by the Football League. Having lost their pre-war ground at Rake Lane, requisitioned by Wallasey Corporation, a lease was obtained for the Tower Grounds. As late as April 1946, a Ministry of Works permit was sought to carry out repairs at the ground, following the US Forces occupation of the site. There were no stands or covered accommodation and the club's first offices and changing rooms comprised two Nissen huts.

At the end of June it was forecast that the playing pitch would be ready within another two weeks, whilst new secretary-manager Neil McBain, a former Scottish international, strived manfully to recruit from scratch a team to represent the club.

There was a strong Scottish contingent amongst the new recruits who joined pre-war favourites Alf Ainsworth, Norman Richardson and Harry Topping. George McGeachie was appointed club captain and the team which represented New Brighton in their first peacetime match, at the Racecourse, Wrexham, was: Corbett; Topping, Richardson, McGeachie, Hill, Paterson, Buist, Wells, Pendergast, A.Ainsworth, Forsyth. New Brighton led 2-1 at the interval, through goals by Buist and Pendergast, but Wrexham rallied to win 3-2. At least 1,000 from Wallasey and district were amongst the crowd of 10,000 and they could not have been too downhearted as the new 'Rakers' had produced some nice football and looked a capable side.

Bradford City were the first visitors to the Tower Grounds on Wednesday 4 September. Torrential rain made for heavy going and defences were very much on top in a goalless encounter. The weather restricted the attendance to a disappointing figure of 6,126 spectators.

The first post-war 'derby' generated great interest and special ferry boats ran direct from Birkenhead to New Brighton, fare 9d, tickets for the match being sold on the boats to ease any possible congestion at the ground. A crowd of 14,291 packed into the Tower and saw New Brighton gain their first win of the season, 2-1.

Victory number-two came at the expense of bottom-of-the-table Accrington Stanley by 4-0, but three heavy defeats followed — notably a 5-1 home reverse against Hull City. The Tigers were also first-round FA Cup opponents at Hull and Major Buckley's team were considered hot favourites. A 4-2 home win against Lincoln City on the Saturday prior to the Cup tie put the Rakers in good heart and they managed to come away with a 0-0 draw, thanks almost entirely to an inspired afternoon's goalkeeping by Alex Corbett.

The replay proved a grim encounter, exhausting to both sides due to the condition of the Tower Grounds pitch, which was a virtual sea of mud. Archie Wells shot a marvellous goal for New Brighton after seven minutes and they held the lead until 15 minutes from time, when Chadwick equalized. Full-time came with the scores level and after 25 minutes of extra-time, Hull scored the decider, despite protests from New Brighton's players that Lester had punched the ball over the line.

Travelling fans were disappointed when a waterlogged Millmoor pitch caused a late postponement of the 7 December fixture at Rotherham United. A week later, New Brighton went down 2-1 at Chester, George McGeachie failing to convert a penalty awarded two minutes from time.

On 21 December the York City game at the Tower was abandoned after 72 minutes due to failing light with the visitors 1-0 ahead. York had little cause for complaint, however, as their own late arrival had delayed the kick-off by 42 minutes. This game attracted the lowest 'gate' of the season — 2,973 spectators.

The Rakers had much the better of the Christmas exchanges with fellow strugglers, Oldham Athletic. At Boundary Park, Oldham were two up within 25 minutes, but two goals from Alf Ainsworth levelled matters at 2-2. In the return match at the Tower, Rakers' supporters were delighted to see their team win 4-0 through goals by Bill Pendergast (3) and Alf Ainsworth.

This year ended on a disappointing note when a crowd of over 5,000 had to be turned away from the Tower when the Wrexham match was postponed due to ground conditions.

The New Year's Day match against Stockport County was only made possible by the efforts of a gang of over 50 men — including players, officials and supporters — working on the pitch every night until midnight. Thankfully, all their efforts were rewarded when 'Cowboy' McLellan scored the only goal of the game after 85 minutes.

At Doncaster, the Rakers did well to hold the runaway leaders of the division to a goalless draw at Belle Vue before a crowd of 14,482. A visit to lowly Southport, who had not won since 7 September, brought a surprise defeat by 2-0. Rochdale won 2-1 at the Tower on 18 January, but the return 'derby' at Prenton Park had everything, two goals in the last two minutes providing a dramatic finish to an exciting game which ended 3-3. After the interval and with the score standing at 1-1, Alexander scored for Tranmere without a New Brighton player touching the ball. Goals from Pendergast (his second) and Alf Ainsworth put New Brighton 3-2 up, but Tranmere equalized in the last minute through Atkinson. There were 13,580 spectators.

A long-overdue first away victory came on 1 February at the Shay, Halifax, Alf Ainsworth's goal proving the decider. Jimmy Buist failed from the spot for New Brighton. Arctic weather conditions wiped out the remainder of February's League fixtures and it was 8 March before a resumption could be made. A rusty-looking Rakers team lost 3-2 to Gateshead, on a pitch which was a mixture of ice and mud at the Tower.

A week later, history was made when manager Neil McBain was obliged to turn out in goal for the Rakers at Hartlepools at the venerable age of 51 years and four months. A prominent centre-half in his playing days, capped three times for Scotland, Mr McBain kept his charge really well, showing remarkable agility and saving many shots. Hartlepools were 3-0 winners on a waterlogged pitch, but the real honours went to McBain who was heartily congratulated by the Hartlepools officials, who insisted that he accept a stiff tot of whisky for his efforts.

The following week saw a spring-like day and much better playing surface at the Tower and the Rakers gained a decisive 4-0 victory over a strong Crewe Alexandra side. By contrast, one week later pumping operations were carried out on the Lincoln pitch until just before kick-off time. The Imps proved more at home on the sticky surface and won 5-1.

A single goal was sufficient to take the points in each of the three Easter fixtures. On Good Friday, Barrow won at the Tower whilst on the Saturday, visitors Southport were beaten rather more easily than the 1-0 scoreline suggested. On Monday, a valuable away win, thanks to a Keith Pritchard penalty, brought the points away from Barrow. The Easter games had seen New Brighton move up from their second-from-bottom position to a position well towards the middle of the table. Successive 3-0 defeats at Rotherham United and at home to Chester once more jeopardized the League position, but an unexpected success by 2-1 at York City moved New Brighton to sixth from bottom at the end of April.

When an injury-weakened Rakers visited Stockport County on 3 May and lost 2-0, sports pages were heralding the onset of the cricket season, on what should have been the last Saturday of the football season. As it was, the severe winter had caused so many postponements that another seven matches had still to be decided. The season finally wound up on 14 June and, thanks to a fighting finale of five undefeated matches, the Rakers finished their initial season of post-war football in 18th place in the table.

A look at the appearances for the season showed that goalkeeper Corbett had missed only one match (due to travelling difficulties which had given manager McBain his solitary post-war appearance) and full-backs Harry Topping and Norman Richardson had ever-present records. Bill Pendergast was the leading goalscorer with 14 of the team's 57 League goals.

In a much later announcement of the retained list, due to the length of the season, it was revealed that 14 players had been offered terms for the 1947-8 season.

In August 1947, New Brighton's playing pitch was said to resemble a cricket ground and an end to the previous season's difficulties with the playing surface was confidently predicted. As sun-bronzed players worked hard in training, the Egremont side of the ground was being cleared of rubble and new girders were delivered, ready for erection to provide covered accommodation for 5,000 spectators.

In almost tropical conditions, 1,500 sunbathers attended the trial match on 16 August, which ended 1-1. Alf Ainsworth scored for the Reds and John Ainsworth for the Whites. The local correspondent correctly forecast that New Brighton's old failing — poor finishing — appeared to be their chief problem.

In the opening League fixture, played in heatwave conditions, New Brighton disappointed their own supporters by losing 2-0 against Bradford City at the Tower, despite having most of the play.

Transport difficulties caused a late arrival at Barrow and gave the team no time for lunch, but the 11 hungry men took a well-earned point, Bill Pendergast opening the season's scoring account in the 1-1 draw. The useful away performance was quickly offset in midweek when Accrington Stanley inflicted the second home defeat in succession, by 1-0.

The early leaders, Wrexham, were held to a 1-1 draw at the Tower, the game featuring a fine debut by the Rakers' new outside-right from Queen of the South, William McLean, and a brilliant penalty save by Alex Corbett, the Rakers' goalkeeper.

Goalkeeper Alex Corbett made a brilliant penalty save against Wrexham but later asked for a transfer and moved to Hull City.

On the same afternoon, the Reserves lost 4-3 at Nelson, Rakers' amateur winger Keith Pritchard having the misfortune to be on the losing side despite having scored a hat-trick.

The season's first win was gained at Lincoln on 10 September, by a 2-1 margin, and a fine repeat performance at Halifax Town gave the side six points from six matches.

A dull, goalless draw against Rochdale at the Tower preceded the season's first 'derby' at Prenton Park. A record crowd for a League fixture there (17,147) saw a full-blooded encounter, but many late arrivals missed the only goal of the match, scored by Tranmere's Des Harlock in the seventh minute. It was the first away defeat of the season, but the following Tuesday saw the team's defensive record ruined as Accrington Stanley scored five at Peel Park. Bill Pendergast hardly deserved to finish on the losing side after scoring a hat-trick, but the Rakers went down 5-3, despite having the lead three times in the match.

October opened with the biggest defeat to date, 4-0 at Southport, and it preceded a depressing run of results which saw the team without a League victory during October and November.

The FA Cup draw paired the Rakers with Marine (Crosby) at the Tower. Marine were lying in third place in the Lancashire Combination, whereas the Rakers were bottom of the Third Division North and without a home win all season. A 'giantkilling' act looked on the cards but, thankfully, it did not happen.

Two records went by the board on 29 November — First Division leaders Arsenal suffered their first defeat of the season, at the hands of Derby County, whilst the Rakers gained their first home win. A crowd of nearly 9,000 spectators were present to see the amateurs from Marine and they showed promising form in the first-half but then faded badly and New Brighton won 4-0. Both Marine full-backs had outstanding games. Strangely enough, both were brothers of famous League goalkeepers, George Burnett (Everton) and Stan Hanson (Bolton Wanderers).

Back to League action and the Rakers added one more to their long list of home failures by going down 2-1 to Gateshead in front of a poor crowd of just over 4,000 spectators.

The second round of the FA Cup took the Rakers to Eastville. Bristol Rovers home record was poor (won 2, drawn 3, lost 5) but they were too good for the Rakers and progressed to round three by a comfortable margin of 4-0.

Two transfer requests, by goalkeeper Alex Corbett and amateur outside-left Keith Pritchard, were granted. Corbett had missed only three matches in two seasons but an injury had let in Dougie Daniels. Pritchard was allowed to move to Marine.

A much-changed team gained a good point at Valley Parade in a 1-1 draw and then gave their supporters a fine Christmas surprise by winning 2-1 at Stockport County. A review of this match was given on the BBC *Sports Special* programme on Christmas evening, in which New Brighton players McGeachie, Daniels, Hitchen and John Ainsworth were all highly commended.

When the return fixture against Stockport County on 27 December was won 1-0, New Brighton's long-suffering supporters were treated to their team's first home League win of the season. It also lifted the side off the bottom of the table, but a New Year's Day defeat by Lincoln City at the Tower put them down again, level on points with Halifax Town and one point behind Hartlepools United.

In early January, Corbett was transferred to Hull City and long-serving Alf Ainsworth departed into non-League football with Congleton Town.

Rain, fog and darkness combined to make the 3 January visit of Barrow a dull affair. The match was played to the tune of foghorns from the Mersey and the local correspondent admitted relief that both goals had been scored at the 'near' end of the field, otherwise the press-box occupants would have had no idea when the goals were scored or who had scored them.

January proved a dismal month, six League matches yielding only four points. In mid-January, the Rakers' Reserves finished their Lancashire Combination fixture at Darwen with seven men and were grateful when the referee abandoned the game after 70 minutes with Darwen 5-2 ahead. Amongst New Brighton's casualties, Harry Topping was felled when he headed the wet, heavy ball. Birkett, Carrigan and Wells all had to leave the field suffering from exposure.

A query in the *Wallasey News* from a supporter asked when the players were going to appear in their 'proper' pre-war colours of maroon and white stripes. The club replied that all their kit had been lost during the war and that striped jerseys had since proved unobtainable. Mr McHarris, the club secretary, took the opportunity to appeal for clothing coupons, as the kit situation was becoming serious. League form was also a serious matter as February brought only one point from four matches, whilst March saw only four points gained out of a possible 12.

In February, manager Neil McBain resigned to take up the post of assistant manager of Leyton Orient. The directors took over team selection and their Monday evening meetings resulted in wholesale changes in team selection and a flurry in the transfer market. Alex Paterson departed to Stockport County whilst a new pair of inside-forwards, Earl (Stockport County) and Brindle (Rochdale), were signed. Amateur centre-forward Ken Rainford made his League bow and Ronnie 'Jet' Birkett was promoted from the Reserves. Unfortunately, there was no improvement in results.

As April opened, five games were left to play but most supporters were already resigned to New Brighton's disappointing season ending with an application for re-election. Easter games had left New Brighton at the bottom of the League. Only one game had been won, the Good Friday meeting with Hull City ending 1-0, thanks to a goal after 15 minutes by Bill Pendergast. A 4-0 reverse at Crewe Alexandra was then followed by a 3-0 defeat at Hull on Easter Monday.

New Brighton pictured at Hull City in March 1948. Back row (left to right): Topping, Hill, McGeachie, Daniels, Hitchen, Hope. Front row: Richardson, Pendergast, Earl, Broughton, Brindle.

The certainty of having to seek re-election faced New Brighton on 10 April. Defeat at Rotherham was not unexpected, but the Rakers took the lead after the interval when Rotherham's full-back, Selkirk, deflected a Ted Redfern shot past his own goalkeeper. This stung Rotherham into action and they rattled in six goals in the second half.

The last match of this unhappy season was against Darlington at the Tower. Only 2,337 spectators bothered to turn up but they were rewarded with a final flourish from the Rakers, who won 2-1 through goals from Earl and Brindle.

The season's average home attendance was 5,229, whilst an average of 9,385 had watched the Rakers' away fixtures.

The end-of-season transfer list revealed one of the club's biggest ever 'clear-outs', 15 players being given free transfers.

On Thursday 24 June 1948 a well-attended meeting of New Brighton AFC shareholders, held at the Sandrock Hotel, New Brighton, was presided over by Dr Tom Martlew. The balance sheet for the year showed a loss of £2,266. The local authorities' settlement of £4,000 for the old Rake Lane ground, which had been requisitioned for housing, was strongly criticized. This seemed fair comment, considering that the Tower Grounds had cost £2,835 in maintenance fees alone during the severe winter of 1947.

A few days prior to the meeting, during a Sunday evening 'Rakers' Concert' at the Tivoli Theatre, the Rakers' new player-manager, Jack Atkinson, had been introduced to the audience. Once into the office, the former Bolton Wanderers centre-half lost no time in recruiting what was virtually a brand-new team.

After suffering a 3-0 defeat at Gateshead in their first game of the season, the Rakers made a good recovery on the following Wednesday evening when they won 2-0 against Carlisle United. The team looked smart in their new strip, the pre-

New Brighton in 1948-9. Back row (left to right): Richardson, McPeake, Grimley, Atkinson, McTaff, Galbraith. Front row: Taylor, Lyon, Roberts, Carter, McClure.

war club colours of maroon and white striped shirts and white shorts, which were being worn for the first time for some years. The team which beat Carlisle lined up: Grimley; Hope, Richardson, McTaff, Atkinson, McPeake, Taylor, Lyon, S.Roberts, Russell, Carter. The only players remaining from the previous season were full-backs Jimmy Hope and Norman Richardson.

Admission prices for this season were paddock 2s, covered stand 1s 6d, ground 1s 3d; for boys, HM Forces or half-time entrants the price was 9d.

A 1-1 draw against Hartlepools was eventful for the 9,093 spectators, not least for the fact that the visitors missed two penalties. Tom Grimley saved the first one, taken by Hawkins, whilst Hartlepools' winger Isaacs struck the crossbar with a second. On their travels, the Rakers drew 2-2 at Carlisle and won 2-0 at Darlington and after five matches had six points.

The topsy-turvy form of early season football was demonstrated when Stockport County came to the Tower and notched their first win of the season. Alex Paterson, the former Rakers player, had a storming game for the visitors, obviously feeling quite at home at the Tower Grounds. Rochdale were the next team to take the points from the Tower, by a 2-1 scoreline. Moss, the Rochdale inside-forward accepted a fortunate rebound off the referee to score a simple winner for the visitors.

Greatest interest in the Stockport County match on 15 September was centred around the debut of Walter Galbraith, the Rakers' new full-back from Clyde. He made an impressive debut but, despite other good displays by Jimmy Hope and Ted Redfern, Stockport won by the only goal of the game.

Nothing could have been more satisfying for the Rakers' supporters than to see their team return to winning form at the expense of their local rivals, Tranmere Rovers. Past 'derbies' at Prenton Park had favoured the Rovers, who had won nine to New Brighton's five, with two draws. A crowd of 16,336 — about a thousand less than the previous season's record attendance there — saw the Rakers gain their first League win at Prenton since season 1934-5, when they also won 1-0.

Unfortunately, the 'derby' success proved to be isolated and a dismal sequence of seven consecutive defeats followed. In this barren spell, only two goals were scored and the shot-shy Rakers were in urgent need of a marksman to finish off their approach work. In the single-goal home defeat by lowly Oldham Athletic at the Tower on 9 October, Bill McClure received his marching orders and was later suspended for a month. Rock-bottom was reached in a 5-1 defeat at Accrington Stanley and the following week, high-flying Rotherham United continued their run of success at the Tower by 1-0, taking their season's record to — played 12, won 11.

A 4-1 defeat at Boothferry Park was only remarkable for the number of spectators present — 31,039 constituting the largest 'gate' in a match involving New Brighton since January 1939, when 36,004 attended the FA Cup fourth-round replay at White Hart Lane, Tottenham.

On 6 November, Don Carter, New Brighton's record signing from Blackburn Rovers, made his debut at the Tower against Doncaster Rovers. The visitors recorded their fourth successive away win, by 1-0.

In the best display for several weeks, a point was gained in a 1-1 draw at Bradford City. News of the FA Cup draw revealed that New Brighton were to meet Carlisle United, at home, in the first round.

On the Saturday prior to the Cup tie, the Rakers introduced Ernie Eaves at centre-forward against Halifax Town. The young amateur provided the opening for Tommy Lyon's goal — the first home goal since 11 September — and scored himself in a confidence-boosting 2-0 win. Eaves was ineligible for the first-round FA Cup tie, having played for Newton-le-Willows in an earlier round, but the team managed without him, winning 1-0 thanks to a goal by Lyon after 18 minutes.

A fine solo goal by Don Carter gave New Brighton the points against Mansfield Town at the Tower on 4 December and then it was back to FA Cup business

New Brighton player-manager Jack Atkinson made his name with First Division Bolton Wanderers before the war and ended his League career with the Rakers.

and a second-round visit to Bradford City. A 'gate' of over 18,000 at Valley Parade saw a scrappy game with too much rough play and big kicking. After 90 goalless minutes, the referee decided that it had become too dark to permit extra-time to be played and a replay was booked for the following Saturday at the Tower.

The second game was little better than the first, but a scrambled goal by Tommy Lyon after 80 minutes proved sufficient to put the Rakers through to the third round. When the draw was made New Brighton were booked for a visit to Bramall Lane to meet First Division Sheffield United.

Two hard-fought Christmas games against York City resulted in a 3-1 home win on Christmas Day, whilst York won 2-1 on Boxing Day. A New Year's Day visit to Hartlepools United preceded the third round of the FA Cup. New Brighton, with three changes due to injuries, brought in Hope, Redfern and Russell but went down 3-1. At this point their League record was: P 22 W 6 D 3 L 13 F 20 A 33 Pts 15 Position 20th.

New Brighton had a strong following in the crowd of over 28,000 at Bramall Lane. Injury victims Walter Galbraith and Steve McTaff were replaced by Ted Redfern and Jim Russell. The Rakers kicked off in unfamiliar colours of blue shirts and white shorts. They started well and led their First Division opponents at the interval, but Sheffield United moved up a gear in the second half to win a rousing tie 5-2. The goal sequence was: Jones (United) 20 minutes, Carter (New Brighton) 25 minutes, Latham (own-goal for New Brighton) 38 minutes, Jones (United) 50 minutes and 63 minutes, Hagan (United) 71 minutes, Warhurst (United) 84 minutes.

After the excitement of the Cup, it was back to League fare and the Rakers' form showed an overall improvement, the defence particularly being strengthened by the introduction of Bob Bowman, a new full-back from Kilmarnock. January and February fixtures saw only ten goals conceded but the attack managed to score only eight in the same period, of which Fred Taylor claimed five from outside-right.

On 5 February the return 'derby' against Tranmere Rovers at the Tower saw the Rakers complete the double over their neighbours, 2-1, watched by the best attendance of the season, 11,990.

After winning at Southport on 26 February, through a late goal by Fred Taylor, New Brighton stood fourth from the bottom of the Third Division North with 23 points and 13 games to play, comprising six aways and seven homes. Another re-election application was a grim prospect indeed and the team's performances during March did nothing to ease the position.

On a snow-covered Boundary Park the Rakers crashed 4-2 to Oldham Athletic. Against lowly visitors, Accrington Stanley, New Brighton scored first but lost 3-1 to give Accrington their first away win of the season. A 1-1 draw at Rotherham United was an unexpected bonus and the month ended with a visit from the leaders, Hull City. By managing to subdue Raich Carter, Hull's silver-haired genius, the Rakers earned a point in a goalless draw.

April was a busy month and it began with a 2-1 defeat at Doncaster. On 9 April, Bradford City were the visitors They stood one point below New Brighton in the table and put up a hard fight before a single goal by Ernie Eaves settled the game in New Brighton's favour.

By winning two of their three Easter Holiday fixtures, New Brighton greatly enhanced their prospects. With only four matches remaining — three at home — they needed only four points to ensure an absolutely secure position. Wins against Wrexham and Barrow brought safety and the programme wound up with a 2-1 defeat at Barrow and a 2-2 draw against Gateshead at the Tower. The final table saw New Brighton in 17th position with 36 points from 42 matches and a goal-difference of 46-58.

In March 1949 at Boundary Park, New Brighton went down 4-2 to Oldham Athletic.

All that remained was the Liverpool Senior Cup. In a hastily concluded competition, the Rakers played in both the semi-final and the Final within the space of five days.

On Monday 9 May, New Brighton beat Everton at Goodison Park, thanks to an extra-time goal by Ernie Eaves. On the Friday following, a crowd estimated at 10,000 gathered at the Tower for the Final against Tranmere Rovers. Obviously still feeling the effects of their gruelling Monday game at Goodison, the Rakers were always struggling and Tranmere won 3-1 after being 3-0 ahead at the interval.

Hopes for the new season rested mainly on the shoulders of new centre-forward Dick Yates, the burly leader signed from Carlisle United. A proven goalscorer and one of the most forceful leaders in Third Division football, Yates was expected to provide the down-the-middle thrust that had been so sadly missing in 1948-9. Other new signings included Arthur Shepherd, a winger from Liverpool, defenders Alf Lees and Les Barton from Bolton Wanderers, and inside-forward Jackie Jones from Doncaster Rovers and formerly Wrexham.

All five were included in the New Brighton team which opened the season on 20 August with a home game against Darlington. A crowd of just over 8,000 saw Shepherd's 16th-minute goal clinch the points.

Monday's visit to Hartlepools proved unproductive. Grimley, Barton and Shepherd all received fairly severe knocks and were virtually passengers during the second half of the game which Hartlepools won 2-0. The season's first 'derby' at Prenton Park was approached with some confidence, New Brighton having won both games the previous season. Just over 14,000 spectators saw a typically bruising encounter

73

Arthur Shepherd, a winger from Liverpool, scored within 16 minutes of his debut for the Rakers.

in which New Brighton went down 2-1. Fred Taylor was reintroduced at outside-right for the Hartlepools return game at the Tower and provided the centre from which Stan Roberts headed the only goal of a rather dull encounter.

Stockport County inflicted the season's first home defeat on 7 September. Young debutant goalkeeper Bobby Williams — son of Horace Williams, the pre-war Rakers' centre-forward — was beaten almost immediately after the kick-off and Stockport County ran out 3-1 winners. The referee was more unpopular than usual in this match, making any number of mysterious decisions, and was escorted from the field by two policemen at the end of the game.

Just a fortnight later, the same opponents provided New Brighton with their first away win of the season, at Edgeley Park. The Rakers' forward line served up some inspired football to gain a sparkling 2-0 win.

Despite all the efforts of Dick Yates, Chester took a point from the Tower in a 3-3 draw. Against one of his former clubs, Yates headed two classic goals and provided the opening for Don Carter to add the third.

New Brighton qualified for the Liverpool Senior Cup Final on 28 September by beating Everton 1-0 at the Tower, Jackie Jones scoring the winning goal 15 minutes after the interval.

A 2-0 win at Southport was no mean feat, as it was the Sandgrounders' first home defeat. In-form Jackie Jones opened the scoring after four minutes, Dick Yates adding a second.

Visitors Crewe Alexandra took both points from the Tower in a 2-0 win which put them at the top of the Third Division North, ahead of Doncaster Rovers on goal-average. The game could have taken a different turn when New Brighton were awarded a penalty after 15 minutes, but Don Carter blasted the ball practically straight at the alert Crewe goalkeeper, Ellson.

After New Brighton picked up a useful point with a 1-1 draw at Barrow, Lincoln City provided attractive opposition at the Tower on 22 October. Led by Scottish wartime international, Jock Dodds, and with their new signing, former England inside-forward Jacky Robinson, the visitors were brimful of finesse. Their short-passing game was well countered by a Rakers' defence on the top of its form and Arthur Shepherd scored the game's only goal after 21 minutes.

The first hat-trick by a New Brighton player for two years accounted for Carlisle United at the Tower, Dick Yates being the successful marksman in the 3-2 victory. Bill McClure, only recently transferred from New Brighton to Carlisle United, was kept quiet by Alf Lees.

By drawing 2-2 at Mansfield, the Rakers became only the second club to take a point from Field Mill this season. Dick Yates was again on the mark with both of the Rakers' goals.

The draw for the first round of the FA Cup saw New Brighton unfortunate to be the only Merseyside club drawn to play away from home, at Doncaster Rovers.

A fortnight after the season's first hat-trick, Stan Roberts whipped home another against Accrington Stanley, who were beaten 3-0 at the Tower. The team were enjoying a fine spell of form, having scored eight goals, including two hat-tricks, in three consecutive games.

In the FA Cup tie at Doncaster, Tom Grimley was outstanding in New Brighton's defence but he had no chance with the five goals which Doncaster scored. At only one point in the game did New Brighton look likely to make a great fight of it. Just before half-time, Don Carter beat Doncaster's goalkeeper but saw his shot skim the crossbar. A minute later, though, he scored with a fine drive. Then the Rakers were awarded a penalty, but Carter missed from the spot. The home forwards, with player-manager Peter Doherty in irresistible form, would have beaten most teams on the day and progressed to the second round by a 5-1 margin.

In a game when the rain poured continuously and the pitch resembled a collection of miniature boating lakes, the Rakers and Oldham Athletic splashed their way to a goalless draw at the Tower. In the 17th minute, a goal-bound Jackie Jones shot was punched off the line by Oldham's centre-half Hurst. Matt McPeake's penalty, however, was brilliantly saved by Ogden, the Oldham goalkeeper.

An attractive but stiff Christmas programme saw Tranmere the visitors on 24 December, followed by a visit from League leaders Doncaster Rovers on Boxing Day. A return trip to Belle Vue was scheduled for the Tuesday and it was a notable achievement which saw the Rakers take three points from the programme, with two goalless draws and a 2-2 draw at the Tower on Boxing Day. In the latter game, the Rakers came within 30 seconds of beating the League leaders, but a spectacular headed goal by Peter Doherty saved his team from defeat.

The year ended with a 1-1 draw against Halifax Town, this being the team's seventh successive home game without defeat. Unfortunately, New Brighton's goalscorer, Don Carter, suffered a gashed thigh and had to be taken to hospital.

The Liverpool Senior Cup Final first leg — the Final this season being contested over two legs — was against Tranmere Rovers at Prenton Park. The Rovers placed a firm retaining hand on the trophy when they won 2-0, to give themselves a useful margin to take into the second leg, scheduled to be played later in the season.

On 12 January it was announced that Mr Richard Whitby had been unanimously elected chairman of New Brighton AFC in succession to Dr Tom Martlew, who had held the post for the past 29 years. The change was brought about by Dr Martlew's recent ill health and in recognition of his long and honourable association with the club, the doctor was elected life president.

In a sea of mud the Rakers went down 4-0 at Rochdale, but the run of unbeaten home games was maintained when Bradford City were beaten 1-0.

A fortunate opener at Wrexham — Steve McTaff's innocent looking lob into the goalmouth being totally misjudged by the Wrexham goalkeeper — was followed by a second from Stan Roberts, a fine shot after a nice combined move. The Rakers allowed the initiative to slip from their grasp, however, and Wrexham levelled matters at 2-2.

February began with a visit to Chester which resulted in a 2-0 defeat, whilst the third successive away fixture was at York City who occupied bottom spot in the league table, but the Rakers' notoriously irregular away form saw them squander several choice openings in a game which they should have won.

Back at the Tower, a ninth-minute goal by Jackie Jones enabled New Brighton to record their first-ever double over Southport. The win moved the team up five places in the table and maintained their record of being unbeaten at home since October.

Telford Bannerman, leading goalscorer in the Reserve team, was introduced for the visit to Peel Park. The Rakers showed much the best approach work, but a combination of bad luck and poor finishing saw them defeated by 3-0.

A visit from Wrexham, one point ahead of New Brighton in the table, featured a starring performance from Jackie Jones. Although he did not appear on the score-sheet, the Rakers' stocky little inside-forward created all the openings in New Brighton's 3-1 victory.

On Wednesday 15 March, a mixed New Brighton XI travelled to Holly Park to play a friendly game against South Liverpool. It was the Rakers first experience of football under floodlights, and in an enjoyable game, South Liverpool won 2-1. Players had some difficulty in judging the flight of the ball, particularly when it was coming out of the lights. There were rather too many shadows on the playing area and when the white paint began to wear off the ball, it became practically impossible to follow.

A 2-1 win at Lincoln City was probably the team's best achievement of the season. Atkinson and Grimley were the heroes of a defence which was almost continually under pressure. Lincoln scored first, but two opportunist goals by Arthur Shepherd won the day.

Rotherham United ended New Brighton's long unbeaten home run. Reduced to ten men after only 15 minutes when Shepherd sustained an ankle injury, the Rakers were beaten 3-0.

After gaining an unexpected point at Carlisle United in a goalless draw, the Rakers disappointed their supporters by going down 2-1 at home to Mansfield Town, after being a goal up inside five minutes.

The busy Easter programme left the Rakers with no fewer than six first-team players on the injury list and a weakened side was desperately unlucky to return from Gateshead empty handed on Easter Monday. Ahead through a Jackie Jones goal after three minutes, the lead was held until the 85th minute when Ingham equalized. Two minutes later, Campbell scored Gateshead's winner.

After New Brighton beat Barrow 2-0 at home on 15 April, Norman Richardson's benefit game against Bolton Wanderers on the following Wednesday proved an enjoyable exhibition of the finer arts of football for the crowd of 3,500. Bolton fielded nine of the side which had drawn against Blackpool the previous Saturday and their methodical approach work and crisp ground passing kept the Rakers' defenders busy. Bolton won 3-1, Webster (two) and Dillon being their scorers. Stan Roberts scored for New Brighton.

Eaves, Redfern and Fitzpatrick, the latter making his League debut, were introduced for the visit to Oldham Athletic. Just before the interval, Oldham scored twice

Oldham goalkeeper Fred Ogden collects the ball during the game between the Latics and New Brighton at Boundary Park in April 1950, when the Rakers went down 3-0.

and went three up after 53 minutes. Ernie Eaves went close on several occasions for the Rakers, but their final away match of the season ended in a 3-0 defeat.

The League programme was completed with a solid win over York City. The visitors, who needed a point to avoid having to apply for re-election, fought hard. They were level at 1-1 after 60 minutes, but the Rakers regained the initiative and ran out 3-1 winners.

All that remained was the second leg of the Liverpool Senior Cup Final and, in a disappointing display at the Tower, the Rakers went down 3-0, losing 5-0 on aggregate. It was the second season running in which Tranmere had defeated New Brighton in the Final.

By finishing 14th in the table, New Brighton achieved their best placing since season 1937-8. Their record was very similar to 1948-9, with 14 wins from 42 matches. Two extra points from ten draws, as opposed to eight draws the previous season, saw the side finish three places higher in the Third Division North. Goals, as ever, had been a scarce commodity, only 45 being scored in 42 matches.

The most significant statistic, however, was the average home attendance of 5,457. Season 1948-9 had seen an average of 6,861 and the consequences of this slump were revealed in mid-June. Player-manager Jack Atkinson was not to be retained because of 'stringent economy measures'. Within a week of Atkinson's dismissal, Walter Galbraith, the Scottish full-back and team captain, was named as the club's new player-manager.

On Tuesday, 25 July 1950, New Brighton players reported to the Tower for the new season and were welcomed by chairman Richard Whitby, vice-chairman Cllr George Young, directors Harry Pemberton and Harry Smith and new manager — but old colleague — Walter Galbraith. Lunch was taken at Mr Whitby's New Brighton restaurant and after an afternoon's loosening-up, followed by an hour in the swimming pool, the players were entertained to the first performance of *Melody Inn* at the Floral Pavilion.

Walter Galbraith (dark suit) after his appointment as New Brighton's player-manager.

A newly-laid third-of-a-mile running track, a returfed pitch and a new coat of paint all round gave the Tower Ground a pleasing appearance. Season tickets — at £2 the cheapest in the League — were put on sale, with an earnest request from Walter Galbraith to the Wallasey public to take up the tickets in better quantities than the previous season, when only 80 had been sold.

It was supreme irony that, in what proved to be New Brighton's last campaign as a Football League club, that they made their best-ever start to a season.

The team which opened the season at Halifax with a 2-0 win contained only two new recruits. The line-up was: Grimley; Lamont (from Kilmarnock), Galbraith, Stirland, Lees, Barton, Bannerman, J.Jones, Roberts, Carter, Alldis (Tranmere Rovers).

On the following Tuesday, Wallasey firemen spent all afternoon attempting to drain a waterlogged pitch, but at kick-off time several large, ankle deep puddles still remained. Southport won the toss and New Brighton defended the 'deep end'. A single goal by Jackie Jones after nine minutes settled the issue.

Against Hartlepools United, New Brighton made a rousing opening and after half an hour, Jackie Jones opened the scoring. Despite being well on top throughout the first half, the Rakers failed to add to their lead. After the interval it was a different story as Hartlepools dominated the exchanges with former Raker, Bill McClure, their dangerman. The visitors hit the upright twice but were held out by a gallant defensive display.

August ended with a visit to Southport and the Rakers completed an early season double, thanks mainly to a magnificent performance from goalkeeper Tom Grimley and a 20th-minute goal by Tel Bannerman.

When the Rakers travelled to Gateshead on 2 September, they were Third Division North leaders, the only team in the Football League with no goals against and the only team in their section to have won all their matches. It was a wonderful

Galbraith cannot prevent Hartlepools United's Bill Burnett getting in a shot at the Tower Ground during the Rakers' final season in the Football League.

opening to Walter Galbraith's career as a player-manager, but sadly the glory proved fleeting and it was to be three months before the team won again.

A crowd of over 14,000 at Gateshead saw the Rakers' 100 per cent record wrecked by a 4-0 reverse. In the Darlington midweek fixture at the Tower, the Rakers' supporters saw home debutant David Musgrave put New Brighton ahead after only three minutes. Don Carter beat three defenders to notch a brilliant solo goal seven minutes later. With New Brighton fans speculating on fives or sixes, suddenly things started to go wrong. Yates reduced the lead before half-time and the visitors, who suddenly appeared a yard faster on the ball, equalized to share the points.

The season's first home defeat came on 9 September when Crewe Alexandra won 2-0 at the Tower and a midweek journey to Darlington proved entertaining but unrewarding fare for the Rakers, who went down 5-3.

The season's first 'derby' brought joint leaders Tranmere Rovers to the Tower on 16 September. A crowd of 14,495 saw a fast and furious encounter. Dick Yates headed New Brighton in front after seven minutes and they retained their lead until 13 minutes from the end, when Wheeler equalized. Jimmy Jones, introduced in goal in place of Tom Grimley, had an outstanding debut which included saving a penalty.

The next four fixtures all resulted in heavy defeats. At Bradford City, Jimmy Jones pulled off some magnificent saves to limit the margin of defeat to 3-0. A bleak day for the club was 30 September as both the League and Reserve teams were beaten 5-1 by Rochdale. At the Tower, New Brighton were level at 0-0 after 66 minutes when their defence collapsed. Goalkeeper Jones and player-manager Galbraith both conceded penalties, each being converted by ex-Raker George McGeachie. In the Reserves' 5-1 defeat at Rochdale, Norman Richardson missed a penalty before Ernie Eaves scored a consolation goal.

In the match against Rotherham United at the Tower, New Brighton were four goals in arrears after 57 minutes and Stan Roberts was a limping passenger on the wing. In a courageous fight-back the Rakers managed to reduce the arrears to 4-2.

Nine goals against in successive home games brought defensive changes, including the return of transfer-listed Tom Grimley in goal. There was no immediate improvement, however, as a visit to Field Mill saw Mansfield Town easy 4-0 winners. Dick Yates was injured in this match, which proved to be his farewell Football League appearance.

The return of Norman Richardson to the rearguard on 21 October did much to shore up a leaky defence and in his first senior appearance of the season, no goals were conceded for the first time since 29 August. Unfortunately, the Rakers failed to score themselves, hitting the woodwork on no fewer than four occasions. An unchanged team travelled to Barrow and another sound defensive display earned a 1-1 draw.

Former Rakers' goalkeeper Dougie Daniels gave an inspired display against his old club in a 1-1 draw against Accrington Stanley at the Tower. The next home fixture saw the visit of League newcomers Scunthorpe United, who became the fourth visiting team this season to take the points in a 2-1 win.

The draw for the first round of the FA Cup seemed unlikely to lift the gloom as the Rakers were drawn to visit Port Vale, the Third Division South side, at their new stadium, opened only a few months earlier. Defensive errors by New Brighton presented Port Vale with three goals in the first half-hour of the tie and, despite a spirited fight-back in which Don Carter scored twice, the Rakers had left themselves with too much to do and went down 3-2.

The first win in 15 games came on a mud-bound Tower Ground on 2 December, two goals from Arthur Shepherd — playing only his third game of the season —

accounting for visitors Oldham Athletic. The Latics' goalkeeper, Fred Ogden, repeated the previous season's achievement of saving a penalty-kick.

Having won at last, the Rakers proceded to overcome Halifax Town, Hartlepools United and Stockport County in consecutive single-goal victories, equalling their early season burst of four successive victories without conceding a goal. Unfortunately, the run ended with a 4-0 Boxing Day defeat at Stockport County. The home side forced 21 corners in a totally one-sided encounter.

The last home game of 1950, against Gateshead, lasted for 30 minutes at the Tower. Two good goals were seen by 869 faithful supporters, but almost immediately following Stan Roberts' equalizer, the referee was obliged to abandon the game which had been played in a blizzard of increasing severity. The New Year's Day Liverpool Senior Cup game against Tranmere Rovers was also a victim of the weather, due to the condition of the Prenton Park pitch.

The new year opened with a visit from Lincoln City and the Rakers' revival hopes suffered a nasty set-back when the visitors won by the only goal of the game. Three consecutive away fixtures followed and all ended in defeat. The most exciting of the three games was what was to prove the last League 'derby' at Prenton. With a young amateur centre-forward, Jimmy Saunders — plucked straight out of Zingari League football — the Rakers led 3-1 at the interval. In the second half their defence was torn to shreds and Tranmere won 4-3.

The new centre-forward scored twice on his debut, but he was unable to maintain his striking rate and the Rakers followed their 'derby' defeat by going seven matches without scoring a goal. During this spell Bradford City won 6-0 at the Tower and would have scored even more but for the daring and acrobatic performance of Rakers' goalkeeper Jimmy Jones, whose fine performance included a penalty save from McGill.

The year's first point came on 10 February when League newcomers Shrewsbury Town drew 0-0 at the Tower. Five successive League defeats followed and Tranmere Rovers knocked the Rakers out of the Liverpool Senior Cup, winning 3-1 at Prenton Park on 21 February.

Defeat at Rotherham by 5-0 ended with the Millers' centre-forward, Jack Shaw, totalling 38 goals in the season to date — 11 more than the Rakers had scored in total. At York on 10 March, the Rakers introduced Jimmy Guild and Bill Heggie, both players making their Football League debuts. Both played well, but York City took the points by winning 2-0.

The journey from leaders to wooden spoonists was completed on 17 March, when Barrow won 2-1 at the Tower and the Rakers' non-stop tumble down the Third Division ladder was complete. It was a bitter pill for the 1,922 spectators, who braved pouring rain, but they did at least see their team score for the first time in eight League games. Home and away fixtures against Chester had to be postponed because of the state of both grounds and the only Easter game played yielded a point from a 1-1 draw at Accrington Stanley.

Successive home defeats by Carlisle United and Gateshead within the space of four days further diminished hopes of escaping from the bottom of the table. At Scunthorpe the Rakers hung on grimly until 20 minutes from time, but in a late goal-rush the home team ran in six goals without reply. A visit to Bradford saw Bill Heggie introduced at centre-forward. New Brighton took the lead after seven minutes through Jack Finlay, Bradford equalizing after 26 minutes. Jimmy Jones saved a penalty from Elliot before the interval, but the Bradford winger scored the match-winner 20 minutes from time.

When Wrexham visited the Tower on 14 April, the Rakers stood at the foot of the table, three points behind Accrington Stanley and five behind Halifax Town. Inside-forward Jackie Jones had a field day against his former club, recording his

1st PRIZE—
Two Tickets for Match versus SHREWSBURY
2nd PRIZE—
Two Tickets for Match versus MANSFIELD T

N° 397

NEW BRIGHTON
A.F.C. LTD.
TOWER GROUNDS, NEW BRIGHTON

Saturday, 3rd February, 1951
New Brighton v. Bradford C.

OFFICIAL PROGRAMME · · · · TWOPENCE

Rakers' programme from their final League season.

first hat-trick for New Brighton in a 3-0 win. The return game at Wrexham on the following Wednesday was a scrappy affair, but Jack Finlay scored New Brighton's winner after 60 minutes. Wyllie of Wrexham shot wide from the penalty-spot.

The two wins had lifted the team off the bottom spot on goal average but two successive 3-1 defeats, at Oldham Athletic and Chester, pushed them back to bottom position with only three matches left to play.

The remaining trio of fixtures yielded three points and included five goals from makeshift centre-forward, Bill Heggie. Against Bradford Heggie scored two of the team's three goals in a game which featured a great recovery by New Brighton, who were 3-1 down at one stage. Chester were beaten 1-0 on 2 May, Heggie heading the match-winner. In what proved to be the Rakers last-ever Football League match at Shrewsbury Town, two good goals from Heggie were not enough in a 4-2 defeat.

The Rakers' final record was: P 46 W 11 D 8 L 27 F 40 A 90 Pts 30.

Their position in the table was 24th, two points behind Accrington Stanley and four points behind Halifax Town. No player made maximum appearances, but Alf Lees with 44 outings was the season's most consistent performer. Leading goalscorer was Jackie Jones with seven out of the team's 40 League goals. By coincidence, the Rakers' first season in the League (1923-4) yielded only 40 goals and the leading goalscorer on that occasion was Billy Crooks, also with seven goals.

The news that New Brighton had been 'sacked' from the Football League reached Wallasey on the Saturday evening of 2 June 1951. Some weeks earlier, a meeting of the Northern Section clubs had decided to recommend both bottom-placed clubs for re-election. What had happened between this statement and the League's annual

82

meeting can only be a matter for speculation. The fact that successful applicants Workington were attracting crowds of 8,000 for non-League football — when the Rakers' League attendances in 1950-51 had barely averaged 4,000, must have greatly influenced the decision.

Many supporters wrote to the *Wallasey News* on the subject of the Rakers' downfall and one local resident thought that the public of Wallasey 'should be utterly ashamed of themselves for letting such a thing happen'. Another correspondent stated: 'My sympathies are with the directors and with the 1,500 loyal supporters who have stood by the club, win or lose.'

Exactly 50 years earlier, New Brighton Tower had voluntarily left the Football League and disbanded because they could not gain promotion to the First Division at a time when the club's only reason for existing was blatantly commercial. In 1951, those relative handful of supporters who followed the fortunes of New Brighton AFC had harboured no illusions about rubbing shoulders with the likes of Arsenal and Manchester United. Simply to be allowed to continue in the Football League would have been reward enough.

It was a sad time for the club, made even more so by the death, in October that year, of Dr Tom Martlew, life president of New Brighton AFC and, for 29 years, the Rakers' chairman. It would be too much to suggest that he died of a broken heart, but his passing and the demise of the League club with which he had been so closely associated seemed somehow linked.

Once ejected from the Football League, the Rakers had little option but to enter the first team in the Lancashire Combination in 1951-2, in place of the reserve side who had been scheduled to compete in that competition. The directors decided to run as a part-time professional organization, but two weeks after the season began they transferred player-manager Walter Galbraith to Grimsby Town.

The Rakers first game as a non-League club was on 18 August 1951, when 1,000 people saw them lose at Ashton United. There were about 1,800 present for their first home game, another defeat, this time against Clitheroe. At the end of a season marked by a backlog of fixtures, which saw New Brighton playing virtually a game a day in the final week, the Rakers finished in 14th place out of 22 clubs. They made a tongue-in-cheek bid to rejoin the Football League, but with debts amounting to some £2,800, it was hardly surprising that they polled only two votes.

By 1954 the Rakers were still in the lower reaches of the Lancashire Combination and, worse still, had lost the tenancy of the Tower Grounds. They were offered the use of a piece of open ground at Castleway North in Leasowe. They changed at the New Brighton Rugby Club ground, half a mile away.

With poor facilities and now in bottom place in the Combination, in 1955 New Brighton had to ask themselves the question: Could they carry on? A crisis meeting that summer voted in favour of giving it one more try and the Rakers, reprieved from relegation, joined forces with Wallasey Borough FC and returned to the Tower Grounds as joint tenants.

In 1955-6 they finished seventh in the table and enjoyed a reasonable run in the FA Cup, all of which contributed to stabilizing the club's rocky financial position. The following season, however, was to eclipse those achievements.

In 1956-7, New Brighton finished runners-up behind Prescot Cables and won the Liverpool Senior and Junior Cups. Most important of all, they reached the fourth round of the FA Cup. After beating three Football League clubs — Stockport County after a replay, eventual Third Division North champions Derby County and Torquay United in a game which attracted a record attendance to the Tower Grounds — the Rakers met First Division Burnley at Turf Moor.

There are conflicting reports of the attendance for the Torquay game, between 13,000 and 17,000, but the Burnley match attracted 42,000, the biggest attendance ever to see a New Brighton match. Alas, it was there that the fairy-tale ended, for Burnley won 9-0. Nevertheless, the Rakers had profited from their share of bumper gate receipts.

The club were able to pay off all their outstanding debts and purchase the Tower Grounds outright for £8,373. A £5,000 loan from the FA for this purpose was repaid within ten years.

Times were good at New Brighton now. In 1958-9 the Rakers won the Lancashire Combination title, the Liverpool Senior Cup and the Liverpool Combination Cup. They now made a more confident bid for Football League status but with 18 non-Leaguers applying, the votes were scattered and New Brighton's share was a miserly two.

From that peak in their non-League history, New Brighton began the slump which was to end in their extinction. Moderate form in the Lancashire Combination was followed by another attempt to join the Football League in 1962, but again two votes was all they could count upon. The Rakers had further success in the Liverpool Senior Cup but in 1965-6, in a bid to revive their fortunes, they joined the Cheshire League. By 1978-9 the Cheshire League had formed a Second Division and New Brighton — who had applied for re-election no less than three times in the intervening years — were relegated to it. The last bid to join the Football League had been made in 1968. One vote was all that the Rakers could muster and they did not trouble themselves again.

In 1976 the Tower Grounds had been compulsorily purchased by the local council, three years after no less than 11 directors had resigned. The recriminations had been bitter with allegations that the the management who had been in charge in the 'glory' years of the mid-1950s had squandered the cash gained then. The council also came under fire for not providing the town's senior club with a decent home.

The old wooden stand at the Tower Grounds had been badly damaged by fire only a day after the mass resignations and there were accusations that the old board had under-insured it. The new board, meanwhile, kept their intentions to themselves.

Brian Pilkington hammers home Burnley's eighth goal. The New Brighton defenders are goalkeeper Hurst and full-back Heggie. Despite the FA Cup hammering, the Rakers went home with plenty of cash from the gate receipts at Turf Moor.

A £115,000 council bid for the Tower Grounds was apparently rejected at first, but in June 1977 the ground was sold to the local authority for that sum and the directors were accused of 'asset stripping'. Chairman Peter Catchpole, a former Wall of Death rider at the New Brighton Tower Amusement Park, left for Australia and a Board of Trade inquiry looked into the dealings of New Brighton Football Club, paying particular interest to the Rakers' social club.

Some £35,000 was spent on a move to Carr Lane, Hoylake, the former home of the Ellerman Line Sports Club, but the venue was several miles from New Brighton and few Rakers supporters bothered to make the trip every other Saturday. New Brighton spent five miserable seasons there and were for some time under threat of expulsion from the Cheshire League because the ground had no covered accommodation.

Early in 1978, a new club was formed under the name of the Rakers Holding Company. In July a supporters' committee was formed but a year later, with debts now totalling £32,000, it looked likely that the football club would die. In December 1979 it was suggested to Wallasey Council that they built a stadium and leased it back to the club. But the New Brighton club was still required to contribute a considerable amount and, even after the sale of the existing ground, there would be insufficient funds left over after all the club's debts had been met.

Late in 1980, with the manager and players drawing only expenses, it was proposed that a new ground be created at Gardenside in nearby Leasowe. Some 700 local residents signed a petition objecting to that move and the idea was killed-off. Still New Brighton refused to die and in 1981-2 they moved to Vista Park, Greasby, home of Newton FC. The facilities were no better than at Carr Lane and, in any case, New Brighton had already been demoted to the Wirral League.

Relegated again, they spent 1982-3 playing on two unenclosed grounds in Greasby and Bromborough. At the end of that season the club was allowed to die.

It is a sad tale. True, New Brighton Football Club had never enjoyed great prosperity, even in their most successful days in the Football League. But the men who had seen them through the darkest hours deserved better. It is unlikely, of course, that a senior football club will ever again function in New Brighton, for followers of the game have Liverpool, Everton and Tranmere Rovers within a short distance. But the likes of the Rakers should never be forgotten. Their part in the story of the Football League is as important as any.

Homes of the Rakers

ANDHEYS Park, the pre-war home of New Brighton Football Club, was situated off Rake Lane — which the ground was sometimes called — and Osborne Avenue and Earlstown (later Penkett) Road. Before the Rakers moved in, the ground was little more than a sloping, open field but, after purchasing the site in the summer of 1921, the football club moved quickly to construct a compact football ground.

By the time the club had also bought a wide strip of land at the opposite end to Rake Lane, together with a large house called Osborne Mount and a cottage named Sandheys Lodge, they owned some 17,500 square yards of land.

By early August 1921, work had begun on levelling and turfing the pitch and constructing a 1,000-seater stand. The offices and dressing-rooms were situated in the former Sandheys Lodge and Osborne Mount was converted into a social club. The Rakers also constructed a large concrete open paddock area in front of the stand. Later, they erected a covered terrace on the opposite side of the ground.

The 20,000 capacity of Sandheys Park was never seriously tested and in 1932, when the club's financial problems worsened, there were plans to sell the ground for housing, for it was situated in a residential area. New Brighton would have moved to Gorsey Lane, Poulton, to land which the council would purchase and then lease to the club at a rent of £450 per annum. The £5,700 cost of the move — resiting the old stand as well as building a new one — would be offset by the sale of Sandheys Park.

The move was thwarted by local objections and the Rakers soldiered on at Sandheys Park and, in all, spent 20 years there until the ground was badly damaged by German bombs during World War Two. In 1944, Wallasey Corporation requisitioned the site for housing and after a period when prefabricated buildings were used, a permanent estate was established. Alas, nothing remains today of the Sandheys Park football ground.

In 1946, New Brighton re-established the Tower Grounds as a Football League venue. That venue had been created in the 1890s as part of the New Brighton Tower complex and was dominated by the Tower, in its time the tallest structure in the United Kingdom.

The Tower Grounds was first used by New Brighton Tower FC, the club formed in the hope of bringing in revenue to the complex in the winter months. In their three seasons of League football, the ground was a large, oval-shaped arena surrounded by a running track and a wide-banked cycle track. Set back from the perimeter was a large ornate stand which included a restaurant on the Tower side. This main stand ran half the length of the pitch. Opposite this was another stand which went the full length of the pitch and had its own refreshment bar.

There were two entrances on the west side and probably another at the south-east corner.

The capacity was huge — there is a claim for a 100,000 crowd who saw a cycle race there in the 1920s — and would have easily accommodated the First Division crowds that the club's owners had hoped for.

After the Tower club folded, the ground continued to stage motor and cycling events and even stock-car racing. The Tower itself was demolished in 1919 and by the time New Brighton FC took over the ground for the first post-war season, it had fallen into disrepair and was far from the grand venue of its former glory. Weeds were everywhere, the stands had all but disappeared and the pitch

The Tower Grounds at New Brighton, dominated by the Tower itself which stood, at 621ft, higher than the 518ft-high Blackpool Tower. Opened at Whitsuntide 1897, it was dismantled in 1919 after a fire.

was a soggy morass. Matters were made worse by the fact that the ground had suffered from its use by the military in wartime. Apparently heavy vehicles had been parked on the pitch and bricks and concrete under a thin layer of turf meant that in the dreadful winter of 1946-7, the pitch was a bog as rain, melted snow and ice could not drain away.

At the end of that season the near 2,000-strong supporters' club donated £700 for new building work, plus £200 for returfing on the pitch.

A stand was built once again on the south side, running half the length of the pitch, and concrete terracing was built at the west end. Covered standing areas were later established opposite the main stand and at the curved east end. After New Brighton FC bought the ground, floodlights, a social club, theatre and restaurant were progressively erected at the Tower Grounds.

Alas, the facilities were not to last for long and after the alleged mismanagement of the club, they fell into disrepair, suffering from neglect and vandalism. The base of the old Tower was eventually removed when Wallasey Council bought the site and today a second home of League soccer in New Brighton lies beneath a modern housing estate.

A SKETCH by Councillor K. Kihna, architect, giving an impression of how New Brighton Football Club's ground at the Tower will look if the Board's plan to buy the ground and erect stands and covered accommodation are successful. The concrete cycle track will broken up at the Molyneux Drive end and "stepped" to give a "Spion Kop" effect. Spectators will be brought within twelve or fifteen feet of the playing pitch, creating much more atmosphere than exists at present.

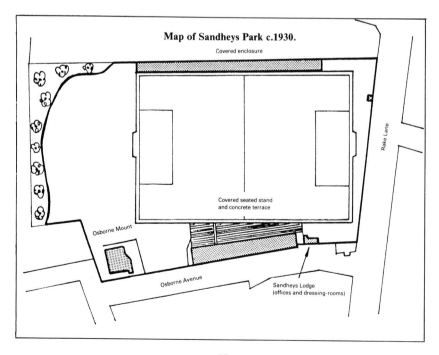

Map of Sandheys Park c.1930.

Covered enclosure

Rake Lane

Covered seated stand
and concrete terrace

Osborne Mount

Osborne Avenue

Sandheys Lodge
(offices and dressing-rooms)

88

New Brighton Tower

BEFORE the turn of the century, New Brighton had grown into a flourishing seaside resort. The town's excellent beaches attracted day-trippers from the densely populated Merseyside area and each weekend, crowds would pour across the river to sample the attractions. One major feature was the New Brighton Tower complex and the far north-east tip of the Wirral Peninsular was dominated by the Tower, a structure which rivalled the Eiffel Tower in Paris.

The Tower provided grand views of the coast as well as fairground amusements and walks. In its shadow was the Tower Athletic Ground, which was built in the 1890s and it was this which prompted the New Brighton Tower and Recreation Company to form a football club which would quickly aspire to Football League status.

Although the Tower was busy in the summer, when the holiday season brought people to New Brighton, the place was largely deserted in winter — and the owners decided that they must do something to generate income in the off-season. Thus, New Brighton Tower FC was born, not out of some young lads' needs to play soccer, but as a blatantly commercial enterprise. Thus, on 8 May 1897, the company announced its intention to create 'a strong Association club which will be run next season'.

Indeed, they had already applied for membership of the Football Association, stressing that the club would run its own affairs and not be simply a tool of the parent company. And to prove how serious they were, it was announced that Jack Robinson, the current England goalkeeper, was to be signed.

This news rocked football but, although Robinson duly signed for New Brighton Tower, an FA commission, sitting in Manchester on 11 August 1897, ruled that the signing was invalid because the Tower club were not affiliated. Only when they had become members of the Cheshire FA did the authorities relent. Even then, one newspaper commented tartly: 'If Robinson thinks he can enhance his reputation by joining a mushroom organization like the New Brighton club, whose purse may not always be as heavy as at present, he has done well to leave Derby County.' The move apparently did Robinson no harm, for he maintained his England place and went on to play in an FA Cup Final for Southampton.

The reality was that New Brighton Tower's purse *was* heavily loaded and no new member of the Football League, before or since, can have joined in such a wealthy position, funded as they were by the Tower company. There was certainly a great deal of ill-feeling directed at the Tower club. They were refused admission to the Lancashire FA and entry into its prestigious cup competitions, although they were allowed to become members of the Lancashire League, which they joined for the 1897-8 season.

Although the club had originally faced difficulties in signing good quality players — basically because of the initial uncertainty over the FA's attitude — they eventually amassed quite an array of talent. As well as Jack Robinson, New Brighton Tower also boasted international stars like the Everton pair, Alf Milward (England) and Smart Arridge (Wales). Arridge was bitter at missing the 1897 FA Cup Final, after playing for Everton in the first three rounds, and he was eager for a move from Goodison.

Tower also had the services of Scottish internationals Gow and Hamilton (both

Smart Arridge (left) and Donald Gow (above) were two international players signed by the New Brighton Tower management to boost the prospects of the fledgeling club.

formerly of Sunderland) and Dewar (late of Blackburn Rovers). Other players with League experience were Tearney (Blackburn Rovers), Hammond and Henderson (both Sheffield United) and McEleney (Burnley). John Goodall, the former Preston, Derby and England centre-forward, was to join them in October 1899, during their second season in the Football League.

Under the watchful eye of trainer Jack Hunter, the former Blackburn Rovers star, New Brighton Tower began their career in the Lancashire League on 1 September 1897, with a 2-1 win over Halliwell at the Tower Grounds. The attendance was a disappointing 500, although the weather was quite appalling and at one stage it looked as though the torrential rain would cause the game to be abandoned.

New Brighton's second game was also at home, a 4-0 win over Ashton United. The team for this game was stronger than for the initial match, when registration wrangles were still being ironed out.

New Brighton Tower's first set-back came in a 4-1 defeat by Liverpool in a charity game, but the next match — Tower's first away game — attracted a crowd of 9,000 to Halliwell, where the Towerites, as they were soon known, won 1-0 to go top of the table.

Tower's first FA Cup game was on 25 September 1897, when they won 6-0 at Middlewich before a crowd of 1,200, and so the season progressed with a series of highlights. A reasonable home attendance saw Tower beat South Shore 5-0 in their fourth Lancashire League game and then came a surprise 1-0 defeat at Southport Central, followed by another shock reverse, this time at Stockport where 7,000 saw the game.

Tower then made further progress in the FA Cup, beating Garston Copper Works 6-0 in a game which attracted barely 700 to the Tower Grounds. Fairfield disbanded

90

before they could meet Tower in the next round and that took the New Brighton club into the fourth qualifying round and a game at Crewe. Some 10,000 fans saw the sides draw before New Brighton won the replay.

Seven thousand people saw Tower beat Stockport County 1-0 to move into the first-round proper — and that was where New Brighton Tower's Cup dreams ended. They went down 2-0 to West Bromwich Albion in front of 15,897 spectators at The Hawthorns.

New Brighton Tower's league form had not been suffering, despite this lengthy Cup run, and by the New Year they were back on top of the table. They were still attracting big attendances away from home — 8,000 each at Oldham County and St Helens — but during the season the Tower Company suffered two major blows. In November, a fire destroyed the roof of the grandstand at the Tower Athletic Ground. And on 1 April 1898, the Tower itself caught fire. Although one man died, the damage to the structure was not as serious as at first thought, but the repairs required put further financial strain on the Tower company — and subsequently on the football club.

However, by the end of the season, the average attendance at the Tower Grounds had crept up to around 1,000 and when they beat Southport Central 1-0 on 25 April, in the last league game of the season, they were already assured of the Lancashire League championship.

Five days later the trophy and medals were presented after a match against the Rest of the League, but there was dismay when a strong Everton side beat Tower 3-0 in the Liverpool Senior Cup Final at Goodison in front of a 3,000 crowd.

On 29 May 1898, New Brighton Tower were elected to the Second Division of the Football League after receiving 29 votes at the League's annual meeting. Secretary J.C.Bulmer was soon on the lookout for new players, but there was a problem over Alf Milward. He had been playing for New Brighton Tower for a year but now that the club were members of the Football League, Everton insisted on a £200 transfer fee before he could be registered.

Tower were allowed to postpone their first League game, against Darwen, whilst the wrangle was sorted out and so their debut in the competition came at home to Gainsborough Trinity on 10 September 1898, when a good crowd saw Tower win 3-2. The team was: Haddow; Stephenson, Arridge, McCartney, Hammond, Allison, Coupe, Cunliffe, Hargreaves, Hill and Becton. The scorers were Cunliffe, Becton and Hammond.

New Brighton Tower FC were now attracting new supporters and many of them were dissatisfied with the way the club was being run. At a meeting at the Albert Hall, Victoria Road, on 13 September, it was agreed to send a deputation to the directors. These fans wanted a bigger say in the running of the club and the board's response was positive, issuing a further 3,000 one-pound preference shares. The directors also agreed that if the new shareholders wished to elect their own committee, then the businessmen would stand down.

Back on the field, New Brighton visited Hyde Road, Manchester, on 17 September and earned a creditable 1-1 draw with Manchester City in front of a 6,000 crowd. A week later, Milward and McEleney made their Football League debuts for Tower in a 2-2 draw against Darwen at the Tower Grounds. Despite the return of two fine players, however, the attendance was a disappointing 3,500.

By 15 October, Tower were still unbeaten, although they had drawn five of their seven games. A week later, they scored a marvellous third victory, hammering fancied Small Heath (later to become Birmingham City) 4-0. Again, though, the attendance at the Tower Grounds gave cause for concern as fewer than 4,000 turned up for a potentially attractive fixture.

This time, New Brighton Tower had no luck in the FA Cup, going down 4-2 at Glossop to a club who were also in their first season in the Football League.

Tower's game at Grimsby on 12 November gave some indication of the trials and tribulations of League soccer before the turn of the century. The railway carriage in which the team was travelling was shunted into a siding and the rest of the train carried on without it. Tower eventually made it, kicked-off 30 minutes late and managed a 2-2 draw.

The following week, Newton Heath (later Manchester United) inflicted upon New Brighton Tower their first defeat, winning 3-0 at the Tower Grounds. It was 7 January, though, before New Brighton tasted their first away reverse in the Second Division, when Gainsborough beat them 3-1.

Attendances were still poor, despite Tower's promotion form, and barely 3,000 fans had bothered to turn up for the Christmas Eve fixture against Leicester Fosse, who were also pushing hard for a place in the First Division.

On 14 January, New Brighton Tower's record attendance was set when a crowd of around 10,000 saw Billy Gillespie give Manchester City a 1-0 win. City were heading for the title that season and the attendance was swelled by thousands of Manchester fans who made the day trip to the seaside to cheer on a side which included Billy Meredith.

Two weeks later, New Brighton Tower rejoiced in a 6-0 win over Walsall — but only 1,600 were at the Tower Grounds to see it. In February there was a controversial match against Burton Swifts. The result was a 1-1 draw, but the

Alf Milward (above) and John Goodall (right), both England internationals who were persuaded to sign for Tower. After joining the League the club had to renegotiate Milward's transfer from Everton.

92

Towerites claimed that they had been 'robbed' because two of the three match officials were from Burton.

When Tower visited Leicester Fosse on 22 April, both teams were still in with a chance of promotion. There were 10,000 present and this time many New Brighton fans were in the crowd for an away game. Their vociferous support spurred Tower on and they took the lead before falling away to lose 4-1. Promotion hopes were dashed and it was no consolation that Fosse also failed to gain a First Division place, Glossop joining Manchester City in the top flight at the end of the season.

Still, there was hope and the first public trial match of the 1899-1900 season attracted 2,000 spectators to see New Brighton Tower's new signings. There were 3,000 to see the first game — a 2-0 win over Burslem Port Vale on 2 September — but the crowds began to dwindle as New Brighton Tower's fortunes faltered. Three thousand saw Gainsborough beaten 5-0 and about the same number saw Woolwich Arsenal win 2-0 in December. But only 2,000 had been present when high-flying Small Heath earned a 2-2 draw a few weeks earlier.

That autumn, New Brighton Tower had tried to revive their flagging fortunes by signing Derby's John Goodall, who played for Preston North End's epic double-winning side of 1888-9.

The Christmas Day game against The Wednesday, who were on their way to the Second Division championship, drew a crowd of 6,000 to the Tower Grounds and New Brighton earned a 2-2 draw in what was later described as one of the best games ever seen at that venue.

In the FA Cup, however, New Brighton Tower had already suffered some embarrassment and attendances had been abysmal. Despite their Football League status they had to start in the qualifying rounds and began with a home game against Birkenhead, who were hammered 5-0. The attendance was disappointing, despite the attractions of a local derby, and when Wirral Railway were despatched in the next round, even New Brighton's reputation as a League club could attract no more than 500 to the Docks Station ground of their opponents. Tower's Cup campaign ended with a 3-2 defeat by South Liverpool at the Shorefields Ground.

By the New Year, New Brighton Tower were 11th in the Second Division, a huge disappointment after the promises of the previous season. And matters got worse. The rest of the 1899-1900 campaign was frittered away. Although the last game of the season — at home to Barnsley in a match that had been postponed earlier — was won 6-2, there were less than 1,000 spectators present.

A final placing of tenth would not have been considered a great disaster at most clubs, but New Brighton Tower FC was a commercial organization and the owners, for all their protestations to the countrary, saw profit as the ultimate goal. That could only be achieved if the club won promotion to the First Division. They promised that money was available to strengthen the team for the following season.

New Brighton Tower retained ten players for the start of 1900-01 and the newcomers included Cunliffe, who returned to the club from Portsmouth, Fred Barrett, a former Scottish international from Newton Heath, and Jack Farrell from Stoke.

Tower could hardly have hoped for a better start to the season. After a goalless draw against Blackpool they won 5-0 at Stockport and when the first home game came around, some 4,000 fans, encouraged by early results, attended the game against Small Heath. New Brighton were held to a goalless draw by the team which was to be promoted as runners-up at the end of the season.

Then followed a 5-2 defeat at Grimsby and the fickleness of New Brighton's football supporters became apparent. Despite the fact that the team was still fairly well placed in the Second Division, only 2,000 turned up for the next home game, when Lincoln City were beaten 2-0. Thereafter a pattern emerged where Tower had a good home record — indeed, they remained unbeaten all season at the Tower Grounds — but struggled on their travels.

Nevertheless, by the turn of the year they were fourth in the table, albeit eight points adrift of leaders Grimsby. People had ceased to be interested in New Brighton Tower, however, and barely a dozen fans followed the team away from home. In the FA Cup, New Brighton Tower went out 5-1 at First Division Wolves. Attendances at the Tower Grounds hovered under the 3,000 mark and even a remarkable 5-0 hammering of Grimsby, the eventual champions, failed to convince the public.

With this lack of support, the players could hardly be blamed for lacking incentive and the final two games of the season arrived with Tower out of the running for promotion. The last away game produced a point at Barnsley and then New Brighton Tower beat Woolwich Arsenal 1-0 in front of a 'moderate' attendance in what turned out to be their final game. Ironically, their last goal was scored by an opponent, Arsenal's Jimmy Jackson turning the ball through his own goal in a scrappy match played on a bone-hard pitch.

A final position of fourth in Division Two would again have been welcomed by most clubs but this was no ordinary club, with priorities based upon continued League status and anything else a bonus. Nevertheless, there was little hint of the bombshell to come, even when the directors released 32 of the club's 45 players. At least they had retained 13 for the following season. And the fixtures were published showing that Tower would begin the 1901-02 campaign with a home game against Burslem Port Vale on 7 September.

But there was to be no following season for New Brighton Tower FC. On 4 September 1901 it was announced that the club would be unable to fulfill their fixtures. The Football League were furious at such late notice but the act was done. There was no public meeting of concerned fans, no wealthy benefactor stepping in to keep the club alive. New Brighton Tower FC had been formed to win a First Division place and make money. In three seasons as a League club they had failed. Closure was the only option as far as the businessmen were concerned.

Rakers' Managers

Bert Pelham
1922-1931

WHEN New Brighton AFC made their first appearance at Sandheys Park, for the FA Cup qualifying tie against Whiston Parish on 10 September 1921, a crowd of 4,307 were present as the referee started the game. Few of the spectators could have dreamed that the referee would subsequently become the Rakers' secretary, and later secretary-manager, and that during his period of service, the team would hit the headlines by defeating the Corinthians and Sheffield Wednesday, amongst others, in the FA Cup competition.

Bert Pelham was appointed secretary in August 1922 and secretary-manager in August 1927. During his spell of almost nine years with New Brighton, he initially helped the club gain election to the Third Division North of the Football League and subsequently earned a reputation for unearthing 'rough diamonds'. Amongst his most notable recruits were Jimmy Dunne, the prolific goalscoring centre-forward who gained Irish international honours; Peter Kelly, whose career was later blighted by a knee injury sustained in Notts County's service; and Jimmy Smedley and Len Carr, two of the Rakers' most outstanding servants.

Bert Pelham left New Brighton in April 1931 to join Southport as secretary-manager. In his first full season in charge, Southport reached the fourth round of the FA Cup, where they met Newcastle United and drew 1-1 at St James' Park before a crowd of 45,000. In the replay at Haigh Avenue, an all-time record crowd of 20,010 saw another 1-1 draw. The third match, played at Hillsborough in heavy conditions, resulted in a crushing 9-0 defeat for Southport. After finishing seventh in 1931-2, Southport were 12th in 1932-3 but Bert Pelham did not last the season, being rather surprisingly dismissed in March 1933. After a long spell out of the game, he returned to Southport in September 1939 as manager, staying throughout the six years of war. He died on 1 April 1977, in his 94th year.

Bill Sawyer
1933-1940

AFTER two years without a paid official, New Brighton appointed Bill Sawyer as secretary-manager on 21 March 1933. He quickly proved to be a lucky mascot, as one day after his appointment New Brighton beat Liverpool in the semi-final of the Liverpool Senior Cup. Three days later, a victory over Third Division North leaders Hull City moved the Rakers off the foot of the table.

Appointed honorary secretary of Everton in 1918, Bill Sawyer served as a director at Goodison Park and for ten years was chairman of the club's financial committee. In a 40-year association with both amateur and professional football, Sawyer was a founder of the South Liverpool club and their secretary for ten years. He also helped form Wigan Borough FC, the Liverpool Football League and the Liverpool Midweek Hospital Cup competition.

A shrewd judge of a player, Bill Sawyer's greatest achievement at Rake Lane was his 1937-8 side, which cost less than £100 to build but which enjoyed the most profitable and eventful FA Cup run in the history of the club, sharing gate receipts totalling £5,292.

In recognition of his services, New Brighton awarded Bill Sawyer a benefit and Everton visited Sandheys Park to play in his benefit match in April 1938. Sawyer died after a short illness at his home in Seabank Road, Wallasey, on 27 June 1940, at the age of 69 years.

Jack Atkinson
1948-1950

A MEMBER of the Durham Schoolboys side which included Raich Carter, Jack Atkinson joined New Brighton as player-manager after being with Bolton Wanderers since 1931, in which time he recorded 240 Football League appearances.

His first experience of management came during the war years when he was in charge of the British troops in Austria team. The BTA team became the first to beat the renowned 8th Army team, for whom Tom Grimley — later to join New Brighton — was goalkeeper.

Joining New Brighton in the summer of 1949, Atkinson had to start practically from scratch and soon built up a very workmanlike team. His personal influence was instrumental in bringing to the Tower such players as Alf Lees and Les Barton from Bolton Wanderers and Don Carter from Blackburn Rovers. One of his biggest disappointments, however, was his failure to secure the signature of Bert Trautmann from St Helens Town, the German goalkeeper electing to join Manchester City, with whom he achieved fame.

Having joined the Rakers at their lowest ebb, Jack Atkinson's two seasons in charge coincided with the club's best post-war performances and his dismissal — for economy reasons — proved, in hindsight, an unwise decision. A keen golfer with a handicap of seven, he left football to become a licensee in Bolton.

Neil McBain
1947-1948

NEIL McBain was appointed New Brighton's first post-war secretary-manager in June 1946, one week after Jack Breedon — the former Manchester United goalkeeper — had withdrawn, because of his wife's disinclination to leave her home in Leeds.

Three times capped by Scotland in the 1920s, Neil McBain was a gifted sportsman, being a brilliant golfer and good enough at billiards to have recorded a 157-break in 1928.

In a lengthy managerial career, McBain put in three separate spells of service at Watford and Ayr United, having served as player, manager and scout with both clubs. He was still engaged on Everton's scouting staff in 1968, in which year, incidentally, he celebrated his golden wedding anniversary and was living about a minute's walk from the Ayr United ground.

A sound personal knowledge of football north of the border was reflected in the strong contingent of Scots players recruited, as he signed up virtually a brand new team for New Brighton's return to football for the first time in five years.

Bad weather and the state of the Tower Ground did not help the team's cause during the 1946-7 season, although a late fighting finale pulled the side clear of trouble and into 18th place. Neil McBain resigned his post in February 1948 with the team again in deep trouble, after a dreadful start to the campaign which saw the first home League win achieved as late as 27 December.

Famous for his emergency appearance as goalkeeper for New Brighton in 1947, at the age of 51 years and four months, Neil McBain died in 1974 at the age of 79 years.

Walter Galbraith
1950-1951

ONE of the youngest Football League managers at the time of his appointment in August 1950, Walter Galbraith's new career opened brightly as the Rakers headed the Third Division North after four consecutive wins that month. However, the season ended with New Brighton in 24th place and he left in August 1951 to join Grimsby Town, after the Rakers had lost their Football League status.

In a lengthy managerial career, Walter Galbraith's spell at Accrington Stanley coincided with the best run in that club's history. Having joined them when they were bottom of the Third Division North, he improved their position to such an extent that they finished in the top three for four consecutive seasons. In 1955, Accrington Stanley became the first English club since Sunderland in 1902 to field an all-Scottish team in the Football League.

Taking over at Bradford in November 1958, after they had been relegated to Division Four, he was successful in getting them on the way back into Division Three in season 1960-61, before leaving to manage Tranmere Rovers in January 1961 and Hibernian in November of the same year. His final appointment in senior football was with Stockport County, who originally recruited him as chief scout in July 1968, but he served as their manager from August 1969 to April 1970, after the departure of Jimmy Meadows.

Who's Who of the Rakers

AINSWORTH, Alphonso   **1935-39 and 1946-47**
Inside-forward. 5ft 6ins. 10st 6lbs.
Born: Manchester, 31 July 1931. Died: Rochdale,
25 April 1975.
Debut v Stockport County (h) 14 September 1935.
Appearances: 180; Goals: 48.
Career: Ashton Athletic; Manchester United 13
February 1934; RAKERS 14 September 1935 (fee
£100); Accrington Stanley, Rochdale and Oldham
Athletic (wartime guest); RAKERS (re-registered)
10 August 1946; Congleton Town December 1947.
Alf Ainsworth graduated to Manchester United via
Ashton Athletic, who were champions of the
Palatine League in his first season with them. In
a lengthy career with New Brighton, either side
of World War Two, he was recognized as one of
the most skilful ball players in the lower divisions.
His playing style was neatly summed up in the local
Press, following one of his early appearances in
the Rakers' colours: 'Probably the smallest man
on the field, but the judicious passing of this nimble-
footed, newly-signed inside-right was one of the
biggest influences in a greatly improved New
Brighton attack.'

AINSWORTH, John   **1947-48**
Inside-forward.
Born: Probably in the Wallasey area.
Debut v Darlington (h) 24 May 1947.
Appearances: 14; Goals: 3.
Career: Local junior football; RAKERS amateur
18 March 1947; Ellesmere Port Town August 1948.
Jack Ainsworth — no relation to Alphonso
Ainsworth (*qv*) — was first tried in the Rakers'
Reserve team at Clitheroe on 22 March 1947 and
scored twice in a 4-2 win. His senior debut followed
two months later, the 1946-7 season running until
mid-June due to severe weather which caused many
matches to be postponed. Ainsworth was on the score-
sheet in his second League appearance at the Tower,
against Carlisle United, and earned the following
Press verdict: 'Ainsworth, the amateur leader, rather
slow but keen, robust and aggressive, netted one of
the season's best goals'. In the 1947-8 season he
contested the number-nine jersey with Bill Pendergast,
but an ankle injury, sustained on New Year's Day
1948, hampered his progress.

ALLDIS, Gilbert John   **1950-51**
Outside-left.
Born: Birkenhead, 26 January 1920.
Debut v Halifax Town (a) 19 August 1950.
Appearances: 12.
Career: Tranmere Rovers amateur 13 May 1938,

professional 6 October 1939; RAKERS 7 July 1950
to 31 July 1951; Prescot Cables 1951-2; Bangor
City 1952-3.
In the Rakers' last season of League football, Gil
Alldis was an outside-left in the opening four
matches of the campaign, all of which yielded
maximum points. At the end of September, the
Rakers headed the table and were the only team
in the Football League with no goals scored against
them. Things were never as good again, as Alldis
lost his place to David Musgrave and the team
went 15 matches before winning again. Alldis first
signed for Tranmere Rovers as an 18-year-old,
during season 1938-9, and made his League debut
in the Rovers' single season of Second Division
football. In this campaign, they totalled only 17
points and were relegated.

ALLEN, Frank   **1933-35**
Inside-forward or half-back. 5ft 8ins. 11st 10lbs.
Born: Altofts, near Normanton, 5 May 1901.
Debut v Doncaster Rovers (a) 26 August 1933.
Appearances: 51; Goals: 18.
Career: Altofts; Castleford Town; Barnsley 20
February 1926; Bangor City August 1928; Clapton
Orient 26 January 1929; Southport 3 June 1929;

Nelson 7 August 1930; Barrow 2 January 1931;
RAKERS 16 August 1933; Le Havre (France) June
1935; Ollerton Colliery.
Frank Allen was an industrious 90-minute trier,

100

who blossomed out as a very useful wing-half during his spell at Barrow. He was never a prolific goalscorer, despite his first-half hat-trick against Southport — one of his previous clubs — in April 1934. Much of his best work for the Rakers was in the right-half position, but he was unable to hold his place when Jim Smedley was free from injury.

ALLMARK, John Joseph   **1938-39**
Outside-right. 5ft 9⅔ins. 11st 7lbs.
Born: Liverpool, 26 May 1912; Died: 1981.
Debut v Darlington (a) 3 December 1938.
Appearances: 5; Goals: 2.
Career: Colwyn Bay; Manchester City 7 January 1937; RAKERS 10 May 1938 to cs 1939.
Allmark's recruitment coincided with the close of the 1937-8 season, when he became the first of two new wingers signed for the following campaign, Jimmy Stein, the former Everton star, being the other newcomer. Allmark lost his place after an indifferent start and was subsequently unable to dislodge Horace Small. He spent the greater part of the season in the Lancashire Combination side, who recorded over a century of goals to finish in seventh place, 15 points adrift of champions, South Liverpool.

AMERY, Charles Siddall   **1932-36**
Utility. 5ft 9⅔ins. 11st 5lbs.
Born: Heswell, 16 September 1910; Died: Liverpool, late 1979.
Debut v Accrington Stanley (h) 3 September 1932.
Appearances: 117; Goals: 9.

Career: Heswall FC; Tranmere Rovers amateur 10 August 1931; RAKERS amateur 24 August 1932, professional 26 September 1932; Tranmere Rovers 29 January 1936; Stockport County 12 February 1938 (fee £100), released on a free transfer 9 June 1939.
Initially recruited as an inside-forward, Charlie Amery proved a highly versatile performer, subsequently appearing as a half-back and full-back. Match reports invariably mentioned his ability to kick the ball tremendous distances — almost a prerequisite in defenders of his era. When ne returned to his former club, Tranmere Rovers, in January 1936, he moved from the bottom to the top of Division Three North, but the Rovers failed to sustain their promotion challenge, finishing in third place.

ATKINSON, John Edward   **1948-50**
Centre-half. 6ft 1in. 13st 1lb.
Born: Washington, Co Durham, 20 December 1913.
Debut v Gateshead (a) 21 August 1948.
Appearances: 52.
Career: Durham Schoolboys; Washington Colliery;

101

Bolton Wanderers 2 September 1931; Everton & Blackpool (wartime guest player); RAKERS 21 July 1948, released on free transfer 31 July 1950. *International honours: England Schools; FL XI v Combined Wales/Ireland XI 1935.*
'Big Jack' Atkinson, for two years a popular player-manager of the Rakers, graduated through the 'A' and Central League teams of Bolton Wanderers. He was the youngest member of the 1934-5 side which won promotion to the First Division and also appeared in the 1935-6 FA Cup semi-final, when Bolton were beaten by West Brom after a replay. He saw active service in Africa, Sicily, Italy and Austria as an NCO in the Lancashire Fusiliers, rejoining Bolton Wanderers after his demob. Although well into the veteran stage as a player, he was an inspirational pivot. One amusing verdict on his play was: 'Atkinson was as difficult to pass, as New Brighton rock is to chew'.

BAINES, Peter C   **1947**
Inside-forward.
Born: Australia.
Debut v Carlisle United (a) 15 November 1947.
Appearances: 2.
Career: Monsall FC; Oldham Athletic amateur 11 November 1937; Wrexham 19 April 1943; Grimsby Town; Halifax Town; Hartlepools United;

Liverpool & Middlesbrough (wartime guest player); Wrexham (re-registered) 21 May 1946; Crewe Alexandra 1 November 1946 (In exchange for J.Boothway); Hartlepools United 21 June 1947;

RAKERS (trial) 17 October 1947; Carlisle United (trial) 13 December 1947.
The dusky complexioned Peter Baines made only a handful of Football League appearances in post-war football, despite his association with five clubs in the Northern Section of the Third Division. A thrustful, scheming inside-forward who was able to use either foot successfully, Baines' career spanned the war years and, during season 1944-5, he netted 27 League and Cup goals for Wrexham. Briefly on trial at New Brighton, 'Darkie' Baines — as he was soon nicknamed — played twice in the League side without winning a permanent engagement.

BAKER, Frederick   **1930-31**
Half-back.
Debut v Nelson (h) 24 January 1931.
Appearances: 4.
Career: Mold; RAKERS amateur 21 August 1930 to cs 1931.
Fred Baker was one of two amateur players from Mold — the other being N.Baker, an outside-left who did not appear in the Rakers' first team. Whether the two Bakers were related has not been established. Fred Baker first deputized for Bobby Morrison, who was serving a period of suspension for something that he said to the referee in the Hartlepools match. Baker was on the winning side on his debut, 'doing all that was required of him', according to one match report. His opportunities, however, were few, due to the often experienced wing-halves on the books. In addition to Morrison, the Rakers also fielded Tom Lewis and Archie Pollock in the right-half berth during the course of the season.

BALL, Harold   **1932-33**
Centre-half or Centre-forward.
Debut v Mansfield Town (a) 5 September 1932.
Appearances: 1.
Career: Colwyn Bay; RAKERS amateur 24 August 1932 to cs 1933.
With Parle an early-season injury victim and with Kitching unavailable because of his duties as a schoolmaster, New Brighton found themselves short-handed for their midweek visit to Mansfield. Harry Ball, a young amateur, who had appeared at both centre-half and centre-forward in the Rakers' Reserve team, was introduced at inside-right. His Football League debut and New Brighton's first visit to Field Mill resulted in a 5-1 defeat.

BANNERMAN, Telford Gordon   **1949-51**
Winger or Centre-forward. 5ft 9ins. 11st.
Born: Coupar Angus, Perthshire, 17 September 1924.
Debut v Wrexham (a) 29 January 1949.
Appearances: 35; Goals: 3.
Career: RAF Weeton (Blackpool Services League) 1943; Lockeehard FC (Dundee); Coupar Angus Juniors; Dundee; Blairgowrie Juniors cs 1948;

Kilmarnock (trial) during season 1948-9; RAKERS 29 January 1949 to 31 July 1951.

Tel Bannerman, an enthusiastic and speedy winger, showed steady improvement throughout his two and a half years with the Rakers. His debut was disappointing and he made only one appearance in his first season. In 1949-50 he switched wings in the Reserve side, in order to develop his left foot, as he had been inclined to be rather one-footed. He headed the Reserves scoring list in 1949-50, with 12 goals, and in the Rakers' last season of League football he finally established himself, making 26 first team appearances, at outside-right and centre-forward.

BARLEY, Henry Frank   **1932-34**
Outside-right. 5ft 6½ins. 10st 12lbs.
Born: Grimsby, 1905.
Debut v Rotherham United (a) 27 August 1932.
Appearances: 21; Goals: 4.
Career: Humber United (Grimsby); Grimsby Town 12 August 1929; Hull City 27 May 1931; RAKERS 10 August 1932; Notts County 2 February 1934; Scunthorpe United August 1934; Bristol Rovers 10 May 1935; Barrow 23 May 1936; Kidderminster Harriers July 1937.

Harry Barley was a small but skilful winger, who possessed a hard shot. In the home League game

against Darlington in November 1933, his goal was struck with such force that it burst the net and floored a small boy standing about 25 yards behind the goal. One month later, in the FA Cup first-round replay at Mansfield, his second-half hat-trick

included one penalty and one long-range strike direct from a free-kick. Harry Barley left New Brighton for Notts County, but his best return in first-class football came with Barrow in 1936-7, when he scored eight goals in 40 appearances.

BARTON, Leslie   **1949-51**
Full-back or Half-back. 5ft 7ins. 11st.
Born: Rochdale, 20 March 1920.
Debut v Darlington (h) 20 August 1949.
Appearances: 64; Goals: 1.
Career: Bolton Wanderers amateur 23 August, professional 10 September 1946; RAKERS 11 August 1949; Linfield 26 October 1951 (fee £67).

Les Barton was one half of a dual signing by Rakers' manager, Jack Atkinson, from his old club Bolton Wanderers. Both Barton and Alf Lees proved resolute defenders for New Brighton. A regular member of Bolton Reserves, Barton was equally effective at full-back or half-back. Initially recruited to fill the right-back position left vacant by the release of Bowman, he subsequently appeared on both flanks as full-back and half-back. A typical Press comment was: 'Barton worked like a Trojan, was quick to the tackle and constructive in his clearances.'

BAXTER, Leslie   **1935-36**
Half-back. 5ft 8ins. 10st 12lbs.
Born: Clay Cross, Derbyshire, 1913.
Debut v Tranmere Rovers (h) 31 August 1935.
Appearances: 11.
Career: Chesterfield Junior football; Chesterfield 30 June 1932; Scarborough season 1934-5; RAKERS 10 July 1935 to cs 1936.

In two seasons with Chesterfield, Les Baxter did not feature in their League side. He began as a forward but was converted to wing-half and was selected to represent the Midland League versus the Champions (Grimsby Town Reserves). In one season with Scarborough, he was ever-present in League and Cup matches. With New Brighton, he lost his place to Norman Greenhalgh after appearing in the first seven matches of 1935-6, which yielded only three points. Later in the season, another wing-half recruit from Bolton Wanderers, Billy Wright, provided further competition in the middle line.

BEATTIE, David   **1926-29**
Half-back. 5ft 8½ins. 11st 7lbs.
Born: Renton, Dumbarton, 23 August 1903.
Debut v Ashington (a) 15 January 1927.
Appearances: 29.
Career: Scottish junior football; RAKERS 22 October 1926; Clydebank 30 April 1927; RAKERS 22 June 1927 to cs 1929.

In two separate spells with the Rakers, David Beattie proved a useful reserve in any of the three half-back positions. His best spell came in a ten-match run at the end of the 1927-8 season, when only one match was lost. It was during this spell

that one critic wrote: 'Beattie was a virile initiator of forward movements and ever-ready to tackle back in defence'.

BECKETT, William   **1934-36**
Outside-left. 5ft 6ins. 10st.
Born: Kirkdale, 4 July 1915.
Debut v Rochdale (a) 15 December 1934.
Appearances: 25; Goals: 4.
Career: Liverpool Schoolboys; Litherland; RAKERS amateur 29 June 1934, professional 2 November 1934; Tranmere Rovers 16 July 1936; South Liverpool 17 September 1936; Blackpool 22 April 1937: Bradford City 7 July 1938; Watford 24 May 1939; Northampton Town 28 June 1947 to cs 1948.
Billy Beckett played at left-half for Liverpool Schoolboys, but subsequently developed skill as a winger, a position best suited to his lightweight physique. His best League return came in his first season when, as a 19-year-old, he won the first-team spot from Frank Kenyon. During this season, Beckett appeared in 22 League matches and scored three goals. In his spell with New Brighton he kept fit during the summer months by his association with the North Liverpool American Baseball Club.

BEEDLES, Norman   **1935-36**
Full-back. 5ft 9½ins. 13st 1lb.
Born: Ardwick, Manchester, 13 June 1907. Died: Bebington, Wirral, 14 August 1972.
Debut v Tranmere Rovers (h) 31 August 1935.
Appearances: 19; Goals: 1.
Career: Local junior football; Stockport County amateur 9 April 1930, professional 17 April 1930; Barnsley 3 July 1934; RAKERS 12 July 1935 to 18 March 1936.

An experienced, solidly-built full-back, Norman Beedles spent five years with Stockport County and a season with Barnsley prior to joining the Rakers. He began the 1935-6 season as first-choice right-back, but lost his place after appearing in the first 16 matches, in the last five of which 23 goals were conceded. He was one of four players transfer-listed on 14 March 1936, McMullan, Lloyd and Johnson being the others.

BIRD, Charles Denton   **1934-37**
Goalkeeper. 5ft 9ins. 11st 5lbs.
Born: Hoylake, October 1914. Died: Birkenhead 1984.
Debut v Southport (h) 9 February 1935.
Appearances: 31.
Career: Hoylake; RAKERS amateur 5 December 1934, professional 2 January 1935 to cs 1937.
An outstanding debut for New Brighton Reserves at Lytham in December 1934 — which resulted in their first away win of the season — paved the way for an early professional engagement for Charlie Bird. He quickly won a first-team place

from Tony Carr but, unfortunately, this highly promising young goalkeeper sustained a knee injury at Chesterfield in September 1935 which necessitated an operation. He went on the injured list again when the 1936-7 season opened and did not figure in the first team in this, his final season.

BIRKETT, Ronald   **1947-48 & 1951-52**
Outside-right. 5ft 9ins, 10st 8lbs.
Born: Warrington, 21 July 1927.
Debut v York City (h) 17 May 1947.
Appearances: 8.
Career: Garswood St Andrew's; Crompton's Recs; Manchester City amateur 2 May 1945, professional

29 January 1946; RAKERS 21 January 1947; Oldham Athletic 10 August 1948; Accrington Stanley 11 July 1949; RAKERS 1951-2.

During his first spell with New Brighton, Ronnie 'Jet' Birkett, a slim, speedy winger, had many outstanding games in the Rakers' Reserves. Several hat-tricks, including one four-goal return against Darwen in June 1947, were followed by similar feats in 1947-8. In this season, Birkett scored in five consecutive Lancashire Combination matches during January-February 1948 and was the Reserves' leading goalscorer. Unfortunately, for all his electrifying pace and whole-heartedness, Birkett lacked experience at top level and was unable to make the senior right-wing position his own. Brother of Wilf Birkett, a goalkeeper with Everton, Southport and Shrewsbury Town and Cliff Birkett, a Schoolboy international who assisted Manchester United and Southport.

BOOTH, Robert   1925-26

Half-back. 5ft 8ins. 11st 10lbs.

Born: West Hartlepool, 20 December 1890.

Debut v Barrow (a) 29 August 1925.

Appearances: 12; Goals: 1.

Career: Spennymoor; Blackpool 9 May 1912; Birmingham 27 May 1920; Southend United 12 July 1922; Swansea Town 25 June 1923; Merthyr Town 7 March 1925; RAKERS 28 May 1925 to cs 1926.

'A very quiet hard worker, who never becomes

ruffled,' was one verdict on this veteran wing-half. He lost his first-team place to Harry Gee after a promising start, which included a goal on his first appearance at Sandheys Park. Earlier in his career, Booth made six appearances in Birmingham's Second Division championship side in 1920-21.

BOWER, Ronald William Charles   1930-35

Full-back. 5ft 7ins. 11st 4lbs.

Born: Wrexham, 17 November 1911.

Debut v Rochdale (a) 27 December 1932.

Appearances: 24.

Career: RAKERS amateur 4 July 1930; South Liverpool June 1935; Bolton Wanderers 7 January 1936 (fee £500); Millwall 4 June 1937; RAKERS season 1940-41 (wartime guest); Folkestone Town November 1945.

Associated with New Brighton on amateur forms for five years, Ronnie Bower made the bulk of his League appearances during the 1933-4 season. The following term he found less opportunities, when Ratcliffe and Carr were the regular full-back pairing. After leaving the Rakers, his form with South Liverpool induced Bolton Wanderers to pay a fee for his services, but he made only three First Division appearances for the Trotters. He did not appear in the first team at Millwall.

BOWMAN, Robert Craig C   1949

Full-back.

Born: Motherwell, 21 October 1920.

Debut v Darlington (h) 15 January 1949.

Appearances: 18.

Career: Dalziel School; Arthurlie 1935; Kirkintillock Rob Roy; Queens Park 1936; Third Lanark 1943-44; Dundee June 1945; Alloa Athletic July 1946; Dundee May 1947; Kilmarnock August 1948; RAKERS 15 January to 31 July 1949. Subsequent whereabouts unknown until 1956, when he was appointed assistant manager to Third Lanark, of which club he later became a director.

A star in Scottish schoolboy football, Bob Bowman was with Dalziel School when they won both the Scottish Intermediate and Senior Shields. In a lengthy spell with Queens Park, he played many games alongside Walter Galbraith (qv), and gained a Scottish Amateur League medal. He made an impressive debut for the Rakers, despite the atrocious condition of the badly waterlogged Tower pitch. An outstanding feature of his play was his clever anticipation and interception of dangerous passes. A regular in the Rakers' rearguard throughout his brief stay, his release in the close season was totally unexpected, as he had done as much as anyone to help New Brighton win through their gruelling end-of-season struggle to avoid having to seek re-election.

BRADSHAW, George Fredrick   1932-34

Goalkeeper. 5ft 8½ins. 10st.

Born: Southport, 10 March 1913; Died: Southport 28 August 1989.

Debut v Barrow (h) 21 September 1932.

Appearances: 83.

Career: St Simons's Boys Brigade; High Park Villa (Southport); RAKERS amateur 24 August 1932, professional 20 September 1933; Everton 26 November 1934 (fee £500); Arsenal 18 March 1935 (fee £2,000); Doncaster Rovers 20 May 1936; Bury 3 June 1938; Oldham Athletic 6 July 1950 to 31 July 1951.

George Bradshaw first encountered New Brighton FC in October 1931, when playing for High Park Villa in the George Mahon Cup. It was a painful meeting, too, as he was carried off the field after saving a Ben Twell penalty which hit him in the face. When he joined the Rakers the following season, Bradshaw quickly won a first-team place and thereafter had no serious rivals before his move to Everton. On the small side for his position, but

very sound and with cat-like agility, Bradshaw played as an amateur during his first season, residing in Southport and assisting his father in a grocery business. When he left Rake Lane he became the fourth professional goalkeeper on Everton's books. His stay at Goodison was brief, as Arsenal signed him a few hours before the transfer deadline in 1935, following the shoulder injury sustained by their English international, Frank Moss, at Goodison Park. Bradshaw's final move in League circles, to Oldham Athletic, came in his 37th year.

BRINDLE, John James   **1948**
Inside-forward. 5ft 11ins, 11st 12lbs.
Born: Blackburn, 12 July 1917; Died: Blackburn, 1975.
Debut v York City (h) 6 March 1948 (scored one goal).

Appearances: 9; Goals: 3.
Career: Blackburn Rovers amateur 1934; Accrington Stanley 1939-40; Burnley 13 March 1943; Howard & Bullough FC (Lancashire Combination) November 1943; Rochdale 29 September 1945; Chelsea 6 March 1946 (fee £1,000); Rochdale 9 August 1947 (fee £500); RAKERS 6 March 1948; Rhyl August 1948.

Jack Brindle's sojourn with New Brighton saw him pitched straight into a battle to attempt to lift the side away from the foot of the table and a possible application for re-election. He scored on his first and last appearances in the Rakers' colours, announcing his arrival at the Tower by putting both ball and the York City goalkeeper into the back of the net to register his first goal. An illuminating, if rather wordy description of his debut was: 'Brindle, new, uncertain with strangers as partners in attack, impressed with his robust, energetic yet skillful debut. He seeks the open space, not only to receive a pass, but to place one.'

BROAD, James   **1925-26**
Centre-forward. 5ft 9ins. 11st 7lbs.
Born: Stalybridge, 10 November 1891; Died: Chelmsford, 22 August 1963.
Debut v Bradford (a) 16 December 1925.
Appearances: 11; Goals: 3.
Career: St Mark's (West Gorton); Stalybridge Celtic; Manchester City 12 November 1909; Manchester United cs 1910; Oldham Athletic 23

August 1913; Blackburn Rovers (wartime guest player); Greenock Morton 1918; Millwall Athletic 9 April 1919; Stoke 22 June 1921 (fee £2,000); Sittingbourne 1924; Everton 25 November 1924 (fee £1,400); RAKERS 16 December 1925 (fee £200); Watford 3 September 1926; Caernarfon Town October 1927; Taunton United 21 September 1928;

Fleetwood 22 August 1931; Chelmsford City groundsman later in the same year.

Note: In addition to the above, Broad held overseas posts as coach to Corunna, Las Palmas, Barcelona and Geneva.

One of the game's 'happy wanderers', Jimmy Broad started his football career as a goalkeeper and it was only because a centre-forward did not turn up one day that he took up the position of attack leader. When he crossed the Mersey to join New Brighton from Everton, he had not played a game for three months, but he was good enough to contest the first-team spot with Jimmy Dunne, before the Irishman's move to Sheffield United and subsequent international fame. Broad's winning goal against Sheffield Wednesday in January 1926 put the Rakers into the fourth round of the FA Cup for the first time in their history.

BROADHURST, John William   **1939**
Centre-forward. 5ft 11½ins. 13st 6lbs.
Born: Birkenhead, 11 March 1918; Died: 1979.
Debut v Crewe Alexandra (h) 25 March 1939.
Appearances: 1.
Career: Brookville FC; Tranmere Rovers amateur 16 December 1937, professional 14 January 1938; Southend United 8 August 1938; RAKERS 22 March 1939 to cs 1939.
Signed as cover for the inside-forward berths following the sale of Stamps and Frost, Broadhurst had scored five goals in four Southern Section games and 12 in 11 London Combination games for Southend United. In a very brief stay at Rake Lane he made a solitary League appearance, after an initial run in the Northern Section Cup replay against Wrexham, which New Brighton won 4-3.

BROCK, George Wallace   **1935-37**
Left-half. 5ft 9½ins. 11st 6lbs.
Born: Glasgow, 1915.
Debut v Barrow (h) 11 September 1935.
Appearances: 66; Goals: 4.
Career: Kirkintilloch Rob Roy; trials with Partick Thistle and Airdrie; RAKERS 7 August 1935; Wolverhampton Wanderers 6 March 1937 to cs 1938.
Arriving at New Brighton on a month's trial, George Brock quickly played himself into the first team, after getting his first chance when Len Salmon was out through injury. Brock's debut prompted one critic to write: 'Here is a half-back who should eventually earn a good transfer fee for New Brighton.' Prophetic words, as he did in due course attract a 'substantial' fee when Wolves recruited him. Brock was a free-kick specialist with a powerful shot, at times successful from seemingly impossible distances.

BROUGHTON, Edward   **1947-48**
Outside-right. 5ft 8½ins. 11st 3lbs.
Born: Bradford, 9 February 1925.
Debut v Bradford City (h) 23 August 1947.
Appearances: 4.

Career: Bradford City amateur 28 July, professional 14 September 1945; RAKERS 10 July 1947; Crystal Palace 18 August 1948, retiring due to injury in 1954.
Ted Broughton, who had appeared in wartime football with Bradford City, made his first Football League appearance for New Brighton. By coincidence, his debut on the Tower Ground was against his previous club and he had the misfortune to hit the Bradford City woodwork during the course of the game, which Bradford won 2-0. In a season with New Brighton, after starting as first-choice outside-right, he was quickly deposed and spent much of his time in the Lancashire Combination side. Released in the close season, he found more opportunities with his next club, Crystal Palace, making 37 appearances and scoring four goals in his first season at Selhurst. In a lengthy association with Palace, Broughton occupied every forward position in totalling exactly a century of first-team appearances (96 League and 4 FA Cup).

BROWN, Joseph B   **1935-36**
Outside-right.
Born: 1913.
Debut v Tranmere Rovers (h) 31 August 1935.
Appearances: 16; Goals: 3.
Career: Gateshead amateur 15 July 1932; Jarrow; RAKERS 27 August 1935, released on free transfer 4 August 1936.
Joe Brown did not establish a regular berth in the Rakers' League side until late in season 1935-6 and it was during this time that he was involved in an unusual incident at Rochdale. Entrusted with a penalty-kick, he drove the ball on to the crossbar and volleyed the rebound into the net. The result, of course, was a free-kick to Rochdale.

BROWN, Wilfred   **1934-35**
Outside-right. 5ft 10ins. 11st 8lbs.
Born: Rotherham.
Debut v Accrington Stanley (a) 25 August 1934 (scored one goal).
Appearances: 11; Goals: 2.
Career: Rotherham & Yorkshire Schoolboys; Boston United; RAKERS amateur 11 August 1934, professional 20 October 1934; Rawmarsh Welfare cs 1935; Rotherham United May 1936 to cs 1937.
Signed as an amateur understudy to Frank Kenyon for the outside-right berth, Wilf Brown was quickly introduced into League action when Kenyon was injured in the final pre-season trial match. He made a good debut, too, scoring New Brighton's second goal in their opening 3-1 victory at Peel Park. He was signed as a professional in October, but did not feature in the first team after the mid-season mark, when injuries sidelined both himself and Kenyon, letting in Tommy Lawrence. After leaving Rake Lane, Brown scored 40 goals — including eight hat-tricks — for Rawmarsh Welfare, who won the Sheffield Association League Cup. Given a trial in Rotherham United's Reserve team on the last Saturday of 1935-6, he scored twice against Peterborough United and was signed on

for 1936-7. He stayed for only one season, making 16 appearances and scoring seven goals.

BRYSON, George Maxwell 1921-24
Inside-forward. 5ft 8½ins. 11st 7lbs.
Born: Liverpool, 11 November 1900; Died 1953.
Debut v Wolverhampton Wanderers (h) 1 December 1923.
Appearances: 2.
Career: Seaforth Fellowship; South Liverpool; RAKERS August 1921; Port Sunlight October 1924; Northwich Victoria cs 1925.
In October 1922, George Bryson scored hat-tricks for New Brighton Reserves in three successive

weeks. When the seniors made their bow in the Football League, at Bradford on 25 August 1923, Bryson scored seven goals (five in succession) for the Reserves, who beat Port Sunlight 10-0 in the Liverpool County Combination at Sandheys Park. When he made his Football League debut, he was the leading scorer in the Reserves with 18 goals, but in his two Football League appearances he seemed somewhat out of his depth. He took his goalscoring talents to Port Sunlight for 1924-5 and assisted them to the championship of the Liverpool County Combination. In the following season, when assisting Northwich Victoria, he became the first player to register a goal in the Cheshire County League.

BUIST, James Gibb 1946-47
Outside-right.
Born: Falkirk, 19 June 1918.
Debut v Wrexham (a) 31 August 1946 (scored one goal).
Appearances: 21; Goals: 6.

Career: King's Park; Raith Rovers; Dundee; RAKERS 14 August 1946 to cs 1947; Plymouth Argyle 1 August 1948 to 31 July 1949; Hereford United; Gloucester City.
Jimmy Buist was the Rakers' first post-war goalscorer, nine minutes into the first Football League meeting with Wrexham at the Racecourse, after a gap of six years. He was also the first League goalscorer on the Tower Ground but an early injury, sustained at Bradford City, halted his progress. A progressive winger with clever footwork, Buist's return of six goals in 1946-7 included two penalties, taken left-footed, although his position on the field was outside-right. In a single season with Plymouth Argyle, Buist made only one League appearance in the 1948-9 side which narrowly avoided relegation from Division Two.

BULLOCH, Hugh Cairns 1936-39
Centre-half. 5ft 11ins. 12st 7lbs.
Born: Larkhill, nr Motherwell, 2 June 1908.
Debut v Hull City (h) 26 September 1936.
Appearances: 82; Goals: 3.
Career: Royal Albert; Greenock Morton; Portadown 1932-3; Newcastle United 29 November 1935 (fee £1,325); RAKERS 3 September 1936; Portadown player-manager January 1938; RAKERS May 1938 to September 1939.
An inspiring captain and king-pin of the defence, Hugh Bulloch set his clubmates a fine example of unyielding, wholehearted defensive play, whilst also finding time to assist his forwards. He played a major part in the Rakers' successful Cup run in 1937-8, when they shared gate receipts amounting to £5,292 in four rounds. New Brighton's directors showed their appreciation by releasing him in January 1938 to take up the position of Portadown manager. They were pleased to welcome him back, however, for 1938-9, when he lost his centre-half berth to Steve Hughes after an enforced injury absence. He recovered in time to take the right-back position in place of Willis Vaughton, a broken leg victim in February 1939.

BURKE, Joseph William 1935
Inside-forward. 5ft 8ins. 10st 10lbs.
Born: Jarrow 1913.
Debut v Chesterfield (a) 7 September 1935.
Appearances: 2.
Career: Jarrow St Bedes; Gateshead 16 June 1933; RAKERS 28 June 1935 to 30 October 1935; Wigan Athletic April 1936.
'An inside-forward who can forage to some purpose,' was the verdict of one critic following the pre-season trials. Joe Burke was part of an extensive recruiting campaign in the summer of 1935, the Rakers having transferred three players (Davis, Ratcliffe and Butler) to Oldham Athletic and released ten on free transfers, including Len Carr and Jimmy Smedley. Burke's debut was delayed, due to a bout of influenza, but in the event, he made only two appearances in the Rakers' colours, not featuring in the first team after Alf

Ainsworth was signed from Manchester United. Later in the same season, Burke joined Wigan Athletic in their run in to the Cheshire County League championship, which they won with a margin of 13 points, scoring 136 goals. The Rakers finished the same campaign on the bottom of Division Three North, having conceded 102 goals.

BURTON, Matthew   **1923-25**
Outside-left. 5ft 9½ins. 11st 8lbs.
Born: Grassmoor, near Chesterfield 1897.
Debut v Bradford (h) 1 September 1923.
Appearances: 16; Goals: 6.
Career: Everton during World War One; Stoke 20 January 1920 (fee £75); Wrexham 22 August 1921; RAKERS 12 July 1923; Rhos 1925-6; Connah's Quay December 1927.
A lively winger, not averse to a first-time shot, Burton was Wrexham's leading goalscorer in season 1921-2. In New Brighton's first season of League football he was understudy to Peter Quinn, but managed to make 15 appearances and score five goals. He also scored the only goal of the Cheshire Senior Cup Final replay against Tranmere Rovers on 7 May 1924, bringing the trophy back to

BUTLER, Charles Reginald   **1933-35**
Half-back or Inside-forward. 5ft 11ins. 11st 8lbs.
Born: Barry, Glamorgan, 20 March 1908; Died: Hendon 1983.
Debut v Walsall (h) 30 August 1933.
Appearances: 69.
Career: Army football; Barry Town; Charlton Athletic amateur 3 March 1928; Cardiff City 31 July 1930; Thames 9 October 1930; Blackburn Rovers 30 November 1931; Bath City (loan) 1932; RAKERS 11 August 1933; Oldham Athletic 4 July 1935 (fee £200); Tranmere Rovers 1 July 1936 to February 1937; Cork City 15 July 1937; South Liverpool December 1937.
International honours: Wales Schoolboys.

Wallasey for only the second time in its history (former winners being New Brighton Tower in 1898). After scoring — from what was described as a seemingly impossible angle — against Accrington Stanley in his only League appearance of 1924-5, he was injured in the first-round tie of the Cheshire Cup against Witton Albion on 20 December 1924 and did not appear again.

One of comparatively few footballers to have worn the red and blue quarters of Thames FC during their brief Football League career, Charlie Butler had assisted four League clubs, but made only the same number of appearances before joining the Rakers. In two seasons with New Brighton he was usually first choice at either wing-half or inside-forward. He was probably best in the middle line, where his coolness and prompt tackling and the thought put into his distribution made him a potent factor. He was one of three New Brighton players who joined Oldham Athletic in the summer of 1935.

BUXTON, Arthur   **1937-40**
Centre-half or Full-back. 5ft 10½ins. 12st.
Born: Barlborough, Derbyshire, 1912.
Debut v York City (a) 18 December 1937.
Appearances: 54.
Career: Worksop Town; Wrexham 28 May 1930;
Bangor City July 1933; Wellington Town 1934-5;
RAKERS 10 August 1937; Wrexham (wartime
guest player).
After suffering a broken ankle in Wrexham's pre-
season trial in August 1932, Arthur Buxton was
released at the season's end and spent the next four
years outside the League. In three seasons with
Wellington Town he made 140 appearances, twice
helping his club to the Birmingham League title.
He joined New Brighton as a left-back, but in the
Rakers' Combination team he was moved to centre-
half. After his promotion to the first team and the
subsequent departure of Hugh Bulloch, he took over
the roll of pivot with great success. In 1938-9, Buxton
reverted to left-back, securing the first-team berth
after Harry Topping had started as first choice for
the position.

CAMPBELL, Kenneth   **1922-23 and 1929-31**
Goalkeeper. 5ft 11ins. 11st 10lbs.
Born: Cambuslang, 6 September 1892; Died: 28
April 1977.
Debut v Darlington (h) 23 November 1929.
Appearances: 55.
Career: Rutherglen Glencairn; Cambuslang

Rangers; Liverpool 9 May 1911; Partick Thistle
April 1920 (fee £1,750); RAKERS June 1922; Stoke
16 March 1923; Leicester City 12 November 1925;
RAKERS 16 November 1929, retired May 1931.
*International honours: 8 Scottish caps. 1
appearance for Scottish League.*
*Club honours: Liverpool, FA Cup runners-up 1914.
Partick Thistle, Scottish Cup winners 1921.*
'Kenny Campbell's canary-coloured jersey quite
caught the eye,' commented one reporter in
September 1922, during the Scottish international
goalkeeper's first spell with New Brighton. His
form, also eye-catching, ensured that he did not
remain long in Lancashire Combination circles.
When he returned to New Brighton, about seven
years later, he had been out of football for two
months and had decided to retire. He quickly
proved, however, that he was by no means finished,
inspiring a mid-season rally which took the club
from the bottom to a mid-table finish. In business
as a sports outfitter in Wallasey, Campbell was
a leading figure in the establishment of football
competitions for the area's unemployed in the early
1930s.

CARNEY, Eugene Francis   **1922-23, 1924-25 and 1926**
Outside-left. 5ft 9ins. 11st 12lbs.
Born: Bootle, 1895; Died: Bootle, 4 December 1952.
Debut v Bradford (h) 30 August 1924.
Appearances: 46; Goals: 3.

Career: South Liverpool; Pontypridd; Rochdale 18
May 1921; RAKERS August 1922; Reading 21
May 1923; Mold 4 February 1924; RAKERS 24
July 1924; Caernarfon Athletic 1925-6; RAKERS
3 March 1926 to May 1926; Caernarfon Athletic;
Sandbach Ramblers September 1929.

Club honour: Pontypridd, Welsh Cup runners-up 1920-21.

Unique in having three separate spells with the Rakers, Gene Carney was a clever worker on the left flank, if at times inclined to 'dally too much with fancy footwork', according to one critic. During his season with Rochdale he scored with the first penalty-kick to be awarded in Division Three North, on 27 August 1921 when Rochdale beat Accrington Stanley 6-3. His final spell with New Brighton came shortly after the club had transferred Jimmy Dunne and Peter Kelly. He was later Mayor's Attendant in his native Bootle.

CARR, Anthony Grey   1934-35
Goalkeeper. 5ft 10½ins. 12st.
Born: Seaton Delaval, 18 May 1901; Died: 1968.
Debut v Barrow (a) 1 December 1934.
Appearances: 12.
Career: Seaton Delaval; Newport County 20 May 1922; Sheffield Wednesday 20 May 1924 (fee £720); Seaton Delaval; Preston North End 16 October 1926 (fee £475) to cs 1928; South Shields 13 July 1929; RAKERS 3 October 1934 to June 1935.

A qualified aviator, Tony Carr had been out of football for some time and was living in Wallasey when the Rakers obtained his signature. He was quickly back into League action when George Bradshaw was transferred to Everton. During his Preston North End days, Carr was the proprietor of a motor haulage business in Seaton Delaval. At cricket, he was accomplished enough to have appeared at Minor Counties level with Durham.

CARR, Leonard William   1927-35
Full-back. 5ft 10½ins. 11st 12lbs.
Born: Sheffield, 19 September 1901; Died: 1981.
Debut v Darlington (a) 27 August 1927.
Appearances: 302; Goals: 2.

Career: St Bart's (Sheffield); Mansfield Town; Sheffield Wednesday amateur 26 May 1925; Barnsley 18 May 1926; RAKERS 18 June 1927; South Liverpool player-manager June 1935.

'New Brighton with a team of Carrs would soon rise in the table,' commented the *Athletic News* in November 1929. Len Carr's career with New Brighton covered eight seasons. His all-action style earned him the nickname 'Comedy' Carr, but his consistently high standard saw him clock up the club's record total of appearances and made him one of the personalities of the Third Division. On Monday 18 September 1933, a crowd of 4,311 attended his benefit, taken jointly with Jimmy Smedley, when Everton's Cup winning side — including Dixie Dean — drew 2-2 against the Rakers. The revived South Liverpool club took him as their player-manager and he quickly fashioned them into one of the most attractive and successful sides in the Combination.

CARR, Stanley Rushton   1948
Full-back.
Born: Southport, 1 June 1926.
Debut v Gateshead (a) 21 August 1948.
Appearances: 1.
Career: Brockhouse FC; Southport amateur 18 August, professional 29 October 1945; RAKERS (trial) 19 August 1948; Clitheroe 16 September 1949.

In a month's trial with New Brighton, Stan Carr made his solitary Football League appearance. During his spell with Southport he was in the Forces for much of the time, but made 11 appearances at right-back during season 1945-6.

CARTER, Donald Frederick   1948-51
Forward. 5ft 8ins. 11st.
Born: Midsomer Norton, 11 September 1921.
Debut v Doncaster Rovers (h) 6 November 1948.
Appearances: 105; Goals: 19.
Career: Welton School; Somerset County Schoolboys; Norton St John's; Stourbridge FC April 1938; Bury 28 January 1939; Blackburn Rovers 12 June 1944 (fee £5,000); RAKERS 6 November 1948; Northwich Victoria cs 1951.

Without revealing the exact amount involved, it was reported that Don Carter had cost New Brighton 'a fee four times bigger than the club has ever paid for a player'. News of his signing followed closely the announcement that Bill McClure, the Rakers' outside-left, had been suspended for a month after being sent off in the match against Rotherham United on 23 October. In his first season, Carter occupied every forward position except inside-right, but from 1949 to 1951 he operated on the left flank, either as inside-forward or on the wing. He was a consistent, hard-working forward, prepared to do more than his fair share of 'fetching and carrying'. During the war he joined the RAF as a wireless operator, but in 1943 was transferred to the Army and spent two and a half years in the Tank Corps.

CARTER, Herbert J   **1931-33**
Half-back.
Born: Wallasey.
Debut v Hull City (h) 19 September 1931.
Appearances: 5.
Career: RAKERS amateur 20 August 1931, professional 26 August 1932; Winsford United cs 1933.
A wholehearted reserve half-back, first introduced as deputy to Archie Pollock, Bert Carter was one of six players tried at right-half during the 1931-2 season. By contrast, in the left-half spot, Jimmy Smedley appeared in every match. In the following season a more settled pattern emerged, with Smedley, Ratcliffe and Robb the regular middle line.

CHALLINOR, Samuel   **1923-24**
Half-back. 5ft 11ins. 12st.
Born: Middlewich, 2 April 1900.
Debut v Bradford (a) 25 August 1923.
Appearances; 40 Goals: 2.
Career: Everton during World War One; Brentford August 28 1920; Halifax Town 26 July 1921; Accrington Stanley 8 June 1922; RAKERS 14 June 1923; Mold 23 August 1924.
Club honour: Mold, Welsh League champions 1924-5.

The release of Sam Challinor into non-league football after only one season with the Rakers was unexpected, as he proved to be a fine driving force from left-half in New Brighton's first season of League football. He was the first player to score a League goal at Sandheys Park, against Bradford, and it gave New Brighton their first-ever win in the competition. In the 1921-2 season, Challinor was Halifax Town's captain in their initial Football League season.

CHAMBERS, Robert   **1928**
Centre-half. 5ft 11ins. 12st 7lbs.
Born: Newcastle upon Tyne, 11 December 1902.
Debut v Barrow (h) 25 August 1928.
Appearances: 1.
Career: Brighton West End (Newcastle); Lincoln City 24 August 1921; Burnley 10 March 1922; Rotherham County 5 June 1923; Torquay United 1925-6; Carlisle United cs 1926; Exeter City 8 August 1927; RAKERS 14 July 1928 to 15 October 1928; Colwyn Bay; Hurst August 1929.
'A keen tackler with the ability to distribute the ball well,' was one one verdict on Bob Chambers after New Brighton's pre-season trials. Recruited

to fill the gap left by Jack Reid's departure to Ireland, Chambers failed to reproduce his practice-match form on his debut, which resulted in a disappointing home defeat on the opening Saturday of 1928-9. Chambers spent the remainder of the season in the Reserves, often as centre-forward. He started his career as a forward and was Lincoln City's leading goalscorer in 1921-2.

CLEMENT, Archibald Ernest   **1931-33**
Full-back. 5ft 9ins. 12st 2lbs.
Born: Grays, Essex, 27 November 1901; Died: Chatham, 9 May 1984.
Debut v Gateshead (h) 29 August 1931.
Appearances: 78.
Career: Grays Athletic; Whistable cs 1924; Chatham; Millwall 26 May 1928; Watford 13 June 1930; RAKERS 18 August 1931; Yeovil & Petters United August 1933; Southport 21 June 1934; Sittingbourne; Canterbury Waverely 1938-9; Chatham player-coach August 1939.
Archie Clement missed only four matches in his

two seasons with New Brighton, forming an effective last line of defence with Len Carr. Sound and resourceful, and one of the most consistent members of the Rakers' defence, he was initially recommended to New Brighton by Watford's manager, Neil McBain (*qv*). He worked in the Naval Dockyard, Chatham up until his retirement in 1966.

CLEWLOW, Sidney John   **1939 and 1946-47**
Half-back. 5ft 9½ins. 10st 8lbs.
Born: Wallasey, 8 November 1919.
Debut v Darlington (a) 19 October 1946.
Appearances: 1.
Career: Wallasey Schoolboys; St Joseph's CYMS; Poulton Victoria; RAKERS amateur 11 January, professional 16 February 1939; Wolverhampton Wanderers 11 May 1939; Aberdeen (wartime guest player); RAKERS 2 August 1946 to cs 1947.
Sid Clewlow was an outstanding schoolboy footballer whose unruffled approach and constructive ideas from wing-half attracted League club scouts. Within three months of signing professional forms for New Brighton, he was snapped up by Wolves just prior to World War Two. It was seven years later, however, when he made his solitary Football League outing, after rejoining the Rakers after the war.

COLLINS, Legh Richman   **1924-25**
Half-back. 5ft 7½ins. 11st.
Born: Liverpool, 1901.
Debut v Bradford (h) 30 August 1924.
Appearances: 11.
Career: Liverpool City Schoolboys; Wigan Borough amateur 17 November 1921, professional 4 February 1922; Nelson 8 May 1923; RAKERS 19 July 1924; Crewe Alexandra 31 October 1925; Stalybridge Celtic.
Legh Collins, a neat footballer and keen tackler, shared the left-half berth with Harry Gee during 1924-5, when the Rakers finished third in the table. In May 1925 he was chosen to represent the Midland Combination versus the Champions (Chesterfield). At Wigan Borough, he appeared in their first season of League football and with Nelson he made 13 appearances in their only season of Second Division football.

COCHRANE, George Napier   **1950-52**
Inside-forward. 5ft 10ins, 11st 6lbs.
Born: Glasgow, 27 February 1931.
Debut v Stockport County (a) 26 December 1950.
Appearances: 2.
Career: Arthurlie; RAKERS 17 July 1950; Cork cs 1952.
Billed as 'an inside-forward with a future' when he joined the Rakers from Scottish junior football, George Cochrane showed plenty of energy and ideas in the Reserves. He developed so well that he was selected for his Football League debut whilst still only 19 years old. Unfortunately, New Brighton lost their Football League status at the end of Cochrane's first season at the Tower. Nevertheless, he was one of four part-time professionals — Jim Hope, Ted Redfern and Bill Hounslea being the others — who were selected for the Rakers' first team on 18 August 1951, when New Brighton made a reappearance in the Lancashire Combination, after a gap of 29 years.

COPITCH, William   **1925-26**
Outside-left. 5ft 6ins. 10st 4lbs.
Born: Higher Cheetham, Manchester, 1899.
Debut v Chesterfield (a) 6 March 1926.
Appearances: 3; Goals: 1.
Career: Junior football; Blackburn Rovers 7 May 1920; Tranmere Rovers 25 July 1921; Stockport County 27 December 1924; RAKERS 21 August 1925 to cs 1926.
A star in New Brighton's pre-season trials, Copitch was signed after scoring in the game held on 18 August. He was unable to establish himself beyond the reserve team, for whom he scored four goals from outside-left when they won the Victoria Central Hospital Cup Final, against Harrowby. Of Jewish descent, he had a younger brother, Israel, who was known as Jack Copitch and was a goalkeeper with Southport in the 1925-6 season.

CORBETT, Alexander McLennan   **1946-48**
Goalkeeper. 6ft. 12st 4lbs.
Born: Saltcoates, Ayrshire, 20 April 1921.
Debut v Wrexham (a) 31 August 1946.
Appearances: 58.
Career: Annbank United; Ayr United 1945; RAKERS 15 July 1946; Hull City 12 January 1948; Dartford August 1949; Weymouth; Hartlepools United 20 July 1953 to 30 October 1953.
A tall, red-haired goalkeeper with good anticipation and handling, Alex Corbett missed only one match during season 1946-7. Travelling difficulties prevented him from reaching Hartlepools United on 15 March 1947 and a piece of soccer history was made when New Brighton's manager, Neil McBain (*qv*) deputized, thus becoming the oldest player to appear in a Football League match. An ankle injury sustained at Rotherham on 22 November 1947 let in reserve goalkeeper Duggie Daniels, whose form was such that Corbett was unable to regain his place. Listed at his own request in December, Corbett was quickly snapped up by Hull City. At Halifax on 13 September 1947, Corbett saved his second penalty in successive weeks, a feat recorded in most of the Sunday papers of the time.

COWPER, Peter Poole   **1928-30**
Outside-right. 5ft 8½ins. 11st 2lbs.
Born: Bolton, 1 September 1902. Died: Clifton, nr Preston, 26 September 1962.

Debut v Doncaster Rovers (a) 1 September 1928 (scored one goal).
Appearances: 71; Goals: 19.
Career: Burns Celtic; Parkside Rangers; Atherton; Bolton Wanderers (trial); Wigan Borough (trial); Rossendale United 1923-4; West Ham United 12 June 1924; Grimsby Town 9 June 1927; Lancaster Town April 1928; RAKERS 25 August 1928; Southampton 13 June 1930; Southport 15 March 1932; Carlisle United 30 July 1932; Wigan Athletic July 1933; Altrincham 10 September 1934; Prescot Cables 1936-7.
Although just short of his 26th birthday when joining New Brighton, Peter Cowper had a variety of experience. He had an excellent first season with the Rakers, his 16 goals (all scored from the outside-right position) making him the club's leading goalscorer. After leaving the League scene, he gained a Cheshire County League championship medal with Wigan Athletic in 1933-4 and a runners-up medal with Altrincham the following season. He scored for Prescot Cables when they visited New Brighton Reserves in December 1936.

CRITCHLOW, Richard Harold   **1922-26**
Full-back. 5ft 9ins. 11st.
Born: Birkenhead, 1897.
Debut v Accrington Stanley (a) 3 September 1923.
Appearances: 10.
Career: Runcorn; RAKERS 12 August 1922 to cs 1926.

After Jimmy Niven damaged a cartilage at Chesterfield in New Brighton's fourth Football League match, Dick Critchlow was given his opportunity. 'Wild in his kicking but a good attack breaker,' was one verdict on his debut and after four games, Ted Glover was introduced and held the position. Back in the Reserves, Critchlow captained them to the Liverpool County Combination championship and the Cheshire Senior Cup.

CROOKS, William J   **1922-25**
Inside-forward. 5ft 8ins. 10st 4lbs.
Born: Belfast, 12 December 1900.
Debut v Bradford (a) 25 August 1923.
Appearances: 33; Goals 7.
Career: Glentoran; Manchester United 13 March 1922; RAKERS 19 August 1922; Belfast Celtic cs 1925.

International honours: 1 Irish cap v Wales in 1922, Irish League, 3 appearances in 1921.
The only player to appear in a full international whilst on New Brighton's books was Bill Lacey, who won his final Irish cap during 1924-5. Billy Crooks could well have been the first, however, had not New Brighton's officials declined to release him for the game against England in October 1922. Irish selectors were turned down as the international clashed with an FA Cup qualifying tie and the Rakers were also without inside-left Dai Williams, who was suspended. A pre-League signing by the Rakers, Crooks found more success after New Brighton joined the Football League, his light build and ball-playing style lacking the ruggedness needed in Lancashire Combination circles.

CURR, Robert   **1928-33**
Full-back. 5ft 7½ins. 10st 7lbs.
Born: Liverpool, 1906.
Debut v South Shields (h) 26 January 1929.
Appearances: 33.
Career: Orrell FC; Everton 20 November 1926;
Lancaster Town August 1928; RAKERS 23
November 1928 to cs 1933.
The elder of the Curr brothers, Robert had the
somewhat unenviable task of understudying Len
Carr as the first-team full-back clocked up his
record appearances total. In August 1931, Curr
took over the captaincy of the Reserves from his
brother.

CURR, Wallace   **1929-33**
Wing-half. 5ft 7ins. 10st 10lbs.
Born: Liverpool, 4 April 1908; Died: Tameside 1981.

Debut v Port Vale (a) 9 September 1929.
Appearances: 8.
Career: Everton amateur 27 August, professional
20 November 1926; RAKERS 15 August 1929 to
cs 1933.
A wing-half with attacking inclinations, Wally Curr
twice scored four goals in a match for the Reserves
in 1930-31, each quartet including a penalty. His
goalscoring exploits won him a first-team call in
April 1931, but in his three-match run at inside-
forward both he, and the Rakers, failed to find
the net.

DANIELS, Douglas   **1947-48**
Goalkeeper. 5ft 10ins, 11st.
Born: Manchester, 21 August 1924.
Debut v Gateshead (h) 6 December 1947.
Appearances: 25.
Career: RAF football; Manchester City amateur
(trial) 18 August 1945; RAKERS 26 August 1947;
Chesterfield 29 July 1948; Accrington Stanley 10
October 1949 to cs 1953.
Duggie Daniels received excellent Press notices —
despite operating behind a leaky defence — after
coming into New Brighton's first team in November
1947. His first game was in the FA Cup first-round
tie against Marine and the 4-0 victory was the
Rakers' first home win of the season. The *Liverpool
Echo* commented: 'Daniels looks like making a first
class goalkeeper, he shows clean, sure handling and
sound anticipation'. Other contemporary reports
mentioned the fact that he was extremely speedy
for a goalkeeper — useful when having to make
a quick dash off his line. During his early days
with New Brighton, Daniels was still serving in the
RAF but was handily placed at the nearby West
Kirby camp. After leaving New Brighton, he spent
a thankless season as understudy to Chesterfield's
highly-respected goalkeeper — and Justice of the
Peace — Ray Middleton. With Accrington Stanley,
Daniels made 112 appearances in a four-year stay
at Peel Park.

DANIELS, John F   **1948-49**
Goalkeeper. 6ft 1in, 12st 3lbs.
Born: Sutton, St Helens, 8 January 1925.
Debut v Crewe Alexandra (a) 18 April 1949.
Appearances: 3.
Career: St Helens Schoolboys; Sutton Celtic, Clock
Face FC (St Helens Junior League); British Cider
(St Helens Senior League); Lincoln City 14 May
1946; RAKERS 11 March 1948 to 7 May 1949.
John Daniels played for two seasons as a centre-
half for Sutton Celtic and first became a goalkeeper
with Clock Face FC. Two seasons later, he joined
British Cider and gained St Helens Senior League
medals in successive seasons. First appearing for
New Brighton Reserves as an amateur trialist on
31 January 1948, he was signed as a part-time
professional two months later. Understudy to
Duggie Daniels (who was no relation) in his first
season and Tom Grimley in 1948-9, Daniels' three
League appearances for the Rakers came within

the space of four days over the Easter period in April 1949. He conceded only three goals in his trio of appearances, which resulted in two wins and one defeat. Daniels' uncle, Richard Jones, was a Welsh international inside-forward.

DAVIDSON, Charles Alfred　　　　**1928-30**
Outside-left. 5ft 8ins. 12st 2lbs.
Born: Kirkdale, Liverpool, 10 October 1904; Died: Ormskirk 26 November 1978.
Debut v Hartlepools United (a) 1 December 1928.
Appearances: 34; Goals: 6.
Career: Kirkdale; RAKERS 20 August 1928; Southport 26 September to 14 December 1931; Blundellsands 4 March 1932 to 7 May 1932; Macclesfield Town August 1932 to May 1933.
Signed as understudy to Jimmy Dickie, Davidson's chance came when the Scottish winger was transferred to Bristol City in December 1928. He took over with some success, missing only one match in the rest of the season and scoring six goals in 27 appearances. After being transfer-listed at a fee of £250 in May 1929, he was re-signed in the August, but spent the season in the shadow of George Pither, a vastly more experienced winger.

DAVIES, Glynn Ivor　　　　**1931-32**
Outside-left.
Born: Swansea, 24 November 1909; Died: Morriston 5 September 1985.
Debut v Walsall (h) 9 September 1931.
Appearances: 3.
Career: Swansea Town amateur 28 November 1926; Connah's Quay 1930-1; RAKERS amateur 25 August 1931; Casuals 1931-2; Bristol University; Norwich City amateur 21 June 1933.
International honours: Welsh Amateur & FA Amateur XI.
In the 1931-2 season, when New Brighton scored only 38 goals in 42 matches, five outside-lefts were tried, two being amateurs. Davies had an early opportunity, but failed to do himself justice in a poor side. He won Welsh Amateur recognition whilst still a schoolboy and also had a final Welsh Schools trial at Rugby Union. He was later a master at Kimbolton School.

DAVIS, Thomas Lawrence　　　　**1933-35**
Centre-forward. 5ft 10ins. 12st 10lbs.
Born: Dublin, 1911.
Debut v Doncaster Rovers (a) 26 August 1933.
Appearances: 76; Goals: 50.
Career: Midland Athletic; Cork; Shelbourne; Exeter City (trial); Boston Town; Torquay United 18 June 1932; RAKERS 16 August 1933; FC de Metz (France) 15 May 1935; Oldham Athletic 5 June 1935 (fee £250); Tranmere Rovers 26 February 1938; York City 6 June 1938; Workington July 1939; Belfast Distillery 24 August 1941; VVV (Venlo) Holland, manager-coach August 1947.
International honours: 2 Republic of Ireland caps 1937-8; 1 Northern Ireland cap 1937.
Released on a free transfer by Torquay United after a season in their Reserve side, Tommy Davis, a

strong and bustling leader, proved an excellent capture for the Rakers. Despite suffering at times from lack of support, he nevertheless scored 24 goals in his first season and 26 in 1934-5, twice netting four goals in a match. After breaking his contract with French side, FC de Metz, to join Oldham Athletic in June 1936, he was suspended by the FA for three months from 31 August 1936. In a second season at Boundary Park, his 33 goals in 39 matches remains the club record for the highest number of goals by a player in one season.

DENWOOD, Wilfred　　　　**1925**
Outside-left.
Born: Bury 1900.
Debut v Nelson (a) 7 March 1925.
Appearances: 5.
Career: Bacup Borough; RAKERS 4 February 1925; Nelson 27 August 1925 to cs 1926.
Wilf Denwood, a recruit from Lancashire Combination football, spent much of his spell with the Rakers in their Midland Combination side. On Easter Monday 1925, he played in two games. In the morning he scored once at Anfield for New Brighton Reserves in their 5-0 win against Fairres FC in the Liverpool Challenge Cup Final. In the afternoon he was on the mark again, scoring once in the 4-0 win against Halifax Town Reserves at Sandheys Park.

DICKIE, James　　　　**1927-28 and 1932-33**
Outside-left. 5ft 7ins. 10st 7lbs.
Born: Montrose, Forfarshire, 22 September 1903.
Debut v Darlington (a) 27 August 1927.
Appearances: 83; Goals: 19.
Career: Buckie Thistle; Preston North End (trial) 26 January 1925; Buckie Thistle 9 March 1925; Preston North End 26 January 1926; Forres

Mechanics May 1926; St Johnstone January 1927; RAKERS 24 August 1927; Bristol City 1 December 1928 (fee £1,550); Chester July 1930; Macclesfield Town 1931-2; Chester 28 August 1932; RAKERS 22 September 1932; retired May 1933.

Originally signed on one month's trial, Dickie struck such an effective vein that he was signed for the season, long before the trial period was up. He was New Brighton's best forward in 1927-8 and the only one of the front line retained for 1928-9. He commanded a sizeable fee when Bristol City signed him in December 1928. Listed by Bristol City at £750 in 1930, Dickie had a spell outside the League

with Chester and Macclesfield. When Bristol City waived their fee, he rejoined Chester, eventually returning to New Brighton in 1932. When the Rakers won the Liverpool Senior Cup for the first time in their history, in April 1933, Dickie scored a hat-trick from outside-left in the 6-0 victory over Southport.

DIXON, Matthew   **1930**
Centre-half. 6ft. 12st.
Born: Byker, Newcastle upon Tyne, 1906.
Debut v Stockport County (a) 1 September 1930.
Appearances: 2.
Career: Walker Park; Everton 6 December 1928; Preston North End 27 May 1929; Barrow 30 January 1930; RAKERS 19 August 1930; Connah's

Quay September 1930; Nantwich Victoria 11 October 1930; Wigan Athletic; Bacup Borough July 1933.

Signed at a time when a replacement for Walter Wadsworth was being sought, Matt Dixon and former Raker, Jack Reid, were contenders for the centre-half role as the 1930-31 season opened. 'Lacking polish', was one verdict on Dixon's debut and he was released shortly after Billy Matthews, the Welsh international centre-half, was signed from Stockport County.

DORRANS, Owen   **1931**
Inside-forward. 5ft 7½ins. 10st 9lbs.
Born: Stevenston, Scotland, 1905.
Debut v Chester (h) 3 October 1931.
Appearances: 3.
Career: Cowdenbeath; Raith Rovers cs 1925; Greenock Morton cs 1929; Wigan Borough 17 January 1931; Stevenston FC; RAKERS (trial) 3 October to 6 November 1931.
A foot injury, which necessitated his removal to hospital, brought a painful conclusion to Dorrans' trial with New Brighton. He had not impressed greatly during his brief stay, despite showing plenty of spirit and working hard. In each of his three outings, the Rakers were defeated, failing to score on each occasion. During a lengthy spell in Scottish football, Dorrans helped Raith Rovers to promotion from Division Two in the 1926-7 season.

DUFF, James   **1931**
Outside-right. 5ft 8ins. 10st 11lbs.
Born: Scotland, 1910.
Debut v Walsall (h) 9 September 1931.
Appearances: 4; Goals: 1.
Career: Glasgow Celtic; RAKERS (trial) 20 August to 26 October 1931; Southport (trial) 3 November to 14 December 1931.
Injury to Parle in the local 'derby' at Tranmere gave Jimmy Duff an early taste of League action. Despite finding the net in his second appearance at Barrow, he lost his place in a welter of team changes brought about by the team's dreadful start to the season. Back in the Reserves, he was sent off in the George Mahon Cup tie against High Park Villa at Sandheys Park on 10 October. During the course of this game, two players were taken to hospital, two Park Villa players cautioned, New Brighton were awarded two penalties and won 6-3. In a short trial period with Southport, Duff made four reserve-team appearances, but failed to win a permanent engagement.

DUFF, Stanley Douglas   **1939**
Outside-left. 5ft 8½ins. 11st 7lbs.
Born: Liverpool, 1919.
Debut v Doncaster Rovers (h) 11 March 1939.
Appearances: 3.
Career: Earle FC; Leicester City amateur 27 August 1935, professional 20 February 1936; Tranmere Rovers 10 May 1937; Waterford (Ireland) cs 1938; Chester 5 December 1938; RAKERS 2 February 1939 to cs 1939.

117

International honours: England Schoolboys.
Signed by Leicester City as a professional when he was only 17 years old, Stan Duff was a regular member of their London Combination XI. A desire to return to Merseyside saw him choose Tranmere Rovers, after Charlton Athletic had expressed an interest in signing him. One of his best games for Tranmere was against the Rakers in October 1937. In a sensational period of six minutes in the second half, Tranmere scored four times, Duff netting one of the goals. In a brief spell with the Rakers, his debut resulted in the team's heaviest home defeat of the season, Doncaster Rovers winning 6-3.

DUGGINS, Alfred E   **1925-26**
Outside-left. 5ft 9ins. 12st.
Born: Aston, Birmingham.
Debut v Barrow (a) 29 August 1925.
Appearances: 13; Goals: 3.
Career: Redditch FC; Aberdeen cs 1922; Heart of Midlothian cs 1923; Preston North End 18 January 1924; Walsall 26 May 1924; RAKERS 17 July 1925 to cs 1926.
International honour: England Juniors v Scotland Juniors.
Alf Duggins' football career was launched in Scotland when he was recruited by the Dons after appearing at Aberdeen in a junior international match during season 1921-2. He was one of several specialist outside-lefts on the Rakers' books during 1925-6, being one of five to occupy the berth during the season. He began as first choice, but lost his place after a poor display against Crewe Alexandra in September. His unhappy afternoon included a penalty attempt 'shot six yards wide' according to one match report. During World War One, he was awarded the DCM whilst serving in the Machine Gun Corps

DUNNE, James   **1925-26**
Centre-forward. 5ft 9ins. 11st 9lbs.
Born: Dublin, 3 September 1906; Died: 1949.
Debut v Rochdale (h) 7 November 1925 (scored one goal).
Appearances: 8; Goals: 6.
Career: Shamrock Rovers; RAKERS 7 November 1925; Sheffield United 20 February 1926 (fee £500); Arsenal 2 October 1933 (fee £8,250); Southampton 16 July 1936 (fee £1,000); Shamrock Rovers player-coach 12 June 1937.
International honours: 7 Irish caps, 1928-33.
Club honour: Arsenal, Division One champions 1933-4.
Induced by New Brighton's goalkeeper, Bert Mehaffy, to try his luck in England, the young, ginger-haired centre-forward, Jimmy Dunne, arrived at Sandheys Park for a month's trial in November 1925. Considered good enough only for the reserve team of Shamrock Rovers and straight off the boat from Ireland — on which he had been sea-sick *en route* — Dunne nevertheless showed promise on his goalscoring debut. He was not destined to remain with the Rakers for long, as Sheffield United recruited him after about three

months, during which time he had scored seven goals in ten League and Cup appearances. At the end of his first season at Bramall Lane he was placed on the transfer list. Fortunately for Sheffield United there were no takers and his subsequent goalscoring feats were to net him a total of 143 goals, which included 41 in the 1930-31 season, when he was

the First Division's leading goalscorer. When he joined Arsenal in October 1933, he became one of eight forwards on the Gunners' books who, together, had a combined aggregate amounting to 971 Football League goals — (Jack 265, Dunne 149, Lambert 116, Coleman 98, Bastin 93, Hulme 92, Bowden 89 and James 69). His nephew, Tommy Dunne, was a half-back with Leicester City, Exeter City, Shrewsbury Town and Southport.

EARL, Albert Thomas   **1948**
Inside-forward. 5ft 6½ins. 11st 4lbs.
Born: Gateshead, 10 February 1915.
Appearances: 9; Goals: 1.
Career: Dunston CWS; Bury 28 March 1932; Rhyl Athletic 1936-7; York City 3 July 1937; Accrington Stanley (wartime guest); Stockport County 23 August 1946; Rochdale 8 November 1947; RAKERS 6 March 1948; Northwich Victoria August 1948.
Signed just prior to the 1947-8 season's transfer

'deadline', Earl partnered left winger Johnny Forsyth in seven of his nine games for the Rakers, at the conclusion of which New Brighton had to apply for re-election. The brief wing partnership was said to lack understanding, as additional new recruits — Brindle and Rainford — were introduced late in the season. Earl's career spanned the war. Beginning at Bury as a 17-year-old, he made 35 appearances (seven goals) and also assisted York City (58 appearances, nine goals). In the first season of peacetime football, Earl scored 11 goals in 30 appearances for Stockport County, who finished the 1946-7 season in fourth place in Division Three North.

EAVES, Ernest   **1948-51**
Centre-forward. 5ft 10ins. 10st 13lbs.
Born: Bryn, near Wigan, 4 January 1927.
Debut v Halifax Town (h) 20 November 1948 (scored one goal).
Appearances: 14; Goals: 3.
Career: Earlestown Central School; Wigan Technical College; Newton Juniors; Newton YMCA. (Liverpool County Combination); Newton-le-Willows; RAKERS amateur September 1948, professional 4 August 1950, released on a free transfer 5 May 1951.
A youthful, lightweight amateur centre-forward, Ernie Eaves could hardly have wished for a better Football League debut. He provided one goal and scored himself in the 2-0 win against Halifax Town, giving the Rakers their first home win for almost three months. He was Cup-tied and unavailable for the following week's game, the FA Cup first-round tie against Carlisle United. Inexplicably, he was not called upon again until four months later, when he appeared in ten out of the last 11 matches of the season, as five wins and three draws lifted the Rakers from the foot of the table and into the safety of 17th place. During National Service in the Fleet Air Arm, he served in the Far East and represented the RN in Hong Kong.

EDGE, Thomas   **1922-24**
Outside-right. 5ft 9ins. 11st.

Born: Leigh, Lancashire, 28 April 1898.
Debut v Bradford (a) 25 August 1923.
Appearances: 26; Goals: 2.
Career: Brook Valley; Stockport County (during World War One); Manchester City 17 October 1919; Treherbert cs 1920; Oldham Athletic 25 January 1921; Exeter City 27 May 1921; Blackpool 11 May 1922; RAKERS April 1922 to cs 1924.
Representative honour: Southern League v Central League at Wolverhampton, 25 March 1922.
A speedy winger who had given Lancashire Combination defenders lots of trouble in the season prior to the Rakers' Football League debut, Tommy Edge began as first-choice outside-right in 1923-4 and did well to hold off the challenge of the emerging Ernie Whitter. An ankle injury ended Edge's First Division career with Oldham Athletic in 1921.

EGAN, William   **1933-34**
Full-back.
Debut v Crewe Alexandra (h) 25 February 1933.
Appearances: 1.
Career: RAKERS amateur 10 February 1933 to cs 1934.
Considering the *Wallasey News* report on Bill Egan's debut, which took place on a quagmire after heavy snow, it was surprising that he featured only once in the Rakers' first-team: 'The amateur W.Egan — who deputized for Carr — was not only a resolute tackler and sure kicker, but showed that he also possessed speed and stamina. His clearances were frequently applauded, and he deserved all the praise bestowed upon him.' Egan's lack of opportunity was due to the fact that he was understudy to Len Carr, the club's long-serving, record-appearance full-back.

ELLIOT, Robert   **1935-36**
Outside-left. 5ft 8ins. 10st 7lbs.
Born: Carlisle, 1912.
Debut v Tranmere Rovers (h) 31 August 1935.
Appearances: 38; Goals: 1.
Career: Carlisle United amateur 19 March 1934; Preston North End 15 December 1934; RAKERS 18 July 1935; Bath City August 1936; Aldershot 15 June 1937 to cs 1938.
A lightly-built, nippy winger, Bob Elliot had no serious rivals for the outside-left position during 1935-6. He did not, however, survive the general 'clear-out' at the end of that season, which saw New Brighton make their third application for re-election. After assisting Bath City to sixth place in the Southern League in 1936-7, he was one of eight new forwards signed by Aldershot for 1937-8.

EVANS, Nicholas   **1947**
Outside-right.
Born: Trimdon, 23 November 1925.
Debut v Hartlepools United (a) 15 March 1947.
Appearances: 1.
Career: Hesleden FC; RAKERS amateur 15 March 1947.
Whilst the debut of Neil McBain for the Rakers at the record-breaking age of 51 years and four

months is well documented, the Football League debut of Nicholas Evans — in the same match — is less well-remembered. The Rakers arrived at Hartlepools two men short after fog had caused travelling difficulties. The son of a Hartlepools United official, Mr Nicol Evans, young Nicholas was signed on amateur forms on the spot and gave a creditable display at outside-right. Evans junior, a regular inside-left with Hesleden in the Hartlepools & District League, was invited to a dinner-dance with the Rakers' party at their West Hartlepool hotel on the Saturday evening. No doubt he must have found his day unforgettable.

FINLAY, John　　　　　　　　**1951**
Outside-right. 5ft 8½ins, 11st.
Born: Glasgow, 1 July 1925.
Debut v Mansfield Town (h) 3 March 1951.
Appearances: 15; Goals: 2.
Career: Clyde; RAKERS 5 March 1951; Leeds United 15 June 1951 to July 1952 (joint transfer with W.C.Heggie for a combined fee of £6,000); Yeovil Town 1952-3; Walsall 7 August 1953 to 15 June 1954.
Although Jack Finlay's signing came too late to save the Rakers from 24th place and subsequent loss of League status, the Scottish winger added punch to the right wing and formed a good understanding with his inside partner, Jackie Jones. The last professional to be signed by New Brighton whilst a Football League club, Finlay's stay at the Tower was brief, Leeds United signing him and Bill Heggie in June 1951. After only one Second Division appearance at Elland Road, Finlay had a spell in the Southern League before Walsall signed him for the 1953-4 season. In this campaign, he was one of 41 players used by the Saddlers in the League as they finished 24th in Division Three South.

FITZPATRICK, Peter P　　　　**1949-50**
Inside-forward.
Born: Bebington, 27 April 1929.
Debut v Oldham Athletic (a) 22 April 1950.
Appearances: 1.
Career: RAKERS amateur 1949-50; Bolton Wanderers (trial) 9 August to 3 September 1950.
A star in the Rakers' Colts XI in Division Two of the West Cheshire League, 'Fitz' won a rapid promotion to the Reserves, playing in the Lancashire Combination. Undoubtedly a clever ball-player, if at times inclined to be a little too individualistic, he was only five days short of his 21st birthday when he made his solitary Football League appearance at Boundary Park.

FLOOD, Leslie Thomas B　　　**1925-35**
Goalkeeper. 6ft 1in. 11st.
Born: Bristol, 1904.
Debut v Tranmere Rovers (a) 11 February 1928.
Appearances: 38.
Career: Wallasey Town; Wallasey Trams; RAKERS amateur 21 February 1925 to cs 1935; Thorndale FC.

Tall, pencil-slim, and wonderfully agile, amateur goalkeeper Les Flood had a ten-year association with the Rakers. An employee of Wallasey Tramways, his longest spell of action at Rake Lane was in the 1928-9 season when, as deputy for the injured Bert Mehaffy, he made 21 appearances, in eight of which he kept a 'clean sheet'. The quality of his performances were clearly revealed by the fact that he was beaten only 25 times in his 21 appearances, whilst Irish international Mehaffy conceeded 46 goals in the same number of matches.

FOGG, William Henry　　　　　**1936-37**
Half-back. 5ft 8ins. 11st.
Born: Birkenhead, 9 March 1903; Died: 29 July 1966.
Debut v Port Vale (h) 2 September 1936.
Appearances: 32; Goals: 1.
Career: Wirral Railways; Tranmere Rovers amateur 21 August 1924, professional 19 January 1925; Bangor City 19 May 1926; Huddersfield Town 8 May 1928 (fee £20); Clapton Orient 22 August 1933; RAKERS 20 August 1936 to cs 1937.
Good positional sense and judgement in distributing the ball were Billy Fogg's chief strengths. His lengthy career began at outside-right, but Huddersfield Town converted him to wing-half. In 1929-30, when Huddersfield Town won their way to Wembley, he played in all the rounds but missed the Final due to injury. By permission of the FA, he was granted a medal. A keen golfer, he won the challenge cup in the handicap division of the Merseyside Professional Footballers' Golf Championship at the Wootton course on 5 October 1936.

FORSYTH, John Thomson　　　**1946-48**
Outside-left.
Born: Dumbarton, 20 December 1918.
Debut v Wrexham (a) 31 August 1946.
Appearances: 64; Goals: 4.
Career: Dumbarton; Luton Town 29 August 1942; Grimsby Town (wartime guest, 1943-4); RAKERS 15 July 1946; Chester 14 July 1948 to 14 June 1949.
One of a bevy of Scots recruited by manager McBain for the Rakers' first season of peacetime football. A diminutive outside-left, Forsyth became a professional with Dumbarton before his 18th birthday. His career was interrupted by the war, when he saw service in Tobruk before being captured and spending three years as a PoW in Italy and Germany. A consistent performer, Forsyth made 32 appearances in each of his two seasons with New Brighton and another 32 in his one season with Chester.

FOULKES, James　　　　　　　**1925-28**
Goalkeeper. 5ft 10½ins. 11st 4lbs.
Born: Prescot.
Debut v Crewe Alexandra (h) 26 September 1925.
Appearances: 6.
Career: Prescot; RAKERS 7 May 1925 to cs 1928.
Jim Foulkes played Rugby League with St Helens Town before transferring to soccer with Prescot.

He first caught the eye of the Rake Lane officials in May 1924, when he was unbeaten in two matches which took the George Mahon Cup to Prescot. After drawing 0-0 against New Brighton Reserves at Sandheys, Prescot won the replay, at Burscough, by 1-0. Good reflexes and a safe pair of hands made him a good man to have in reserve, but he was afforded few opportunities due to the fine form of Bert Mehaffy. A crown-green bowls champion he was the father of W.A.'Billy' Foulkes, the Manchester United and England defender who recorded 567 League appearances in 21 years at Old Trafford.

FOULKES, William David   1936-38
Inside-forward. 5ft 6½ins. 11st.
Born: Flint, North Wales, 1912.
Debut v Southport (h) 19 December 1936 (scored two goals).
Appearances: 18; Goals: 3.
Career: Southport amateur 5 September 1931; Arsenal amateur 21 May 1932; Flint Town; RAKERS amateur 13 November 1936, professional 3 December 1936, released on free transfer 6 July 1938.
International honours: Welsh Amateur v Scotland in 1934 and 1935 (two caps).
Commenting on Foulkes' selection for his New Brighton debut, the local Press recorded: 'His reserve-team displays have fully merited promotion. He is not big, but has football ability, and plays a move ahead of the game.' His first senior game was at Stockport and he scored in the first half, but the game had to be abandoned 14 minutes from time, due to fog. He did even better the following week, scoring twice in a 3-1 win against Southport, one of his former clubs.

FRIEL, John Patrick   1950-51
Inside-forward. 5ft 10ins, 11st 8lbs.
Born: Glasgow, 1 September 1923.
Debut v Darlington (a) 13 September 1950.
Appearances: 3.
Career: Third Lanark; RAKERS 20 June 1950 to 16 April 1951; Queen of the South; Torquay United 14 October 1952 to 30 June 1953.
John Friel was the first player signed by Walter Galbraith, after his appointment as player-manager. When Friel made his League debut for the Rakers, he was one of six team changes, three positional, in the wake of an early season crop of injuries. After a promising debut at Darlington, when he was said to show a nice turn of speed, he also joined the injury list. A dislocated wrist sidelined him for a spell and he was subsequently unable to dislodge either Carter or Jones, the experienced pair of first-team inside-forwards. When New Brighton published their retained list in May 1951, Friel was one of six professionals not kept on. He did not feature in the first teams of either of his subsequent clubs, Queen of the South and Torquay United.

FROST, Arthur Douglas   1938-39
Centre-forward. 5ft 11½ins. 12st.
Born: Liverpool, 1 December 1915.
Debut v Halifax Town (h) 24 September 1938 (scored one goal).
Appearances: 23; Goals: 18.
Career: Army football; RAKERS amateur 23 July, professional 19 August 1938; Newcastle United 4 March 1939 (fee £2,515); RAKERS wartime guest from October 1939; Southport wartime guest 1943; South Liverpool 1946-7.
A recruit from the South Lancashire Regiment, Arthur Frost played himself into the Rakers' first team by his goalscoring feats and sense of positional play. Eight goals in five days brought the Reserves' total to 29 goals in seven games, 19 of which had come in their last three matches. He scored the winner after 70 minutes in his Football League debut match at Halifax and his subsequent goalscoring exploits made him a great favourite. Sadly, he became just another asset to be realized due to lack of public support. His last League goals, against Hartlepools, were witnessed by only 1,453 spectators.

GAFFNEY, Peter   1925-26
Centre-half. 6ft. 12st 6lbs.
Born: Straiton, Strathclyde, 1900.
Debut v Hartlepools United (h) 10 April 1925.
Appearances: 19; Goals: 3.
Career: Hamilton Academical; Alloa 1921; Doncaster Rovers 15 June 1923; Barrow 1 June 1924; RAKERS 2 April 1925; Coventry City 24 June 1926; Ashington 27 August 1927.
Injury to regular pivot Jack Reid midway through 1924-5, saw four other players tried before Gaffney's signing brought much needed stability to the Rakers' defence. A promotion winner with

Alloa in 1921-2, Gaffney had an extended run at centre-forward with New Brighton in 1925-6, following the sale of Jimmy Dunne to Sheffield United.

GALBRAITH, Walter McMurray   1948-51
Full-back. 5ft 10½ins, 11st 8lbs.
Born: Glasgow, 26 May 1918.
Debut v Stockport County (a) 15 September 1948.
Appearances: 109; Goals: 1.
Career: Strath Bungo School; Strathclyde Juniors; Clyde FC 1939; Queen's Park FC 1941; Clyde FC 1946; RAKERS 15 September 1948 (fee approx. £1,000); appointed player-manager 19 June 1950; Grimsby Town 29 August 1951 (fee £660); Accrington Stanley player-manager 27 June 1953 (retiring as a player May 1954); Bradford manager November 1958; Tranmere Rovers manager January 1961; Hibernian manager November 1961; Stockport County chief scout July 1968, appointed manager August 1969 to April 1970.

Although Walter Galbraith was perhaps better known for his lengthy managerial career, on the field he was a cultured, consistent defender. One report in 1950 stated: 'In a patchy Rakers' defence, the flurry and bustle of others was accentuated by the ice-cold display given by skipper Galbraith — surely the best left-full-back in Division Three.' Twice a Glasgow Cup winner with Queens Park and Clyde, in his early days Galbraith joined his father's old soccer team, Strathclyde Juniors. In his first game for Clyde, which was a Cup tie, he scored the only goal of the match from left-half. A commercial traveller before joining New Brighton, Galbraith was appointed captain in August 1949 and succeeded Jack Atkinson as player-manager in June 1950.

GALE, George Warrington   1938-39
Goalkeeper. 6ft. 12st 8lbs.
Born: 1916.
Debut v Chester (a) 31 August 1938.
Appearances: 18.
Career: Cardiff City amateur, professional 29

January 1935; Bangor City cs 1935; Northwich Victoria during 1935-6; RAKERS 10 August 1938 to cs 1939.
Signed as understudy to Willie Hawthorn, George Gale was soon called upon when the first-team goalkeeper was injured in the first match of the season. His debut at Chester resulted in a 3-1 win and he earned good Press notices for a confident display of clean handling. He graduated with Cardiff City, starting in their 'A' team in 1934. During the 1934-5 season he turned down the opportunity to join Bradford, who were managed by former Cardiff wing-half, Bill Hardy.

GEE, Harry   1923-27
Half-back. 5ft 8ins. 11st 7lbs.
Born: Haydock, 25 December 1894.
Debut v Accrington Stanley (a) 8 September 1923.
Appearances: 87; Goals: 7.

Career: Haydock St James; Newton Common Recs.; Burnley amateur, professional 9 August 1922; RAKERS 12 July 1923; Exeter City 8 August 1927; Runcorn August 1931.
As a schoolboy, Harry Gee played Rugby for Lancashire Schools, but the former bookmaker's clerk switched codes so successfully that he made his bow in senior football with First Division Burnley. His debut, at Turf Moor, came on 21 October 1922, when 40,919 spectators — the Clarets' all-time record attendance — witnessed the local 'derby' against Blackburn Rovers. Joining the Rakers for their first Football League season, he was reserve

to Sam Challinor in 1923-4, becoming firmly established as a senior in the following term. His shrewd promptings from left-half were a feature during the Rakers' best-ever season, when they secured third place in the table. In the 1925-6 season, his penalty against Sheffield Wednesday set the Rakers on their way to the fourth round of the FA Cup for the first time in their history. His League career was ended at Exeter when he broke an ankle. He eventually received £280 in compensation and returned to Wallasey as a newsagent. Gee became an alderman and served on the Wallasey Council from 1943 to 1959. He retained a life-long interest in the Rakers and was chairman of the Supporters' Club for many years.

GLOVER, Charles Edward   1922-24
Full-back. 5ft 7ins. 10st 8lbs.
Born: Bootle, Liverpool, 7 April 1902.
Debut v Halifax Town (h) 29 September 1923.
Appearances: 32.
Career: Bootle Schoolboys; Stanley FC; South Liverpool; RAKERS August 1922; Everton 14 May 1924 (fee £750 plus the proceeds of a match); Southport 14 July 1925; Wigan Borough 5 August 1927; New York Giants (USA) August 1928; New York Ameriks; Brookhatton FC 1935; Phalzer SC 1941; Later managed Brooklyn SC.

Ted Glover began the 1923-4 season as the Rakers' third-choice right-back, but after injury had sidelined Jimmy Niven, he won his place after Dick Critchlow had deputized for four matches. Glover's form was so outstanding that Everton signed him at the end of the season. The Merseysiders added the not inconsiderable fee of £750 to the proceeds of a match at Sandheys Park, which Everton won

4-0. After a season in reserve at Goodison, he next assisted Southport (55 appearances) and then Wigan Borough (12 appearances). He departed from Liverpool on 28 July 1928, on the White Star Liner *Celtic*, to join New York Giants FC. Glover enjoyed a most successful career in the States, being nominated for the Soccer Hall of Fame in 1965 at a dinner given by the American Soccer League at the Sheraton Atlantic Hotel. Married to the former Grace Armstrong, daughter of James Armstrong, the Secretary of the US Soccer Football Association. A bank security officer, Ted Glover now lives in retirement, in Colarado.

GREATREX, George Kenneth   1930-33
Goalkeeper. 5ft 9ins. 11st 7lbs.
Born: Liverpool, 16 May 1904; Died: 1981.
Debut v Gateshead (h) 15 September 1930.
Appearances: 25.
Career: Orrell; Wrexham amateur 20, professional 30 August 1928; RAKERS 29 July 1930; Crewe Alexandra (trial) 7 September to 20 October 1933; Runcorn; Stoneycroft St Paul's FC during 1935-6.

After understudying Scottish international Kenny Campbell in his first season, and the ever-present Stan Walker in 1931-2, Ken Greatrex began 1932-3 as first-choice goalkeeper. He did not hold the position for long, however, as the emerging amateur George Bradshaw proved far too good for reserve football. Greatrex's last game for New Brighton, on the last Saturday of the 1932-3 season, was against his former club, Wrexham. It was a vital meeting, as the Rakers, fifth from bottom, needed one point to ensure that they would not finish in the re-election zone. In a tense encounter at Rake Lane, Wrexham won 2-0 leaving New Brighton in 21st place and re-election applicants along with Darlington. In May 1932, when New Brighton made their debut in Division One of the English Baseball Association, Ken Greatrex scored seven runs in New Brighton's 27-run victory against Oakfield Social at Rake Lane.

GREENHALGH, Norman   1935-38
Full-back. 5ft 9ins. 10st 6lbs.

Born: Bolton, 10 August 1914.
Debut v Southport (a) 5 October 1935.
Appearances: 77; Goals: 8.
Career: Bolton junior football; Bolton Wanderers amateur 11 May, professional 6 September 1933; RAKERS 2 October 1935; Everton 29 January 1938; Bangor City 1948.
International honour: England v Scotland, wartime game, 1939.
Club honour: Everton, Division One champions 1938-9.
Apart from injuries and an operation for appendicitis in January 1937, Norman Greenhalgh was a regular first-team player throughout his stay at Rake Lane. Outstandingly versatile, Greenhalgh began at right-half, but when he deputized in goal temporarily for the injured Hawthorn in the first-round Cup tie against Workington in November 1937, he had then played as goalkeeper, full-back, half-back and forward. A move across the Mersey to Everton saw him partner left-back Willie Cook at Goodison Park and Greenhalgh was ever-present in Everton's League Championship season in 1938-9.

GRICE, Robert   **1932**
Centre-forward. 5ft 10½ins. 12st 8lbs.
Born: Sutton, St Helens, 12 March 1907.
Debut v Hartlepools United (a) 29 October 1932.
Appearances: 3.
Career: Runcorn; Peasley Cross Athletic cs 1931; RAKERS (trial) 29 October 1932; Peasley Cross Athletic 6 December 1932; Oldham Athletic 10 January 1933; Southport 20 June 1935; Stalybridge Celtic 8 August 1936; Clitheroe October 1936.
A total of 55 goals for Peasley Cross Athletic in 1931-2, together with nine in the season in which New Brighton signed him, suggested that Bob Grice might improve an attack which had been goalless for the previous three weeks. He appeared at Hartlepools a few hours after signing and his debut cost New Brighton a fee of two guineas (£2.10p), for playing him before the registration was completed. 'Lacking pace', was one verdict. 'Over eager' was another and it was obvious that he found life in the Third Division less rewarding than the Liverpool County Combination. A second chance in League football came after he had switched to a defensive role and he made 26 appearances for Oldham Athletic and 40 for Southport, before moving back into non-League football.

GRIFFITHS, William T   **1935-37**
Centre-forward. 5ft 7ins. 11st 5lbs.
Born: Pontefract, 1914.
Debut v Tranmere Rovers (h) 31 August 1935.
Appearances: 24; Goals: 7.
Career: Upton Colliery; Goole Town; Sunderland 14 February 1934; RAKERS 13 July 1935 to cs 1937.
A knee injury sustained after only three minutes of the game at Rotherham on 23 November 1935 ended Billy Griffiths' season. Despite recovering and scoring prolifically in the Lancashire Combination, he could not dislodge the young, up-

and-coming Dennis Westcott. His ill-luck continued into 1936-7 when another injury, in the first trial match in August, sidelined him until the end of October. He was to make only nine appearances in what proved to be his final season.

GRIMLEY, Thomas William   **1948-51**
Goalkeeper. 6ft 1in. 13st.
Born: Dinnington, Sheffield, 1 November 1920.
Died: Great Barr, Birmingham, 4 November 1976.
Debut v Gateshead (a) 21 August 1948.
Appearances: 94.
Career: Dinnington & Thurcroft Schools; Sheffield & South Yorkshire Schoolboys; Barnsley (trial); Wolverhampton Wanderers (trial); Swallownest FC; West Bromwich Albion trialist 10 September 1938 amateur 27 October 1938 professional 19 April 1939; RAKERS 18 August 1948; Hednesford Town 20 July 1951; Rugby Town 16 August 1952, retired cs 1957. West Bromwich Albion scout 1957-62.
Reserve goalkeeper for England Boys, Tom Grimley left school at 15 and started to work in a brickyard. West Brom signed him just before the war and he quickly graduated to their Reserves. A Military Policeman from 1940, he served for five years in the Middle East and Italy. A sound goalkeeper, with good anticipation and handling, Grimley was a Rakers regular for two seasons before losing his place to Jimmy Jones.

GUILD, James   **1950-51**
Wing-half. 5ft 10ins, 12st.
Born: Glasgow, 10 December 1928.
Debut v York City (a) 10 March 1951.
Appearances: 2.
Career: Clelland Hawthorne Juveniles; Dunoon Athletic May 1950; RAKERS 23 September 1950 to 31 July 1951.
When Jimmy Guild made his debut for New Brighton Reserves against Darwen, he found himself directly opposed to Ray Westwood, the former Bolton Wanderers star inside-forward. It was a severe test for a young player, but Guild impressed with his quick tackling and constructive distribution. In the same match, he had the referee and linesman initially baffled by his terrific throw-ins. Guild was the Scottish record holder for the throw, having beaten Haddow's (Clyde FC) record of 40 yards by three yards in the summer of 1950. Out of competition, Guild had thrown as far as 45 yards. He was one of many Scots players 'captured' by Bert Niven, the Rakers' long-serving Scottish scout. At the time of joining the Rakers, Guild was in his final year as an apprentice carpenter.

GUTTERIDGE, George   **1924-25**
Half-back. 5ft 8½ins. 11st.
Born: Prescot.
Debut v Doncaster Rovers (h) 28 March 1925.
Appearances: 2.
Career: Prescot Cables; RAKERS 16 June 1924 to cs 1925.
Reserve centre-half George Gutteridge made only

Appearances: 6.
Career: Hamilton Academical; RAKERS 11 August 1925 to cs 1926.
Pre-season prospects for the Rakers, reviewed in the *Liverpool Echo* in August 1925, named Hannah and Wilson as 'promising understudies' to Duggins for the outside-left spot. Before the end of October, all three had been tried and it was not until an old favourite, Gene Carney, returned in March, that the position was considered satisfactorily filled. Hannah's first appearance at Rake Lane resulted in New Brighton's first-ever victory over Southport, on 10 October 1926.

HARLEY, Alexander John   1927-28
Centre-forward. 5ft 9½ins. 11st 10lbs.
Born: Edinburgh, 17 July 1898; Died: Cardiff 9 February 1984.
Debut v Halifax Town (h) 17 September 1927 (scored one goal).
Appearances: 27; Goals: 14.
Career: Bonnyrigg FC (Midlothian); Bathgate; Heart of Midlothian cs 1925; Caernarfon Town cs 1926; RAKERS 8 July 1927; Millwall 25 June 1928 (fee £350); Rhyl Athletic September 1929; Norwich City (trial) 11 September to 5 November 1930.

two senior appearances during his season with New Brighton. At a time when Jack Reid's absence through injury was causing problems, Gutteridge's debut was not a happy one, the Rakers losing their unbeaten home record. He did better the following week at Durham, in a 0-0 draw, but the arrival of Gaffney from Barrow saw Gutteridge back in the Reserves. On Easter Monday 1925 he scored twice at Anfield when New Brighton Reserves won the Liverpool Challenge Cup Final against Fairres, 5-0.

HAMILTON, Herbert   1923-24
Full-back. 5ft 9½ins. 11st 10lbs.
Born: Wallasey, 27 March 1906.
Debut v Ashington (a) 22 December 1923.
Appearances: 1.
Career: Harrowby; Poulton Rovers; RAKERS amateur 19 December 1923; Everton 1 October 1924; Preston North End 17 May 1927; Chesterfield 4 June 1931 (fee £250); Tranmere Rovers 12 May 1937; Accrington Stanley 10 November 1938; Marine FC 1939-40.
Club honours: Chesterfield, Division Three North champions 1935-6; Tranmere Rovers, Division Three North champions 1937-8.
'Duke' Hamilton showed great tackling skills and other defensive abilities when he made his Football League debut for New Brighton as a 17-year-old. His meteoric rise from junior football to an appearance in a Third Division North game proved to be the start of a long, successful career. A Third Division North championship medal winner twice in as many seasons, with Chesterfield and Tranmere Rovers, Hamilton was a beneficiary with Chesterfield, for whom he made 192 appearances in six seasons.

HANNAH, George   1925-26
Outside-left.
Debut v Lincoln City (a) 3 October 1925.

A reserve for the Scottish Schoolboys team in 1913-14, Alex Harley actually made his goalscoring reputation in Wales. He came to New Brighton from Caernarfon with a record of 54 goals in season 1926-7. Horace Williams' transfer to Blackpool gave Harley his chance and he responded well, being particularly prominent in

FA Cup ties, scoring six goals. These included four against Rhyl Athletic, scored in succession in the second half in the Rakers' 7-2 victory. During his spell with the Hearts club, Harley worked as a librarian in Edinburgh.

HAWKSWORTH, Ernest   **1926-27**
Inside-forward. 5ft 7½ins. 11st 8lbs.
Born: Rochdale, 6 December 1894. Died: Rochdale, 17 July 1961.
Debut v Durham City (h) 30 October 1926.
Appearances: 17; Goals: 2.
Career: Sudden Villa; Rochdale 1912-13; Hull City (wartime guest); Blackburn Rovers 22 March 1919 (fee £500) to cs 1925; RAKERS 26 October 1926; Bury (coach) September 1927.
Ernest Hawksworth first joined Rochdale as an amateur and after only two reserve-team matches,

was promoted to the first team. When war came, he joined the First Dragoon Guards and during his military training in York made a number of appearances for Hull City. After being transferred to the Royal Scots, he fought in France, being twice wounded. He spent nine months in hospital but was able to resume with Rochdale after his demobilization in January 1919. He was soon snapped up by Blackburn Rovers and scored 35

goals for them in 96 matches before returning to his families' tailoring business in 1924. Brought out of retirement by the Rakers in 1926-7, he formed a good left-wing partnership with New Brighton's Irish international, David Lyner.

HAWTHORN, William   **1936-39**
Goalkeeper. 6ft. 12st 7lbs.
Born: Glasgow, 1910.
Debut v Oldham Athletic (a) 29 August 1936.
Appearances: 108.
Career: Alloa Athletic; Bradford 16 March 1933; Airdrieonians 1934-5; RAKERS 21 August 1936 to September 1939.
Willie Hawthorn was so successful on joining New Brighton that he did not miss a first-team match for two years. He was injured whilst saving a penalty-kick against Stockport County in the opening fixture of 1938-9 and eventually was out of the side for three months. He recovered in time to complete his century of League appearances for New Brighton during the season. After the war, he worked in Scotland as a representative for an oil and petroleum company.

HAYDON, Cecil   **1937-39**
Inside-forward or Winger. 5ft 10ins. 11st.
Born: Birkenhead, 24 May 1919.
Debut v Oldham Athletic (h) 21 January 1939.
Appearances: 1.
Career: Victory Social (Birkenhead League); RAKERS amateur 31 December 1937, professional 16 February 1939; Derby County 5 June 1939; Doncaster Rovers 3 October 1945; Rochdale 2 July 1948 to cs 1949.
Cecil Haydon, who had occupied every forward position in the reserve team, got his chance after the departure of Jack Stamps. Strangely enough, he was to follow Stamps to Derby County about five months later. Moving to Doncaster Rovers, where he was mainly in reserve, he played four matches in 1946-7 when the Rovers won the Third Division North with a record-breaking 72 points, including 37 in away matches.

HEGGIE, William Campbell   **1951**
Full-back. 5ft 11ins, 12st.
Born: Scone, 7 June 1927.
Debut v York City (a) 10 March 1951.
Appearances: 10; Goals: 5.
Career: Perth City BC; Earngrove FC; Jeanfield Swifts (fee £75); RAKERS 9 February 1951; Leeds United 15 June 1951 (joint transfer with J.Finlay for a combined fee of £6,000): Wrexham 31 July 1952; Winsford United 30 November 1954; Accrington Stanley 10 February 1955 to 30 June 1955; RAKERS August 1955.
A product of the same Perthshire junior club which launched the career of Frank Christie, the Liverpool and East Fife half-back. Bill Heggie was considered one of the most promising full-backs North of the border, yet it was as a centre-forward that he made his mark with New Brighton. It was a bold experiment — and perhaps one born of desperation

126

— which saw Heggie converted from full-back to a match-winning centre-forward. It was unfortunate that the experiment had not been tried a month earlier, as it may well have made the difference between success and failure in the season which saw New Brighton lose their League status. A coal merchant by trade, Bill Heggie returned to the Rakers in the summer of 1955 and was part of the wonderful FA Cup run in season 1956-7, when New Brighton reached the fourth round.

HENDERSON, Robert D   1931-32
Outside-left.
Debut v Gateshead (h) 29 August 1931
Appearances: 11.
Career: Burnley amateur, signing professional 10 September 1929; RAKERS 18 August 1931 to cs 1932.
In 11 League appearances for the Rakers, Bob Henderson, a young reserve winger from Burnley, did not appear on the winning side until the last two games of the season. It was the only occasion on which the team won two consecutive matches. Henderson was one of five outside-lefts tried during the course of the season. The most regular choice was Peter Miller, normally an inside-forward.

HIGGINS, Frank   1926-31
Half-back. 5ft 9½ins. 11st 7lbs.
Born: Birkenhead.
Debut v Southport (a) 5 March 1927.
Appearances: 13.
Career: Wirral Railways; RAKERS amateur 4 August 1926, professional 29 September 1926 to cs 1931.
Although Frank Higgins' debut resulted in the Rakers conceding seven goals for the first time in their history, he had the satisfaction, less than two months later, of assisting in a 7-2 win against Nelson. One of five local amateurs to be given a trial in the pre-season 'Stripes v Whites' on 21 August 1926, he was to prove a valuable clubman and an able deputy in any of the three half-back positions.

HILL, Maurice   1946-48
Half-back. 5ft 9½ins, 11st 2lbs.
Born: Halifax, 2 May 1920; Died: 1966.
Debut v Wrexham (a) 31 August 1946.
Appearances: 73.
Career: Anfield Road School (Liverpool); Park Side FC; Everton amateur 9 May 1938, professional 15 May 1939; RAKERS; Tranmere Rovers & Stockport County (wartime guest); RAKERS 20 July 1946 to 1 May 1948; South Liverpool; Skelmersdale United manager 1959.
Although Maurice Hill was born in Halifax, he first played football in Liverpool. His association with Everton began when he was only 16-years-old, but he did not sign amateur forms with them until two years later. A former 'Bevin Boy', Hill first assisted New Brighton as a wartime guest in season 1939-40 and signed on a permanent basis

after the war. At home in any position in the middle line, Hill was an ideal wing-half, coolness and excellent ball-control being the main features of his play.

HIRD, Harry   1924-26
Inside-forward. 5ft 7½ins. 11st 8lbs.
Born: Bolton, 1898.
Debut v Bradford (h) 30 August 1924.
Appearances: 13; Goals 3.
Career: Bolton Parish Church; Westhoughton Naval Gun Factory; Horwich RMI; Bury 4 June 1919; Blackpool 30 May 1922 (fee £200); Horwich RMI 1923-4; RAKERS 22 August 1924 to cs 1926.

In his first two seasons at Gigg Lane, Harry Hird scored 20 goals in 57 appearances and was leading goalscorer in 1919-20. Thereafter, he had less success and failed to gain a permanent first-team place with either Blackpool or New Brighton.

HITCHEN, Henry   1946-48
Half-back. 6ft, 12st 2lbs.
Born: Liverpool, 22 October 1922.
Debut v Hull City (h) 26 October 1946.
Appearances: 70; Goals: 2.
Career: Litherland SS Football; Formby FC;: RAKERS amateur 26 August, professional 19

September 1946; Sheffield United 13 May 1948 (fee approx. £3,000); Bury 20 May 1953 to cs 1954.
Club honour: Sheffield United, Division Two champions 1952-3.
Harry Hitchen first played football for a church team in Litherland, his home district. When war broke out he joined the Royal Marine Commandos and saw service in Burma, China and Egypt. It was in Services football that he developed as a centre-half and on leaving the forces he joined Formby. He was quickly spotted by the Rakers and made tremendous progress, becoming a steady and reliable pivot. He eventually brought New Brighton a fee, said to be the biggest the club had ever received, when he moved to Sheffield United in May 1948. Having ended season 1947-8 with the Rakers bottom of the Third Division North, Hitchen's first campaign at Bramall Lane saw his new team finish bottom of Division One. In his final season, however, the Blades were the champions of Division Two. Harry Hitchen's career figures were 226 appearances and 17 goals.

HODDINOTT, Francis Thomas　　　**1927-28**
Inside- or Centre-forward. 5ft 8ins. 11st 10lbs.

Born: Brecon, 26 November 1894; Died: Southend, November 1980.
Debut v Darlington (a) 27 August 1927.
Appearances: 23; Goals: 6.
Career: Aberdare Athletic; Watford August 1920; Chelsea 3 June 1921 (fee £3,500); Crystal Palace 23 May 1923; Rhyl 1926-7; RAKERS 29 May 1927; Newark Town August 1928; Grantham Town June 1931.
International honours: 2 Welsh caps, 1921.
Club honours: Rhyl, Welsh Cup runners-up 1927.
Frank Hoddinott was brought back into League football by New Brighton after he had spent a season with Rhyl, one of the giantkillers of the 1926-7 FA Cup competition. His early-season wing partnership with Dickie proved extremely fruitful, the Welsh international showing touches of dazzling footwork and constructive flair. Before turning to football, Hoddinott almost became a professional boxer. During the war years he won the Army Lightweight Boxing Championship. As an athlete, he had many successes to his credit in the 100 yards, quarter-mile handicaps and high-jump events. In a distinguished war career he was mentioned in despatches for his work in the Mesopotamian Campaign and was demobbed with the rank of Regimental Sergeant-Major and holder of the Meritorious Service Medal.

HOGGAN, Matthew　　　**1935-36**
Centre-half. 5ft 11ins. 12st 7lbs.
Born: Standford, Fife.
Debut v Tranmere Rovers (h) 31 August 1935.
Appearances: 38.
Career: Raith Rovers January 1928; RAKERS 14 August 1935 to cs 1936.
Said to have missed only six games in as many seasons with Raith Rovers, Matt Hoggan also missed six games during his season with New Brighton. During his absence — due to an ankle injury — the Rakers conceded 24 goals in losing six successive matches, which included first-round knock outs in both the Northern Section Cup and the FA Cup. His return restored confidence and a much brighter display all round, when Carlisle United were beaten 3-0. Unfortunately, his sterling work as captain lacked good quality support and New Brighton were unable to avoid a third re-election application.

HOPE, James Gordon　　　**1947-51**
Utility player. 5ft 10½ins, 11st 6lbs.
Born: East Wemyss, Fife, 4 October 1919.
Debut v Lincoln City (a) 10 September 1947.
Appearances: 43.
Career: Wemyms College; East Fife; RAKERS 6 August 1947 to 31 July 1951, re-signing in August 1951 to assist the Rakers in their early Lancashire Combination days.
The son of a professional footballer who had assisted Stoke City and Raith Rovers in the 1920s, Jimmy Hope was employed in the building trade

when he first signed professional forms with East Fife just before the war. He joined the Royal Engineers, served in France with the BEF and was evacuated from Dunkirk. After a spell in India, he was demobbed in 1945 and returned home to play for East Fife. After one season, he signed for

New Brighton. In a long spell at the Tower Grounds, Hope proved an adaptable footballer. Originally a right-half, he subsequently appeared at outside-right, centre-half and full-back. As a utility player, he proved invaluable to a club which generally lacked strength in numbers and adequate reserve cover.

HOUGH, William   **1930**
Half-back. 5ft 7½ins. 10st 13lbs.
Born: Greenfield, Wales, 1910.
Debut v Chesterfield (h) 8 November 1930.
Appearances: 4; Goals: 1.
Career: Connah's Quay; Holywell Arcadians; RAKERS amateur 26 August 1930, professional 11 September 1930; Preston North End 12 December 1930; Blackburn Rovers 11 December 1936 to 1942.
Club honours: Blackburn Rovers, Division Two champions 1938-9. Football League War Cup runners-up v West Ham United 8 June 1940.
An iron-foundry worker, who was unable to get time off from work to travel to Halifax after first being selected, Bill Hough did not have to wait very much longer before making his Football League debut. In only four appearances he did enough to

draw the scouts, this despite his playing in the unaccustomed role of inside-forward. He arrived at New Brighton as a half-back, but his subsequent fame came as a full-back, a position which he first adopted with Preston North End. He helped Preston into the First Division in 1933-4, as runners-up to Grimsby Town. He went one better, when Blackburn won promotion to the top flight as champions in the last peacetime season.

HOUNSLEA, William Hudson   **1946-48**
Full-back.
Born: Liverpool, 15 August 1926.
Debut v Bradford City (a) 20 December 1947.
Appearances: 16.
Career: Unity Boys; RAKERS amateur 29 July 1946, professional 29 January 1948; Chester 9 August 1948; Winsford United 2 November 1948; RAKERS August 1951.
Consistent displays in the Rakers' Reserves earned Bill Hounslea his chance and he replaced Harry Topping at right-back after the second-round FA Cup tie at Bristol Rovers, which the Rakers lost 4-0. A full-back who showed good anticipation and made his job look simple, Hounslea's introduction — along with goalkeeper Daniels — tightened the Rakers' defence considerably. Recruited from the same junior club as Ted Redfern (qv), Hounslea joined Chester after being granted a free transfer in May 1948. He later returned to play for New Brighton in their first season of non-League football.

HOWARD, Frederick   **1924**
Centre-forward. 5ft 10ins. 12st 6lbs.
Born: Walkden, 1893.
Debut v Doncaster Rovers (a) 16 February 1924.
Appearances: 10; Goals: 4.
Career: Walkden Wednesday; Manchester City amateur 2 October, professional 10 October 1912; Pontypridd; Ayr United & Clyde during 1922-3; Port Vale 3 July 1923; RAKERS 13 February 1924; Wrexham 1 October 1924 to cs 1925.
Fred Howard's claim to fame was his remarkable success when making his Football League debut for Manchester City against Liverpool at Hyde Road on 18 January 1913. Within the first 13 minutes he recorded a hat-trick and added a fourth goal after 20 minutes of the second half. The goalkeeper on the receiving end was Scottish international Kenny Campbell (qv). By a strange coincidence, Howard's debut for New Brighton was in a friendly fixture against Stoke, Kenny Campbell again being the goalkeeper. On this occasion, however, he did not get on to the score-sheet. With New Brighton, Howard had more success in scoring goals than in stopping them. On 1 March 1924, he took over in goal from the injured Bert Mehaffy at Rochdale. It was after the retirement of Mehaffy that Rochdale scored five of their six goals — four of which should have been saved according to one match report.

HOWSON, George Sherple   1927-28
Full-back. 5ft 9ins. 12st.
Born: Bolton.
Debut v Darlington (a) 27 August 1927.
Appearances: 11.
Career: Little Hulton United August 1922; Bristol
City 27 August 1925; RAKERS 29 May 1927; Bath
City July 1928; Exeter City 19 June 1929; Bath
City August 1930.
Stockily-built 'Sam' Howson, as he was popularly
known, found limited opportunities in his one
season with the Rakers. He was one of three new
full-backs signed for 1927-8 and he lost out to Len
Carr and Jock McDonald, who became the usual
pairing. In a season with Exeter City, between spells
with Bath City, Howson made 13 appearances for
the Grecians, his highest return in a Football
League season.

HUGHES, Stephen   1938-39
Centre-half. 6ft 1in. 12st 7lbs.
Born: Aigburgh, Liverpool, 1913.
Debut v Barnsley (a) 14 January 1939.
Appearances: 17.
Career: Old Collegians; Liverpool amateur 9
February 1937; Oldham Athletic amateur 21 May
1937; Stalybridge Celtic November 1937; RAKERS
amateur 23 February 1938 to September 1939, but
continuing as a wartime player until April 1942.
In November 1940, the *Liverpool Echo* rated Steve
Hughes 'next to Arsenal's Bernard Joy as the best
amateur centre-half in present-day football'. A
surveyor with Liverpool Corporation, Hughes did
so well as deputy to club captain, Hugh Bulloch,
that the Irishman was unable to win back his
position after recovering from injury. Hughes
continued as the Rakers' pivot during wartime
football, until an RAF posting took him away from
Merseyside.

HULLETT, William   1937
Centre-forward. 5ft 11ins. 11st.
Born: Liverpool, 19 November 1915; Died: Cardiff,
6 September 1982.
Debut v Lincoln City (h) 9 January 1937 (scored
one goal).
Appearances: 13; Goals: 8.
Career: Everton amateur 16 September,
professional 28 December 1935; RAKERS 8
January 1937; Everton 7 May 1937; Plymouth
Argyle 19 October 1937; Manchester United 16
March 1939; Southport (wartime guest); Merthyr
Tydfil; Cardiff City 7 February 1948; Nottingham
Forest 27 November 1948; Merthyr Tydfil cs 1949,
later appointed manager.
Second-highest goalscorer for New Brighton in
1936-7, despite playing in only 13 matches, Bill
Hullett was without League experience when he
joined the Rakers, but proved to be a great
opportunist. In scoring seven goals in his first seven
matches, he netted five on opponents' grounds,
seeming to play better away than at home. 'Takes

a lot of shaking off the ball and has a terrific volley,'
reported one journalist. He proved a consistent
goalscorer for subsequent clubs, Plymouth Argyle
(20 goals in 27 appearances) and Nottingham Forest
(15 goals in 27 appearances).

IDDON, Richard   1928-29
Forward. 5ft 8ins. 11st.
Born: Tarleton, Lancashire, 22 June 1901.
Debut v Barrow (h) 25 August 1928.
Appearances: 11; Goals: 2.
Career: Tarleton FC; Preston North End amateur
26 August, professional 25 October 1921; Chorley
1923-5; Manchester United 7 May 1925; Chorley
cs 1927; Morecambe later in the same season;
RAKERS 12 May 1928 to cs 1929; Lancaster Town
December 1929.
Described as 'a front line leader of the worrying type'
in the 1930-31 issue of the *Lancashire Daily Post
Annual*, Iddon certainly had proved to be a handful
for Lancashire Combination defences, scoring 37
goals in only 29 appearances for Lancaster Town,
Combination champions in 1929-30. A Lancashire
Junior Cup winner with Chorley in 1923-4, Iddon
had scored 31 goals in the season prior to his joining
New Brighton (seven for Chorley and 24 for
Morecambe). He was a good goalscorer in New
Brighton's Reserve team, four goals against Mold
in December winning him a first-team recall. He failed
to capitalize, however, and was unable to establish
himself, despite being usefully versatile in his ability
to occupy any of the forward positions.

INGHAM, Thomas L   1936-37
Outside-left. 5ft 5ins. 10st 7lbs.
Born: Prestwich, 1917.

Debut v York City (h) 2 May 1936.
Appearances: 2.
Career: Manchester North End; Bolton Wanderers amateur 24 October 1935; RAKERS amateur 16 March 1936, professional 5 August 1936; Altrincham 4 September 1937.

Invited for trials at Rake Lane in February 1936, Tom Ingham was signed on amateur forms after three weeks and went on to make his Football League bow when only 19 years of age. He was one of only a handful of players offered terms for the following season, but it was Irish import, Paddy Shiels, who dominated the outside-left position in 1936-7. Ingham's solitary appearance in this term came at Accrington Stanley, when an injury-weakened New Brighton team were beaten 5-0.

JENKINS, Eric Trevor   **1925-31**
Centre-forward.
Born: Wallasey, summer 1904.
Debut v Halifax Town (a) 31 August 1931.
Appearances: 1.
Career: Local junior football; RAKERS amateur 25 August 1925 to cs 1926. Re-registered 19 August 1931 to cs 1932.

Eric Jenkins first signed amateur forms for New Brighton in August 1925, but he found little opportunity in the Midland Combination side, who were invariably able to field a forward line of experienced professionals. Re-registered after a gap of six years, Jenkins made his Football League debut less than a fortnight after signing. Early-season injuries to Ben Twell and Leo Stevens saw Jenkins drafted into the side to visit The Shay. In a goalless draw, he was reported to lack confidence in front of goal. The Rakers should have won, though, Peter Miller missing a penalty.

JOHNSON, Cyrus William   **1935-36**
Centre-forward. 5ft 8ins. 12st 4lbs.
Born: Hoylake 1906.
Debut v Barrow (a) 2 September 1935.
Appearances: 10; Goals: 6.
Career: Nantwich Victoria cs 1932; RAKERS 12 August 1935, transfer listed 14 March 1936.

Of only moderate height, but strongly built, Johnson was a leader of the bustling, go-ahead type. His best performance came in the home game against Carlisle United, when he completed a hat-trick to give the Rakers their third win of the season after 18 matches. On the same afternoon, two of the Westcott brothers were assisting New Brighton Reserves at Chorley. Dennis was shortly to capture the first-team jersey, after netting nine goals in eight reserve-team matches. Johnson was released, along with McMullan, Beedles and Lloyd, before the end of the season.

JOHNSON, Ernest L   **1937-39**
Half-back. 5ft 7ins. 11st 2lbs.
Born: Sheffield, 1917.
Debut v Rotherham United (h) 13 November 1937.
Appearances: 8.
Career: Sheffield United amateur, professional 12 May 1936; Nottingham Forest 16 August 1937; RAKERS 22 October 1937 to cs 1939.

Ernie Johnson, a keen, workmanlike, young half-back spent two seasons with the Rakers without getting much chance to show what he could do in the first team. Signed as a professional by Sheffield United at 19 years of age, he spent four years at Bramall Lane before moving to Nottingham Forest for a season. He was without League experience when he joined New Brighton, initially for a month's trial. As understudy to Billy Fogg in 1937-8 and Leslie Turner in 1938-9, he found few opportunities.

JOHNSON, Richard Kemp   **1929-31**
Centre-forward. 5ft 9½ins. 12st.
Born: Gateshead, 1895; Died: West Derby, Liverpool, January 1933.
Debut v Carlisle United (h) 21 September 1929.
Appearances: 74; Goals: 23.
Career: Felling Colliery; Liverpool 27 January 1920; Stoke 20 February 1925 (fee £1,200); RAKERS 21 September 1929; Connah's Quay August 1931.
Club honours: Liverpool, Division One champions 1922-3; Stoke, Third Division North champions 1926-7.

'A forward who uses his brains as well as his feet,' was one local Press comment on Dick Johnson, whilst the *Athletic News* said of him in November 1929: 'The crafty one of the five, Johnson possessed admirable ball control. In fact, he seemed out of his class.' His 17-goal return for the Rakers in 1929-30 included three hat-tricks.

JONES, James   **1922-27**
Full-back. 5ft 7½ins. 10st 9lbs.
Born: Newburn-on-Tyne, 1889.

Debut v Bradford (a) 25 August 1923.
Appearances: 141; Goals: 1.
Career: Gateshead; Blackpool 11 June 1913; Bolton
Wanderers 16 March 1920 (fee £1,000); RAKERS
5 August 1922, retired cs 1927.
Coolness under pressure and steady judgement were
prominent features of Jimmy Jones' play. The
former Bolton Wanderers player was the Rakers'
first captain in the Football League, when he
replaced Alex Finney, who had moved in the
opposite direction, to Burnden Park. Jones' only
goal for New Brighton, the winner against
Hartlepools United in November 1923, was struck
from the half-way line. His wind-assisted shot
completely deceived Summerfield, the Hartlepools'
goalkeeper.

JONES, James Alfred   1950-51
Goalkeeper. 5ft 10ins, 12st 6lbs.
Born: Birkenhead, 3 August 1927.
Debut v Tranmere Rovers (h) 16 September 1950.
Appearances: 32.
Career: Everton amateur 7 May, professional 1
December 1945; Ellesmere Port Town; Everton 2
August 1948; RAKERS 19 August 1950; Lincoln
City 20 August 1951 (fee £408); Accrington Stanley
19 February 1954; Rochdale 13 September 1955,
retired June 1961 to become a licensee in Lincoln.
*Club honour: Lincoln City, Third Division North
champions, 1951-2.*

Jimmy Jones' New Brighton debut was in the *Boy's
Own* category, as he almost single-handedly defied
an onslaught from Third Division North leaders,
Tranmere Rovers. He was voted 'man of the match'
after making any number of magnificent saves, was
knocked out when diving at a forward's feet and
topped everything by saving a penalty. Jones
established himself, at the expense of Tom Grimley,
in the Rakers' final League season and enjoyed a
successful career with three other Northern clubs
which saw him clock up 331 League appearances.

During season 1958-9, when he was playing for
Rochdale, he missed half of the season due to eye
trouble and afterwards wore contact lenses.

JONES, John   1949-51
Inside-forward. 5ft 8ins. 11st 4lbs.
Born: Wrexham, 9 April 1921.
Debut v Darlington (h) 20 August 1949.
Appearances: 77; Goals: 11.
Career: Junior football; Wrexham 21 June 1947;
Doncaster Rovers 28 July 1948; RAKERS 4 August
1949; Ellesmere Port Town cs 1951.
Signed as part of a 'renovated' attack for 1949-50
by manager Jack Atkinson, Jack Jones had played
in six matches for Doncaster Rovers in 1948-9, but
was unable to regain his place after a leg injury.
Rarely absent during his two years with the Rakers,
Jones proved an industrious worker, always striving
to engineer openings for his colleagues. His skilful
style was outlined in an August 1949 match report:
'Jones has one of the neatest body feints I have
seen in the Division and it was a joy to see him
sending the defence the wrong way before slipping
the ball through to his wingman'. In the Rakers'
final League season, his ninth-minute goal which
enabled New Brighton to record their first-ever
double against Southport was described as one of
the best goals ever seen at The Tower Ground.

KELLY, Peter   1924-26 and 1929-30
Inside-forward. 5ft 7ins. 11st 7lbs.
Born: Tyldesley, 20 March 1901.
Debut v Bradford (h) 30 August 1924.
Appearances: 63; Goals: 20.
Career: Tyldesley Celtic; Chorley; RAKERS 20
August 1924; Notts County 18 February 1926 (fee

£1,500); RAKERS 8 October 1929; Chorley July 1930.

'Possesses clever ball control and a vigorous style,' commented the *Lancashire Daily Post Annual* in 1923-4, when Peter Kelly was the utility man of the Chorley team. With New Brighton, the former collier was normally seen at inside-forward and his all-action style eventually realized a useful fee, First Division Notts County recruiting him shortly after they had knocked the Rakers out of the FA Cup in January 1926. A knee injury eventually curtailed his Notts career and when he returned to Rake Lane, he was unable to reproduce the form which had made him such a favourite. He made only eight appearances before leaving on a free transfer. Kelly had another, rather unusual, sporting pastime. He was a champion all-in wrestler.

KENYON, Frank   1934-35
Winger. 5ft 9ins. 11st.
Born: Chorlton, 22 February 1912; Died: Rhuddlan, Rhyl, 1978.
Debut v Darlington (h) 1 September 1934.

Appearances: 13; Goals: 3.
Career: Wardley Colliery Welfare; Charlton Athletic 5 December 1932; RAKERS 8 August 1934; Ashington June 1935.
It took New Brighton four months to secure their first home League victory in 1934-5, so it was not surprising that the selectors indulged in fairly extensive team changes in the hopes of hitting upon a winning combination. Frank Kenyon was used on both wings before losing his place, when Lawrence and Beckett became established wingers. In the Rakers' five-hour long FA Cup tie against Southport, which ended in success for New Brighton at Goodison, it was Kenyon's remarkable goal from the touch-line which set them on their way to a 2-1 victory.

KERR, Jasper   1933-34
Full-back. 5ft 8ins. 11st 4lbs.
Born: Burnbank, Scotland, 1903.
Debut v Doncaster Rovers (a) 26 August 1933.
Appearances: 10.
Career: Larkhill Thistle; Bathgate September 1923; Everton 28 December 1923; Preston North End 11 March 1927 (fee £3,000); RAKERS 27 July 1933; Lancaster Town August 1934.

Hailing from Burnbank, a productive Scottish nursery, Jasper Kerr crossed the border to join Everton, but made his mark with Preston North End. His career at Deepdale spanned 121 appearances and was ended by a broken leg in December 1931. He was out of football and working as a commercial traveller when New Brighton signed him, but a knee injury, sustained in the FA Cup replay at Mansfield in November, ended his career. He was amusingly summed-up in the *Lancashire Daily Post Annual* for 1930-31 thus: 'A Scot who neither smokes nor drinks, but yet is a cheerful, good-hearted fellow.' A member of a noted Scottish footballing family, his elder brother was a well-known right-back with Hamilton Academical and his father also played at professional level.

KILSHAW, Frederick   **1946-47**
Inside-forward.
Born: Wrexham, 24 August 1916.
Debut v Doncaster Rovers (h) 7 September 1946.
Appearances: 8; Goals: 1.
Career: Army football; Leicester City 4 January 1945; RAKERS 31 July 1946; Prescot Cables season 1947-8.
A wartime discovery by Leicester City, who recruited him from Army football, Fred Kilshaw occupied both inside-forward positions during his season at the Tower Grounds. He was the third inside-left tried within the space of three matches, as the first post-war campaign opened with manager McBain shuffling his new recruits in search of a winning blend. Dropped after a five-match run in September, Kilshaw failed to regain his place in the first team. Perhaps on the small side for the rigours of Third Division football, Kilshaw nevertheless was a good initiator in the Lancashire Combination side, his style — and physique — being very similar to that of Alf Ainsworth, the Rakers' long-serving inside-forward.

KIRK, Henry   **1928-29**
Inside-forward. 5ft 8½ins. 11st 4lbs.
Born: Dillington, Yorkshire.
Debut v Barrow (h) 25 August 1928 (scored one goal).
Appearances: 27; Goals: 9.
Career: Worksop Town; Bristol City 29 March 1920; Plymouth Argyle 20 June 1921; Exeter City 4 March 1922; Plymouth Argyle 28 May 1922; Exeter City 30 September 1922 (fee £250); Charlton Athletic 13 May 1926 (fee £150); Bath City 1927-8; RAKERS 24 August 1928; South Shields 9 August 1929; Bath City September 1930.
Harry Kirk was known throughout footballing circles as 'Jazzo' Kirk, on account of his talents as a ukulele player and entertainer. Although a Yorkshireman, he first came out with Bristol City, joining them at the time of their FA Cup semi-final appearance in March 1920. He next shuttled between two Devon clubs, Exeter City and Plymouth Argyle, having two separate spells of service with each. He was Exeter's leading scorer in consecutive seasons between 1923-25, and was the first Grecian to score four goals in a League match, at Portsmouth on 3 March 1923. With New Brighton, he formed a productive partnership with Jimmy Dickie, before the Scottish winger departed to Bristol City. In the game against Chesterfield at Rake Lane on 10 September 1928, Kirk scored for New Brighton within 15 seconds of the kick-off.

KIRKMAN, Gerald   **1938-39**
Half-back. 5ft 10ins. 11st 3lbs.
Born: Bolton, 1912.
Debut v Crewe Alexandra (a) 19 November 1938.
Appearances: 2.
Career: Bolton YMCA; Bolton Wanderers 28

November 1929; Reading 6 May 1936; RAKERS 6 September 1938 to cs 1939.
Gerald Kirkman had few opportunities with New Brighton as he spent his time understudying the consistent Len Turner. In the Lancashire Combination side he was described as 'a clean and stylish half-back with good constructive ideas'. Throughout his football career, Kirkman had not managed to graduate beyond reserve-team football. In a seven-year association with Bolton Wanderers he made only one Football League appearance. He also had a solitary outing with Reading. In his New Brighton debut, the Rakers went down 7-1 at Crewe, after goalkeeper Gale had been injured in attempting to save the fifth goal and had to leave the field.

KIRSOPP, William Henry James   **1923-24**
Inside-forward. 5ft 8ins. 11st.
Born: Liverpool, 21 April 1892; Died: 1978.
Debut v Durham City (h) 12 September 1923.
Appearances: 14; Goals: 1.

Career: Wallasey Borough; Everton 25 April 1914; Bury 20 May 1921 (fee £400); Grimsby Town 29 September 1922 (fee £50); RAKERS 19 June 1923; Crystal Palace (trial) August 1924.
Club honours: Everton, Division One champions 1914-15.
When Billy Kirsopp left Wallasey Borough for Everton, he did so on the day of the 1914 FA Cup

134

Final. He quickly found fame at Goodison, winning a Football League Championship medal with Everton after first coming into the side on New Year's Day 1915. He returned 'home' to New Brighton, after spells with Bury and Grimsby Town, to assist the Rakers in their first season of League football. A resourceful forager at inside-right, Kirsopp had stiff competition from Billy Crooks, the Irish international inside-forward.

KITCHING, Harry 1932-36
Inside-forward. 5ft 8½ins. 11st 5lbs.
Born: Grimsby, 1905.
Debut v Rotherham United (a) 27 August 1932.
Appearances: 39; Goals: 7.
Career: Junior football; Grimsby Town 24 August 1923; Boston Town August 1926; Worksop Town 1927; Lincoln City 9 May 1928; Tranmere Rovers 10 August 1931; RAKERS 13 August 1932 to cs 1936.
A Birkenhead schoolmaster, Harry Kitching's best footballing days were spent with Lincoln City. During three seasons with the Imps, he scored 28 goals in 58 appearances, turning out regularly in the 1930-31 campaign in which Lincoln scored 102 goals in finishing as runners-up — by a point — to Chesterfield. In four seasons at Rake Lane, he proved a hard-working inside man, a typical comment being: 'He strove desperately from beginning to end to work openings.'

LACEY, William 1924-25
Inside-forward. 5ft 8ins. 11st 9lbs.
Born: Wexford, 20 September 1889.

Debut v Bradford (h) 30 August 1924.
Appearances: 7.
Career: Dublin Shelbourne; Everton 27 May 1908; Liverpool 28 February 1912 (in an exchange transfer for Gracie & Uren); Belfast United and Linfield wartime guest; RAKERS 9 August 1924; Dublin Shelbourne cs 1925; Cork Bohemians.
International honours: 23 Irish caps. 2 Victory International appearances 1919.
Club honours: Liverpool, FA Cup runners-up 1914. Division One champions 1921, 1923; Dublin Shelbourne, Irish Cup runners-up 1908; Linfield, Irish Cup winners 1919.
There can be little doubt that Bill Lacey's best footballing days were behind him by the time he arrived at Rake Lane. Nevertheless, in his 35th year, he became the only New Brighton player to appear in a full international. Sadly, in the game against England, he received an injury which resulted in New Brighton making a £200 claim for compensation from the Irish FA. He did not play again for the Rakers, undergoing a knee operation in March 1925. In a career which contained many highlights, his two goals for Ireland against England at Middlesbrough in February 1914 helped his country to a memorable first international success in England, by 3-0.

LAMONT, William Turnbull 1950-51
Full-back. 5ft 11ins, 12st 2lbs.
Born: Glasgow, 25 December 1926.
Debut v Halifax Town (a) 19 August 1950.
Appearances: 27.
Career: Hugh McGowan Juveniles (Govan); Kilmarnock July 1947; RAKERS 22 July 1950; Tranmere Rovers 11 September 1951 (fee £330); Cowdenbeath 30 June 1956.
International honours: Scottish Juvenile v England.
Bill Lamont, who made his debut in the Scottish League Second Division as a 21-year-old, was one of several new signings made by player-manager Galbraith in the summer of 1950. Following successive home defeats, by 5-1 and 4-2, Lamont lost his place in early October and did not reappear in the League side until almost four months later. He was out of action for six weeks due to suspected cartilage trouble and was not able to resume full-time training until mid-December. After leaving New Brighton, Lamont gave excellent service to Tranmere Rovers. In a five-year stay at Prenton Park, he totalled 143 appearances and scored three goals.

LAWRENCE, Thomas 1934-37
Outside-right. 5ft 7ins. 10st 4lbs.
Born: Hoylake, 1910.
Debut v Darlington (a) 5 January 1935.
Appearances: 55; Goals: 7.
Career: Hoylake; Runcorn; RAKERS amateur 17 December 1934, professional 23 January 1935; South Liverpool July 1937.
Given his first chance following injuries to regular wingers, Brown and Kenyon, Tommy Lawrence's introduction at outside-right had much to do with

the rejuvenation of the Rakers' attack. His entry into League football maintained a family tradition, his father having played with Burton Town and Tranmere Rovers, whilst a cousin, Eddie, was a Welsh international half-back whose club's included Clapton Orient, Notts County and Bournemouth. A keen golfer, Lawrence was a prizewinner in the handicap division of the Merseyside Professional Footballers' Golf Competition at the Woolton course in October 1936.

LAWTON, John Wesley   **1935-36**
Inside-forward. 5ft 8ins. 11st 7lbs.
Born: Wallasey, 1910.
Debut v Carlisle United (h) 14 December 1935.
Appearances: 18; Goals: 4.
Career: Wallasey Grocers; RAKERS amateur 29 November 1935, professional 2 January 1936, released on a free transfer 4 August 1936.
In a meteoric rise, Jack Lawton progressed from Wallasey Grocers FC to the Football League, within the space of a fortnight. His two Lancashire Combination appearances in between had done enough to suggest that he would not be out of place in the Third Division. A former Grocers' teammate of Dennis Westcott, the two young Wallaseyans found themselves reunited in the Rakers forward line in mid-season, each player making 18 appearances. In the close season, their paths took opposite directions. Westcott departed to Wolverhampton Wanderers and subsequent football fame, whilst Lawton was released on a free transfer.

LAYCOCK, Frederick Walter   **1927-28**
Inside-forward. 5ft 9ins. 11st 7lbs.
Born: Sheffield, 31 March 1900.
Debut v Darlington (a) 27 August 1927.
Appearances: 28; Goals: 14.
Career: St Mary's (Sheffield); Rotherham Town; Sheffield Wednesday 8 March 1924; Barrow 21 July 1924; Nelson 16 March 1925; Mansfield Town August 1926; RAKERS 31 July 1927; Peterborough & Fletton United September 1928; Darlington 20 September 1929; York City 24 June 1930; Swindon Town 29 May 1931; Derry City July 1933; Witton Albion October 1934; Nuneaton Town October 1935.
A player of the 'move every year' fraternity, Fred Laycock is thought to be the only player in the history of the game to be transferred while a game in which he was taking place was in progress. This occurred on the last day for transfers in 1925, when he was playing for Barrow on Rotherham United's ground. More than one club with representatives at the ground sought his signature. In the event, he was called from the pitch to sign forms, thus finding himself in the curious position of playing for Barrow, whilst a Nelson player. Adept at 'nodding 'em in', a high percentage of Laycock's goals came from deft use of his head. Despite losing

his place in the Rakers' attack for eight matches in October/November 1927, Laycock finished the season as joint leading goalscorer with Harley.

LEADBETTER, John Herbert   **1922-25**
Half-back. 5ft 7ins. 10st 6lbs.
Born: Prescot, 1899.
Debut v Grimsby Town (a) 27 October 1923.
Appearances: 1.
Career: Whiston Parish; RAKERS 29 July 1922; Connah's Quay cs 1925.
One of a pair of brothers who assisted New Brighton prior to their Football League entry. Alan Leadbetter (who did not appear in a League match) actually scored twice against the Rakers for Whiston Parish, when Rake Lane staged its first-ever match. Jack Leadbetter, a small but tenacious wing-half, appeared in only one Football League match. During Max Reid's absence due to suspension, he played in a goalless draw at Grimsby Town.

LEES, Alfred   **1949-51**
Centre-half or Full-back. 5ft 11ins. 11st 2lbs.
Born: Worsley, 28 July 1923.
Debut v Darlington (h) 20 August 1949.
Appearances: 72.
Career: Junior football; Bolton Wanderers 2 August 1948; RAKERS 11 August 1949; Crewe Alexandra 6 September 1951 (fee £330) to 30 June 1956.
When manager Jack Atkinson sought a suitable

replacement for his own centre-half position, he returned to his old club, Bolton Wanderers, for Alf Lees. A regular Central League player at Burnden, Lees was not unlike Atkinson in his style of play, being a cool, deliberate defender with a good sense of anticipation. A broken bone in his foot saw him on the casualty list for a spell during 1949-50, but thereafter he was rarely absent. He proved a bargain buy for Crewe Alexandra, recording 185 League appearances in a five-year stint at Gresty Road.

LEONARD, John   **1936-37**
Centre-forward. 5ft 9½ins. 11st 4lbs.
Born: Scotland, 1914.
Debut v Hull City (h) 26 September 1936 (scored one goal).
Appearances: 8; Goals: 2.
Career: Renfrew & Lanark United; Hibernian; Southport (trial) 4 June 1936; RAKERS 26 September 1936 to cs 1937.
Released by Southport after three reserve-team appearances, Jack Leonard celebrated his debut with the Rakers by heading a 'picture goal' against Hull City, within a few hours of signing. He was on the mark again in October against Wrexham in the first-round Northern Section Cup game, his winning header being the first goal conceded by Wrexham at the Racecourse that season. Unable to hold his position in the League side, Leonard proved a prolific goalscorer for the Reserves, twice hitting five goals in a match.

LEWIS, Thomas Henry **1927-31 and 1932**
Half-back. 5ft 9½ins. 11st.
Born: Greenfield, Wales, 1903.
Debut v Tranmere Rovers (h) 1 October 1927.
Appearances: 99; Goals: 4.
Career: St Mary's (Greenfield); Connah's Quay; Manchester United (trial); Chester 1923; Crewe Alexandra 23 January 1924; Holywell Arcadians; Rhyl Athletic; RAKERS 30 September 1927; Connah's Quay September 1931; Holywell Arcadians September 1932; RAKERS 25 February 1932; Holywell Arcadians September 1933.
International honour: Welsh FA XI in Canada 1929.
Tommy Lewis filled many positions during his career. He was usually right-half or centre-half for the Rakers, but occasionally played at inside-forward and on the right wing. A cool-headed player, methodical rather than dashing, his strategy and skill counter-balanced a slight lack of pace. Lewis was one of only two players to win international recognition whilst on the Rakers' books, Bill Lacey, the Irish international, being the other.

LIGGINS, Alfred G   **1932-34**
Outside-right. 5ft 9ins. 10st 10lbs.
Born: Poulton, 1912.
Debut v Tranmere Rovers (h) 16 January 1931.
Appearances: 76; Goals: 13.
Career: Liverpool Schoolboys; Poulton Rovers; Little Sutton; Everton amateur 10 August 1929 to 15 February 1931; Liverpool amateur 13 June 1931;

RAKERS amateur 14 January 1932, professional 13 August 1932 to cs 1934; South Liverpool.
A talented all-round sportsman, Alf Liggins broke into the Rakers' first team as a 20-year-old amateur. A winger with all the necessary attributes, he was always prepared to cut in for a shot when the opportunity presented itself. A leg injury sustained in 1933-4 gave him much trouble, eventually causing him to leave first-class football. As an

opening batsman with four different Liverpool Competition clubs, he twice led the League averages. In 1948, he was the only player in the League to total 800 runs. He made his Minor Counties debut for Cheshire in 1949, heading their batting with an average of 38. He was awarded his cap in 1950.

LIGHTBODY, John William   **1927-28**
Centre-forward.
Born: Newcastle-upon-Tyne, 10 March 1905; Died:
New Forest, 1979.
Debut v Lincoln City (a) 18 February 1928 (scored
one goal).
Appearances: 1; Goals: 1.
Career: Sunderland amateur 21 April 1926;
Liverpool, 1 November 1926; RAKERS 3
November 1927; Fulham 27 August 1928; Grays
Thurrock October 1928.
Despite being associated with four different senior
clubs, Lightbody made only one Football League
appearance. In this, he had the satisfaction of
scoring the winner for New Brighton in an excellent
victory at Lincoln City. Despite this useful start,
he was displaced by new signing, W.D.Roberts,
the ex-Bolton Wanderers centre-forward. When he
made his debut for New Brighton Reserves, Jack
Lightbody scored a goal within a minute of the
kick-off. In December 1927, he scored five goals
in a remarkable match against Rhos, the Rakers'
Reserves running out narrow winners by 6-5.

LINDSAY, Thomas   **1931**
Outside-left. 5ft 6½ins. 11st 4lbs.
Born: Renfrew, 11 March 1900.
Debut v Hull City (h) 19 September 1931.
Appearances: 7.
Career: Renfrew Juniors; Ardeer Thistle;
Kilmarnock August 1924; Alloa cs 1926; Reading
27 July 1927; Wigan Borough 23 August 1928;
Rochdale 24 July 1929; Watford 27 September
1930; RAKERS (trial) 17 September 1931;
Southport (trial) 18 November 1931; Chester 1
January 1932; Prescot Cables 15 February 1932;
Wrexham 26 July 1933; Leyland Motors April
1934.
Before the mid-season mark in 1931-2, New
Brighton had used four different outside-lefts. Tom
Lindsay was by far the most experienced, but he
failed to win a permanent contract after playing
in seven consecutive League matches in his two
months' trial. The Rakers won against Doncaster
Rovers on his final appearance, but the previous
six matches had all been lost, and the attack had
failed to score in five consecutive games.

LIVINGSTONE, Allan McKenzie   **1925-26**
Inside-forward. 5ft 7½ins. 11st.
Born: Alexandria, Dumbartonshire, 2 December
1899; Died: 1970.
Debut v Durham City (h) 4 December 1925.
Appearances: 6.
Career: Vale United; Everton (trial); Dumbarton
Harp; Hull City 5 May 1921; Scunthorpe United
1922; Hartlepools United (trial) October 1924 to
14 November 1924; Crewe Alexandra 12 October
1925; RAKERS 10 November 1925; Clapton Orient
18 December 1926; Merthyr Town 29 June 1927;
Swansea Town 1 June 1928 (fee £95); Ayr United
September 1929; East Fife cs 1931; Walsall 28

September 1931; Oswestry Town November 1931;
Colwyn Bay December 1931; Chester 21 April 1932;
Colwyn Bay July 1932 returning to Scotland during
the season but re-joining Colwyn Bay January 1933;
Ayr United; Mansfield Town August 1933;
Stockport County 28 November 1934 to cs 1935.
*Representative honour: Glasgow League v Western
League.*
'A Scottish footballer who likes a move' proved
to be something of an understatement by the
Wallasey & Wirral Chronicle in November 1925,
as Allan Livingstone had hardly made a start in
his wandering career. Described during his New
Brighton spell as 'a clever constructive footballer
and willing forager', he was not a good finisher.
His highest seasonal total was three goals for
Merthyr Town in 1927-8. His elder brother, Dugald
Livingstone (1898-1981), was a full-back with
Aberdeen, Glasgow Celtic, Everton and Tranmere
Rovers and held managerial posts with Newcastle
United, Fulham and Chesterfield.

LLOYD, Norman   **1935-36**
Half-back. 5ft 11½ins. 11st 13lbs.
Born: Salford, 1912.
Debut v Oldham Athletic (a) 9 November 1935.
Appearances: 5.
Career: Manchester Central; Manchester City 13
May 1932; RAKERS 1 November 1935, released
on a free transfer 14 March 1936.
Norman Lloyd's signing was to provide defensive
cover, following early-season injuries to first-team
defenders Hoggan and Brock. Lloyd's first game
in the Rakers' colours was at centre-half against
Southport, in the first round of the Northern
Section Cup, which New Brighton lost 2-0. Worse
was to follow and his handful of Football League
appearances resulted in several heavy defeats, four
games producing a goal-average of 1-19. Oddly
enough, he was dropped after a 3-0 win against
Carlisle United.

LONG, Wilfred R   **1946-47**
Outside-left. 6ft, 12st 4lbs.
Born: Wallasey, 28 December 1922.
Debut v Bradford City (h) 4 September 1946.
Appearances: 2.
Career: Wallasey junior football; Earle FC; Everton
amateur; RAKERS amateur 10 July 1946 to cs 1947.
New Brighton's post-war debut on the Tower
Grounds featured an all-amateur left-wing pairing
of Wilf Long and Keith Pritchard. Of the two, Long
found the step from junior football more difficult
and made only one more senior appearance during
the season. At reserve level, however, he was
prominent and ended the season as top goalscorer
in the Lancashire Combination side with 11 goals.

LOWNDES, William   **1933-34**
Centre-forward.
Born: Wallasey, 1909.

Debut v Crewe Alexandra (h) 25 February 1933 (scored one goal).
Appearances: 13; Goals: 10.
Career: Egremont United; RAKERS amateur 22 February 1933, professional 20 April 1933, retired due to injury cs 1934.

Fifty-six goals for Egremont United in 1932-3 attracted the Rakers' scouts and Billy Lowndes obliged by scoring four goals in succession for New Brighton Reserves on his debut. On the strength of this initial showing he was promoted to the first team. Opposed to Fred Keenor, the Welsh international centre-half, he marked his Football League debut by scoring the first of his ten goals (in 13 appearances). Amongst his goals were a hat-trick against Hartlepools United and four against Darlington, which included a six-minute hat-trick in the first half. By complete contrast, his second — and final season — proved disastrous. Injured in the pre-season trials, he was unable to play for two months and never recovered his fitness or form. His last two appearances in the first team resulted in a 6-0 League reverse at Gateshead and the record 11-1 defeat at Wrexham in the Northern Section Cup.

LUMBERG, Arthur Albert   1935-36
Full-back. 5ft 8½ins. 11st 8lbs.
Born: Connah's Quay, 20 May 1901; Died: Wrexham, 16 February 1986.

Debut v Wrexham (h) 16 November 1935.
Appearances: 2.
Career: Connah's Quay; Mold; Wrexham, 20 November 1924; Wolverhampton Wanderers 21 May 1930 (fee £650); Brighton & Hove Albion 16 June 1933 (fee £250); Stockport County 31 May 1934 to 17 January 1935; Clapton Orient 1 February 1935; Lytham cs 1935; RAKERS 13 November 1935; Winsford United cs 1936; Newry FC player-manager cs 1938; Wrexham Old Boys coach in the 1950s.

International honours: 4 Welsh caps 1929-32.
Club honour: Wrexham, Welsh Cup winners 1925
Recruited by New Brighton in the midst of an injury crisis — Hoggan, Brock and Salmon all being sidelined — Albert Lumberg was thought to have the experience necessary to steady the Rakers' defence. He made his debut against one of his former clubs, Wrexham, and the Welshmen overran the Rakers 4-0. One week later, in what proved to be his final Football League appearance, Rotherham beat New Brighton 5-0. Lumberg first came into prominence with Wrexham, having a taste of First Division action with Wolverhampton Wanderers in 1932-3, but the bulk of his 215 League appearances were made during his six seasons with Wrexham. A nephew, also named Albert Lumberg, signed for Wolverhampton Wanderers in December 1935.

LYNER, David   1926-27
Outside-left. 5ft 9ins. 10st 10lbs.
Born: Belfast.
Debut v Nelson (a) 15 September 1926.
Appearances: 21; Goals: 1.
Career: Owen O'Cork FC; Glentoran; Belfast Distillery; Glentoran; Manchester United 9 August

1922; Kilmarnock 14 December 1922 to cs 1924; Queens Island; Clydebank January 1925 (fee £100); RAKERS 13 September 1926 to cs 1927.
International honours: 1 Victory International appearance, 1919. 6 Irish caps 1920-23; Irish League representative, 7 appearances.
Club honours: Glentoran, Irish Cup winners 1914, 1917.
One of two experienced outside-lefts recruited for the 1926-7 season, David Lyner contested the first-team spot with George Shelton, the former Sheffield Wednesday and Exeter City winger. After a quiet start, Lyner showed signs of his international pedigree during an extended run of first-team duty, before losing his place, along with his inside partner, Ernie Hawksworth. Two-footed, Lyner was at home on either flank and appeared for his country on both wings.

LYON, John   **1921-24**
Centre-forward. 5ft 10½ins. 12st 3lbs.
Born: Prescot, 3 November 1893.
Debut v Bradford (a) 25 August 1923.
Appearances: 28; Goals: 5.
Career: Prescot; Hull City 18 October 1913; Leeds United 4 July 1920 (fee £300); Prescot; RAKERS 20 August 1921; Mold 2 August 1924; Prescot 1926-7.
Club honour: Mold, Welsh National League (Northern Section) champions, 1924-5.
In New Brighton's first two seasons, Jack Lyon did as much as anyone to bring the club into the position which resulted in their election to the Football League in 1923. In all competitions he recorded 40 goals in 1921-2 and 38 in 1922-3. Sadly, on the Rakers elevation to League football, he was unable to reproduce the scoring prowess which had gained him such prominence in the Lancashire Combination. Perhaps the root of the problem was revealed in a September 1923 match report: 'Lyon is too one-footed to be a natural centre-forward'. Certainly, he much favoured his left foot and his return of only four goals in 38 appearances suggested that his methods had found less success against Football League defenders. He was back on the goal trail again after leaving New Brighton, leading the Mold attack which scored 92 goals in 30 matches in season 1924-5. His elder brother, Samuel Lyon, was a centre-forward with Hull City and Barnsley before World War One. A younger brother, James, was an inside-forward with Derby County and Wrexham in the 1920s.

LYON, Thomas King   **1948-49**
Inside-forward. 5ft 9ins. 11st 7lbs.
Born: Clydebank, 17 March 1915.
Debut v Gateshead (a) 21 August 1948.
Appearances: 36; Goals: 7.
Career: Clydebank High School; Clydebank Juniors; Motherwell 1932; Albion Rovers 1933; Blackpool 16 March 1937; Chesterfield 16 September 1938; RAKERS 24 July 1948 to 7 May 1949; Prescot Cables; Oswestry Town late 1949.
Club honour: Blackpool, Lancashire Cup winners v Blackburn Rovers 8 May 1937.

Tommy Lyon tasted his first cup victory when his team won the Scottish Schools Intermediate Cup in 1927 and he was still at school when he played with Clydebank Juniors. During war service he was a quarter-master sergeant in Burma and represented the English Northern Command at football. In a season with New Brighton he did an excellent job. As arch-schemer and prompter, he did much to knit together what was virtually a new team under player-manager Jack Atkinson. An attack of 'flu in late season appeared to slow him down and he lost his place after appearing in 40 consecutive League and FA Cup matches. The son of a former head shipwright from Clydebank, who played in good class amateur soccer, Tommy's elder brother played for Glasgow Celtic before being injured during the war.

McBAIN, Neil   **1947**
Goalkeeper (emergency). 5ft 8ins.
Born: Cambeltown, 15 November 1895; Died: 1974.
Debut v Hartlepools United (a) 15 March 1947.
Appearances: 1.
Career: Campbeltown Academicals; Ayr United cs 1914; Portsmouth and Southampton (wartime guest player); Manchester United 22 November 1921 (fee £5,000); Everton 23 January 1923 (fee £4,000); St Johnstone July 1926 (fee £1,000); Liverpool 9 March 1928; Watford 24 November

1928, appointed player-manager May 1929 to 1931, then manager only to August 1937; Ayr United manager season 1937-8; Luton Town manager 1 June 1938 to 5 June 1939; RAKERS secretary-manager June 1946; Leyton Orient assistant manager February 1948, manager from April 1948 to 1949; Ayr United manager 1955-6; Watford manager August 1956 to February 1959; Ayr United manager January 1963. Other post-war engagements included scouting posts with Watford, Mansfield Town, Everton and Chelsea, also a coaching position with Estudiantes de la Plata FC, Argentina.

International honours: Scottish international, three caps 1922-24.

When Neil McBain appeared as New Brighton's goalkeeper on 15 March 1947, at the age of 51 years and 4 months, he created two Football League records. He became the oldest player to appear in a Football League match, a record previously held by Halifax Town's trainer, Bob Suter, who played as emergency goalkeeper in April 1929, at the age of 48 years and 10 months. The span of McBain's career also constituted a record. His debut in first-class football was as a centre-forward with Ayr United in March 1915, thus his playing career spanned two world wars and 32 years. In pre-war days, McBain was a stylish half-back who toured Canada and the USA with the Scottish party in 1921 and represented his country against England, Ireland and Wales.

McCLURE, William   **1948-49**
Outside-left.
Born: Shotts, Lanarkshire, 16 May 1921.
Debut v Gateshead (a) 21 August 1948.

Appearances: 45; Goals: 7.
Career: Calder School; Eastfield Heatherbell 1936 to 1940; Fauldhouse United 1944; Douglasdale 1945; Albion Rovers 1946; Preston North End 10 December 1947; RAKERS 20 July 1948; Carlisle United 17 October 1949; Hartlepools United 1 August 1950.
A former collier and Royal Marine, Bill McClure's debut for Albion Rovers was traumatic. They lost 9-0 and McClure was injured and put out of action for several weeks. With New Brighton he proved a speedy and clever winger. He scored the best goal of the season on Christmas Day 1948, against York City at the Tower. It was his second and New Brighton's third goal in a 3-1 win. The *Wallasey & Wirral Chronicle* reported: 'Receiving from Carter near the corner flag, McClure dribbled along the dead-ball line, beating two defenders before swerving back towards the middle of the field and finishing with a scorching drive into the far corner of the net.' For season 1949-50, a reshuffled forward line was employed, but Carter and McClure remained as the left-wing pairing. In early October, however, McClure requested a transfer and was quickly snapped up by Carlisle United. His career figures were 184 appearances, 34 goals.

McCOSH, John McLoughlan   **1931-32**
Inside-forward. 5ft 10ins. 11st 10lbs.
Born: Coylton, Ayrshire, 29 March 1904.
Debut v Gateshead (h) 29 August 1931 (scored one goal).
Appearances: 24; Goals 2.
Career: Auchinleck Talbot; Ayr United cs 1925; Cowdenbeath cs 1928; Queen of the South cs 1929; Exeter City 2 June 1930; RAKERS 18 August 1931 to cs 1932.
Club honours: Ayr United, Scottish League Second Division champions, 1927-8.
The scorer of New Brighton's first goal of the 1931-2 season, John McCosh nevertheless lost his place after eight matches. These had yielded only four goals and a solitary point. He regained his place later in the season, when an improvement coincided with a more settled team formation. In Scottish football, he was successful in his final season with Ayr United, who scored 117 goals in 38 matches to take the championship with a nine-point margin over Third Lanark. He was leading goalscorer for Queen of the South in 1929-30 with 11 goals. In a season with Exeter City he was unable to win a place in the first team, who progressed to the sixth round of the FA Cup. He did well in the Reserves, however, assisting them to the championship 'double' of the Western Section of the Southern League and the Western League.

McCRAE, David   **1934**
Centre-forward. 5ft 7½ins. 11st.
Born: Bridge of Weir, Renfrewshire, 23 February 1900; Died: 1976.
Debut v Accrington Stanley (h) 25 August 1934.
Appearances: 11; Goals: 1.

Career: Beith FC; Manchester City (trial); Bury (trial) 25 January 1922; St Mirren 1923-4; RAKERS 6 August 1934; Queen of the South 7 November 1934.
International honours: 2 Scottish caps, 1929.
Club honour: St Mirren, Scottish Cup winners 1925-6.
Four goals in the two pre-season trials suggested that David McCrae would be the man to bring the Rakers' approach work to a successful conclusion. New Brighton opened the 1934-5 season with a good win at Accrington Stanley, watched, incidentally, by the smallest League attendance of the day. Despite this promising start, McCrae was given not the slightest chance of living up to his reputation, by the subsequent lack of support for his efforts. After scoring only once in 11 League matches he returned to Scotland, his contract cancelled 'by mutual consent'. McCrae's ten years with St Mirren produced the magnificent total of 222 goals in 319 appearances. His brother James (*qv*) also assisted New Brighton in 1924-5.

McCRAE, James   1924-25
Centre-half. 5ft 10½ins. 11st 12lbs.
Born: Bridge of Weir, Renfrewshire, 8 March 1897.
Debut v Ashington (a) 8 November 1924.
Appearances: 6.
Career: Clyde; West Ham United June 1919; Bury

2 December 1920 (fee £750); Wigan Borough 17 September 1923; RAKERS 1 November 1924; Manchester United 11 August 1925.
Club honour: Bury, Lancashire Cup runners-up 1922.
Jimmy McCrae had an unrewarding spell with New Brighton. In his debut at Rake Lane, against Stalybridge Celtic in the first round of the FA Cup, he sustained concussion after ten minutes and at the conclusion of the game did not even know the result. One week later, at Doncaster, he was injured and was out of action for a month. His failure to establish a place was disappointing, as he had featured regularly with all of his previous clubs. In a season at Old Trafford, after leaving the Rakers, he appeared in the FA Cup semi-final, when the all-Manchester affair ended 3-0 in favour of City. Employed as a cashier during his Bury spell, McCrae totalled 181 Football League appearances, scoring 16 goals. Brother of David McCrae (*qv*).

McDONALD, John   1927-31
Full-back. 5ft 10½ins. 12st.
Born: Dykehead, 4 January 1896.

Debut v Doncaster Rovers (h) 31 August 1927.
Appearances: 160; Goals: 3.
Career: Motherwell; Airdrie season 1919-20; Everton 30 April 1920 (fee £2,200); RAKERS 25

August 1927 (fee £750); Connah's Quay August 1931.

Representative honour: Scottish League v Football League, 5 April 1919.

In the matter of years of service, 'Jock' McDonald was the veteran of New Brighton's team, having started his career with Motherwell before World War One. An inspiring captain, he lasted the pace as well as any and what he lacked in speed was more than counter-balanced by his strategy and skill. In seven seasons at Goodison Park, he made 208 League appearances, being appointed club captain in August 1921.

McGEACHIE, George   1946-48
Right-half. 5ft 9ins, 11st.
Born: Calder, 26 October 1916.
Debut v Wrexham (a) 31 August 1946.
Appearances: 63; Goals: 4.
Career: Gairdoch Juveniles; St Johnstone cs 1937;

RAKERS 17 July 1946; Leyton Orient 28 July 1948; Crystal Palace 5 June 1951; Wigan Athletic cs 1952, retiring due to ill health January 1953.
Following his demob from the Argyle and Sutherland Highlanders, George McGeachie was recruited by Rakers' manager Neil McBain. He was the oldest of the Scottish contingent and proved an excellent signing, being a regular at right-half

during his two seasons at the Tower. An inspirational footballer with a rare fighting spirit, he combined dour defensive qualities with excellent distribution. When manager McBain left New Brighton to join Leyton Orient, he lost little time in recruiting McGeachie to his new club. In season 1950-51, when playing for Rochdale, McGeachie scored twice — both penalties — against New Brighton at the Tower Grounds. McGeachie retired from football due to bronchial trouble at the age of 36 and was later a greengrocer in Falkirk.

McKENNA, John   1927
Left-half.
Debut v Darlington (a) 27 August 1927
Appearances: 4.
Career: Bohemians; RAKERS 13 August 1927; Mansfield Town September 1927.
After appearing in the first four matches of the 1927-8 season, John McKenna lost his place to a combined challenge from Bobby Morrison and Jimmy Smedley — two of New Brighton's finest wing-halves. Following the briefest of stays, McKenna was transferred to Mansfield Town, at that time a Midland League club.

MACKIE, Thomas Forbes   1947-48
Left-back. 5ft 10½ins, 11st 10lbs.
Born: Burntisland, 30 March 1918.
Debut v Lincoln City (a) 10 September 1947.
Appearances: 2.
Career: St Johnstone; RAKERS 12 May 1947; Chester 9 August 1948; Stalybridge Celtic 22 November 1949.
As deputy to long-serving left-back Norman Richardson, Mackie had little opportunity during his season with the Rakers. Nevertheless, in the two matches in which he did appear he gave promising displays and finished on the winning side on both occasions. Later in the season, Mackie displayed wonderful versatility when deputizing in goal — due to the non-arrival of John Daniels — at Darwen. In his unaccustomed role Mackie gave a brilliant display and it was not until two minutes from time that Darwen drew level at 2-2.

McLEAN, William   1947-48
Outside-right.
Born: Scotland.
Debut v Wrexham (h) 6 September 1947.
Appearances: 12; Goals: 2.
Career: Queen of the South; RAKERS 13 August 1947 to cs 1948.
A bustling winger with neat footwork, McLean, along with Archie Wells, made a dangerous right-wing pair in the early stages of the 1947-8 season. The former Queen of the South man had a particularly good debut at Wrexham, when New Brighton took a point from the Third Division leaders. Unfortunately, an ankle injury sustained at Rotherham on 22 November proved more troublesome than had been first thought and it was not until late February that he made a re-appearance in the Reserves.

143

McLELLAN, Alastair Alexander   **1946-48**
Inside-forward. 5ft 10ins, 12st.
Born: Glasgow 16 April 1922.
Debut v Rochdale (a) 14 September 1946.
Appearances: 34; Goals: 7.
Career: Glasgow Schoolboys; Shettleston Juniors;
Raith Rovers; Huddersfield Town (wartime guest);
Albion Rovers; RAKERS 17 July 1946; Tranmere
Rovers 18 May 1948; Morecambe August 1949;
Prescot Cables and South Liverpool during season
1950-51.

International honour: Scottish Schoolboys.
'A good bustler who packs a dynamic shot', was
one 1948 verdict on McLellan, who was popularly
known as 'Cowboy' — cartoons of the time often
picturing him complete with chaps and spurs. The
source of the unusual nickname remains a mystery,
but one suggestion was that it referred to his
'bronco-busting' style of bursting through defences.
He also carried a 'big gun' in either foot. A medical
student prior to being called up, McLellan served
as an air-gunner in the RAF and was badly
wounded over Germany. A talented musician,
today he lives in Wallasey and is physiotherapist
to Tranmere Rovers.

McMULLAN, Samuel   **1935-36**
Goalkeeper. 5ft 11ins. 12st 10lbs.
Debut v Barrow (h) 11 September 1935.
Appearances: 8.
Career: Dundalk; Ards; RAKERS 24 August 1935,
released 7 April 1936.
Club honour: Ards, Irish Cup winners 1927.
*Representative honours: 3 appearances for the Irish
League in 1929.*
One of three goalkeepers used by the Rakers in
the 1935-6 season, Sam McMullan deputized for
Charlie Bird, making his Football League debut
in a 3-2 defeat by Barrow. He was then displaced
by the amateur, Ernie Temple, and did not feature
again until mid-October. On his recall, he conceded
30 goals in an eight-match run. He was released
before the end of a season in which New Brighton
conceded over a century of goals.

McMURRAY, Campbell   **1925-26**
Left-back. 5ft 10ins. 11st 10lbs.
Born: Glasgow, 27 June (year not established).
Debut v Chesterfield (h) 24 October 1925.
Appearances: 1.
Career: Strathclyde; Glasgow Ashfield; Hull City
January 1920; Workington 1922; York City cs 1923;
RAKERS 12 September 1925 to cs 1926.
After experience with two of the premier junior
sides in Glasgow, McMurray began as a
professional with Hull City. He found himself cast
in a reserve role, making only four League
appearances. During his venture into non-League
football, he was converted from the middle line
into a full-back. With the Rakers for a season, he
was deputy to Jimmy Jones and, apart from his
solitary League outing, spent the season in the
Midland Combination team.

McPEAKE, Matthew   **1948-50**
Half-back. 5ft 10ins. 11st 8lbs.
Born: Ballymena, Co Antrim, 19 June 1919.
Debut v Gateshead (a) 21 August 1948.
Appearances: 50; Goals 2.
Career: Larne FC 1936; Sligo Rovers 1937;
Ballymena United 1939; Chester, Marine and
Tranmere Rovers (wartime guest); Everton 22 July
1946; Grimsby Town 18 June 1947; RAKERS 26
July 1948 to 6 May 1950.
When Matt McPeake played his first game for Sligo
Rovers, Dixie Dean, then Rovers' centre-forward,
was on top form and scored with five headers.
Moving to England in 1940, McPeake took a job
at Hootton Aircraft Works. During his five years
there, he played in wartime football. In one
particularly memorable match he scored for
Tranmere Rovers against Blackpool, but it was
about the only kick that he had, as Blackpool won
15-3. When he joined Everton in 1946, he was
switched from outside-left to left-half. He did not
appear in the League with either Everton or
Grimsby Town, but was a regular with New
Brighton until 1949-50, when a groin strain and
leg injury combined to end his season in January

144

1950. In June 1950 he was on New Brighton's transfer list and awaiting a specialist's verdict on whether he could play soccer again.

McPHERSON, Lachlan   1933-35
Inside-forward or half-back. 5ft 9½ins. 12st.
Born: Cambuslang, Lanarkshire, July 1900.
Debut v Doncaster Rovers (a) 26 August 1933.
Appearances: 53; Goals: 3.
Career: Cambuslang Rangers; Notts County 18 May 1921; Swansea Town 23 June 1924; Everton 3 January 1930 (fee £5,000); RAKERS 24 August 1933; Hereford United player-coach July 1935.
Club honours: Notts County, Second Division champions 1922-3; Swansea Town, Third Division South champions 1924-5. Welsh Cup runners-up 1926; Everton, Second Division champions 1930-31.

'Lachy' McPherson learned his football in the same school as Scottish international inside-forward, Andy Wilson, coming to the fore with Cambuslang Rangers. He was spotted by Swansea officials when Notts County and Swansea were undertaking a summer tour to Denmark in 1923. One year later, he moved to Vetch Field and assisted the Swans to the Third Division South championship. Everton paid a hefty fee for him in January 1930, but was unable to steer them clear of relegation. The following season, however, they regained their place in the First Division. An influential player, either as a forward or wing-half, he made maximum appearances for the Rakers in his first season. One early Press comment on his style was: 'New Brighton's attack is now blending successfully, following a better general understanding of McPherson's subtleties.' In 1934-5, injuries, both on the field and off, curtailed his season. He had the misfortune to be involved, as a pedestrian, in a road accident which injured both his ankles.

McPHERSON, Peter Copeland   1934-35
Inside-forward. 5ft 9½ins. 11st 4lbs.

Born: Livingston Station, Mid Calder 19 March 1912.
Debut v Doncaster Rovers (h) 6 October 1934.
Appearances: 4.
Career: Shotts Battlefield; Dalkeith Thistle; Hibernians 8 August 1932; Barnsley 12 August 1933; Southport (trial) 14 June to 4 October 1934; RAKERS 10 October 1934; Le Harve (France) June 1935; Portadown; Hibernian; Heart of Midlothian; Waterford September 1938; St James' Gate (Dublin); Harrow Town (coach) 1947-8.
Peter McPherson's first English club was Barnsley, but he made only one League appearance in the side which won the Third Division North championship in season 1933-4. With New Brighton, he did not appear on the winning side in his four League outings, but his play in the Lancashire Combination side earned him consistently good notices. He was the Reserves' most successful marksman with 18 goals, signing off at Rake Lane on 4 May 1935 with a hat-trick in a 6-1 win over Accrington Stanley Reserves.

McTAFF, Stephen   1948-51
Half-back. 5ft 10ins, 10st 8lbs.
Born: Burnopfield, Durham, 11 March 1922.
Debut v Gateshead (a) 21 August 1948.
Appearances: 100; Goals: 3.
Career: Byemoor School; North-West Durham Schoolboys; Eden Colliery; East Tamfield; Bradford 14 May 1945; RAKERS 28 July 1948; York City 27 October 1951 to cs 1952.
One of new player-manager Jack Atkinson's first signings after his appointment in July 1948, Steve McTaff proved a sound investment and was rarely absent from first-team duty, apart from a spell of injury in 1950-51. McTaff was quick to tackle, quick to recover and if beaten, was prepared to chase his man the length of the field. One contemporary match report stated: 'McTaff sticks to his man like fly-paper,' — a household commodity perhaps unfamiliar to younger readers!

MAHER, Edward   1929-30
Goalkeeper.
Debut v Halifax Town (a) 19 October 1929.
Appearances: 4.
Career: Everton amateur, signing professional 1 December 1928; RAKERS 14 October 1929 to cs 1930.
Ted Maher had made only one reserve-team appearance before being selected for his Football League debut at Halifax. He was beaten four times at The Shay, after the Rakers were reduced to ten men due to an injury to Tommy Lewis. The handful of first-team games in which he featured contained some heavy goalscoring. They were (New Brighton's score first): 0-4, 0-5, 4-1 and 0-5. At this point, the Rakers were successful in persuading their former goalkeeper, Kenny Campbell, out of retirement.

MAJOR, William Henry   **1932-34**
Centre-half. 5ft 11ins. 12st 6lbs.
Born: Wallasey, 1915.
Debut v Walsall (h) 17 December 1932.
Appearances: Poulton FC; RAKERS amateur 29
June 1932; Tranmere Rovers 11 May 1934 to cs
1937.
An outstanding amateur footballer, Bill Major
represented Lancashire in the Northern Counties
Amateur championship during season 1933-4. He
was also selected for the North in the England
Amateur international trial against the South at
Wimbledon on 6 January 1934. A strong and
dominant defender, Major was sought by several
clubs during his spell at Rake Lane, but he preferred
to remain an amateur so that he could continue
with his milk delivery business. When he did leave
Rake Lane, his transfer was subject to two Football
League commissions of enquiry. The second
commission ruled that Major had been improperly
approached by a Tranmere Rovers director, but
without the knowledge of all the members of the
club's board. The director concerned was
suspended, Major was fined £10, and Tranmere
had to pay the costs of the two hearings. After
all the excitement, Major made only eight
appearances in three seasons at Prenton Park, being
appointed captain of the Rover's Reserve side in
August 1935.

MATHIESON, Allan   **1923-27**
Inside-forward. 5ft 10½ins. 13st 4lbs.
Born: Belfast.
Debut v Chesterfield (h) 29 August 1923.
Appearances: 127; Goals: 37.
Career: Glentoran; Luton Town 1919-20; Exeter
City 12 August 1922 (fee £250); RAKERS 20
August 1923 to cs 1927; subsequently played in
USA and Canada.
International honours: 2 Irish caps, 1921.
A glance at the figures given for Allan Mathieson's
height and weight when he joined the Rakers, were
no doubt in part the reason for Press comments
such as: 'The tactician of the line was the ponderous
Mathieson'. Another, even less kind verdict was
'statuesque.' Despite his bulky frame, he was a
scientific player with delicate footwork and some
memorable goals to his credit. When he was capped
in March 1921, Third Division Luton Town created
a record by supplying three forwards for an
international. Mathieson and Louis Bookman were
Ireland's left-wing pair, and Ernest Simms was
England's centre-forward. They were all on Luton's
books at the time.

MATHIESON, John   **1926-27 and 1929-30**
Inside-forward. 5ft 11ins. 11st 6lbs.
Born: Ireland, 1905.
Debut v Accrington Stanley (a) 6 November 1926.
Appearances: 11; Goals: 3.
Career: Barr FC; Shelbourne; Glentoran;
RAKERS 6 November 1926; Dundalk July 1927;

Belfast Celtic 10 October 1929; RAKERS 14
August 1929 to cs 1930.
John Mathieson, younger brother of Allan (*qv*),
had two separate spells at Rake Lane. During his
first season, he had an early run in the League
side, but was said to lack ball control. He had
obviously improved as the season drew to a close,
for his eight-match run in the first team yielded
three goals. After a two-year spell with Dundalk,
he returned to New Brighton — who had retained
his registration — but he did not get in to their
League side. Mathieson was well-known as a boxer
in Ireland.

MATTHEWS, Robert William   **1930-32**
Centre-half. 6ft 1½ins. 13st 5lbs.
Born: Plasbennion, near Ruabon, 4 April 1897;
Died: Wrexham, 18 December 1987.
Debut v Tranmere Rovers (h) 11 October 1930.
Appearances: 41; Goals: 1.

Career: Colwyn Bay FC; Liverpool 1916; Bristol
City 2 March 1922; Wrexham 5 November 1923
(fee £350); Northwich Victoria; Barrow 13
November 1925; Bradford 31 January 1926;
Stockport County 9 May 1930; RAKERS 11
October 1930 (exchange for Joseph Taylor);
Chester 8 January 1932; Oswestry Town June 1932;
Witton Town September 1932; Sandbach Ramblers
November 1932; Colwyn Bay during 1932-3;

146

Rossendale United August 1933-4; Llangollen FC manager; Blackpool scout.

Club honours: Bristol City, Third Division South champions 1922-3; Wrexham, Welsh Cup winners 1924; Bradford, Third Division North champions 1927-8.

International honours: 3 Welsh caps 1921-6. 2 Victory International appearances 1919.

Billy Matthews, a source of power to the side in both attack and defence, served the Rakers well in the critical part of season 1930-31, when the side fought clear of the foot of the table. A northern-based correspondent aptly described his qualities in 1930: 'Matthews, big, burly and boisterous, was prominent in most things that New Brighton did.' It was especially disappointing, in view of his excellent work during the 1930-31 season, that his form appeared to have deserted him in 1931-2. He lost his place after appearing in the first 11 League matches, which yielded a solitary point. He was placed on the transfer list, at his own request, in October 1931.

MEHAFFY, John Wesley   1924-25

Goalkeeper.
Born: Belfast, 22 December 1896; Died: 3 December 1937.
Debut v Walsall (a) 12 January 1924.
Appearances: 5.
Career: Glentoran; RAKERS 1 January 1924; Rotherham County 24 January 1925 (fee £525); Dundalk cs 1927; Coleraine 5 July 1929.
Representative honours: Irish League, 2 appearances, 1921-3.
Club honour: Glentoran, Irish Cup winners 1921.
John Mehaffy was a New Year's Day signing from Glentoran, the same Irish club which supplied McClure, New Brighton's previous reserve-team goalkeeper. A fine goalkeeper in his own right, John Mehaffy was overshadowed by his elder brother, Bert, at Rake Lane. He scored for New Brighton Reserves, from the penalty-spot, in the George Mahon Cup semi-final against Skelmersdale. Following his transfer to Rotherham, the brothers Mehaffy faced each other when Rotherham visited Rake Lane in March 1926, and the Rakers won 5-1.

MEHAFFY, Joseph Alexander Cuthbert 1923-29

Goalkeeper. 5ft 8ins. 10st 7lbs.
Born: Belfast, 10 April 1895; Died: 1970.
Debut v Bradford (a) 25 August 1923.
Appearances: 218; Goals: 1.
Career: Queens Park (Lurgan); Queen's Island; Belfast Celtic; Tottenham Hotspur (trial); RAKERS 7 June 1923; Belfast Celtic 20 August 1929.
International honours: 1 Irish cap, 1922. 2 appearances Irish League, 1921.
One of four goalkeeping brothers, J.A.C.Mehaffy, commonly known as 'Bert', began as a 16-year-old with Queen's Park. During World War One, he served in the Royal Navy and represented the

RN at centre-forward. On his Football League debut for New Brighton, he displayed almost miraculous anticipation and deftness of handling. He was to maintain similar high standards throughout his six years at Rake Lane, often being referred to as 'the best goalkeeper in the Northern Section'. He was one of comparatively few goalkeepers who have taken penalty-kicks in the League. He netted from the spot against Ashington on Boxing Day 1923 and opened the New Year's scoring list in a Liverpool Senior Cup tie against Tranmere Rovers on 9 January. He lost the job in the following month, however, after shooting wide against Doncaster Rovers and having to get back down the field in undignified haste. Mehaffy, who was awarded a benefit match against Tranmere Rovers on 29 April 1929, was brother-in-law to Elisha Scott, the Liverpool and Irish international. The two goalkeepers shared 'digs' in the New Brighton district.

MILLAR, John McVey   1937

Outside-left. 5ft 8½ins. 11st 2lbs.
Born: Coatbridge, 1908.
Debut v Halifax Town (h) 19 October 1937.
Appearances: 1.
Career: Saltcoats Victoria; Kilmarnock August 1927; Barnsley 5 July 1928; Hartlepools United 28 June 1929; Workington cs 1930; Lancaster Town cs 1934; Belfast Glentoran June 1936; Lancaster Town cs 1937; RAKERS (trial) 25 September to 22 October 1937; Rochdale 25 October 1937; Exeter City 16 July 1938 to 25 February 1939; Astley Bridge 1939-40.
'Jock' Millar was invited for a month's trial with New Brighton after playing against their reserves for Lancaster Town, ten days earlier. In 1935, the *Lancashire Daily Post Annual'* said of him: 'Millar should prove the most speedy outside-left in the (Lancashire) Combination seeing that he is reckoned amongst the five fastest professional sprinters in Scotland and has won 45 prizes on the track.' Millar had some noteworthy goalscoring feats to his credit in non-League football. These included 25 in 1930-31 and 27 in 1931-2 for Workington, 26 for Lancaster Town in 1934-5 and 27 for Glentoran in 1936-7.

MILLER, Peter Steadman   1931-35

Inside-forward or winger. 5ft 8½ins. 11st 5lbs.
Born: Bo'ness, 1909.
Debut v Gateshead (h) 29 August 1931.
Appearances: 140; Goals: 22.
Career: Bo'ness United; Falkirk; Watford 7 August 1930; RAKERS 20 August 1931; Le Havre (France) June 1935; Rotherham United 27 January 1936; Port Vale 20 June 1936.
A great footwork artist, Peter Miller began his career as an outside-left, later switching to the inside berth. New Brighton used him as a winger on occasions, but the inside role seemed to be his natural position. He was the Rakers' most successful marksman in 1932-3, with 13 League

MONTGOMERY, John Joseph   **1937-39**
Centre-forward. 5ft 10½ins. 11st 8lbs.
Born: Glasgow, 1915.
Debut v Barrow (h) 28 August 1937 (scored one goal).
Appearances: 57; Goals: 34.
Career: Coltness United; Manchester United 11 May 1936 (fee £500); RAKERS 17 July 1937 to September 1939.
When Jack Montgomery left Coltness United to join Manchester United, the fee of £500 which Coltness received was, at that time, a record for a Scottish junior club. With his excellent sense of positional play and readiness to try a shot, he quickly became a crowd favourite. He was leading goalscorer, by a very large margin, in his first season with 24 League goals (next highest was Alf Ainsworth with nine), six FA Cup and two Northern Section Cup goals. In the 1938-9 season he lost his place to Arthur Frost, but regained it after Frost had been sold to Newcastle United. In this season, the last one of peacetime football, he scored ten goals in 17 League appearances, one in the Northern Section Cup, and 21 in the Lancashire Combination.

MORLEY, Samuel B   **1936-37**
Inside-forward. 5ft 9ins. 11st.
Born: Liverpool.
Debut v Darlington (h) 14 March 1936.
Appearances: 2.
Career: Church Road Services Club (Liverpool); RAKERS amateur 19 February 1936, professional 13 March 1936; Prescot Cables 16 October 1937.
One of the most promising inside-forwards in Liverpool amateur football, Sam Morley was said to have attracted the notice of Belfast Celtic and Newry Town, prior to his trial with New Brighton. After less than a month in the Lancashire Combination side, he was signed as a professional and made his Football League debut. In a forward line that had shown a lack of combination all season, he found it difficult to make his mark and was probably unfortunate to have arrived upon the scene when the Rakers' fortunes were at their lowest ebb.

MORRIS, George Edward   **1937-39**
Left-back. 5ft 8ins. 11st 10lbs.
Born: Birkenhead, 1911.
Debut v Chester (h) 19 March 1938.
Appearances: 14.
Career: Tranmere Rovers amateur; Everton 9 May 1934; RAKERS 26 May 1937 to 1939; post-war with South Liverpool until 1950.
There was keen competition between George Morris and Norman Richardson for the left-back berth after Norman Greenhalgh had been transferred to Everton. Morris ended the season in the first team, but in the following campaign he was crowded out by Harry Topping and Arthur Buxton. One of the longest kickers on the club's books, Morris had been elected captain of the reserve team just before the outbreak of World War Two.

goals in 35 appearances. In 1934, the *Daily Express* commented; 'Miller was the star of the New Brighton attack. He had all the touches of a First Division artist and kept the ball until the right moment to part with it.'

MILLIGAN, Joseph T   **1934-37**
Centre-half. 6ft. 12st 8lbs.
Born: Birkenhead, 29 September 1911; Died: Upton, Wirral, 20 August 1980.
Debut v Mansfield Town (h) 16 January 1935.
Appearances: 12.
Career: Ellesmere Port Town; RAKERS 21 July 1934; Tranmere Rovers 26 February 1937.
Joe Milligan, deputizing for the injured Charlie Amery, faced a daunting League baptism. He was directly opposed to Mansfield Town's centre-forward Johnson, a player approaching a career aggregate of 300 goals. He took the job in his stride and, in a good all round display, played no small part in the comparative subjection of the arch goalscorer, New Brighton winning 2-1. Johnson, incidentally, completed his career total of 300 goals on 6 April 1935 — against the Rakers. In the unaccustomed position of centre-forward, Milligan scored both of New Brighton's goals in extra-time when Tranmere Rovers were beaten 2-0 in the Liverpool Senior Cup Final on 10 May 1935. On the injured list for a considerable spell in 1936-7, Milligan had not made a senior appearance for New Brighton that season when Tranmere signed him in February 1937.

MORRISON, Robert   **1925-31**
Half-back. 5ft 7ins. 10st 10lbs.
Born: Hyde, Cheshire, 31 March 1901.
Debut v Rochdale (h) 7 November 1925.
Appearances: 168; Goals: 4.
Career: Hyde United; Stockport County amateur 22, professional 29 December 1922; RAKERS 27 August 1925 to cs 1931.
A former weaver in a Lancashire cotton mill, Bobby Morrison was rated as one of the most wholehearted half-backs ever to represent the Rakers. A sprightly performer who often turned defence into attack, at times assuming the role of a sixth forward. He was generally first choice with New Brighton, but had an unfortunate time in season 1930-31, a knee injury sustained in a pre-season practice, restricting him to only nine appearances during the season. After retiring from the game he ran a newsagents business in Manchester.

MORTIMER, John McCormick   **1949-51**
Full-back. 5ft 8ins. 10st 9lbs.
Born: Birkenhead, 5 December 1923.
Debut v Rotherham United (a) 29 October 1949.
Appearances: 5.
Career: Junior football; Wrexham 1 August 1948; RAKERS 15 October 1949 to 5 May 1951.
Johnny Mortimer had an unfortunate start with the Rakers. A broken leg, sustained in a reserve match at Fleetwood whilst he was still a trialist, saw him out of action for over three months. Given the precarious financial position, it was a sporting gesture by New Brighton's directors to offer him a contract for the remainder of the season. Mortimer recovered very well from his injury, appearing in the final three League matches of 1949-50, but he made only one League appearance during 1950-51.

MURRAY, William Thomas   **1926-27**
Left-half. 5ft 10½ins. 12st.
Born: Alexandria, Dumbartonshire, 9 November 1904; Died: 1940.
Debut v Ashington (a) 15 January 1927.
Appearances: 7.
Career: Scottish junior football; Clydebank; RAKERS 22 October 1926; Clydebank 30 April 1927; Liverpool 28 November 1927; Barrow 31 January 1930; Bristol Rovers 27 December 1933 (fee £250); Folkestone June 1936 (fee £275).
A Scottish scouting tour by New Brighton resulted in the signing of two wing-halves from Clydebank, David Beattie joining Bill Murray in his move to Merseyside. After a brief stay at Rake Lane, during which time he made five appearances at left-half and two at centre-half, Murray returned to Clydebank. After retracing his steps to Merseyside, but this time to join Liverpool, he spent two years in reserve at Anfield. His career blossomed when he moved north to join Barrow. He were re-election applicants in Murray's first season but, before he left Holker Street they had finished 5th, 9th and 8th in consecutive seasons under his splendid captaincy. Murray's total career figures were 189 appearances and ten goals.

MUSGRAVE, David   **1950-51**
Outside-left.
Born: South Shields, 20 April 1928.
Debut v Gateshead (a) 2 September 1950.
Appearances: 35; Goals: 2.
Career: Johannesburg (South Africa); Manchester United 25 December 1947; Northwich Victoria; Fleetwood; RAKERS 23 August 1950; Preston North End (trial) 16 August 1951; Southport 12 October 1951 (fee £300); Accrington Stanley 9 September 1953; Fleetwood cs 1954; Lancaster City November 1954; Winsford United later in season 1954-5; Oldham Athletic (one month's trial) August 1955; Northwich Victoria 1955-6; Winsford United 1956-7.

A South Shields native, David Musgrave was only five-years-old when he emigrated to South Africa with his family. He returned after the war to start his professional career with Manchester United. At one time a trainee in the field of commercial art, Musgrave was arguably the Rakers' best post-war winger. The young, fair-haired, outside-left could send across a perfect centre with either foot and, as one correspondent put it, had 'a pocketful of delightful dummy moves'. After the Rakers failed to gain re-election, he went to Preston North End on trial but moved on to assist Southport and Accrington Stanley. His career figures were 117 appearances and 16 goals — all his senior appearances being made with three clubs who lost their Football League status.

MUSTARD, John   **1936-38**
Outside-right. 5ft 7½ins. 11st 4lbs.
Born: Boldon-on-Tyne, 1905.
Debut v Oldham Athletic (a) 29 August 1936
(scored one goal).
Appearances: 78; Goals: 11.
Career: Crawcrook Albion; Queen's Park Rangers
13 November 1926; South Shields 21 September
1929; Wrexham 5 June 1930; Preston North End
11 May 1932; Burnley 16 March 1933; Southend
United 27 December 1933; Crewe Alexandra 26
July 1934; Wrexham 13 May 1935; RAKERS 22
July 1936 to 29 December 1938.
Jack Mustard, a noted sprinter and penalty-taker,
was recruited by New Brighton as part of a new
and experienced forward line for season 1936-7.
He captained the side in early matches, but asked
to be relieved of the job in early October, stating
that his outside-right berth 'was not a suitable
position from which to supervise players'. Handily
versatile, for two seasons he was a regular on either
flank, but lost his place in 1938-9, when Jimmy
Stein (former Everton) and Horace Small were the
established wingers. In the early part of 1938-9,
Mustard scored from the penalty-spot in three
successive games for the Rakers' Reserve team. His
career record was 319 appearances and 65 goals.
His best seasonal return was with Crewe Alexandra
in 1934-5, when he scored 17 goals in 38
appearances.

NIVEN, James H   **1922-25**
Right-back. 5ft 8ins. 11st 6lbs.
Born: Liverpool, 8 September 1900.
Debut v Bradford (a) 25 August 1923.
Appearances: 37.
Career: Tranmere Rovers amateur 1 September
1921; RAKERS 19 August 1922; Flint Town 15
August 1925; Bangor.
After Jimmy Niven appeared in most matches in
1922-3 as full-back partner to Jimmy Jones, the
pair were entrusted with the responsibility of being
the last line of defence when the Rakers opened
their Football League programme in August 1923.
Of his League debut, one writer said: 'Niven stood
out for his timely interventions, and his tackling
was a revelation of full-back play'. Alas, a damaged
cartilage ended his season after only four matches
and it was almost a year before he appeared with
the first team again. He recovered to make 33
appearances in 1924-5, the Rakers' best League
season, when they finished in third place. Jimmy
Niven's father, James B.Niven, was capped for
Scotland in 1885.

OAKES, Alfred William   **1929-31**
Inside-forward. 6ft. 11st 10lbs.
Born: Bewdley, Worcs, 22 July 1901; Died: Bristol
25 December 1967.
Debut v Barrow (a) 31 August 1929.
Appearances: 54; Goals: 15
Career: RAF Uxbridge; Chesham United; Millwall
Athletic 26 June 1923; Reading 17 May 1925; Rhyl
Athletic cs 1926; Worcester City; Birmingham 23

February 1927 (fee £300); Rhyl Athletic June 1928;
RAKERS 14 August 1929; Wigan Borough 26 June
1931; Frickley Colliery November 1931;
Stalybridge Celtic August 1932.

Alf Oakes arrived at Rake Lane from Rhyl Athletic
with a big reputation, having scored 47 goals for
the Welsh club in 1928-9. He began quietly with
New Brighton but, once established after
Christmas, he began to live up to his reputation.
He was particularly dangerous from corner-kicks
or in meeting high centres, when he used his height
to full advantage. Oakes was Wigan Borough's
leading goalscorer when they withdrew from the
Football League on 26 October 1931. As their
record was completely expunged, his four goals do
not appear in official records.

PAGE, Thomas   **1929-30**
Inside-forward. 5ft 7ins. 11st 4lbs.
Born: Kirkdale, Liverpool, 15 November 1888.
Died: Gloucester, 26 October 1973.
Debut v Barrow (a) 31 August 1929.
Appearances: 8; Goals: 1
Career: Carada FC (Bootle); Pembroke; Liverpool
15 April 1911; Rochdale 11 June 1911; Everton
19 June 1913; St Mirren cs 1914; Wartime guest
player with South Liverpool and Rochdale; Port
Vale 8 June 1920 (fee £400); RAKERS 26 August
1929 to cs 1930.
*Club honours: St Mirren, Scottish Victory Cup
winners, 26 April 1919.*
Tommy Page was one of several footballing

brothers, the most notable being Louis Antonia Page, the English international. Aside from Neil McBain's debut for New Brighton at the age of 51 years and 4 months, Tom Page would probably qualify as the oldest debutant under any normal circumstances. He was 40 years and 9 months old when he appeared at Barrow in his first game for New Brighton. A comment on his play at Rake Lane was: 'Despite his undoubted cleverness in the outfield, Page is not the type of inside-forward that is required. The Rakers could do with a man with less science and more thrust.' The bulk of Page's career was spent with Port Vale, for whom he recorded over 300 Football League appearances.

PARKER, John   1928-29
Inside-forward.
Born: Stoke, 1895.
Debut v Barrow (h) 25 August 1928.
Appearances: 38; Goals: 8
Career: Shrewsbury Town; Nottingham Forest, 11 February 1920 (fee £100), released on free transfer May 1920; Stalybridge Celtic; RAKERS 25 August 1928; Rhyl Athletic July 1929.
A recruit from the Cheshire County League, Jack Parker was the star of the second pre-season trial at Rake Lane, scoring four of the Stripes' six goals. Adept in any of the three inside-forward positions, Parker opened the game out well and showed a readiness to have a shot. He missed only four matches in his one season with New Brighton. Much earlier in his career, Parker appeared in five Football League matches for Nottingham Forest during season 1919-20.

PARLE, James   1931-33
Inside-forward or winger. 5ft 8ins. 10st 10lbs.
Born: Liverpool, 1907.
Debut v Gateshead (h) 29 August 1931.
Appearances: 65; Goals: 9

Career: Bootle Celtic; Birmingham amateur 8th, professional 24 August 1928; Chesterfield 9 May 1929; Walsall 23 May 1930; RAKERS 5 August 1931; Crewe Alexandra (trial) 12 September to 20 October 1933; Worcester City; Yeovil & Petters United June 1934; Newport County 26 June 1935 to cs 1936.
Jimmy Parle joined New Brighton as an outside-right, beginning in this position in his first season. He had not done very well up to January but, when switched to inside-forward, his performances did much to lift the team away from the foot of the table. In a spell of non-League football, he was inside-right in the Yeovil & Petters team who were champions of the Southern League (Western Section) and Southern League Cup Finalists in 1934-5. They were also one of the shock sides in the FA Cup competition, defeating Crystal Palace 3-0, Exeter City 4-1, before losing 6-2 to Liverpool in the third round. In his final season of League football, Parle scored eight goals in 35 appearances for Newport County in 1935-6.

PATERSON, Alexander   1946-48
Half-back or Inside-forward.
Born: Hardgate, 18 March 1922.
Debut v Wrexham (a) 31 August 1946.
Appearances: 67; Goals: 10
Career: Alloa Athletic; RAKERS 15 July 1946; Stockport County 13 March 1948; Barrow 28 August 1953; Halifax Town (trial) August-September 1954.
In New Brighton's first post-war season, Alex Paterson, generally a left-half, was tried at inside-left over the Easter period 1947. He scored twice against Darlington and then scored one in the next four consecutive fixtures, — six goals in five games. He began the 1947-8 season in the inside-left role and whilst unable to maintain his earlier goalscoring ratio, he impressed with his ball control and aerial ability. Paterson was transferred to Stockport County just prior to the 'deadline' in March 1948 and A.T.Earl, the Stockport inside-forward, moved in the opposite direction during the same month. Paterson stayed for five years at Edgeley Park, making 160 appearances.

PEGG, Frank Edward   1933-34
Outside-left. 5ft 6½ins. 10st 3lbs.
Born: Beeston, Notts, 2 August 1902.
Debut v Doncaster Rovers (a) 26 August 1933.
Appearances: 41; Goals: 8
Career: Sawley United; Loughborough Corinthians; Derby County (trial); Blackpool (trial) 27 August to 14 November 1924; Nelson (trial) 24 December 1924; Sunderland 12 May 1925; Lincoln City 6 May 1926; Bradford City 8 May 1931 (in exchange for B.A.C. Hall); Norwich City 15 June 1932; RAKERS 11 August 1933; Great Yarmouth 1934.
Frank Pegg was first spotted when playing for his local club in the South Derbyshire village of Sawley. His best form was seen in the first three of his five seasons with Lincoln City, in which he recorded

leading goalscorer in both of his seasons at the Tower. His tally of 26 goals included two hat-tricks, the last of which, scored at Accrington Stanley in September 1947 was unique in that he became the only New Brighton player to score a hat-trick and finish on the losing side.

PITHER, George   **1929-31**
Outside-left. 5ft 8½ins. 11st 2lbs.
Born: Kew, Surrey, 24 June 1899; Died: Tunbridge Wells, 3 January 1966.
Debut v Barrow (a) 31 August 1929.
Appearances: 79; Goals: 10
Career: Richmond Wednesday; Isleworth Town; Brentford amateur 20 August, professional 8 September 1921; Millwall Athletic 20 May 1922; Bristol Rovers 21 August 1924; Torquay United August 1925; Merthyr Town 4 May 1926; Liverpool 26 November 1926; Crewe Alexandra 26 May 1928 (fee £100); RAKERS 14 August 1929; Tunbridge Wells Rangers August 1931; Margate September 1932.
Representative honour: London Combination v London League, March 1924.
Aside from a dozen appearances with First Division Liverpool, the greater part of George Pither's career was spent in the Third Division. He scored 11 goals in 38 appearances for Crewe Alexandra in 1928-9 and gave good service to New Brighton for two seasons, appearing in all matches in his final term. New Brighton's officials must have regretted their decision to release him, for in 1931-2, no fewer than five outside-lefts were tried, eventually leading to the re-signing of Jimmy Dickie.

POLLOCK, Archibald   **1930-32**
Half-back
Debut v Wigan Borough (h) 13 September 1930.
Appearances: 26
Career: Peasley Cross Athletic; RAKERS 21 August 1930 to cs 1932.
Archie Pollock, a recruit from the Liverpool County Combination, began with New Brighton as a half-back, first showing promise in the August 1930 public trials. In his first season, either in the first or second team, he filled so many positions that it was difficult to judge which was his best, for on every occasion he showed ability and adaptability. He was unfortunate during 1931-2 to sustain a troublesome hip injury which ended his season in January, this after he had established himself at right-half in the seniors.

PRITCHARD, Keith   **1946-47**
Inside-forward or Winger.
Born: Wallasey, 20 October 1919.
Debut v Bradford City (h) 4 September 1946.
Appearances: 25; Goals: 8.
Career: Oldershaw School; Wallasey FC; Northern Nomands October 1936; New Brighton Baptists; RAKERS amateur 13 July 1946; Liverpool Marine 27 December 1947.

106 appearances and scored 44 goals. He proved a consistent winger for the Rakers after joining them on a free transfer from Norwich City. On his third appearance for New Brighton, against Barrow on 2 September 1933, he shot wide from the penalty-spot. It was said to be his first such miss for three seasons. One minute earlier, New Brighton's skipper McPherson had also missed from the spot.

PENDERGAST, William James   **1946-48**
Inside-forward.
Born: Pen-y-groes, 13 April 1915.
Debut v Wrexham (a) 31 August 1946 (scored one goal).
Appearances: 69; Goals: 26.
Career; Rhyl Juniors; Crewe Alexandra amateur 21 December 1934; Wrexham amateur 26 August to 19 December 1935; Manchester United 20 December 1935; Wolverhampton Wanderers 10 January 1936; Bristol Rovers 7 May 1936; Chester 21 July 1938; RAKERS 1 August 1946; Rhyl cs 1948.
The Rakers' attack was subject to many early changes in the 1946-7 season, but Bill Pendergast retained his number-nine jersey, toiling with industry, tenacity and ideas as the new team sought blend and balance. A seasoned campaigner, Pendergast was at times accused of squandering opportunities. Nevertheless, he was the club's

An accomplished amateur all-round sportsman, Keith Pritchard represented the Public Schools at rugby and first appeared for Northern Nomads — the famous Northern amateur soccer team — when he was only 17-years-old. With Wallasey FC he scored 33 goals in season 1935-6 and followed with 21 goals in the first seven matches of 1936-7. During wartime Army service he was CQMS with the Lancashire Fusiliers and played in representative Army football both at home and abroad. A natural footballer, ideally built, strong and fast, Pritchard was arguably the best amateur ever to wear the Rakers' colours. A prolific reserve-team goalscorer, his senior return of eight goals in 25 appearances — mainly from outside-left — was a fair reflection of his abilities.

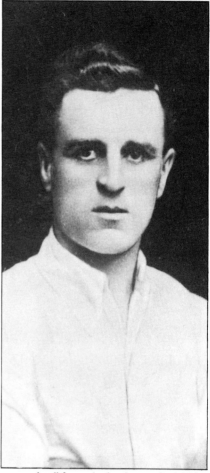

QUAYLE, Charles James   **1932-33**
Centre-forward.
Born: Kirkdale, Liverpool, 1907
Debut v Rotherham United (a) 27 August 1932.
Appearances: 11; Goals: 2.
Career: Seventh Kings FC (Bootle); RAKERS amateur 24 August, professional 5 September 1932; Accrington Stanley 9 September 1933; Shrewsbury Town August 1934; Drumcondra August 1935; Crystal Palace 30 July 1936; Bradford City 4 June 1938.
Charlie Quayle was not a stranger to Rake Lane when he signed amateur forms in August 1932. Three months earlier, he had scored ten runs for New Brighton on their debut in the English Baseball Association at Rake Lane. He was a surprise choice for the first team. Despite having shown plenty of dash and perseverance in the public trials, he was considered hardly ready for League football. Nevertheless, in his second appearance, against Mansfield Town, his winner was taken like a veteran, cleverly lobbing over the visitor's goalkeeper following a long throw-in from Robb. He lost his place after playing in the opening nine League matches, having scored two of the Rakers' ten goals. A long spell of injury followed and he was in the Reserves towards the close of the season, scoring both goals in their 2-0 victory in the Liverpool County Challenge Cup Final, against Garston Reformers, at Anfield .

QUINN, Peter   **1923-24**
Outside-left. 5ft 7½ins. 11st.
Born: Sunderland, 1892.
Debut v Bradford (a) 25 August 1923 (scored one goal).
Appearances: 30; Goals: 2.
Career: Junior football; Blackpool 2 December 1910; Preston North End 11 March 1920 (£3,000); Fleetwood cs 1921; Bury February 1923 (£1,125); RAKERS 27 July 1923 to May 1924.
Club honours: Preston North End, FA Cup runners-up 1922.
Peter Quinn, the scorer of New Brighton's first goal in the Football League, was a lightly-built player who relied on skill to achieve his ends. He had recovered well from a broken leg sustained during his short spell with Bury. In a distinguished military career, Quinn returned from active service with the Military Medal and Bar. Whilst in France, he played for the British Military team in representative matches. Whilst with Blackpool, the *Lancashire Daily Post* described Quinn as 'the club's best outside-left since H.P.Hardman'.

RAINFORD, Kenneth S   **1948**
Centre-forward. 6ft, 12st 2lbs.
Born: Saughall Massie, 4 November 1926.
Debut v Chester (h) 20 March 1948.
Appearances: 3; Goals: 1.
Career: New Brighton Baptists; RAKERS amateur 10 February 1948; Prescot Cables season 1948-9.
Described as 'a neat ball player who gets results' on his signing amateur forms in February 1948, Ken Rainford had scored over 50 goals in junior league football during 1947-8. He quickly earned

a senior outing, being promoted after scoring the winner for the Reserves against Chorley. His goal on this occasion was described as 'a perfect example of amateur opportunism, dogged determination and soccer skill'. In his final League appearance, at Gateshead, Rainford scored New Brighton's goal in a 3-1 defeat and was said to be 'the only bright spark in a dull forward line'. An elder brother, Reginald H.Rainford, was also an amateur on the Rakers' books during 1930-31 but he did not appear in the first team.

RATCLIFFE, Beaumont   **1931-35**
Half-back or full-back. 5ft 10½ins. 11st 12lbs.
Born: Bolton-on-Dearne, Yorkshire, 24 April 1909.
Debut v Hartlepools United (a) 10 October 1931.
Appearances: 131; Goals: 4.
Career: Bolton Albion; Bradford amateur 23 December 1930; Charlton Athletic (trial) September 1931; RAKERS 3 October 1931; Le Havre (France) cs 1935; Oldham Athletic 28 June 1935 (fee £500); guest player with RAKERS, Liverpool and Arsenal during World War Two; Reading 24 May 1946; Watford 27 May 1948; Runcorn player-manager June 1949.

During four years with New Brighton, Beau Ratcliffe appeared in both full-back positions, all the half-back berths and, when selected to lead the attack against Rotherham United on 31 December 1932, he scored twice in three minutes to give New Brighton their first home win for four months. After a brief spell with Le Havre, he returned to England to join Oldham Athletic, staying for four seasons and making 156 appearances. Returning to Rake Lane as a guest player in 1939-40, he was right-back in a fine side which achieved some memorable victories, including wins against Stoke City, Manchester City and Manchester United.

RAWSTHORNE, Joseph   **1931-32**
Centre-forward.
Debut v York City (h) 17 October 1931.
Appearances: 9; Goals: 2.
Career: Rhyl Athletic; RAKERS amateur 17 October 1931 to cs 1933.
New Brighton first encountered Joe Rawsthorne when he scored the winner against their Reserves for Rhyl Athletic in the semi-final of the Pyke Cup on 28 March 1931. He began well in the Rakers' Reserves, scoring four against High Park Villa in September 1931. His Football League debut came shortly afterwards and, although he missed two 'golden chances', he was responsible for some good work, despite lacking experience. His two goals at Spotland in November were well taken, but they proved insufficient to improve the Rakers' miserable League record of three points from 14 matches. Although re-registered on amateur forms in August 1932, Rawsthorne did not appear in the League side during this, his final season.

REDFERN, Edward   **1947-52**
Half-back and Forward. 5ft 7ins. 10st 6lbs.
Born: Liverpool, 24 June 1920.
Debut v Wrexham (a) 17 January 1948.
Appearances: 22.
Career: Unity Boys; RAKERS amateur 16 June 1947, professional 29 January 1948; Caernarfon Town August 1952.
Ted Redfern sampled the Anfield atmosphere at a very early age when his school, St Saviour's, lost to Christ Church, Everton, in the Liverpool and District Schoolboy's Cup Final in the early 1930s. He played for Unity Boys on either side of the war, joining the Rakers along with Bill Hounslea (qv) and Brian O'Brien from the same club. A valuable clubman, able to occupy most outfield positions with equal faculty, Redfern made 13 appearances in 1947-8, typically appearing at right-half, inside-right and outside-right during the season.

REID, John Walkinshaw   **1921-28 & 1930**
Centre-half. 5ft 10½ins. 11st 8lbs.
Born: Riccarton, near Kilmarnock, 18 June 1898.
Debut v Bradford (a) 25 August 1923.
Appearances: 174; Goals: 9.
Career: Belfast Distillery; RAKERS 27 August 1921 (fee £750); Ballymena August 1928; Bangor (Ireland) cs 1929; RAKERS 23 August 1930; Belfast Distillery 5 November 1930.
Club honours: Ballymena, Irish Cup winners 1929.
A New Brighton stalwart for seven years in his first spell, Jack Reid was rarely absent from the first team. His only spell of inactivity came during 1924-5, when a knee injury saw him miss half of the season. Reid was a centre-forward before coming to New Brighton and for Distillery he scored twice past Bert Mehaffy in the County Antrim Shield Final. He made his (non-League) debut for New Brighton as a centre-forward, but

Debut v Bradford (a) 25 August 1923.
Appearances: 109; Goals: 2.
Career: Belfast Distillery; RAKERS 27 August 1921; Portadown August 1927; Canadian football August 1932.
An enthusiastic wing-half with a biting tackle, Max Reid proved a fine servant to the Rakers, sharing with his younger brother, Jack (*q.v.*) a joint benefit in 1926. Their benefit match, billed 'Irish XI v Scottish XI', included most of the notable Merseyside international players of the day. An injury on New Year's Day 1926, sustained in the match against Doncaster Rovers, ended his season prematurely.

REID, Thomas   1928-30
Centre-forward. 5ft 8½ins. 11st.
Born: Airdrie, 1901.
Debut v Barrow (h) 25 August 1928.
Appearances: 7; Goals: 1.
Career: Clyde; Ayr United; Port Vale 24 August 1922; Clapton Orient 21 January 1927 (fee £230); Northwich Victoria season 1927-8; RAKERS 20 August 1928 (fee £50) to cs 1930.
After leading the Rakers' attack in the first five games of the 1928-9 season, Tom Reid sustained a knee injury at South Shields. This resulted in a cartilage operation and he did not play again until the following season. He was again first-choice leader when the 1929-30 campaign opened, but was deposed by Joe Taylor after only two matches. The newcomer seized his opportunity, ending the season as leading scorer with 21 goals in 35 appearances. In four seasons with Port Vale, for whom he started as an outside-left, Reid's best seasonal return was 17 appearances and two goals in 1923-4. In a brief stay with Clapton Orient, he helped them narrowly avoid relegation. Needing to win their final League fixture at Reading to avoid the drop, they managed, by a penalty, to win 1-0.

an injury to club skipper Billy Hulme saw him tried at centre-half. He did so well that he retained the position for the next seven years. Max Reid, one of his six brothers, all of whom played soccer, was a New Brighton teammate, whilst younger brother, Bob, played in America. The Reid family moved to Belfast when Jack was two years old and the Irish FA enquired about his availability for the international against England in October 1922, thinking that he was Irish. The New Brighton directors had to advise them of his Scottish birth. Not, one feels, something that would have stood in his way these days!

REID, Maxwell Walkinshaw   1921-27
Right-half. 5ft 8½ins. 11st.
Born: Kilmarnock, 1 June 1893.

RICE, Arthur   1933-34
Wing-half. 5ft 8½ins. 10st 7lbs.
Born: Liverpool.
Debut v Accrington Stanley (h) 4 November 1933.
Appearances: 1.
Career: RAKERS amateur 7 June 1933; Manchester United amateur 20 December 1934, professional 12 February 1935; Stockport County 6 August 1936; Crewe Alexandra 11 July 1938 retiring during World War Two.
On Arthur Rice's selection for his Football League debut at Accrington, the *Wallasey News* commented: 'Rice, a young amateur left-half, whose polished and distinctive style in the Reserves has been so impressive, is being introduced into New Brighton's team today'. Despite winning a professional contract at Old Trafford, Rice did not appear in Manchester United's first team. In two seasons with Stockport County, he sampled both promotion and relegation in making 15 appearances. During season 1938-9 he was playing at inside-forward with Crewe Alexandra and scored four goals against York City in an 8-2 win on 27 December 1938.

'MAX'

George Green

155

RICHARDSON, Norman　　　　　　**1936-51**
Full-back. 5ft 9½ins, 11st.
Born: Hamsterley, Durham, 15 April 1915.
Debut v Gateshead (a) 22 February 1936.
Appearances: 213.
Career: Blackhall Mill School; Medomsley Juniors
1930; Bolton Wanderers 9 May 1933; RAKERS
20 February 1936 to 5 May 1951; Chorley; Bangor
City.
Before signing professional forms with Bolton
Wanderers as an 18-year-old, Norman Richardson
played for Medomsley Juniors and was a teammate
of Ephraim 'Jock' Dodds, the Scottish wartime
international centre-forward. Signed from Bolton,
along with Norman Greenhalgh in 1936,
Richardson was a sure-footed defender with a
deadly tackle, despite being one of the lightest full-
backs in the division. During wartime service with
the Royal Scots Fusiliers, Richardson served for
four years in Burma. He returned to New Brighton
after the war to become one of only a handful of
players whose careers spanned both Rake Lane and
the Tower Grounds. During his 14 years association
with the Rakers 'Richie' occupied every position
except goalkeeper. He was awarded a benefit in
April 1950, when 3,500 spectators saw the visit of
Bolton Wanderers to the Tower Grounds. Norman
Richardson's brother, also a left-back, had a fine
soccer record, spending two seasons with
Wolverhampton Wanderers and ten with Linfield,
where he gained Irish Cup winners' medals in 1934,
1936 and 1939.

ROBB, David　　　　　　**1932-33**
Wing-half. 5ft 11ins. 12st 3lbs.
Born: Leith.
Debut v Rotherham United (a) 27 August 1932.
Appearances: 34.
Career: Bruntonians FC (Musselburgh); Dundee
cs 1924; Charlton Athletic (trial); Wigan Borough
20 September 1926; Chesterfield 22 May 1930;
RAKERS 19 August 1932 to 25 April 1933.
*Club honours: Bruntonians, Scottish Junior Cup
winners 1923-4; Chesterfield, Division Three North
champions 1930-31.*
David Robb first came to the fore with Wigan
Athletic, managed at that time by Angus
McKinnon, who later became the Rakers' trainer-
coach. Moving to Chesterfield, Robb made 23
appearances in their promotion-winning side. A
burly, forceful, half-back with a sure tackle, he
missed only one match for the Rakers before
requesting his release to take up a business
appointment in Scotland.

ROBERTS, Charles Leslie　　　　　　**1936-38**
Inside-forward. 5ft 10ins. 12st 7lbs.
Born: Halesowen, 28 February 1901; Died: 29 May
1980.
Appearances: 40; Goals: 11.
Career: Junior football; Aston Villa amateur 8
August 1921; Chesterfield 13 May 1922; Sheffield
Wednesday 13 June 1923 to 10 March 1924;
Merthyr Town 4 August 1924; Bournemouth &
Boscombe Athletic 19 December 1924; Bolton
Wanderers 4 February 1925 (fee £1,500); Swindon
Town 24 June 1927; Brentford 2 June 1930;
Manchester City 7 January 1931; Exeter City 26
February 1932; Crystal Palace 22 July 1932; Chester
19 January 1934; Rotherham United 18 October
1934; Scunthorpe United August 1935; RAKERS
18 July 1936 to May 1938.
'A player of abundant experience who thinks a
move ahead,' was the *Wallasey News* verdict on
Leslie Roberts in August 1936. He was the type
of player who remained in demand because of his
constructive skills and ability to probe out the weak
spots in opposing defences. In a nomadic career,
in which he made just short of 300 League
appearances and scored 81 goals, Roberts' longest
spell was with Swindon Town, where he made 106
appearances and scored 31 goals.

ROBERTS, Peter Lawrence　　　　　　**1948-49**
Inside-forward. 5ft 6½ins. 10st 7lbs.
Born: Sherburn, Co Durham, 16 July 1925.
Debut v Oldham Athletic (h) 9 October 1948.
Appearances: 3.
Career: East Durham Schoolboys; Sherburn Hill
BC; Newcastle United amateur 1945; Leeds United
amateur 19 August, professional 4 September 1946;
RAKERS 13 July 1948 to 7 May 1949.

When Peter Roberts was selected as centre-forward for his Football League debut, the Rakers had scored only two goals in their previous six outings. In three first-team matches, in which he occupied three different forward positions, the Rakers lost each game and scored only one goal. As a junior, Roberts scored 42 goals for Sherburn Hill Boys Club and took part in the Boys' Club Cup Final against South Shields. After three drawn games, the clubs decided to share the trophy. A reserve-team player with Leeds United, Roberts was an all-round sportsman, spending his summers with Whitkirk CC, a prominent amateur cricket club in Leeds.

ROBERTS, Stanley   **1948-51**
Inside-forward. 5ft 8ins. 11st.
Born: Wrexham, 10 April 1921.
Debut v Gateshead (a) 21 August 1948.
Appearances: 103; Goals: 25.
Career: Rhosddu School; Hightown Athletic; Cross St FC (Wrexham & District League); Wrexham amateur season 1939-40, re-registered 28 September 1946, professional 10 January 1947; RAKERS 22 July 1948; Ellesmere Port Town cs 1951.
As a schoolboy, Stan Roberts scored one of the two goals which gained his school the Denbighshire & District Cup. With Cross Street in the Wrexham & District League, he scored 78 goals, which brought him to Wrexham's notice just before the outbreak of war. After serving in the RAF Regiment in India and Singapore, he rejoined Wrexham, making his Football League debut on Christmas Day 1946. After 27 appearances and nine goals for Wrexham, he was recruited by new Rakers manager, Jack Atkinson. In a three-year spell at the Tower he retained his place on the strength of his midfield creativity, which effectively kept the attack on the move.

ROBERTS, William David   **1928**
Centre-forward. 5ft 7½ins. 11st 4lbs.
Born: Rainhill, near Prescot, 9 January 1904.
Debut v Hartlepools United (h) 25 February 1928 (scored one goal).
Appearances: 16; Goals: 10.
Career: Saltney FC; Northwich Victoria; Huddersfield Town 8 May 1923; Tranmere Rovers 18 May 1925; Winsford United cs 1926; Buckey United; Bolton Wanderers 28 January 1927 (fee £250); Flint Town 19 January 1928; RAKERS 23 February 1928; Prescot Cables 1928-9.
When the Rakers' Reserves were beaten 3-2 by Flint on 3 January 1928, the best forward on view was W.D.Roberts, the Flint centre-forward. He joined New Brighton shortly afterwards and celebrated his entry into the side by scoring the winner against Hartlepools United. A clever opportunist, who certainly pepped up the Rakers' attack in a late season burst which took them into tenth place in the League.

ROBERTSON, Alexander H   **1923-28**
Half-back or Inside-forward. 5ft 11½ins. 12st 3lbs.

Born: Liverpool.
Debut v Wolverhampton Wanderers (h) 1 December 1923.
Appearances: 3.
Career: Harrowby; Northern Nomads; Liverpool amateur during season 1918-19; Oldham Athletic amateur 11 February 1922; Harrowby October 1922; RAKERS amateur 21 November 1923, and subsequently re-registering on amateur forms on four separate dates, the last being 22 November 1928; Northern Nomads.
International honours: English Amateur v Wales 1921
Club honour: Northern Nomads, FA Amateur Cup winners 1926
An outstanding amateur, Alex Robertson made infrequent appearances, but was prominent in the matches in which he took part. In the old school of attacking pivots, his shrewd distribution continually put the forwards into action. He was at inside-right for Northern Nomads when they won the FA Amateur Cup by a record margin of 7-1 at Sunderland in 1926.

ROBINSON, William   **1928-30**
Full-back. 5ft 8ins. 10st 7lbs.
Born: Birkenhead.
Debut v York City (a) 18 September 1929.
Appearances: 1.
Career: Local junior football; RAKERS 8 October 1928 to cs 1930.
Bill Robinson's Football League debut came in the midst of an injury crisis, when the Rakers were forced to make four last-minute changes in the selected team to travel to York City, the Third Division newcomers. The makeshift team had an unhappy afternoon, being well beaten by 3-0 after Robinson's full-back partner, Jock McDonald, had missed from the penalty-spot.

ROSCOE, John   **1929-30**
Inside-forward or Winger. 5ft 9ins. 11st 0lbs.
Born: Prescot, 1908.
Debut v York City (a) 18 September 1929.
Appearances: 16; Goals: 5.
Career: Prescot Cables; Everton 23 August 1928; RAKERS 23 August 1929; Prescot Cables 1930-31; Rotherham United 28 July to 14 December 1931; Prescot Cables; Lancaster Town 1933-35; Prescot Cables cs 1935; South Liverpool January 1936.
Jack Roscoe did not make a big impression in Football League circles, although his career aggregate of eight goals in 21 appearances suggested that he had something to offer. He was a prolific Lancashire Combination marksman, scoring an average of over 50 goals per season for four seasons after leaving Rotherham United. This included 52 in 42 matches for Lancaster Town in the 1933-4 season. When he played against the Rakers' Reserves at Sandheys on 23 April 1938 for South Liverpool, his team won 3-2 to retain the Lancashire Combination championship — with four games still

GEORGE GREEN

to play. Roscoe's contribution at this point was 39 Combination and 25 Cup goals. South Liverpool's final goal tally was 177 in 42 matches and they were League champions with a ten-point margin.

ROSE, Leslie Eric Ronald   **1935-36**
Inside-forward. 6ft. 11st 8lbs.
Born: Weston-super-Mare, 30 November 1914;
Died: Trowbridge, August 1987.
Debut v Oldham Athletic (a) 9 November 1935.
Appearances: 2.
Career: Trowbridge Town; Everton amateur trialist 17 August to 27 September 1934; Bristol Rovers 4 October 1934; Bath City August 1935 RAKERS (trial) 2 November 1935; Bath City; Hartlepools United 20 June 1938 to September 1939.
The Rakers used 30 players in League matches during 1935-6 and Leslie Rose was amongst the trialists, playing in successive games which were lost 6-0 and 4-0. When he made his debut at Oldham, he was one of seven changes from the previous week. He first wore the Rakers' colours at Southport, in the first round of the Third Division North Cup, and was hurt in a 2-0 defeat played in inclement weather and watched by only 600 spectators who paid just £28 in gate receipts. Rose did not appear in Bristol Rovers' League side, but made 12 appearances — mainly at wing-half — for Hartlepools United.

RUSSELL, James Walker   **1948-49**
Inside-forward. 5ft 10ins. 11st.
Born: Edinburgh, 14 September 1916.
Debut v Gateshead (a) 21 August 1948.
Appearances: 24; Goals: 1.
Career: Edinburgh Schoolboys; Queens Park; Heart of Midlothian; Sunderland 9 June 1934; Norwich City 18 May 1938 (fee £1,500);

Middlesbrough and Carlisle United (wartime guest); Crystal Palace December 1946; RAKERS 20 July 1948; Fleetwood cs 1949.
International honours: Scottish Schoolboys, three appearances v Ireland (2) and Wales.
When Jim Russell netted from the penalty-spot against Bradford City on 13 November 1948, his goal brought the Rakers their first point for eight weeks. Up to the mid-season point, Russell's skill, ball-control and swinging crossfield passes had made him the side's outstanding forward. Sadly, his form fell away to the point where he lost his place in mid-February. He was unable to get back into the side as a late season burst of form lifted them clear of the foot of the table. An outstanding schoolboy footballer and a professional with Sunderland at 17 years of age, Russell lost his best footballing years to the war.

SALMON, Leonard A   **1934-36**
Half-back 5ft 7½ins. 10st 8lbs.
Born: West Kirby, 24 June, 1912.
Debut v Hartlepools United (a) 13 October 1934.
Appearances: 30; Goals: 2.
Career: Hoylake; RAKERS amateur 13 August, professional 3 October 1934; South Liverpool 8 August 1936; Burnley during World War Two; Tranmere Rovers September 1946 to cs 1947.
Club honour: South Liverpool, Welsh Cup winners v Cardiff City 4 May 1939.
Len Salmon, a steady young player with good distribution, had a good first season with the Rakers, appearing in 20 League games at right-half. In 1935-6 he was tried at inside-left and scored one goal and provided another against Stockport County in the Rakers' first win of the season. He lost his place shortly afterwards, however, to the newly-signed Norman Greenhalgh, and was then sidelined for four months with a knee injury. In three seasons with South Liverpool prior to the war, Salmon was centre-half in their three successive Lancashire Combination championships. In season 1935-6, Salmon's younger brother, Leslie, an inside-forward who graduated from West Kirby Central, played in the Rakers' Reserve team.

SANDERSON, Frederick Cecil   **1927-28**
Half-back or Inside-forward. 5ft 9ins. 11st 10lbs.
Born: Seaton Delaval, 13 September 1902; Died: Whitley Bay, 26 July 1977.
Debut v Darlington (a) 27 August 1927.
Appearances: 11; Goals: 1.
Career: Seaton Delaval; Newport County 16 August 1923; Stockport County 27 July 1926 (fee £200); RAKERS 6 July 1927; Blyth Spartans August 1928.
A reserve-team player with both Newport County (12 appearances) and Stockport County (two appearances), Fred Sanderson began as first-team right-half with the Rakers, but soon lost his place. Rather surprisingly, he was dropped after the season's best performance, a 6-0 win against Ashington. A workmanlike, adaptable footballer, Sanderson was later reintroduced at inside-right.

SAUNDERS, Leonard James   **1951**
Centre-forward. 5ft 11ins, 12st 10lbs.
Born: Liverpool, 7 January 1928.
Debut v Tranmere Rovers (a) 20 January 1951
(scored two goals).
Appearances: 4; Goals: 2.
Career: West Derby Albion; Stoneycroft FC;
RAKERS amateur January to March 1951;
Stoneycroft FC.
Despite being directly opposed to Harold Bell —
Tranmere Rovers' record-breaking centre-half —
Jimmy Saunders scored twice on his Football
League debut for the Rakers. His goals came before
half-time at Prenton Park and at the interval the
Rakers led their local rivals 3-1. Unfortunately,
the story-book ending was denied by Tranmere,
who fought back to win 4-3. Saunders, a plumber
in his father's Liverpool business, began his football
career with West Derby Albion, where he was a
teammate of Don Woan, the Liverpool winger. For
three seasons Saunders averaged about 50 goals
per season in the Zingari League and the Rakers
gambled by pitching him straight into a local 'derby'
attended by over 12,000 spectators. His two-goal
debut certainly justified his selection but in three
subsequent outings, both he and the Rakers failed
to score. The team went from 26 December 1950
to 10 March 1951 — 11 League matches — and
scored only three goals, Saunders' two plus an own-
goal.

SAVAGE, Jack   **1926-27**
Full-back.
Born: Ireland.
Debut v Tranmere Rovers (h) 22 January 1927.
Appearances: 11.
Career: Belfast Distillery; Larne August 1924;
RAKERS 26 June 1926 to cs 1927.
*Representative honours: 2 appearances Irish
League in 1921.*
Twice an Irish League representative during his
Distillery spell, Jack Savage made the bulk of his
Rakers appearances during April and May, when
the regular left-back, Jimmy Jones, was on the
injured list. Despite some impressive displays in
a good run-in to the season, Savage was part of
a sweeping clear-out in the close season to make
way for a new defensive set-up built around new
signings, Len Carr and Jock McDonald.

SAYER, Stanley Charles   **1925**
Centre- or Inside-forward. 5ft 6ins. 11st 7lbs.
Born: Chatham, 2 February 1895; Died:
Westbourne, Dorset, 5 April 1982.
Debut v Barrow (a) 29 August 1925 (scored two
goals).
Appearances: 12; Goals: 5.
Career: Army football; Ramsgate Town; Millwall
Athletic 20 January 1921 (fee £25); Northfleet
August 1922 (fee £25); Tranmere Rovers 15 March
1923 (fee £25); RAKERS 8 July 1925; Wigan
Borough 6 November 1925; Lincoln City 6 March

1926; Southend United 13 July 1927; Dartford
1929.
Signed to replace New Brighton's record-breaking
centre-forward, Jonah Wilcox, Stan Sayer gave early
promise, scoring six goals in the final public trial
and two against Barrow on the opening Saturday
of the season. A brainy player who worked well
with his wingers, Sayer was a provider of opportunities rather than an outright goalscorer. He did
not remain long with the Rakers, assisting three clubs
during 1925-6, when he made 39 appearances and
scored 13 goals. During his Tranmere Rovers days,
he was leading goalscorer in 1922-3 with nine goals,
despite having played in only eight matches. He was
leading scorer again in 1923-4 and, in 1924-5, he
was inside partner to the emerging Dixie Dean. His
career figures were 190 appearances and 51 goals.

SEARCH, John   **1935-36**
Centre-forward. 6ft 1½ins. 12st 10lbs.
Born: Liverpool, 5 February 1915.
Debut v Southport (a) 5 October 1935 (scored one
goal).
Appearances: 6; Goals: 3.
Career: Liobians FC; Lucem FC; Liverpool
amateur 12 May 1933; RAKERS amateur 2 August
1935; Runcorn 1936 to 1949 when he retired as
a player and was appointed club chairman.
Leading goalscorer in the Zingari League when he
led the Lucem's attack, John Search joined New
Brighton after two seasons in reserve at Anfield.

159

After scoring ten goals in Lancashire Combination fixtures, he was given his chance in the League side. He marked his debut with a brilliant goal against Southport. After receiving a pass on the half-way line, he made a fine individual run before netting. He went on to score in each of his next two matches, but his goals dried up as the team's form plummeted, his last three appearances coinciding with defeats of 6-0, 4-0 and 5-0. He had a distinguished war record, reaching the rank of Lt-Colonel. In representative Army football in Italy, he played alongside Stan Cullis and other internationals. A testimonial at Runcorn raised £240 in 1949, after he had retired as a player.

SHAW, Robert E   1932-33
Centre-forward.
Born: Litherland.
Debut v Doncaster Rovers (h) 19 November 1932 (scored two goals).
Appearances: 6; Goals: 3.
Career: Runcorn; Liverpool Cables 1931-2; RAKERS amateur 14 November 1932 to cs 1933.
First given a trial in the Rakers Reserves on 12 November, the young centre-forward made his Football League debut only a fortnight later. He was on the score-sheet within 25 minutes with a fine headed goal and scored again three minutes from time to give New Brighton a 4-3 lead, only for Doncaster Rovers to equalize in the final seconds. After six matches he lost his place during a goalless Christmas programme. Later in the same season, the Rakers fielded two other amateur centre-forwards, J.N.Stevens and W.Lowndes, both of whom made scoring debuts.

SHELTON, George   1926-27
Outside-left. 5ft 10½ins. 11st 4lbs.

Born: Sheffield, 1899; Died: Exeter, 24 February 1934.
Appearances: 24; Goals: 3.
Career: Attercliffe FC; Sheffield Wednesday 23 January 1920; Exeter City, 13 May 1922; RAKERS 27 July 1926 to cs 1927.
In League and cup matches during 1926-7, the outside-left berth was equally shared between George Shelton and David Lyner. Shelton began with Sheffield Wednesday, being one of 42 players used by the Owls in League matches during 1919-20, a season which ended in their relegation from the First Division. After three seasons of mainly reserve football at Hillsborough, Shelton moved to Exeter City, initially as understudy to the Grecian's long service winger, John Dockray. After four years at St James' Park (75 appearances, 7 goals) he joined New Brighton, recording his 100th League appearance during the season. After retiring from football, he returned to Exeter and became licensee of the Bull Hotel, Goldsmith Street. He was only 34 years old when he died, after a short illness.

SHEPHERD, Arthur Leslie   1949-51
Winger. 5ft 8ins. 11st.
Born: Liverpool, 11 May 1922.
Debut v Darlington (h) 20 August 1949 (scored one goal).
Appearances: 30; Goals: 10.
Career: Liverpool 22 April 1946; Wrexham wartime guest during season 1945-6; RAKERS 10 August 1949; South Liverpool August 1951.
On the mark within 16 minutes of his debut for the Rakers, Arthur Shepherd, the younger brother of Liverpool full-back Bill Shepherd, was a strong, go-ahead type of player with plenty of punch near goal. In 1949-50 he appeared on both wings and at centre-forward, scoring eight goals in 22 appearances. He was not alone in finding less success in 1950-51, although his two goals against Oldham Athletic on 2 December ended a run of 14 games without a victory. It was the start of a run of four consecutive wins, but insufficient, in the event, to lift the side to any prolonged improvement in their final season of League football.

SHIELS, James Patrick   1936-38
Outside-left. 5ft 7½ins. 10st 10lbs.
Born: Antrim, 1911.
Debut v Oldham Athletic (a) 29 August 1936.
Appearances: 57; Goals: 8.
Career: Ballymena; Dolphin FC; Belfast Celtic; RAKERS 11 June 1936 to cs 1938.
Club honour: Ballymena, Irish Cup winners 1929.
Paddy Shiels began with the Rakers as an inside-forward, but was considered rather lightweight for the position and was moved to outside-left. He had a difficult time in adapting his game, but made continued improvement as the season progressed, playing a part in most of the Rakers' goals after the mid-season mark. A cartilage injury halted his progress in 1937-8. Injured in the match at Carlisle

United in October, it was a coincidence that his comeback game should also be against the same opponents, when they were the visitors in March 1938.

SHIRLEY, Alexander G   **1946-47**
Outside-right.
Born: Milngavie, 31 October 1921.
Debut v Lincoln City (h) 23 November 1946 (scored two goals).
Appearances: 18; Goals: 3.
Career: Dundee United; Bradford and Halifax Town (wartime guest); RAKERS 11 October 1946; Bradford City 15 August 1947; Mansfield Town, one month's trial August 1948.

GARTH

Alex Shirley scored twice on his debut for New Brighton Reserves against Clitheroe in October 1946 and, one month later, gave a repeat performance by scoring two first-half goals on his Football League debut, against Lincoln City at the Tower. Transferred to Bradford City after one season with the Rakers, Shirley made his debut for the Yorkshire team against New Brighton at the Tower. Anxious to impress against his former colleagues, he forced Rakers' goalkeeper Corbett into action with the first shot of the season, almost immediately after the kick-off.

SMALL, Horace H   **1937-40**
Outside-right. 5ft 6ins. 10st 8lbs.
Born: Connah's Quay, 1913.
Debut v Carlisle United (a) 23 October 1937.

Appearances: 50; Goals: 2.
Career: Flint Amateurs; RAKERS amateur 19 January, professional 22 September 1937 to June 1940.
Injury to Paddy Shiels gave Horace Small the chance to establish a regular place when, to cover the loss of the Irish winger, the Rakers switched Jack Mustard from outside-right to outside-left and introduced Small on the right wing. An extract from the *Wallasey News* match report on his debut said: 'Small played a splendid game and produced football of a high standard. The work of Ainsworth and Small as a right-wing pair was proof that height and weight do not mean everything in football. They had an excellent understanding, and kept the ball on the floor.' In the short-lived Third Division North season of 1939-40, Scottish international Bobby Main had taken over as first-team outside-right but, by October, Small was back and scored the Rakers' first goal in wartime League football.

SMEDLEY, James Henry   **1927-35**
Wing-half. 5ft 8½ins. 11st 4lbs.
Born: Stapleford, Notts, 12 July 1904.
Debut v Crewe Alexandra (a) 10 September 1927.
Appearances: 279; Goals: 12.
Career: Johnson & Barnes Athletic (Nottingham); trials with Chester and Bolton Wanderers; RAKERS amateur 9 September 1927, professional 16 September 1927 to 1 June 1935.
Representative honour: Welsh League XI March 1928.

One of New Brighton's best-ever half-backs, Jimmy Smedley was a hosiery operator who began playing with his works team in the Notts Combination League. A splendidly consistent footballer, Smedley was often in the transfer news. Leicester

City, in particular, were very keen to sign him, but he remained at Rake Lane for eight seasons, always prepared to give his last ounce to help his side to victory. After establishing himself in season 1927-8, Smedley missed only seven League matches in the next five seasons. In his final two seasons, injuries took their toll, but his final total of 279 appearances stands as a wonderful tribute to his consistency. Len Carr (qv) and Jimmy Smedley shared a benefit match, when Everton brought their first team, and the FA Cup, to Rake Lane on 18 September 1933. The game attracted 4,311 spectators, almost 300 more than the average home League gate for the season. It was a fine tribute by the sporting public of Wallasey for two of the club's most popular performers.

SMITH, Walter   1937-39
Inside-forward. 5ft 7ins. 10st 7lbs.
Born: Airdrie, 1914.
Debut v Rochdale (a) 20 November 1937.
Appearances: 16; Goals: 3.
Career: Kirkintilloch Rob Roy; St Mirren; East Stirlingshire; Stranraer; RAKERS 17 November 1937 to September 1939.
Walter Smith, a hard-working inside-forward, found few opportunities with the Rakers. When first introduced, as deputy for Alf Ainsworth, he was reported to 'work the ball well and finish strongly'. He was not at his best in heavy conditions, however, and played his best games as an emergency winger. In this position he appeared to find more opportunity to express his traditional Scottish ball-control.

SPENCER, Samuel   1923-25 and 1931-32
Half-back. 5ft 10½ins. 11st 6lbs.
Born: Middlesbrough, 18 January 1902; Died: Wallasey, 3 January 1987.
Debut v Durham City (h) 12 September 1923.
Appearances: 16.
Career: Stoke amateur 28 August 1921; RAKERS 12 July 1923; Mid Rhondda cs 1925; Aberdeen November 1925; Bristol Rovers 2 June 1928; Newry; Port Vale August 1929; RAKERS 11 August 1931 to cs 1932; Winsford United player-coach 23 September 1933.
As deputy half-back in his first spell with the Rakers, Sam Spencer's first-team outings were limited, although he made a good substitute for Jack Reid when the senior pivot was injured during the 1924-5 season. Returning to New Brighton for a second spell, after sampling football in Scotland, Wales and Ireland, he appeared as wing-half and outside-right during 1931-2. A scout for several League clubs after retiring as a player, Sam Spencer was a past president of the Wirral Youth Football League.

STAMPS, John David   1938-39
Inside-forward. 5ft 10ins. 11st 6lbs.
Born: Thrybergh, 2 December 1918.
Debut v Southport (h) 12 November 1938 (scored one goal).

Appearances: 12; Goals: 5.
Career: Silverwood Colliery; Mansfield Town 11 October 1937; RAKERS 12 August 1938; Derby County 19 January 1939 (fee £1,500), wartime guest with Fulham, Southampton and Rotherham United; Shrewsbury Town 17 December 1953; Burton Albion August 1954, player-coach June 1955 and in various managerial capacities until October 1959.
Club honour: Derby County, FA Cup winners 1945-6.
A free-transfer signing from Mansfield Town, Jack Stamps, a successful member of the Rakers' Reserves' attack with 11 goals in 13 matches, was given his first chance when regular inside-left, Albert Wood, was injured. Many supporters had clamoured for his inclusion earlier and they could well have been right, for it took him only seven minutes to get on to the score-sheet against the League leaders, Southport. Undoubtedly benefiting from the experience and skill of his wing partner, Jimmy Stein, Stamps made such rapid progress that his departure from Rake Lane was not unexpected. A quick, hard-shooting and penetrative forward, Stamps scored twice against Charlton Athletic on his debut for Derby County. He repeated the feat when Derby won the first post-war FA Cup Final in April 1946. The scorer of exactly 100 League goals for Derby County, Stamps became totally blind in later life.

STEIN, James   1938-9
Outside-left. 5ft 10½ins. 11st 10lbs.
Born: Coatbridge, Lanarkshire 7 November 1907.
Debut v Stockport County (h) 27 August 1938.
Appearances: 39; Goals: 5.
Career: West Lothian; Dunfermline Athletic; Everton 20 April 1928 (fee £1,500); Burnley 1 October 1936; RAKERS 4 June 1938 to September 1939.
Club honours: Dunfermline Athletic, Scottish League Division Two champions, 1925-6; Everton, Division One champions 1931-2. Division Two champions, 1930-31. FA Cup winners 1933.
Jimmy Stein first made his name by helping Dunfermline Athletic to win promotion to the First Division of the Scottish League. In eight years with Everton he was often referred to as 'the man who helps Dixie Dean to most of his goals'. He was also a good goalscorer himself, frequently on the mark with his cutting-in tactics and quick shooting. In December 1930 he scored four goals from outside-left against Plymouth Argyle in a 9-1 win at Goodison. In the same season he was one of six Everton players to record a double-figure total of Football League goals. It was only the second time that it had been done, Stockport County being the first in 1928-9. A broken leg in Everton's 1935 tour of Switzerland sidelined him until February 1936 and ended his Everton career. After two years with Burnley he joined the Rakers. With New Brighton his subtle skills make him a great favourite, his work on the left wing adding class and power to the attack. He was sent off the field,

162

for the only time in his career, whilst with New Brighton. In view of his previously unblemished record he was fined three guineas (£3.15) but was not suspended.

STEVENS, George Leopold   **1930-32**
Centre-forward.
Born: Wallasey, 18 March 1910; Died: 1987.

Debut v Rochdale (h) 6 December 1930 (scored two goals).
Appearances: 54; Goals: 33.
Career: Wallasey Trams; RAKERS amateur 5 December 1930, professional 29 January 1931; Everton 11 June 1932 (fee £500); Southend United 3 November 1933 (fee £100); Stockport County 13 June 1936 (fee £150); Crewe Alexandra 11 July 1938 to September 1939; wartime guest player with Oldham Athletic during 1943-4.
Club honour: Stockport County, Division Three North champions 1936-7.
Leo Stevens burst on to the Rake Lane scene in December 1930. The slim, fair-haired, tram conductor scored twice on his Football League debut and his fine opportunist skills made him leading goalscorer in the 1930-31 and 1931-2 seasons. Everton signed him prior to the 1932-3 season but, as Dixie Dean's understudy, he made only two First Division appearances. He proved a prolific marksman for all of his subsequent clubs, his career figures being 180 appearances, 112 goals. One of 13 children, two of his five brothers also played for the Rakers. John N. (*qv*) and Bill, who did not play in the League side.

STEVENS, John N   **1931-33**
Centre-forward.
Born: Wallasey.
Debut v Accrington Stanley (a) 7 January 1933 (scored two goals).
Appearances: 3; Goals: 3.
Career: Wallasey amateur football; RAKERS amateur 24 August 1931; Runcorn cs 1933; Ellesmere Port Town January 1934.
Jack Stevens emulated his elder brother, Leo, by scoring twice on his Football League debut for the Rakers. As a utility player in the reserve side, he was brought into the first team as a last-minute replacement for influenza victim, Jimmy Smedley. From centre-forward he scored New Brighton's first two goals in an entertaining encounter which Accrington Stanley won by 5-4. During the German blitz on Wallasey in the summer of 1941, Jack Stevens was awarded the George Medal for the two-hour rescue of a woman and a child from a bombed and extensively damaged house in Manor Road. He showed complete disregard for his own safety in the midst of falling debris and continued enemy action. He won another four life-saving medals during the course of the war.

STIRLAND, Cecil John   **1950-51**
Half-back. 6ft, 11st 10lbs.
Born: Ardwick, Manchester, 15 July 1921.
Debut v Rochdale (a) 14 January 1950.
Appearances: 51.
Career: Junior football; Doncaster Rovers amateur 19 May, professional 19 July 1938; RAKERS 10 January 1950; Scunthorpe United 13 August 1951 (fee £300).
Club honour: Doncaster Rovers, Third Division North champions 1946-7.
Cec Stirland signed professional forms with

Doncaster Rovers a few days after his 17th birthday, but the war intervened and he did not appear in their League side until season 1946-7. In this campaign he made 38 appearances in the Rovers' record-breaking side which totalled 72 points and scored 123 goals. Unfortunately, with much the same team, they were relegated after only one season in Division Two. A first-rate team man, sound without being spectacular, Stirland was a first-team regular during his stay with New Brighton. He left in 1951 to join Scunthorpe United for their second season in the Football League.

TARRANT, Fredrick   1934
Centre-forward.
Born: Hoylake, 1913.
Debut v Lincoln City (h) 22 December 1934.
Appearances: 1.
Career: Hoylake; RAKERS amateur 5 December 1934.
One of several Hoylake recruits to assist the Rakers during 1934-5, Fred Tarrant was promoted one week after scoring twice on his reserve-team debut, against Clitheroe. He had less success on his League debut, although he put in two smart headers which brought good saves from McPhail, the Lincoln City goalkeeper. In this season, the Rakers did not win a home League match until Boxing Day 1934.

TAYLOR, Frederick   1948-50
Outside-right. 5ft 9ins. 10st 6lbs.
Born: Burnley, 24 February 1920; Died: 10 April 1983.
Debut v Gateshead (a) 21 August 1948.
Appearances: 55; Goals: 10.
Career: Briercliffe St James'; Lancashire Schoolboys; Burnley amateur 12 May 1936, professional 12 March 1937; RAKERS 29 July 1948 to 6 May 1950.
Fred Taylor joined the office staff of Burnley FC when he was only 15 years old, along with another young hopeful, Tommy Lawton, who became one of the game's finest centre-forwards. In his last season of schools football, Taylor scored 11 goals in a 24-1 victory and totalled over 100 goals in the season. He played for Burnley Reserves at 16½ and was only 17 when he scored twice on his Football League debut against Norwich City in March 1937. In 1940, he joined the RAF and played several times for Tommy Walker's representative team in India. With New Brighton, Taylor was leading goalscorer, from outside-right, in his first season with ten goals in 38 appearances. His goals dried up in the following season, but he was first choice outside-right when a broken ankle — sustained in a training accident — ended his first-class career. He later became a caretaker in Wallasey.

TAYLOR, Joseph   1929-30
Centre-forward. 5ft 7½ins. 11st 2lbs.
Born: Wigan.
Debut v Wrexham (h) 7 September 1929 (scored one goal).
Appearances: 43; Goals: 21.
Career: Tyldesley amateur football; RAKERS

"TERRIER"
TAYLOR
New BRIGHTON.

amateur 26 August, professional 12 September 1929; Stockport County 11 October 1930; Chesterfield 23 February 1936 to cs 1937.
Club honour: Chesterfield, Third Division North champions 1935-6.
Signed on the recommendation of a former New Brighton player, Peter Kelly (*qv*), Joe Taylor showed distinct promise on his debut. Always prepared to work for the ball rather than wait for it, his bustling methods upset several defences during his first season, when he was leading scorer with 21 goals in 35 appearances. After eight matches of the 1930-31 season, Stockport County signed him. In a lengthy stay at Edgeley Park, he made 82 appearances, switching from a forward to a wing-half role midway through his stay. He joined Chesterfield in time to assist them into Division Two, making 15 appearances in their run-up to the championship.

TEMPLE, Ernest Daniel   1935-36
Goalkeeper. 6ft 2ins. 13st.
Born: West Kirby, 1910.
Debut v Stockport County (h) 14 September 1935.
Appearances: 18.
Career: Heswall; Hoylake; Tranmere Rovers amateur 22 August 1931; RAKERS amateur 22 July, professional 18 September 1935; Tranmere Rovers 17 September 1936 to 10 April 1937.
Tall, fair-haired goalkeeper Ernie Temple had a long association with Tranmere Rovers on amateur forms. However, with Welsh international Albert Gray well established at Prenton Park, Temple made only one League appearance. He found more opportunities in a season at Rake Lane, getting an early debut after Charlie Bird was injured in early September. He kept a clean sheet on his debut,

but in a season when 102 League goals were conceded in 42 matches, he was kept busy, being beaten 44 times in his 18 outings — mathematically speaking, about par for the course. When he returned to Tranmere in 1936-7, he was one of four former Rakers on their books, Amery, Butler and Major being the others.

TEMPLEMAN, Joseph   **1929-31**
Inside-forward or Winger. 5ft 7½ins. 10st.
Born: Liverpool.
Debut v Port Vale (h) 2 September 1929.
Appearances: 6; Goals: 1.
Career: Everton amateur 13 May 1927; RAKERS 17 August 1929 to cs 1931.
'A slim lad of virile style and with clever dribbling skills', was an early verdict on Joe Templeman. His style belonged to the old school of dribblers, but at times he beat himself by attempting too much fancy work. Probably lacking the physique for the rigours of Third Division football, Templeman failed to win his spurs at Rake Lane, spending much of his two years in the Reserves.

THOMPSON, Thomas Henry F   **1923-24**
Inside-left. 5ft 7½ins. 11st 6lbs.
Born: Darlington, 1894.
Debut v Bradford (a) 25 August 1923.
Appearances: 6; Goals: 2.
Career: Spennymoor; West Ham United 10 April 1922; RAKERS 15 August 1923 to cs 1924.
Without Football League experience when he joined New Brighton, Harry Thompson appeared in the Rakers' first-ever Football League fixture, but failed to hold his place. Of his debut, the *Wallasey & Wirral Chronicle* reported: 'Although he lacks something in science, Thompson has robust methods and speed in his favour'. Another verdict, following a mid-season appearance against Wigan Borough was: 'Thompson is a dashing forward, but a little over eager and forceful. At times he reminds one of a bull at a gate.'

TOPPING, Henry   **1938-9 and 1946-48**
Left-back. 5ft 9½ins. 11st 8lbs.
Born: Kearsley, 21 September 1913.
Debut v Stockport County (h) 27 August 1938.
Appearances: 72.
Career: Junior football; Manchester City 27 September 1935; Exeter City 12 May 1937; RAKERS 9 July 1938 to cs 1939; RAKERS (re-registered) 29 July 1946; Prescot Cables May 1948.
Harry Topping lost his place to Arthur Buxton after appearing at left-back in the first five League matches of season 1938-9. After the war, in which he was an Army PT instructor, Topping rejoined the Rakers. In 1946-7 he was part of a most consistent rearguard comprising goalkeeper Corbett (41 appearances); Topping (42 appearances) and full-back partner Richardson (42 appearances). After sharing the right-back berth with Bill Hounslea in 1947-8, he departed into non-League football and was awarded a benefit match by Prescot Cables in April 1951.

TURNER, Alfred S   **1951**
Centre-forward.
Born: United States, 26 December 1929.
Debut v Rochdale (a) 17 February 1951.
Appearances: 4.
Career: Port Sunlight; RAKERS amateur 15 February 1951 to cs 1951.
When Dick Yates was transferred to South Liverpool in December 1950, 20-year-old 'A' team centre-forward Alf Turner was promoted to lead the Reserve team against Southport in the Lancashire Senior Cup. Only two months earlier, he had made a scoring debut for the 'A' team at Blackpool. Turner's ultimate promotion came in February 1951 when, in a desperate attempt to infuse more 'pep' into the forward line, he made his Football League debut at Spotland, Rochdale. New Brighton lost 1-0 and Turner was dropped, being reintroduced in late March after scoring a hat-trick for the Reserves against Clitheroe. Sadly, he could not provide a repeat performance during a three-match run in the seniors over Easter and was deposed by Bill Heggie.

TURNER, Leslie Appleby   **1938-39**
Left-half. 5ft 10ins. 11st 10lbs.
Born: Essington, Doncaster, 25 November 1909.
Debut v Stockport County (h) 27 August 1938.
Appearances: 38; Goals: 1.
Career: Conisborough; Huddersfield Town 2 September 1930; Crewe Alexandra 11 July 1932; Doncaster Rovers 18 May 1935; RAKERS 16 July 1938 to September 1939; Rochdale, wartime guest player season 1940-41.
Signed to replace Billy Fogg at left-half, Leslie Turner was the most impressive of the Rakers's newcomers and maintained a consistently high standard during the season. Turner began with Huddersfield Town, but made his Football League debut with Crewe Alexandra, recording 111 appearances in three seasons at Gresty Road. Then followed three seasons with Doncaster Rovers, two of which were spent in the Second Division. He departed Rake Lane after playing in the opening three fixtures of the 1939-40 season, which was abandoned due to the outbreak of war.

TWELL, Benjamin   **1931-32**
Inside-forward. 5ft 6½ins. 12st 0lbs.
Born: Temple Normanton, 30 August 1903; Died: 17 August 1986.
Debut v Barrow (a) 12 September 1931.
Appearances: 11; Goals: 1.
Career: Staveley Town; Matlock Town; Hardwick Colliery; Grassmoor Ivanhoe; Grimsby Town 18 October 1927; Southport 29 May 1929; RAKERS 22 August 1931; Port Vale 29 September 1932; Fleetwood November 1932; Sutton Town 1933-4.
In 11 League outings Ben Twell failed to collect a winning bonus and his general form was disappointing. Injuries did not help his cause, a twisted knee keeping him out of the first four matches of the season and a leg injury sidelining him for six weeks from early October. For New

Brighton Reserves he scored freely, twice netting four in a match. With Southport in 1929-30 he scored three hat-tricks and five goals against Wrexham on Good Friday, 1930. In this season he played in only 16 League matches, yet totalled 20 goals. Earlier in his career, Twell had recorded 50 goals in less than two seasons with Grimsby Town Reserves. A former collier, Twell was still playing football in the Chesterfield & District League when 42 years of age.

VAUGHTON, Willis   1936-39
Half-back or Full-back 5ft 9½ins. 12st 9lbs.
Born: Sheffield, 20 January 1911.
Debut v Oldham Athletic (a) 29 August 1936.
Appearances: 110.
Career: Chapel-en-le-Frith; Atlas Norfolk Works (Sheffield); Huddersfield Town amateur 7 January 1929; Sheffield United 18 May 1934; Boston United player-coach August 1935; RAKERS 11 August 1936 retired due to injury cs 1939.
An amateur with Huddersfield Town before his 18th birthday, Willis Vaughton had a long spell at Leeds Road, but made only two Football League appearances during season 1933-4. A season with Sheffield United followed (three appearances), before he moved into non-League football, from where the Rakers recruited him. A tireless and sure defender who tackled keenly and put the ball to good use, Vaughton's run of 88 consecutive League appearances was ended by a badly fractured leg sustained at Rake Lane on 4 February 1939. A sunny personality, Vaughton was able to accept his accident with fortitude. Whilst being placed on the stretcher prior to being carried from the field he was heard to remark, "Don't forget lads, I like black grapes best."

WADDELL, George Barr   1923
Half-back. 5ft 8½ins. 12st 2lbs.
Born: Lesmahagow, Lanarkshire, 1889; Died: Sible Hedington, Essex, 17 September 1966.
Debut v Hartlepools United (a) 3 November 1923.
Appearances: 3.
Career: Dalzeil Rovers (Motherwell); Burnbank Athletic; Larkhill United; Glasgow Rangers; Kilmarnock (loan) 1912-13; Bradford City 12 June 1914 (fee £1,000); Preston North End 17 September 1920 (fee £1,750); Oldham Athletic 1 July 1922 (fee £250); Birmingham City 13 October 1922 (fee £325); Hamilton Academical 24 July 1923; RAKERS (one month's trial) 1 November 1923; Wolverhampton Wanderers 30 November 1923; Aberaman Athletic player-coach 1924-5; Chorley 28 November 1925; Fraserburgh player-coach; Preston North End assistant trainer and reserve-team coach; Dick Kerr's FC 1930-31; Ribble Motors FC 1931-2.
A veteran Scottish wing-half, who assisted the Rakers briefly during their first Football League campaign, George Waddell was recruited because of Max Reid's suspension and the failure of both Jack Leadbetter and Sam Spencer to deputize adequately. Oddly enough, Waddell was transferred to the Wolves after playing his final

game for New Brighton at Molineux, when the Rakers were comprehensively beaten 5-1 by the eventual Third North champions.

WADE, Edward   1924-28
Inside-forward. 5ft 7½ins. 10st 12lbs.
Born: Blackpool, 29 September 1901.
Debut v Durham City (a) 4 April 1925.
Appearances: 72; Goals: 24.
Career: South Shore (Blackpool); Burnley 13 May 1922; Lytham cs 1923; RAKERS 30 July 1924; Exeter City 11 July 1928 to cs 1929.
After a trial in Burnley's 'A' team, Ted Wade was signed by the Clarets from South Shore FC, who had been Fylde & District League champions for three seasons in succession. After one season he moved to Lytham, in the West Lancashire League, joining New Brighton a year later. In a relatively long spell at Rake Lane, Wade had his best season in 1926-7, when, operating from the inside-right berth, he scored 13 goals in 31 matches. In a season with Exeter City, he scored five goals in nine League appearances and was leading scorer in the Reserves with 24.

WADSWORTH, Walter   1929-30
Centre-half. 5ft 10½ins, 12st.
Born: Bootle, October 1890; Died October 1951.
Debut v Doncaster Rovers (h) 5 January 1929.
Appearances: 55; Goals: 3.
Career: Lingdale; Ormskirk; Liverpool 23 April 1912; Bristol City 14 May 1926; Flint Town player-manager 2 June 1928; RAKERS 5 January 1929; Oswestry Town September 1930.
Representative honours: Football League.
Club honours: Liverpool, Division One champions 1922, 1923; Bristol City, Third Division South champions 1927.

166

Brought back from non-League football by the Rakers when in his 38th year, Walter Wadsworth immediately solved the club's centre-half problem — five players having preceded him in the pivot's role during the first four months of 1928-9. Wadsworth began as a full-back but developed into a fine pivot in Liverpool's championship winning sides of the early 1920s. As captain of Bristol City, he took the Robins into the Second Division as champions in the first season at Ashton Gate. A younger brother, Harold Wadsworth, was a fine winger whose clubs included Tranmere Rovers, Liverpool, Leicester City, Nottingham Forest and Millwall. A lesser known brother, Charlie Wadsworth, remained an amateur, probably due to business calls in connection with his father's haulage business. He was associated with Tranmere Rovers and Liverpool on amateur forms, but is best remembered in the Wallasey district for his many years of service to the Poulton Rovers club, both as an outside-left and as honorary secretary.

WAITES, Sydney Hastings   **1930-31**
Outside-right. 5ft 9ins. 10st 7lbs.
Born: Gateshead, 20 September 1901.
Debut v Lincoln City (h) 30 August 1930.
Appearances: 37; Goals: 6.
Career: Junior Football; Lincoln City 21 August 1922; Newark cs 1924; Halifax Town 14 September 1925; Stockport County 17 May 1928; Boston cs 1929; RAKERS 22 August 1930 to cs 1931.
As the 1930-31 season dawned, the outside-right position was the last to be filled by the New Brighton directorate — as ever, short of funds — and it was not until the time of the first public trial that Sid Waites was signed. His display had shown artistry and speed and his partnership with Dick Johnson, the former Liverpool inside-forward, ensured that he was well supplied with the ball. It proved a fruitful partnership throughout the 1930-31 season, nevertheless, Waites was one of the several players to be released in the close season, due to lack of funds to pay summer wages. In three seasons with Halifax Town, Sid Waites made 96 appearances and scored 13 goals, but he was unable to break into Stockport County's first-team, scorers of 111 goals and Third Division North runners-up in 1928-9.

WALKER, Robert   **1924-5**
Full-back. 5ft 8½ins. 11st 7lbs.
Born: Bradford, 6 April 1903.
Debut v Darlington (a) 3 September 1924.
Appearances: 16.
Career: Wibsey; Bradford City amateur 22 October 1920, professional 2 October 1921; Bradford amateur 1 November 1922; RAKERS 2 July 1924 to cs 1925.
A First Division debut for Bradford City as a 17-year-old was a promising start, but Bob Walker failed to capitalize. He next appeared, some two and a half years later, for the other Bradford club — Park Avenue — in the Third Division North in 1923-4. In a season with New Brighton he was

given an early opportunity when Jimmy Jones was injured on the opening Saturday of 1924-5. In 16 appearances, in which he turned out in both full-back berths, he proved a useful performer. One critic, however, took exception to his 'stonewall tactics and lack of skill'.

WALKER, Wilfred Stanley   **1931-32**
Goalkeeper. 5ft 10½ins. 11st 6lbs.
Born: Waddington, Lincs.
Debut v Gateshead (h) 29 August 1931.
Appearances: 40.
Career: Waddington; Lincoln City 28 August 1925; Gainsborough Trinity; Grantham; Wolverhampton Wanderers 19 April 1928; RAKERS 11 August 1931; Doncaster Rovers 15 June 1932 to cs 1933.

Stan Walker began with a spell on Lincoln City's books, but he did not appear in their first team. When his Football League debut came, it was for Wolverhampton Wanderers at West Bromwich Albion on 28 December 1929. Sadly, it proved to be his only senior game for them as his left leg was broken (Wolves lost 7-3). In his season with New Brighton, Walker played in all League and FA Cup matches (the League being a 40-match programme on account of Wigan Borough's resignation). In this season, the Rakers finished in 20th position, largely due to their inability to score goals, their 38 League goals being the lowest recorded by any club in the Football League in the 1931-2 season.

WALL, Anthony   **1929**
Outside-left.
Debut v Wrexham (a) 1 April 1929.
Appearances: 1.
Career: Local junior football, RAKERS amateur
1 March 1929.
A late replacement for Charlie Davidson at outside-left in the Easter fixture at the Racecourse, Tony Wall's Football League debut resulted in the Rakers becoming the first team to take three points from Wrexham during the 1928-9 season. Wall's debut was made in freak weather conditions, the wind being so strong that Bert Mehaffy, the Rakers' goalkeeper, hit one goal-kick the whole length of the field, and, without touching another player, the ball crossed the opposite goal-line.

WARD, Henry   **1930-34**
Goalkeeper. 5ft 10½ins. 11st 4lbs.
Born: Wallasey.
Debut v South Shields (a) 15 March 1930.
Appearances: 1.
Career: Old Xaverians; RAKERS amateur 14
March 1930.

GEORGE GREEN

HENRY WARD, NEW BRIGHTON.

Henry Ward was called into service after Kenny Campbell sustained a shoulder injury in a Welsh Cup tie against Oswestry and reserve goalkeeper, Ted Maher, was the victim of a last-minute indisposition. Ward, whose only other game for the Rakers in 1929-30 had resulted in the Reserves claiming their first away victory of the season, at Denbigh, gave an assured display on his Football League debut, assisting the Rakers to their second away win of the season.

WATKINS, Wallace Gwyn   **1936-37**
Outside-left. 5ft 8½ins. 10st 4lbs.
Born: Trehafod, 1917.
Debut v Oldham Athletic (a) 29 August 1936.
Appearances: 1.
Career: Trehafod Ex-Schoolboys; Swansea Town amateur 9 February 1935; Bolton Wanderers amateur 27 March, professional 9 April 1935; RAKERS 30 July 1936; Oldham Athletic (trial) 21 October 1937.
Wallace Watkin's solitary Football League appearance came at Boundary Park, Oldham, on the opening Saturday of season 1936-7. The Rakers' forward line in this match was: Mustard, Ainsworth, Watters, Shiels, Watkins. In the next match, less than a week later, the forward line was: Fogg, Watters, Shiels, Ainsworth, Mustard. Five changes might have seemed somewhat drastic, but the new combination worked as Port Vale were beaten 2-0. Watkins, who had lacked confidence on his debut, became the first reserve-team player to register a hat-trick in 1936-7, but he did not get another chance in the League side. Five outside-lefts were used that season, during which Paddy Shiels established himself as the regular left winger.

WATTERS, John   **1936-37**
Inside-forward. 5ft 9ins. 10st.
Born: Glasgow, 24 September 1913.
Debut v Oldham Athletic (a) 29 August 1936.
Appearances: 19; Goals: 2.
Career: Glasgow Juniors; Ayr United; RAKERS 25 July 1936; Cowdenbeath 14 August 1937; Stockport County 25 August 1947 to cs 1948.
The son of a former Third Lanark player, John Watters, a lightweight Scottish inside-forward, exhibited speed, ball control and a good positional sense. He was a regular first-team player during the first three months of the 1936-7 season, but then lost his place to W.D.Foulkes, as the line was changed in search of more punch. Watters ended his season in the Reserves, where goalscoring came rather more easily, consecutive games in May being won 6-2 against Droylsden and 10-3 against Rossendale United. In a post-war season with Stockport County, Watters made only five Third Division North appearances, but was second-highest goalscorer in the club's Cheshire League side.

WELLS, Archibald   **1946-49**
Inside-forward. 5ft 9ins, 11st.
Born: Clydebank, 4 October 1920.
Debut v Wrexham (a) 31 August 1946.
Appearances: 37; Goals: 4.
Career: Dalmuir Hearts (Glasgow); Vale of Leven; St Anthony's (Glasgow); Hibernian, Stirling Albion October 1940; Alloa Athletic later during season 1940-41; RAKERS 15 July 1946 to 7 May 1949.
One of a strong contingent of Scots recruited by Neil McBain for the Rakers first peacetime season, Archie Wells was one of two recruits from Alloa Athletic, Alex Paterson (qv) being the other. A

part-time professional with Vale of Leven at 17 and a worker in the engineering trade, Wells was not the only footballer in his family. His father played for Queen's Park for three seasons and won two cup medals. He was also a referee for 20 years. A younger brother, Tommy, was a Scottish Juvenile international. Usually seen at inside-right with the Rakers, Wells was a provider rather than a goalscorer, but his goal in the FA Cup against Hull City at the Tower in 1946-7 was said to be the best of the season. Taken first-time from a pass from Alex Shirley, Wells' shot, taken from a difficult angle, was curled beyond the reach of the Hull City goalkeeper and into the corner of the net.

WESTCOTT, Dennis   1935-36
Centre-forward. 5ft 10ins, 11st 4lbs.
Born: Wallasey, 2 July 1917; Died: Stafford, 13 July 1960.
Debut v Mansfield Town (h) 11 January 1936 (scored one goal).
Appearances: 18; Goals: 10.
Career: Wallasey Grocers; Leasowe Road Brickworks (Wallasey); Everton amateur trialist January/February 1935; RAKERS amateur 11 December 1935, professional 31 January 1936; Wolverhampton Wanderers 13 July 1936 (fee £300); Blackburn Rovers 22 April 1948; Manchester City 15 February 1950; Chesterfield 14 June 1952 to cs 1953.
International honours: England Wartime, four appearances 1940-43. Football League representative v Scottish League, 12 March 1947. Club honours: Wolverhampton Wanderers, FA Cup runners-up 1939. War Cup winners 1942.
Nine goals in eight reserve-team matches led to 18-year-old Dennis Westcott getting his big chance and he obliged by scoring the only goal of the match on his Football League debut. Big, strong and tenacious, he certainly put new life into the Rakers' attack, scoring ten goals in his first 12 appearances and finishing the season as leading goalscorer, despite having played in only 18 matches. Three weeks with Everton's 'A' team early in 1935 did not result in his being offered an engagement at Goodison. The Rakers, however, were quick to offer him a professional contract. He was not destined to stay very long with New Brighton, Major Buckley, the Wolverhampton manager, signing him a few days after his 19th birthday. A prolific goalscorer throughout his career, with a Football League aggregate of 172 goals in 259 appearances, Westcott scored four goals in the 1939 FA Cup semi-final against Grimsby Town. He also obtained 11 of his team's 20 goals during the earlier rounds. In the first post-war season, Westcott netted 37 goals in only 35 appearances for the Wolves. A brother, Ronnie Westcott, played for Arsenal in the 1935-6 season.

WHELAN, George F   1931-35
Outside-left.
Born: Wallasey.

Debut v Tranmere Rovers (h) 16 January 1932.
Appearances: 6.
Career: Poulton Villa; RAKERS amateur 16 January 1931 to cs 1935.
"George Whelan centred with promptitude and showed good speed", was a *Wallasey News* comment in 1932, when the local amateur winger played in six consecutive League matches during January and February 1932. In each game his opposite winger, Alf Liggins, was also an amateur. Whelan had a rapid promotion into League action after first being invited for a trial, playing for the Reserves against Northern Nomads in December 1931. A fortnight later he was one of three Wallasey amateurs in the Rakers' team which drew with Tranmere Rovers. One Press comment was that Whelan's natural over-anxiety, on stepping from local amateur football into the Third Division, was not helped by shouted instructions from touch-line spectators!

WHEWELL, William   1928-9 and 1930-31
Centre-forward. 5ft 10½ins, 10st 7lbs.
Debut v Southport (h) 6 October 1928 (scored once).
Appearances: 46; Goals: 18.
Career: Army football; Poole; RAKERS 11 August 1928; Connah's Quay September 1929; RAKERS 23 August 1930 to cs 1931.

On his Football League debut, Bill Whewell scored one of the two late goals which gave the Rakers an unexpected victory over Southport. Despite his scoring debut, he did not receive very favourable Press reports, but he showed steady improvement and became a fixture in the side. He ended his first season as second-highest goalscorer with 13 in 30 appearances. Out of football due to illness for much of 1929-30, Whewell returned to the Rakers for season 1930-31. Despite the departure of Joe Taylor — the first-team centre-forward — Whewell did not secure the position, which Leo Stevens took over with some success.

WHITE, Alfred   **1937**
Inside-forward.
Debut v Wrexham (a) 3 September 1937.
Appearances: 1.
Career: Bangor City; Northwich Victoria; RAKERS (trial) 3 September to 1 October 1937.
Alf White was signed for a month's trial after scoring — appropriately for the 'Whites' — in the season's first public trial at Sandheys Park. After two reserve-team matches, he was selected for the League side's visit to Wrexham. Having lost heavily on their previous five visits to the Racecourse, the Rakers were not expected to win, but a Norman Greenhalgh penalty secured the points. Back into the Reserve side after his solitary League appearance, White failed to impress in the Lancashire Combination and did not win a permanent engagement.

WHITTER, Ernest   **1923-28**
Outside-right. 5ft 7½ins, 10st 12lbs.
Born: Didsbury, Manchester, 26 October 1900; Died: Manchester, January 1930.
Debut v Bradford (h) 1 September 1923.
Appearances: 172; Goals: 33.
Career: Didsbury FC; Nelson (trial); Bradford City 22 August 1922; RAKERS 22 August 1923; Ashton National 30 June 1928 to his demise.

Ernie Whitter joined New Brighton at the time of their first season of League football. He was understudy to Tommy Edge in his first season, but made the position his own in the next four seasons. Although a Lancashire boy, he crossed the Pennines to enter the professional ranks with Bradford City, remaining for one season before joining the Rakers. Elusive and with a great turn of speed, Whitter could centre well but his main forté was a quick dribble followed by a close-in shot or short pass. In season 1927-8, his two headed goals against the Corinthians secured one of the Rakers' most famous FA Cup victories. Whitter was only 29 years old when he died after an attack of pneumonia.

WILCOX, Jonah C   **1924-25**
Centre-forward. 5ft 11½ins, 12st.
Born: Coleford, Devon, 1896.
Debut v Bradford (h) 30 August 1924.
Appearances: 42; Goals: 35.
Career: Coleford Athletic; Frome Town; Abertillery; Bristol City 1919; Bradford 9 September 1922 (fee £600); RAKERS 17 July 1924; Bristol Rovers 25 August 1925; QPR 10 May 1926; Gillingham 24 August 1927; Kidderminster Harriers July 1929.

Following the pre-season trials in August 1924, the *Wallasey & Wirral Chronicle* accurately forecast that the scoring of goals would be a feature of Joe Wilcox's play. He did, in fact, register the highest number of Football League goals ever by a New Brighton player in one season, his prowess as a scorer being a large factor in the team's best-ever placing of third in the Third Division North. Unfortunately, a clause in his contract stipulated that he would be given a free transfer if required, as domestic reasons necessitated his return to the south. A goalscorer on his debut for both of the Bristol clubs, Wilcox had career figures of 218 appearances and 106 goals.

WILLIAMS, Horace   **1926-27**
Centre-forward. 5ft 7ins, 12st.
Born: Pembroke, 1900; Died: Holywell, 1960.
Debut v Ashington (h) 28 August 1926 (scored three goals).
Appearances: 46; Goals: 38.
Career: Liverpool Regiment; Hibernians 1919-24; Wrexham (trial); Mold 1924-26; RAKERS 1 July 1926; Blackpool 14 September 1927 (fee 'over £1,000'); Peterborough & Fletton United March 1928; Macclesfield September 1928; Caernarfon October 1928; Lovell's Athletic December 1928; Hereford United January 1929; Amiens (France) June 1929; Tunbridge Wells Rangers December 1929; Abergele August 1931; Lucerne (Switzerland) coach October 1931; Denbigh Mental Hospital September 1933; Banbury Spencer manager 1934.

Six goals in the two pre-season trials set the scene for Horace Williams' goal blitz in season 1926-7. A hat-trick on his debut was followed by a further 13 goals in his next ten matches. During this period, the *Wrexham Advertiser* commented: 'Williams may have little constructive ability, but his wingmen know that any centre they get across will seldom be wasted, he is an out and out opportunist'. His goal ratio brought a sizeable fee from Blackpool, but he was not a success at Bloomfield Road, being placed on the transfer list at the end of his first season with them. He subsequently gathered no moss on the non-League circuit.

WILLIAMS, Robert Francis   **1949**
Goalkeeper. 5ft 9ins, 10st 8lbs.
Born: Chester, 24 November 1932.

Debut v Stockport County 7 September 1949.
Appearances: 1.
Career: Saltney Juniors; RAKERS amateur 17 August 1949; South Liverpool 30 December 1950; Chester amateur 1951, professional 14 May 1956 to 12 November 1959.
Bobby Williams was quickly thrust into the limelight following his signing — during the interval of the pre-season trial match in August 1949. An injury to first-team goalkeeper, Tom Grimley, gave Williams an early League debut but the young amateur was beaten immediately after the kick-off. Misjudging a bouncing ball, he allowed it to slip through his fingers and over the goal-line. He soon regained his confidence and went on to make several good saves, but New Brighton suffered their first home defeat of the season by 3-1. Later on, Williams surfaced with Chester as an outfield player, signing as a professional after completing his National Service in the Royal Corps of Signals. He was largely employed in the Cheshire County League side at Sealand Road, but made 17 League appearances, and scored twice, in 1956-7. The son of Horace Williams (*qv*), a noted pre-war goal getter, Bobby Williams probably qualifies as the Rakers' youngest Football League debutant at 16 years and nine months.

WILLIAMSON, Alfred   **1929-30**
Centre-forward.
Born: Wallasey.
Debut v Tranmere Rovers (h) 26 December 1929 (scored one goal).
Appearances: 1; Goals: 1.
Career: Wallasey amateur football; RAKERS amateur 26 December 1929 to cs 1930.
Introduced into the Rakers' Reserve side as a trialist in December 1929, Alf Williamson averaged a goal a game in the Welsh League, leading to his selection for the Boxing Day derby against Tranmere Rovers at Sandheys Park. The *Birkenhead News* commented: 'New Brighton made a bold move in introducing a young local amateur, Williamson, as leader of the attack. Whilst by no means a polished performer, there was no mistaking his keenness and he certainly put life into the home attack.' In what proved to be a solitary Football League outing, Williamson had the satisfaction of scoring New Brighton's last goal in a 3-0 win.

WILSON, Samuel G   **1925-27**
Outside-left.
Born: Ireland.
Debut v Lincoln City (a) 3 October 1925.
Appearances: 12.
Career: Shelbourne; Liverpool (trial); RAKERS 25 August 1925 to cs 1927.
One of five outside-lefts who appeared for the Rakers in League matches during the 1925-6 season, Wilson was a lively winger, but his finishing was not as successful as his midfield play. 'Prominent in flashes but finished rather badly', was one Press comment in January 1926 and, two months later, Gene Carney was signed — for the third time — to solve the

Rakers an unexpected point. Wood occupied a different position in each of his first four games for New Brighton, appearing in successive weeks at inside-right, centre-forward, inside-left and centre-half. In season 1938-9, Wood was injured at Doncaster in early November. This left the way open for Jack Stamps, who held the position until his transfer to Derby County in January 1939.

WOODS, Henry   **1933-35**
Centre-forward. 5ft 10ins, 12st.
Born: Wallasey, 1911.
Debut v Darlington (h) 18 November 1933.
Appearances: 1.
Career: Rainford North End; RAKERS amateur 17 November 1933 to cs 1935.
Harry Woods was promoted to first-team duty only a week after his initial appearances in the Rakers' Reserves. In the Liverpool County Combination fixture against Whiston he scored two goals. There was need for a change in the seniors' attack, self evident by the results in the immediately preceding weeks — 0-2, 0-4, 0-3 and 0-6. Wood's debut ended the depressing sequence as the Rakers beat Darlington 3-2. He was retained in the winning team for the following week's Cup tie against Mansfield Town, but New Brighton failed to turn their sustained superiority to account in a goalless draw and Woods subsequently lost his place in the team. In the following season's trials, Woods scored four for the 'Whites' — a team consisting of the first-team defence and reserve-team attack — against the 'Stripes'. He did not get another chance in the first team, however, as Tommy Davis was ever present and scored 26 goals during the season.

outside-left problem. Retained for a second season, Wilson suffered a serious attack of pneumonia and, whilst he made a complete recovery, he did not play in the first team in 1926-7.

WORRALL, Edwin   **1925-27**
Right-back. 5ft 11ins, 11st 10lbs.
Born: Buxton, 2 October 1891; Died: Chesterfield, 24 September 1980.
Debut v Barrow (a) 29 August 1925.
Appearances: 84; Goals: 2.
Career: The Comrades (Buxton), Sheffield Wednesday 8 May 1910; Guest player with Tottenham Hotspur and Chelsea during World War One; Fulham June 1919; Aberdare Athletic 14 May 1923; Watford 31 January 1925; RAKERS 9 June 1925; Southport 27 May 1927; Shirebrook July 1929; Ripley Town 1930-31; Derbyshire Schools Association coach; Tottenham Hotspur scout.
'A thoughtful and stylish player, who possesses a remarkable sense of anticipation' was the *Lancashire Daily Post's* summing up of Ted Worrall. A contemporary player also offered an illuminating insight when recalling that Worrall rarely kicked the ball more than 20 yards, and that his left foot 'was for standing on' — indicating a one-footed approach. He was certainly a consistent performer, being an ever-present during his two seasons with the Rakers, when he formed a good last line of defence with Jimmy Jones. A clerk

WOOD, Albert   **1938-39**
Inside-forward. 5ft 11ins, 12st 11lbs.
Born: Seaham Harbour, 1906.
Debut v Hull City (a) 5 February 1938 (scored once).
Appearances: 46; Goals: 11.
Career: Seaham Harbour; Sunderland 18 August 1927; Fulham 6 May 1931 (part exchange for J.Temple); Crewe Alexandra 6 June 1935; Tranmere Rovers 7 August 1936 (fee £400); RAKERS 5 February 1938 (fee £100), Hartlepools United 16 June 1939.
Big, broad shouldered Albert Wood was an admirably built inside-forward with a powerful left foot and was not afraid to try a shot anywhere around the penalty area. A foraging type of player, unorthodox in some of his movements and with a most deceptive body swerve, he celebrated his New Brighton debut with a goal within two minutes of the kick-off at Hull City, which earned the

YATES, Richard 1949-50
Centre-forward. 5ft 11ins, 11st 10lbs.
Born: Queensferry, 6 June 1921.
Debut v Darlington (h) 20 August 1949.
Appearances: 43; Goals: 14.
Career: Chester 23 August 1939; Wartime guest player with Wrexham, Reading, Charlton Athletic and Port Vale; Wrexham December 1947; Carlisle November 1948; RAKERS 10 August 1949; South Liverpool 9 December 1950; Colwyn Bay season 1952-3.

Dick Yates, scorer of 36 goals for Chester during 1946-7, was a natural centre-forward with all the desired physical attributes, a powerful shot in either foot and great aerial ability. He made a good start with the Rakers by scoring the first hat-trick for two seasons against one of his previous clubs, Carlisle United. He was club leading scorer in his first season with 13 in 38 appearances, but his form was disappointing in 1950-51, when he did not figure in a winning side in his five League appearances.

in the Borough of Wandsworth council offices during his Fulham spell, Worrall was a nephew of the famous international goalkeeper, Sam Hardy.

WRIGHT, William 1936-40
Right-half. 5ft 10ins, 11st 1lb.
Born: South Hiendley, near Barnsley, 1913.
Debut v Oldham Athletic (h) 29 February 1937.
Appearances: 124.
Career: Frickley Colliery; Bolton Wanderers 15 December 1934; RAKERS 20 February 1936 to January 1940.
Part of a double transfer deal with Bolton Wanderers — long service full-back Norman Richardson being the other recruit from Burnden Park — Billy Wright joined a very poor New Brighton team in the late stages of season 1935-6. Despite early struggles, Wright's wholehearted displays made him a worthy successor to New Brighton's finest right-half, Jimmy Smedley. Remarkably consistent, Wright missed only one game from December 28 1936 to April 29 1939 — a run of 123 League and FA Cup matches. Without a League goal in his career, Billy Wright did score once in the FA Cup for New Brighton, in the 2-2 draw at Crewe in the second round in 1937-8, when the Rakers progressed to the fourth round before losing to Tottenham Hotspur in a replay at White Hart Lane.

Max Reid (right) and his brother Jack (far right) combined to help New Brighton in their first home game.

Match to Remember 1   10 September 1921

New Brighton 3   Whiston Parish 5

THE very first home match of New Brighton FC was the first by a Wallasey professional club since the demise of the old New Brighton Tower team, some 20 years earlier.

Great excitement surrounded this qualifying round of the FA Cup, queues forming early outside Sandheys Park. The Press recorded that a Mr Godwin, father of the club's honorary secretary, was the first spectator through the gates.

The ground was officially opened by Dr Tom Martlew, the chairman of directors, who unfurled the club flag. Prior to the kick-off, the band of the Navy League Homes entertained the crowd. For the benefit of the cameras, Dr Beuverie F.P.McDonald, MP for the borough, kicked-off. The ball was returned to the centre-spot and A.Leadbetter set the game in motion on behalf of Whiston — a team from a small mining village outside Prescot.

A feast of goals proved well worth the price of admission, but Whiston were to be plucky battlers, sweeping New Brighton out of the Cup by a margin of two goals, after having found themselves two goals in arrears in the early stages.

Jack Reid opened the scoring for New Brighton after four minutes, back-heeling a centre from Millward past the bemused Bickerstaffe. Overwhelmingly superior at this stage, New Brighton added to their lead through Jack Lyon, who converted a free-kick taken by Max Reid. In a 20-minute spell before half-time however, Whiston staged a wonderful rally and took the lead through goals by F.Lyon, H.Lyon and A.Leadbetter.

Eight minutes of continual pressure after the interval gave New Brighton the equalizer, David Beattie's drive from 20 yards hitting the back of the net with Bickerstaffe helpless. Then a breakaway by Neve on the Whiston right resulted in Roberts restoring the visitors' lead, this goal being closely followed by another by A.Leadbetter, who was allowed a clear path in which to shoot.

New Brighton: Carpenter; Sheperd, Finney, M.Reid, Hulme, Paterson, Pickup, Beattie, J.Reid, J.Lyon, Millward.
Whiston Parish: Bickerstaffe; Ferney, Owen, J.Leadbetter, Birks, H.Lyon, Neve, Roberts, A.Leadbetter, F.Lyon, Dagnall.

Referee: Mr B.Pelham (Liverpool)   *Attendance: 4,307*

Lancaster Town 0   New Brighton 1

THE most attractive of the Lancashire Combination fixtures for the season resulted in New Brighton taking both points from the leaders. New Brighton's victory was all the more impressive in view of their team not being at full strength. Captain Hulme was still unfit, as was Millward, their dashing outside-left, whilst Eacock contracted influenza before the match. Their places were filled by Mulligan, John Leadbetter and Clarke respectively.

Lancaster Town had not suffered a home defeat since New Year's Day 1921, but this fine record was upset by the Merseysiders, who proved to be the more effective side on the day.

Max Reid captained New Brighton, who won the toss and faced the sun. They began in fine style with Scott grazing the crossbar with a fierce drive in opening exchanges. Jack Lyon almost netted with a drive which saw Abbott well beaten, but the ball rebounded from the angle of the upright and crossbar. There was no score at half-time.

The Lancastrians re-shuffled their forward line after the interval and the changes brought the home side into a more effective unit. After an injury to Jack Lyon, which forced him to retire for attention, New Brighton scored what proved to be the decisive goal. A partial clearance was collected by Mulligan, whose long-range shot hit the crossbar. From the rebound Clarke dashed up and netted, despite strong protests that he was offside.

Lancaster Town did not lose another home game that season and eventually took the championship of the Lancashire Combination, four points ahead of the Rakers who finished in third position.

Lancaster Town: Abbott; Johnson, Alstead, Boothman, Dickson, Robertson, Proctor, Graham, Brown, Macauley, Wilson.
New Brighton: Peck; Shepherd, Finney, M.Reid, J.Reid, Mulligan, Pickup, Clarke, Lyon, Scott, Leadbetter.

Attendance: 3,000

New Brighton inside-left Scott grazed the Lancaster Town crossbar with a fierce drive in the opening stages of the Lancashire Combination game.

Left-back Alex Finney, shortly to leave New Brighton for Bolton Wanderers, had an outstanding game in the Lancashire Junior Cup Final replay against Chorley.

Match to Remember 3

11 March 1922

New Brighton 2   Chorley 1

THIS replayed Lancashire Junior Cup Final at Burnden Park, Bolton, came one month after the original match, a goalless draw played in a snowstorm on the Preston North End ground before 14,000 spectators.

Two excursion trains from Wallasey were filled to capacity, swelling the attendance to over 15,000, with gate receipts of £670 17s 4d being taken.

Both sides played in change colours, New Brighton in red and Chorley in white. The ground appeared to be on the heavy side, but the conditions did not stop Jack Reid from netting with a swirling shot from 30 yards after only six minutes of play.

After Unsworth, the Chorley winger, missed badly by ballooning the ball over the crossbar from a couple of yards out, New Brighton increased their lead through Scott. Winning a race down the middle against the Chorley backs, his first-time drive found the bottom corner, despite Wilcock's brave effort to save. Play was rarely in the New Brighton area as half-time arrived with the Rakers two goals up.

Chorley began the second half in convincing fashion and after 15 minutes, Davis, receiving the ball from Fishwick, gave Peck no chance with a hard shot from close range. Jack Lyon went through but his shot struck the foot of the post. In reply, Kelly was twice wide by less than a foot and then tested Peck with a long-range drive.

Outstanding in the Rakers' rearguard battle at this stage were Alex Finney (shortly destined for Burnden Park) and the brothers Reid. Tension was eased for a moment when John Leadbetter forced Wilcock into carrying the ball more than two paces, but nothing came from the free-kick. Peck saved in brilliant fashion from Kelly and then did well to clear his lines from a well-placed corner forced by Smith. Chorley were making dangerous progress up the right wing when the final whistle went.

After the presentation of the Cup and medals, New Brighton supporters carried captain Hulme shoulder-high off the field.

New Brighton: Peck; Shepherd, Finney, M.Reid, J.Reid, Hulme, Pickup, Leadbetter, Lyon, Scott, Millward.
Chorley: Wilcock; Leather, Hurst, Taylor, Bennett, Culshaw, Smith, Fishwick, Davis, Kelly, Unsworth.

Attendance: 15,213

Sheffield Wednesday 3   New Brighton 0

ALTHOUGH New Brighton's interest in the FA Cup ended at Hillsborough, their run, which started in September, brought them many congratulations and probably did a great deal to advance their claims for League football. Seven victories and one draw brought the Rakers through to the first round proper, and the third-largest attendance of the day packed into Hillsborough with gate receipts of £2,470 being taken.

New Brighton were slow to settle on a larger than usual pitch. Many of their passes fell short of the mark, giving the Wednesday defence, in which Fred Kean and George Wilson were outstanding, few anxious moments.

The form that New Brighton had exhibited against Coventry City and Crewe Alexandra in earlier rounds was not reproduced. Their tactics of keeping the ball close were not suited to the heavy going, whereas the Wednesday (as they were still known in those days) swung the ball about to great advantage.

Rees Williams, the Wednesday winger, constantly outstripped allcomers and the pick of the New Brighton defence was Niven, whilst goalkeeper Kenny Campbell had a fine game in restricting the scoreline to a single goal by Smailes, until the last few minutes when Binks scored two opportunist goals.

A film of the match was taken by Mr Alvin T.Willis, the enterprising proprietor of the King's Cinema, Liscard Road, New Brighton, for showing on the following Saturday.

Sheffield Wednesday: Davison; Bellas, Dickinson, Kean, Wilson, Brelsford, Henshall, Smailes, Binks, Taylor, R.Williams.
New Brighton: Campbell; Niven, Jones, M.Reid, J.Reid, Graham, Pickup, Gault, Lyon, D.Williams, Carney.

Attendance: 36,082

Scottish international goalkeeper Kenny Campbell played magnificently against Sheffield Wednesday.

177

Peter Quinn, the former Blackpool and Preston forward, scored the equalizer after Bradford had taken a first-minute lead.

Match to Remember 5   25 August 1923

Bradford 1   New Brighton 1

NEW Brighton opened their first season of League football, in the Northern Section of Division Three, with a visit to Bradford, the previous season's runners-up. The Park Avenue club had finished only four points behind champions Nelson and lost only one game at home, creating something of a sensation in the FA Cup first round by beating Everton after a draw at Goodison Park.

The *Wallasey News* suggested that the Rakers would do well to earn a point and when, after only 60 seconds play, Bradford took the lead, Wallaseyans amongst the crowd must have feared the worst. An oblique shot from Peel struck Jimmy Niven and was diverted into the net via the far post, leaving Bert Mehaffy helpless.

New Brighton rallied and play became more even as the Rakers settled down. A corner by Peter Quinn was cleared only with difficulty by the home defence and Jack Lyon might have equalized but was crowded out. Mehaffy was next forced into carrying and from the resultant free-kick, Niven saved a certain goal by heading a shot from Peel over the crossbar.

A brilliant run by Turnbull, which brought a wonderful save from Mehaffy, was a feature of the second half opening. At the other end Thompson netted, but the goal was disallowed for an infringement.

New Brighton were on level terms within eight minutes of the resumption. Following a free-kick near the corner flag, Sam Challinor centred the ball and Quinn scored with a shot through a crowd of legs.

Before the close, Mehaffy made two great saves from Wilcox, the home centre-forward, who was destined to star in New Brighton's second season of League football, in which he netted a record 35 goals.

Bradford: Scattergood; Brandon, McCluggage, Fell, Howie, Hubbert, E.Thompson, McLean, Wilcox, Turnbull, Peel.
New Brighton: Mehaffy; Niven, Jones, M.Reid, J.Reid, Challinor, Edge, Crooks, Lyon, T.H.F.Thompson, Quinn.

Attendance: 8,000

Tranmere Rovers 1   New Brighton 2

ON the previous Saturday, a record crowd of 13,112 had packed into Sandheys Park to witness the first meeting of the two local rivals in a Football League game. Commenting on the goalless draw, the local correspondent wrote in the *Wallasey & Wirral Chronicle*: 'Never since Jonah escaped from the whale's stomach and found himself high and dry on the beach has luck been experienced as that which gave Tranmere Rovers a point in the first League derby with New Brighton at Sandheys Park on Saturday.'

It was, therefore, not without optimism that an unchanged Rakers team travelled to Prenton Park to meet the League leaders for the return match, one week later.

Gates opened at 1.30pm for the 3.15pm kick-off and the 5,000 who saw the match went quite wild with excitement when Jack Lyon scored the winning goal in what was the most exciting match in the history of the Sandheys Park club.

Quite early on, Allan Mathieson hit an upright, but after a goalless first half, the burly Irish international centre-forward gave New Brighton the lead. Tranmere's reply was stunning and spectacular. Following a corner-kick taken by Beswick, Halstead headed the ball forward and Sayer, with an overhead kick, caught Mehaffy totally unaware.

A fine pass from Mathieson sent Quinn away and his centre, cut back from the goal-line, was met by Lyon who headed firmly past Mitchell.

Repeated Tranmere attacks were held at bay, with Bert Mehaffy and the brothers Reid particularly outstanding in the Rakers defence.

Tranmere's challenge for the league leadership faded as the season progressed, Wolverhampton taking the championship with Rochdale one point behind in the runners-up spot. The Rakers finished fifth from bottom, their attack never rising to the standard of their defence.

Tranmere Rovers: Mitchell; Jackson, Stuart, Hawarden, Halstead, Campbell, Beswick, Brown, Sayer, Cartman, Buchan.
New Brighton: Mehaffy; Glover, Jones, M.Reid, J.Reid, Challinor, Edge, Kirsopp, Mathieson, Lyon, Quinn.

Attendance: 15,500

Jack Lyon (left) netted the winner. Former Everton star Billy Kirsopp (far left) also had a fine game in this exciting derby fixture.

Irish international inside-forward Allan Mathieson scored twice as Nelson were put on the rack by New Brighton.

Match to Remember 7   1 November 1924

New Brighton 5   Nelson 0

NEW Brighton retained their unbeaten record in home matches and secured their second 5-0 victory of the season, their first being against Rochdale on 17 September. This win lifted them to second place in the Third Division North table, only two points behind the leaders, Darlington, the eventual champions.

The players wore black armbands in a token of respect for the memory of Mr T.P.Overington, vice-chairman of the club, who died during the week.

Except for the opening stages, the game was almost entirely in New Brighton's favour, although a fine shot from O'Bierne brought a spectacular save from Bert Mehaffy, who leaped upwards and backwards to fist the ball around the post. The Nelson goal had some narrow escapes before Peter Kelly headed past Abbott from a corner-kick by Eugene Carney. Wilcox started the movement which led to the second goal, Allan Mathieson manœuvring cleverly before chipping the ball beyond the Nelson goalkeeper.

In the second half, Mathieson was again on the mark after a shot from Kelly had rebounded from the crossbar. Wilcox added a fourth after his initial drive was parried by Abbott. Then a late run by Carney set up the last goal. He skipped past Lilley to deliver a precision centre which Wilcox turned into the net.

Had the Rakers' away form more closely matched their displays at Sandheys Park, they would have done even better than their final placing of third, level on points with Nelson but with an inferior goal-average.

New Brighton: J.A.C.Mehaffy; Walker, Jones, M.Reid, J.Reid, Collins, Whitter, A.Mathieson, Wilcox, Kelly, Carney.
Nelson: Abbott; Lilley, Phyzaclea, Newnes, Ellerington, Braidwood, Moore, Bottrill, Eddleston, O'Bierne, Cameron.

New Brighton 2   Sheffield Wednesday 1

NEW Brighton's victory over Wednesday was the surprise of the FA Cup third round, but their win was fully deserved and if all their chances had been taken, they would have obtained a bigger margin than the odd goal in three.

The Rakers did not give Wednesday time to settle down. Their direct methods rattled the visitors' defence and it was only over-eagerness which prevented the New Brighton inside men from opening the scoring in the first few minutes.

The pace was fast and furious, each goal coming under pressure in turn. After 11 minutes, Froggatt sent Williams away and the winger returned the ball to Trotter, who gave Wednesday the lead.

Undismayed at this reverse, the home side continued their forceful attack. Blenkinsopp brought down Jimmy Broad in the area but the crowd groaned when Brown saved Allan Mathieson's spot-kick. Fortunately for the Rakers, the referee pointed to the spot again, having seen a infringement. Harry Gee took the second kick and made no mistake.

There was no further scoring in the first half, but 18 minutes after the resumption a brilliant solo dash by Whitter left Blenkinsopp and Felton stranded. When he passed inside to Broad, the centre-forward had a clear field. He went close in before beating Brown with a shot which gave the 'keeper no chance.

The Wednesday rallied after this and, during a long period of pressure on the home goal, Bert Mehaffy was called upon to clear dangerous attacks, remaining cool under pressure and being well supported by his co-defenders.

The Rakers had progressed one round further than ever before but, despite a plucky fight, were subsequently beaten 2-0 at First Division Notts County.

New Brighton: Mehaffy; Worrall, Jones, Morrison, J.Reid, Gee, Whitter, Kelly, Broad, Mathieson, Wilson.
Sheffield Wednesday: Brown; Felton, Blenkinsopp, Lowdell, Froggatt, Marsden, R.Williams, Barrass, Trotter, Hill, Prince.

Attendance: 10,376

Former Burnley wing-half Harry Gee was one of the driving forces behind New Brighton's great win over Sheffield Wednesday.

Irish cap David Lyner scored New Brighton's fourth goal and underlined his international pedigree with a fine performance against luckless Stoke.

2 October 1926

New Brighton 5 Stoke City 0

DESPITE being undefeated leaders of the table, with a goal-difference of 24-4 after nine matches, Stoke were given the surprise of their lives by the manner in which New Brighton swept them aside.

Stoke were never allowed to settle and, within the first two minutes of each half, Horace Williams found the net with close-range efforts. Dixon got his hands to the ball, but failed to prevent it from entering the net for the first goal. When Allan Mathieson added a second, he was able to tap the ball into the unattended goal after Dixon had rushed out in an unsuccessful attempt to clear.

New Brighton's third came in the second minute of the second half, Williams netting with a shot from 25 yards. Then Jack Reid was injured following a collision with Johnson and had to leave the field for 15 minutes. Yet, during his absence, the Rakers scored again, Mathieson's centre being driven home by David Lyner. Whitter, who had a brilliant game on the right wing, added the fifth.

Stoke eventually won the championship, returning to Division Two after one season of Third Division football. It was New Brighton, however, who had the best of the two teams only Football League meetings. The Rakers earned a creditable draw in the return fixture on 19 February 1927.

New Brighton: Mehaffy; Worrall, Jones, Morrison, J.Reid, Gee, Whitter, Wade, Williams, A.Mathieson, Lyner.
Stoke City: Dixon; McGrory, Dawson, Sellars, J.E.Beswick, Eastwood, J.Williams, Davies, Wilson, Johnson, Archibald.

Referee: Mr D.H.Asson (West Bromwich)   *Attendance: 9,715*

New Brighton 7   Nelson 2

DESPITE having to play three matches within the space of five days, New Brighton gave one of their best displays of the season. In a game full of incidents and thrills, Nelson showed plenty of ability but finished badly.

The game had been in progress for half an hour before Wade netted the opening goal for New Brighton. Two more, another from Edward Wade and the other from Horace Williams, followed within seven minutes. Shortly before the interval, John Mathieson, brother of the Irish international, added a fourth goal by coolly lobbing the ball over Mace's head as the goalkeeper rushed out to challenge him.

Inside five minutes of the second half — which began in a downpour of rain — Stevenson netted for the visitors. Two minutes later, he further reduced the arrears, beating Mehaffy from the penalty-spot.

It was not long, however, before Whitter replied, accepting an opening provided by Williams. A handling offence by Rigg resulted in a penalty award to New Brighton, from which Williams made no mistake. Just before the close, George Shelton, the only home forward not to have scored, notched the concluding goal as the game was finished in a hailstorm.

Williams was udoubtedly the best forward on view, despite the fact that he was faced by George Wilson, the former Blackpool, Sheffield Wednesday and England player.

Nelson's attack was led by the youthful Jimmy Hampson, who later that year joined Blackpool with whom he won England recognition, before losing his life in a fishing accident off Fleetwood in January 1938.

New Brighton: Mehaffy; Worrall, Savage, Morrison, J.Reid, Higgins, Whitter, Wade, Williams, J.Mathieson, Shelton.
Nelson: Mace; Broadhurst, Rigg, Bailey, Wilson, Simpson, Hoad, Stevenson, Hampson, Sharp, Bedford.

Attendance: 3,104

Nelson's Jimmy Hampson later made his name in Blackpool's colours and was capped by England. He was to lose his life in tragic circumstances.

New Brighton centre-forward Alex Harley (white shirt) and Corinthians' A.G.Bower in a tussle at Rake Lane.

Match to Remember 11   14 January 1928

New Brighton 2   Corinthians 1

FROM their first appearance out of the tunnel to contest this third-round FA Cup tie at Rake Lane, the premier amateur side of the country were obviously something quite out of the ordinary. To avoid a clash of colours — both sides normally wearing white shirts and blue shorts — the amateurs changed into shirts with a dazzling combination of gold, white and mauve stripes. Dressed in these startling colours, the Corinthians took to the field in nonchalant manner, hands in pockets, to begin shooting-in.

In the first half, kicking up the slope, the amateurs played the better, more settled game. Despite the small pitch, the pronounced slope and the sea of mud, they managed to produce a display of attacking football which saw Hartley open their account after Bert Mehaffy had saved in quick succession from Ashton, Hartley and Doggart. The amateurs netted again shortly afterwards, but an offside decision went against them.

Just on half-time and very much against the run of play, Whitter met a well placed left-wing cross from James Dickie and headed beyond Howard-Baker to level the scores.

It was again from the left that the movement started which led to Whitter heading in the winning goal after 25 minutes of the second half.

A lack of full-time training eventually caused the amateurs to tire in the rain and heavy conditions, and the home side won because they stayed the trying course more consistently.

This was undoubtedly one of New Brighton's most famous victories, but some critics wondered what the Corinthians might have done on a dry pitch.

New Brighton: Mehaffy; McDonald, Carr, Lewis, J.Reid, Morrison, Whitter, Hoddinott, Harley, Laycock, Dickie.
Corinthians: B.Howard-Baker; A.G.Bower, A.E.Knight, W.T.Whewell, A.H.Chadder, C.Hunter, R.W.Robins, F.Hartley, C.T.Ashton, A.G.Doggart, Lieut K.E.Hegan.

Referee: Mr Stott (Tamworth)   *Attendance: 9,256*

New Brighton 6   Lincoln City 1

NEW Brighton fielded an unchanged side for the visit of Lincoln City, who occupied fourth position in the table, only one point behind the leaders, Wrexham.

The game opened in sensational fashion when John Parker, receiving a headed pass from Whewell, drove the ball beyond the reach of the Lincoln goalkeeper to open New Brighton's account within 60 seconds of the kick-off. Five minutes later, the same player headed a second from James Dickie's left-wing cross.

Encouraged by these early successes, the Rakers pressed the Lincoln defence hard, but the interval arrived with no further addition to the score-sheet.

After 12 minutes of the second half 'Jazzo' Kirk volleyed New Brighton's third and added another within a minute. Peter Cowper's two goals were also scored within a minute of each other, Dinsdale netting Lincoln's only goal ten minutes before time.

The Rakers were the better side throughout, but Lincoln were considerably handicapped in the second half by the absence of left-back, Yorke, who was taken to hospital suffering from concussion.

Robert Morrison again justified his selection at centre-half and, despite his lack of inches, he was able to contain the much taller Dinsdale. Excellent assistance in the half-back line was given by Jimmy Smedley and Tommy Lewis, who, in addition to stemming the Lincoln forwards, looked after their own front line with a stream of cleverly-placed passes.

New Brighton: Mehaffy; McDonald, Carr, Lewis, Morrison, Smedley, Cowper, Parker, Whewell, Kirk, Dickie.
Lincoln City: Hill; Worthy, Yorke, Bassnett, Foulkes, Hale, Bosbury, Maidment, Dinsdale, Pringle, Pegg.

Referee: Mr G.Hewitt (St Helens)   *Attendance: 4,387*

*'Jazzo' Kirk scored twice in quick
succession as Lincoln City were
hammered by the Rakers at Sandheys
Park.*

185

The former Liverpool star Walter Wadsworth helped New Brighton continue on their winning way with a good win at Feethams, Darlington.

Match to Remember 13   29 March 1930

Darlington 1   New Brighton 2

CONTINUING on their winning way, New Brighton inflicted Darlington's first home defeat of the season. Much of the credit was due to the defence. Jock McDonald and Len Carr were well-nigh invincible, whilst Wadsworth's craft and great experience effectively subdued Wellock, the Quakers' high-scoring leader.

Kenny Campbell's worth to the side was shown in his clean handling under pressure, especially when he dived full-length to hold a penalty-kick from Wellock.

New Brighton also held the whip-hand in attack with Dick Johnson, the former Liverpool and Stoke player, having a large part in both goals. It was his neat cross to George Pither which produced the equalizer, after Darlington had taken an early lead through Rand. Joe Taylor scored the Rakers' winning goal after Johnson had supplied the opening.

Darlington, who a week earlier had beaten the leaders, Port Vale, were contained by a fine display by New Brighton's middle trio. It proved to be a good weekend all round for the Rakers as the Reserves won their Welsh League encounter against Connah's Quay by 8-2 at Sandheys Park.

New Brighton: Campbell; McDonald, Carr, Lewis, Wadsworth, Smedley, Cowper, Johnson, Taylor, Oakes, Pither.
Darlington: Harris; Dickson, Brown, Cassidy, Waugh, McGuire, Rand, Siddle, Wellock, Laycock, Vine.

Referee: Mr A. Taylor (Wigan)   *Attendance: 3,705*

186

New Brighton 5   York City 3

VISITORS York City might have been expected to tire after their heavy FA Cup programme, two second-round matches against Nelson, the first abandoned before full-time, having occupied their attentions in the week prior to their visit to Rake Lane.

In heavy conditions, however, York opened in sprightly fashion. Their passing was neat and accurate and they fully deserved their early lead which came from the head of Gardner, their diminutive centre-forward.

Finding their feet at last, the Rakers stunned York with four goals within the space of ten minutes. There was no dainty stuff. The goals came by direct methods and hard running as they unsettled the York defence. George Pither led the goal-rush, cutting in from the wing to send a tremendous drive high into the rigging. Two minutes later, Tommy Lewis headed past Farmery, whilst Johnson added a couple of absolutely first-class goals. After half an hour, Dick Johnson completed his hat-trick, receiving a special ovation from the Rakers' fans.

A minute from the interval, Laycock, the former New Brightonian, reduced the deficit, following the referee's decision to disallow a goal by Gardner for offside.

After ten minutes of the second half, D.Kelly, given yards of room in which to manoeuvre, beat Ken Greatrex with a fast, oblique drive. Shortly afterwards, New Brighton missed the chance of increasing their lead when Lewis, entrusted with a penalty-kick, missed the upright by a foot.

The closing stages were marked by repeated clearances by Billy Matthews, and right on the final whistle, Laycock failed to take a great chance.

New Brighton: Greatrex; McDonald, Carr, Pollock, Matthews, Smedley, Waites, Johnson, Lewis, Oakes, Pither.
York City: Farmery; Brooks, Johnson, Beck, Davis, Thompson, D.Kelly, Cowie, Gardner, Laycock, Sharp.

Referee: Mr I.Caswell (Blackburn)   *Attendance: 2,233*

Former Everton player Jock McDonald proved an inspirational skipper of New Brighton.

Match to Remember 15   6 February 1932

New Brighton 2   Lincoln City 1

THE League leaders and favourites for promotion were attractive visitors in this 'David v Goliath' encounter. The Rakers took the field in bottom spot with the dismal record of only two victories in 26 matches and a goal-difference of 15-53.

Against all the odds, New Brighton started in sensational fashion with a goal within two minutes by Leo Stevens. The centre-forward had manœuvred well in midfield to send Alf Liggins away on the right. Following up, Stevens scored with a firm header from the winger's finely-judged cross.

This good start heartened players and spectators alike and Stevens was an inspiration in the attack, bringing out the best in the two amateur wingers, Liggins and G.F.Whelan.

Although Lincoln equalized through Hall after 22 minutes, the leaders never appeared in control, being unable to settle against the go-ahead, bustling style of the Rakers.

Stevens' second goal, six minutes after the interval, was the result of perfect control and coolness. Making space for himself by deft footwork in restricted space, he hooked the ball high into the net.

In the Lincoln goal, McPhail was unfortunate to finish on the losing side, for he was kept much busier than his opposite number and made several fine saves, including two from Stevens and one from Whelan from point-blank range.

Stevens and Archie Clement were the outstanding men of the game, but in a fine half-back line, Beau Ratcliffe was a dominant figure.

New Brighton: Walker; Clement, Carr, R.Curr, Ratcliffe, Smedley, A.G.Liggins, McCosh, Stevens, Parle, G.F.Whelan.
Lincoln City: McPhail; Worthy, Smith, Burnicle, Young, Pringle, Cartwright, Keetley, Hall, Riley, White.

Referee: Mr A.H.Kingscott (Derby)   *Attendance: 2,768*

New Brighton 1   Liverpool 0

ONE day after the appointment of Mr William J.Sawyer as secretary-manager — after two years without a paid official — New Brighton greeted his arrival by beating Liverpool in the semi-final of the Liverpool Senior Cup.

Despite having held Liverpool — whose team had included eight men with First Division experience — to a goalless draw at Anfield the previous Saturday, few expected the Rakers to survive this second meeting.

In the event, the Rakers won this semi-final replay to qualify to meet Southport in the Final. The only goal of the match was scored by Billy Lowndes after 28 minutes, when he side-stepped Lucas and shot with such speed that Elisha Scott could only deflect the ball on to the inside of the upright and over the line. This goal gave New Brighton a well-deserved victory — a victory which would have been achieved by a bigger margin if Scott, the great international 'keeper, had not been in such excellent form.

New Brighton played with a vigour and confidence that obviously unsettled the Merseysiders until late in the second half, when the Rakers came under severe pressure. On two occasions, amateur goalkeeper George Bradshaw stood between Liverpool and the equalizer. He made brilliant saves from Gunson and McDougall, whilst in one attack, Archie Clement headed off the goal-line from Taylor.

New Brighton met Southport in the Final at Goodison Park on 25 April, and won the Cup for the first time in their history in a most convincing fashion by 6-1.

New Brighton: G.F.Bradshaw; Clement, Carr, Smedley, Amery, Robb, Liggins, Parle, W.Lowndes, Miller, Dickie.
Liverpool: Scott; Lucas, Dabbs, Savage James, McDougall, Taylor, Bruton, Crawford, Rogers, Gunson.

Attendance: 2,000

New Brighton would have beaten Liverpool by an even bigger margin, had it not been for a fine performance from the great Irish international goalkeeper Elisha Scott (left). A year later, Everton offered £250 for his services but Liverpool refused after a wave of protest letters from supporters.

Inside-left Peter Miller, who later went to play for Le Havre in the French League, opened the scoring for New Brighton and then hit their fifth goal as they routed Darlington.

Match to Remember 17   8 April 1933

New Brighton 7   Darlington 1

THIS match was a personal triumph for Billy Lowndes, New Brighton's amateur centre-forward, and the Rakers' great victory lifted them two rungs up the League ladder, giving them hopes of gathering sufficient points from their remaining games to avoid having to seek re-election.

Darlington started well, but after New Brighton had settled down, it was clear that they had the measure of the Quakers. Peter Miller opened the scoring by manœuvring past two defenders before netting with a great shot. An amazing burst of scoring followed 20 minutes later, Lowndes completing his second hat-trick for the first team, scoring three goals in the space of six minutes.

Their 4-0 interval lead was increased soon after the restart, Miller being the scorer. Alf Liggins added a sixth after 28 minutes and then Hurst reduced Darlington's arrears, but within a minute Lowndes scored his fourth and the Rakers' seventh.

New Brighton's attack did exceptionally well on the day and the forwards received plenty of assistance from a strong half-back line in which Beau Ratcliffe, back after injury, made his first appearance for five weeks.

On the last Saturday of the season, the Rakers needed one point from their final home match to avoid having to seek re-election. In the event, they were beaten by Wrexham, the Third Division North runners-up. Darlington, with four points less than New Brighton, were their companions in distress.

New Brighton: G.F.Bradshaw; Clement, Carr, Smedley, Amery, Ratcliffe, Liggins, Parle, W.Lowndes, Miller, Dickie.
Darlington: Knox; Daglish, Allison, Halliday, Waugh, Hopkinson, Coates, Eden, Brown, Hurst, Bonas.

Referee: Mr J.E.Miller   *Attendance: 3,032*

New Brighton 3   Gateshead 0

THE Rakers' Boxing Day success was their first home win of the season and by defeating Gateshead at Rake Lane they ended a four-month 'hoodoo' and brought welcome relief to their long-suffering supporters.

Irish centre-forward Tommy Davis had his best day of the season, scoring a fine hat-trick, and his tally would have been greater, had it not been for the brilliance of Ince, the Gateshead goalkeeper, who undoubtedly prevented his side from being defeated by a higher margin.

Davis' goals came in the 3rd, 25th and 81st minutes. Two of them were made possible by the artistry of Billy Beckett, the young winger, who gave another impressive display.

Charlie Butler, too, impressed with his deft footwork and vision. Beau Ratcliffe and Len Carr did good work in defence but, after the first two goals, there was a tendency for New Brighton to rely too much on defensive methods.

The Rakers, despite a mid-season recovery which saw them finish in 16th position, nevertheless found themselves in a perilous financial position at the season's close. Total home gate receipts were only £3,510 — their bank overdraft was £12,500. Close-season sales of Davis, Butler and Ratcliffe, all to Oldham Athletic, helped keep the Rakers' ship afloat.

New Brighton: A.G.Carr; Ratcliffe, L.Carr, Butler, Amery, Smedley, Brown, Kitching, Davis, Miller, Beckett.
Gateshead: Ince; Neilson, Burgess, Spedding, Mathison, Rivers, Ferguson, McAinsh, Hales, Gray, Younger.

Referee: Mr J.Rennie (Oldham)   *Attendance: 4,047*

Irish international centre-forward Tommy Davis scored a fine hat-trick and might have had more but for the fine form of Ince in the Gateshead goal.

191

Eighteen-year-old Dennis Westcott took his goals tally to six in five games for New Brighton. Westcott's talents meant that he was soon the target of First Division clubs and Wolves snapped him up for £300 in July 1936.

Match to Remember 19   8 February 1936

New Brighton 2   Southport 1

BY scoring the two goals which gave New Brighton their third successive home victory, Dennis Westcott, an 18-year-old local centre-forward, brought his total to six goals in five games.

With both sides in need of vital points to avoid having to seek re-election, there were plenty of exciting incidents. In their first attack, seconds after the game had started, Southport almost took the lead, McCarthy hitting the upright. Savage, lying on the ground, managed to get his head to the rebound and turned it into the net, but an offside decision had already been signalled.

Both goalkeepers were kept busy and Westcott opened the scoring for New Brighton in the ninth minute, when he got an awkward ball under control and, despite restricted space, beat two defenders before netting from close in. His second goal, another of the same high order, came in the 39th minute.

A minute after the interval, Savage scored for Southport, who also had the ball in the net on three more occasions, two being disallowed for offside and one for a handling offence.

New Brighton's main advantage was at half-back. Len Salmon returned after his long, enforced absence and played well, as did Matt Hoggan and George Brock.

New Brighton: Temple; Greenhalgh, Beedles, Salmon, Hoggan, Brock, Lawrence, Ainsworth, Westcott, Lawton, Elliot.
Southport: Talbot; Seagrave, Marshall, Proudfoot, Grice, Howshall, Carter, Wynne, Savage, Read, McCarthy.

Attendance: 2,264

192

New Brighton 4   York City 1

WITH Bill Hullett absent after sustaining a knee injury, Norman Greenhalgh, normally employed as a full-back, was tried as centre-forward and became the seventh leader of the attack this season.

York, who had taken five out of six points over the Easter holidays, started with a rush, but it was New Brighton who scored first, Greenhalgh celebrating his move into the attack by netting an opportunist goal. A minute before the interval he headed against an upright and the rebound was driven home by Leslie Roberts.

A series of long-ball attacks by York immediately after the restart resulted in Whitelaw heading past Willie Hawthorn to reduce York's arrears. Three minutes later, however, Greenhalgh hooked in a fine goal following a corner. Paddy Shiels completed the scoring with a powerful first-time shot in the 68th minute.

Greenhalgh, in his unaccustomed role, added some dash to the New Brighton forward line and, by scoring twice and making another goal, he had fully justified the experiment.

In conjunction with the Rakers' '50,000 Shillings Fund', an aeroplane, piloted by Mr Eric Ward and carrying the Mayor (Councillor G.L.Reakes), flew over the ground in a height-judging contest. Nearly 500 entry cards were submitted and there were seven winners who correctly judged the 'plane's height to be 1,275 feet. Proceeds of £6 9s resulted!

New Brighton: Hawthorn; Vaughton, Richardson, Wright, Bulloch, Fogg, Mustard, Ainsworth, Greenhalgh, Roberts, Shiels.
York City: Wharton; Fox, Legge, Duckworth, Wass, Hathaway, Scott, Whitelaw, Thompson, Comrie, Spooner.

Referee: Mr H.Taylor (Rotherham)   *Attendance: 3,487*

Norman Greenhalgh became the seventh centre-forward tried by New Brighton in 1936-7. Normally a full-back, Greenhalgh celebrated by scoring an opportunist goal and followed up with a second to help the Rakers to an impressive victory.

193

Spurs' Jackie Gibbons scores his side's third goal in the replay against New Brighton at White Hart Lane.

Match to Remember 21   22 January 1938

New Brighton 0   Tottenham Hotspur 0

NEW Brighton eventually failed in their bid to reach the fifth round of the FA Cup competition but, although they were beaten in the replay, they were far from disgraced.

After playing seven games in four rounds, which were watched by an aggregate of 78,327 spectators who paid £5,292, New Brighton bade farewell to the FA Cup for another season. But it was the almost unanimous verdict of Press and public alike that Tottenham were extremely fortunate to escape defeat at Rake Lane.

On winning the toss, Bulloch elected to face the slope and it was not surprising that Spurs' best half was the first. Prompted by Willie Hall, the brains of their attack, they made a sparkling start. Fortunately, Tottenham found Willie Hawthorn in his best form in the Rakers' goal, whilst backs Willis Vaughton and Norman Greenhalgh (soon to depart to Everton) were sound and dependable.

Alf Ainsworth, described by more than one critic as the best forward on view, was involved in the most hotly-debated incident in the match. Ten minutes before the interval, John Mustard rounded Ward and his centre was met by Alf Ainsworth, whose header flashed into the net. There was a terrific roar and a mascot ran on to the field, but the cheers faded when the goal was disallowed for offside.

In subsequent exchanges, Ainsworth lifted the ball on to the angle of the crossbar and upright, and a fierce challenge on Spurs goalkeeper Hooper, by John Montgomery, saw the ball roll free, but Ward cleared off the goal-line in the nick of time.

Almost on time, A.H.Gibbons, Spurs' amateur international inside-forward, streaked through the New Brighton defence, but his final drive whistled across the face of goal.

Tottenham, who finished the season in fifth place in Division Two, progressed to the sixth round of the Cup, where they lost 1-0 to Sunderland at White Hart Lane.

New Brighton: Hawthorn; Vaughton, Greenhalgh, Wright, Bulloch, Fogg, Small, Ainsworth, Montgomery, Roberts, Mustard.
Tottenham Hotspur: Hooper; Ward, Whatney, Howe, Hitchins, Buckingham, Sargent, Hall, Morrison, A.H.Gibbons, Lyman.

Referee: Mr G.V.Scarle (Wiltshire)   *Attendance: 13,029*

New Brighton 5   Hartlepools United 2

NEW Brighton, who had lost only once in their last seven games, gained a comfortable victory, despite being without regular first-team players Hugh Bulloch, Small and Leslie Turner.

At one point the Rakers looked like registering their highest score for seasons when they netted four goals in the space of 12 minutes during the first half.

Jack Stamps opened the scoring in the 19th minute, when he raced through the middle and beat Wallace with a low, powerful left-foot shot. A minute later, Arthur Frost added a second, heading through after the ball had rebounded off a defender. Alf Ainsworth dribbled through to register number-three in the 28th minute. Three minutes later, Frost rounded the goalkeeper to give the Rakers a 4-0 interval lead.

Hartlepools were a much more vital force after the interval, and their skilful inside-right, Woods, scored two good goals in the 52nd and 67th minutes.

Jimmy Stein completed the goalscoring, adding New Brighton's fifth, from what seemed to be an offside position. The former Everton winger was in his best form and had forged an excellent partnership with 20-year-old Stamps.

On the day following this match, it was no surprise when Stamps was transferred to Derby County, whose manager, George Jobey, had no hesitation in outbidding other interested First Division clubs.

Stamps, a free-transfer signing, who had been without a club for three months when New Brighton signed him in August 1938, scored 12 goals in as many reserve-team games and five goals in 12 first-team games.

Stamps, Norman Greenhalgh and Frost all departed Rake Lane within a period of 14 months, swelling the club's coffers by an estimated £6,500.

New Brighton: Gale; Vaughton, Buxton, Wright, S.Hughes, E.Johnson, Smith, Ainsworth, Frost, Stamps, Stein.
Hartlepools United: Wallace; H.Johnson, Calder, Wright, Thomas, Musgrave, Price, Woods, Diamond, West, Self.

Attendance: 1,453

Young Jack Stamps impressed in his short career with New Brighton and he was one of several players who left Rake Lane to help the club's bank balance. Stamps was particularly successful and scored two goals for Derby County in the first post-war FA Cup Final.

195

Alf Hanson, an immaculate winger with Liverpool before the war, guested for New Brighton and scored a hat-trick against Manchester United.

Match to Remember 23   18 May 1940

New Brighton 6   Manchester United 0

SOME excellent football had been served up by the Rakers in the Western Section during the first season of wartime competition, but one of their very best performances was this victory over Manchester United. Oddly enough, the Rakers had been beaten by exactly the same scoreline a fortnight earlier, at Manchester.

United had a strong side, although they arrived a man short. L.Watson, a Wallasey amateur who had only gone to the match as a spectator, found himself in the famous red jersey at inside-left, later moving on to the wing.

The Rakers started well and kept it up throughout the full 90 minutes, beating their visitors by artistry and good teamwork. Waring and Arthur Frost (2) scored in the first half and Alf Hanson netted a fine hat-trick after the interval.

The Rakers wound up their season with a 0-0 draw against Liverpool at Rake Lane. They finished seventh in the table with 23 points from 22 matches. Manchester United finished in fourth place, three points behind Stoke City, who were the champions.

New Brighton: Hawthorn; Ratcliffe, Buxton, Davis, S.Hughes, Murphy, Small, Waring, Frost, Malam, Hanson.
Manchester United: Breedon; Redwood, Roughton, Warner, Manley, McKay, Toseland, Carey, Smith, L.Watson, Wrigglesworth.

Referee: Mr H Hartles (Runcorn)   *Attendance: 1,800*

New Brighton 10   Tranmere Rovers 1

NEW Brighton crashed into the headlines when they topped a succession of high-scoring victories with this crushing defeat of their local rivals.

Earlier in the season, Tranmere had drawn at Rake Lane and won 5-1 at Prenton, so even the most optimistic of the Rakers' supporters could not have anticipated such a scoreline.

Alf Hanson took over the captaincy of New Brighton, following Steve Hughes' departure for the RAF.

Most of the early attacking was done by Tranmere and Cox had one shot smartly saved by Willie Hawthorn. Anderson gave Tranmere the lead within 11 minutes but, two minutes later, Malam equalized with a low cross-shot.

Prompted by Waring, New Brighton assumed complete control of the game and their attack was driven home relentlessly through the match, five goals coming in each half. Malam scored four, Waring three (one penalty) and Arthur Frost, Dellow and Hanson got one each. Thus all the forward line shared in the honours.

It was unfortunate that B.T.Simpson, Rovers' debutant goalkeeper from Liverpool University, should injure his hand early in the match. He was in no way responsible for the heavy defeat, as the home forwards were in peak form and their greater experience and skill completely swamped the Tranmere defence.

The Rakers possessed one of the best forward lines in football during this season and their double-figure score boosted their goals total to 37 in their last seven matches.

New Brighton: Hawthorn; Cook, Morris, Rawcliffe, Longdon, Davis, Dellow, Waring, Frost, Malam, Hanson.
Tranmere Rovers: B.T.Simpson; A.Wishart, Owen, Davies, W.B.Price, Coley, L.Ashcroft, A.W.Cox, P.Stanley, B.Jones, Anderson.

Referee: Mr J.N.Brown (Ormskirk)   *Attendance: 1,450*

'Pongo' Waring was another guest in Rakers' colours during World War Two. Waring, a great centre-forward with Aston Villa, scored 159 League goals in 216 appearances. But the only medal he won was a Third Division North championship medal with Tranmere Rovers in 1938.

Bury 10   New Brighton 5

EACH goal underwent narrow escapes in the opening minutes of this League War Cup-tie at Gigg Lane. Bury scored first after nine minutes, Urmston heading in from a corner by Roberts. New Brighton equalized after 17 minutes, through Waring, but, five minutes later, Davies converted a penalty, awarded after Lowe had handled. Adams made a splendid save from Livingstone's volley, but was beaten by Davies, who scored Bury's third with a well-placed shot.

Urmston added a neatly-taken fourth goal after 32 minutes and Carter scored number-five, direct from a corner-kick, after 40 minutes.

After the interval, clever football by Bury, in far from ideal conditions, brought another goal by Urmston after 55 minutes. The Rakers at last hit back as Arthur Frost caught the Bury defence spreadeagled when he ran through to reduce the lead after 60 minutes. Within a minute, the Rakers were awarded a penalty-kick when Griffiths handled. Malam made no mistake from the spot.

Clever play by Livingstone opened the way for Urmston to score his fourth goal of the match after 71 minutes. Livingstone was on the mark ten minutes later and, within four minutes, Roberts and Urmston brought the score to double figures. In a late flurry, Malam and Dellow completed the afternoon's fireworks.

The irony of the Rakers heavy defeat was that five of the goals were scored for Bury by T.Urmston, a Wallasey policeman attached to the National Fire Service at Wallasey.

Bury: Russell; Quigley, Gemmell, Livingstone, W.Griffiths, Watson, Roberts, G.Davies, Urmston, Dougal, Carter.
New Brighton: Adams; Parker, Lowe, Davies, Hill, Pilling, Dellow, Waring, Frost, Malam, Bland.

Referee: Mr W.D.Murdoch (Manchester)   *Attendance: 1,500*

Such was the unpredictable nature of wartime football that big scores were fairly commonplace. In this season, for instance, the Rakers lost their opening game 13-1 to Manchester United with Jack Rowley scoring seven goals. Then a 7-2 defeat at Liverpool was immediately followed by a 5-5 home draw in the return game against the Reds. In their last three games of the season, New Brighton lost 5-0 and 5-1 and then scored a 5-0 victory.

The 1940-41 season, however, had produced even more startling results, including a 10-1 win over Tranmere Rovers and an 8-5 succcess at Wrexham. Few games yielded less then six goals and many were into double-figure scorelines.

New Brighton 2   Tranmere Rovers 1

A BIG crowd assembled to witness the first meeting of the Birkenhead and New Brighton rivals in a League match since season 1937-8. Some of the spectators occupied the grass surrounding the touch-line as New Brighton won the toss and were first away, Lloyd clearing.

Tranmere were first to score after seven minutes, a low cross by Ashworth was met by Williamson who headed home. This goal urged New Brighton to greater efforts and, after Lloyd had saved well from Pendergast, Wells capped a smart move with an equalizer after 16 minutes.

New Brighton's wingers were giving the Tranmere backs a torrid time, but Bell marshalled his defence skilfully. Just before the interval, Lloyd saved twice from Pendergast, and Atkinson missed from a few yards.

On the resumption, both sides, in turn, got on the attack, Corbett twice being called into action. Tranmere next had a lucky escape when two New Brighton players got in each other's way in the goalmouth.

A breakaway by Tranmere ended in Burns shooting wide, but the Rovers were being outplayed and Lloyd was called upon three times in as many minutes.

Nine minutes from the end, Keith Pritchard beat Nightingale and crossed. McLellan, running in, hit a terrific shot off the crossbar into the net for the deciding goal.

Pritchard, New Brighton's amateur outside-left, shared the game's honours with Harold Bell, the Rovers centre-half, as being the outstanding player of the match.

New Brighton: Corbett; Topping, Richardson, McGeachie, Hill, Paterson, McLellan, Wells, Pendergast, Kilshaw, K.Pritchard.
Tranmere Rovers: Lloyd; Nightingale, Hodgson, Alldis, Bell, Salmon, Ashcroft, Burns, Atkinson, Williamson, Jones.

Referee: Mr W.H.E.Evans (Liverpool)   *Attendance: 14,291*

Alex Paterson, a wing-half from Alloa Athletic, was signed to play in the Rakers' first post-war season. The following season he scored regularly after being switched to inside-forward but could not maintain his early success in that position.

199

Former Bury and Blackburn Rovers inside-forward Don Carter levelled the scores from Stan Roberts' pass.

Match to Remember 27   8 January 1949

Sheffield United 5   New Brighton 2

NEW Brighton had to make two late changes for this third-round FA Cup tie at Bramall Lane, Galbraith and McTaff being replaced by Ted Redfern — making his first FA Cup appearance of the season — and Jim Russell.

Both teams had to change colours, New Brighton playing in blue shirts and white shorts and Sheffield United in white shirts with red collars and sleeves and black shorts.

A blustery cross-wind made ball-control difficult and there was little to choose between the sides at the start, Smith having to save from Bill McClure in the first minute.

After 20 minutes, Sheffield United took the lead, Jones beating Tom Grimley with a left-foot shot from just inside the penalty area.

The lead was short-lived, for the Rakers were level five minutes later, Don Carter netting from a Stan Roberts pass. The exchanges were fast and furious. Tommy Lyon was playing a storming game, his ball-control and distribution being a major feature.

After 38 minutes the Rakers took the lead, Russell's shot from 30 yards deflecting off the head of Latham, leaving Smith helpless.

United were level within five minutes of the restart, through Jones, and the same player completed his hat-trick after 63 minutes. Sheffield United were plainly showing the difference in class between First and Third Division football. Hagan headed a fourth goal from a Thompson corner-kick and Warhurst completed the scoring after 84 minutes.

At the outset of the game, the Rakers were equally as good as their First Division opponents, working tremendously hard and being faster on the ball. Sheffield United had proved to be a different side after the interval, crowning good approach play with three fine goals.

Sheffield United: J.Smith; Bailey, Cox, Jackson, Latham, Cockroft, Thompson, Hagan, F.Smith, Warhurst, Jones.
New Brighton: Grimley; Redfern, Richardson, Lyon, Atkinson, McPeake, Taylor, Russell, Roberts, Carter, McClure.

Referee: Mr J.W.Topliss (Grimsby)   *Attendance: 28,097*

Shrewsbury Town 4   New Brighton 2

THE Rakers' final Football League fixture came at the end of a season which had earlier seen them proudly at the top of the table, boasting the only unbeaten record in the four Leagues.

Shrewsbury, on the other hand, were completing their first season in the League. An announcement just before the kick-off advised the spectators that the Football League had decided to transfer Shrewsbury to the Third Division South for next season.

Shrewsbury took the lead after only three minutes play. Following a corner-kick by Barker, Gorin's shot struck Alf Lees and was diverted beyond Jimmy Jones. Within a quarter of an hour the Rakers were level, Jack Finlay opening the way for Bill Heggie to beat Egglestone.

Before the interval, Shrewsbury regained the lead when Brown raced clear of Gil Alldis and put the ball over Jimmy Jones as the goalkeeper came off his line.

In the second half the Rakers played the livelier football, but Gorin put the issue beyond their reach with two quick goals. Six minutes from the end, Heggie caught the home defence napping to reduce the lead with his second goal.

Less than a month after this match, New Brighton failed to gain readmission to the Third Division North.

Shrewsbury Town: Egglestone; Smale, Fisher, Bullions, Depear, Crutchley, Dodd, Jackson, Gorin, Brown, Barker.
New Brighton: J.A.Jones; Lamont, Galbraith, Alldis, Lees, Barton, Finlay, J.Jones, Heggie, Carter, Musgrave.

Referee: Mr A.C.Denham (Preston)   *Attendance: 7,320*

Alf Lees (right) put through his own goal in New Brighton's last-ever League game. He continued his League career with Crewe. Outside-left Dave Musgrave moved to Preston on trial after the Rakers failed to gain re-election but finished up with Southport and Accrington Stanley.

New Brighton in the Football League 1923-24 to 1950-51

		HOME					AWAY						
	P	W	D	L	F	A	W	D	L	F	A	Pts	Pos
			DIVISION THREE NORTH										
1923-24	42	9	9	3	28	10	2	4	15	12	43	35	18th
1924-25	42	17	3	1	56	16	6	4	11	19	34	53	3rd
1925-26	42	13	4	4	51	29	4	4	13	18	38	42	12th
1926-27	42	14	2	5	49	21	4	8	9	30	46	46	10th
1927-28	42	10	7	4	45	22	4	7	10	27	40	42	10th
1928-29	42	11	3	7	40	28	4	6	11	24	43	39	14th
1929-30	42	13	4	4	48	22	3	4	14	21	57	40	13th
1930-31	42	12	4	5	36	25	1	3	17	13	51	33	19th
1931-32	40	8	5	7	25	23	0	3	17	13	53	24	20th
1932-33	42	8	6	7	42	36	3	4	14	21	52	32	21st
1933-34	42	13	3	5	41	25	1	5	15	21	62	36	15th
1934-35	42	9	6	6	32	25	5	2	14	27	51	36	16th
1935-36	42	8	5	8	29	33	1	1	19	14	69	24	22nd
1936-37	42	10	8	3	36	16	3	3	15	19	54	37	15th
1937-38	42	12	5	4	43	18	3	3	15	17	43	38	13th
1938-39	42	11	2	8	46	32	4	7	10	22	41	39	16th
	670	178	76	81	647	381	48	68	219	318	777	596	
1946-47	42	11	3	7	37	30	3	5	13	20	47	36	18th
1947-48	42	5	6	10	20	28	3	3	15	18	53	25	22nd
1948-49	42	10	4	7	25	19	4	4	13	21	39	36	17th
1949-50	42	10	5	6	27	25	4	5	12	18	38	38	14th
1950-51	46	7	6	10	22	32	4	2	17	18	58	30	24th
	214	43	24	40	131	134	18	19	70	95	235	165	
TOTAL	884	221	100	121	778	515	66	87	289	413	1012	761	

New Brighton Against Other League Clubs

The Rakers met 37 clubs in the Football League between 1923-4 and 1950-51, all the games being played in the Third Division North. Below is their record against each club. Some clubs modified their names (eg Hartlepools United became Hartlepool then Hartlepool United). In all cases the current name used by each club covers all games under previous names.

		HOME					AWAY				
	P	W	D	L	F	A	W	D	L	F	A
ACCRINGTON STANLEY	42	11	4	6	43	24	5	2	14	27	64
ASHINGTON	12	3	3	0	19	8	1	3	2	8	13
BARNSLEY	6	0	0	3	4	8	1	1	1	3	4
BARROW	42	11	4	6	45	27	4	6	11	23	40
BRADFORD	12	2	3	1	9	7	0	2	4	6	12
BRADFORD CITY	18	3	3	3	6	14	0	3	6	10	23
CARLISLE UNITED	32	11	2	3	37	17	2	7	7	17	26
CHESTER CITY	26	4	3	6	17	20	2	1	10	16	37
CHESTERFIELD	22	4	4	3	17	14	2	0	9	7	22
COVENTRY CITY	2	1	0	0	5	1	0	1	0	0	0
CREWE ALEXANDRA	42	12	1	8	43	24	5	1	15	24	57
DARLINGTON	38	11	5	3	34	18	3	0	16	17	47
DONCASTER ROVERS	34	6	5	6	27	31	1	5	11	10	35
DURHAM CITY	10	4	0	1	14	3	0	3	2	4	6
GATESHEAD	32	6	4	6	24	18	3	1	12	13	41
GRIMSBY TOWN	6	1	1	1	4	6	1	1	1	3	3
HALIFAX TOWN	42	14	4	3	34	16	5	7	9	21	35
HARTLEPOOL UNITED	42	13	5	3	41	22	3	3	15	21	53
HULL CITY	18	3	4	2	12	10	0	2	7	5	28
LINCOLN CITY	36	9	1	8	35	29	3	1	14	13	45
MANSFIELD TOWN	18	5	2	2	13	7	1	1	7	8	29
NELSON	14	5	1	1	20	4	1	2	4	7	15
OLDHAM ATHLETIC	18	3	2	4	10	9	0	1	8	7	27
PORT VALE	6	1	1	1	3	2	0	0	3	4	11
ROCHDALE	42	11	3	7	39	27	0	5	16	14	48
ROTHERHAM UNITED	42	12	3	6	48	27	2	7	12	15	46
SCUNTHORPE UNITED	2	0	0	1	1	2	0	0	1	0	6
SHREWSBURY TOWN	2	0	1	0	0	0	0	0	1	2	4
SOUTHPORT	42	11	6	4	34	21	3	4	14	15	44
STOCKPORT COUNTY	34	8	4	5	21	18	2	5	10	12	30
STOKE CITY	2	1	0	0	5	0	0	1	0	1	1
TRANMERE ROVERS	40	6	7	7	18	19	7	1	12	31	46
WALSALL	18	5	3	1	17	11	2	1	6	7	19
WIGAN BOROUGH	16	6	1	1	24	8	1	3	4	8	16
WOLVERHAMPTON W	2	0	0	1	0	1	0	0	1	1	5
WREXHAM	42	9	8	4	26	20	5	6	10	24	38
YORK CITY	30	9	2	4	29	22	1	0	14	9	36
TOTAL	884	221	100	121	778	515	66	87	289	413	1012

1921-22 Lancashire Combination

Manager: Bob Alty

1	Aug	27	(a)	Hurst	W 3-1 Lyon 2, Hulme	
2	Sep	3	(a)	Atherton	L 1-2 Millward	
3		17	(a)	Rochdale	W 2-1 Beattie, Lyon	1,000
4		24	(h)	Rochdale	W 5-2 Lyon 3 (1 pen), Bryson 2	4,000
5	Oct	1	(a)	Morecambe	W 3-1 Lyon, J.Reid, Millward	
6		15	(h)	Fleetwood	W 2-0 Lyon 2 (1 pen)	5,000
7		22	(h)	Chorley	W 4-1 Lyon 3, Scott	2,000
8		29	(h)	Eccles U	W 2-1 Pickup, Scott	4,000
9	Nov	5	(h)	Hurst	W 5-0 Pickup, Lyon 2 (1 pen), Millward, Newman	3,000
10		19	(a)	Dick Kerr's	W 3-2 Lyon 3	
11		26	(h)	Stockport C	L 1-3 Lyon (pen)	
12	Dec	3	(a)	Eccles U	L 0-1	5,000
13		17	(a)	Stockport C	D 0-0	2,000
14		26	(a)	Skelmersdale	L 0-1	
15	Jan	7	(a)	Leyland	W 4-2 Clarke 2, Pickup, Leadbetter	
16		9	(h)	Skelmersdale	W 4-0 Lyon 3, J.Reid	
17		21	(h)	Bacup Borough	W 2-0 Lyon 2	4,000
18		28	(a)	Gt.Harwood	W 4-0 Scott, Millward, Lyon 2	
19	Feb	18	(a)	Lancaster T	W 1-0 Clarke	3,000
20	Mar	4	(a)	Bacup Borough	L 0-1	
21		18	(a)	Fleetwood	L 0-5	
22		22	(h)	Dick Kerr's	W 3-1 Lyon 3 (1 pen)	2,500
23		25	(h)	Gt Harwood	W 4-3 Pickup, Wright 2, Scott	6,000
24		29	(h)	Morecambe	W 3-0 Wright 2, Lyon	
25	Apr	1	(h)	Leyland	W 3-0 Wright 2, Lyon	6,000
26		8	(h)	Horwich RMI	D 1-1 Wright (pen)	
27		14	(h)	Darwen	L 2-3 Lyon 2	7,000
28		15	(a)	Darwen	W 2-1 Pickup, Wright	4,000
29		17	(h)	Lancaster T	L 0-1	8,500
30		22	(h)	Atherton	W 4-0 Lyon 2, Bury (og), Wright	4,000
31		25	(a)	Rossendale U	L 0-3	
32		29	(a)	Horwich RMI	W 1-0 Wright	1,000
33	May	3	(a)	Chorley	D 1-1 Hulme	
34		6	(h)	Rossendale U	W 2-0 Wright 2 (1 pen)	

FINAL LEAGUE POSITION: 3rd in Lancashire Combination

Appearances

Goals

FA Cup

P	Sep	10	(h)	Whiston Parish	L 3-5 J.Reid, Lyon, Beattie	5,000

Appearances

Goals

Lancashire Junior Cup

	Nov	12	(a)	Burscough R	W 3-1 Lyon, Scott, Millward	2,000
	Dec	10	(h)	Bacup Borough	W 3-1 Lyon 3	4,000
SF		31	(h)	Lancaster T	W 2-0 J.Reid, Lyon	7,000
F	Feb	4	(n*)	Chorley	D 0-0	14,000
R	Mar	11	(n†)	Chorley	W 2-0 J.Reid, Scott	15,213

*Played at Deepdale, Preston. †Played at Burnden Park, Bolton.

Appearances

Goals

204

Carpenter	Shepherd	Finney	Jagger	Hulme	Patterson	Pickup	Beattie	Lyon	McQuarrie	Millward	Reid M	Reid J	Lawson	Bryson	Peck	Newman	Scott	Butler	Mulligan	Eacock	Clarke	Leadbetter JH	Wright	Waine	Ormesher	Upton	Pitt	
1	2	3	4	5	6	7	8	9	10	11																		1
1	2	3		5	6	7	8	10		11	4	9																2
	2	3			6	7	8	9		11	4	5	1	10														3
	2	3		6		7	8	9		11	4	5	1	10														4
	2	3		6		7	8	9		11	4	5		10	1													5
	2	3		6		7		9		11	4	5		10	1	8												6
	2	3		6		7		9		11	4	5			1	8	10											7
	2	3		6		7		9		11	4	5			1	8	10											8
	2	3		6		7		9		11	4	5			1	8	10											9
	2	3		6		7		9		11	4	5			1	8	10											10
	2	3		6		7		9	8	11	4	5			1		10	5										11
	2	3		6		7		9		10	4	5			1	8	11											12
		3		6		8		9		11	4	5			1		10		2					7				13
		3		6				9		11	4				1	8	10		2					7				14
	2	3		6		7		9		11	4	5			1		10									8		15
		3		6		7		9		11	4	5			1		10		2	8								16
	2	3		6		7		9		11	4	5			1		10				8							17
	2	3		6		7		9		11	4	5			1		10				8							18
	2	3				7		9			4	5			1		10		6		8	11						19
	2	3		6		7		9		11	4	5			1		10				8							20
	2	3		6		7		9		11	4	5			1		10					8						21
		3		6		7		9			4	5			1		10		2		8	11						22
		3		6		7		9			4	5			1		11		2		8		10					23
	2	3		6		7		9			4	5			1		11				8		10					24
	2	3		6		7		9			4	5			1		11				8		10					25
	2	3		6				9			4	5	1							8		11	10	7				26
	2	3		6		7		9			4	5	1								8	11	10					27
		3		6		7		9			4	5			1				2		8	11	10					28
		3		6		7		9			4	5			1				2		8	11	10					29
	2	3		6		7		10			4	5		11	1	8							9					30
		3		6				10			4	5			1	8			2				9	7			11	31
		3		6				10			4	5			1	8	11		2				9	7				32
		3		6				10			4	5			1		11		2		8		9	7				33
		3		6				10			4	5			1		11		2				9	7	8			34
2	23	34	1	32	3	28	5	34	2	20	33	32	4	5	28	10	22	1	12	2	12	7	12	7	1	1	1	
				2		5	1	34		4		2		2		1	4				3	1	12					

1 own-goal

Carpenter	Shepherd	Finney	Jagger	Hulme	Patterson	Pickup	Beattie	Lyon	McQuarrie	Millward	Reid M	Reid J	
1	2	3		5	6	7	8	10		11	4	9	P
1	1	1		1	1	1	1	1		1	1	1	
							1	1				1	

Carpenter	Shepherd	Finney	Jagger	Hulme	Patterson	Pickup	Beattie	Lyon	McQuarrie	Millward	Reid M	Reid J	Lawson	Bryson	Peck	Newman	Scott	Butler	Mulligan	Eacock	Clarke	Leadbetter JH	Wright	Waine	Ormesher	Upton	
	2	3		6		7		9		11	4	5			1	8	10										
	2	3		6		8		9		11	4	5			1		10							7			
	2	3		6		7		9		11	4	5			1		10									8	SF
	2	3		6		7		9		11	4	5			1		10				8						F
	2	3		6		7		9		11	4	5			1		10				8						R
	5	5		5		5		5		5	5	5			5	1	5				2			1		1	
								5		1		2					2										

1922-23 Lancashire Combination

Manager: Bob Alty until 15 March 1923

1	Aug	26	(a)	Fleetwood	W 2-0 Leadbetter, Gault	
2	Sep	2	(h)	Rossendale U	W 3-0 Williams 2, Carney	7,000
3		5	(a)	Great Harwood	D 2-2 Williams, Crooks	
4		9	(h)	Atherton	W 6-0 Crooks 2, J.Reid, Carney, Lyon 2	7,000
5		16	(a)	Leyland	L 0-1	
6		30	(a)	Darwen	D 1-1 Lyon	5,000
7	Oct	14	(a)	Chorley	D 0-0	5,053
8		28	(h)	Horwich RMI	W 3-2 Leadbetter, Lyon 2 (1 pen)	
9	Nov	25	(h)	Eccles U	W 2-0 Williams, Lyon	4,000
10	Dec	23	(h)	Great Harwood	W 7-0 Williams, Gault 2, Lyon 2, J.Reid, Carney	1,500
11		25	(h)	Skelmersdale	W 5-0 Carney, Lyon 3, J.Reid	4,000
12		26	(h)	New Cross	W 1-0 Lyon	5,000
13	Jan	1	(h)	Hurst	W 2-0 Lyon, J.Reid	3,500
14		3	(a)	Skelmersdale	L 0-1	
15		20	(a)	Rossendale U	L 1-3 Lyon	
16		27	(a)	Rochdale	D 0-0	
17	Feb	10	(h)	Morecambe	W 4-0 Lyon 4	
18		17	(a)	Hurst	W 2-0 Lyon, Williams	
19		24	(a)	Morecambe	D 1-1 Lyon	2,000
20	Mar	3	(a)	New Cross	L 0-2	
21		10	(h)	Rochdale	W 6-1 Lyon 3, Williams 2, Royle	4,000
22		24	(h)	Chorley	L 0-1	5,000
23		30	(h)	Fleetwood	L 1-2 Bryson (pen)	6,000
24	Apr	2	(h)	Lancaster T	L 1-2 Gault	
25		7	(h)	Dick Kerr's	W 5-1 Lyon 2, Bryson, Gault 2	3,000
26		11	(a)	Atherton	L 1-2 Lyon	
27		14	(h)	Darwen	W 4-1 Gault, Lyon 2, J.Reid	5,000
28		16	(a)	Bacup Borough	W 2-0 Lyon, Carney (pen)	
29		18	(a)	Horwich RMI	D 1-1 Leadbetter	
30		21	(a)	Lancaster T	D 0-0	3,000
31		26	(a)	Dick Kerr's	D 0-0	
32		28	(a)	Eccles U	L 0-3	
33		30	(h)	Bacup Borough	W 3-2 Scott, Gault, Williams	
34	May	5	(h)	Leyland	D 3-3 Gault 2, Williams	

FINAL LEAGUE POSITION: 4th in Lancashire Combination

Appearances
Goals

FA Cup

P	Sep	23	(h)	Chester	W 4-2 Lyon 3, Carney	7,300
1Q	Oct	7	(a)	Northwich V	W 1-0 Carney	
2Q		21	(a)	Witton Albion	W 2-1 Leadbetter 2	
3Q	Nov	4	(a)	Sandbach R	W 5-0 Lyon 2, M.Reid, Williams 2	
4Q		18	(h)	Crewe A	D 1-1 Crooks	8,000
R		22	(a)	Crewe A	W 1-0 Pickup	5,000
5Q	Dec	2	(h)	Coventry C	W 3-0 Lyon 3	10,000
6Q		16	(h)	Clapton	W 1-0 Williams	
1	Jan	13	(a)	Sheffield W	L 0-3	36,082

Appearances
Goals

Lancashire Junior Cup (Exempt until second round)

2	Nov	11	(h)	Prescot	W 7-1 J.Reid 2, Crooks 2, Lyon, Williams 2	
3	Dec	9	(h)	Bacup Borough	L 0-1	

Appearances
Goals

Campbell	Niven	Jones	Reid M	Reid J	Graham	Pickup	Gault	Williams	Leadbetter A	Carney	Crooks	Lyon	Brophy	Glover	Beattie	Royle	Neilson	Leadbetter JH	Critchlow	Oakes	Voas	Bryson	Lawrenson	Edge	Balfour	Scott	
1	2	3	4	5	6	7	8	9	10	11																	1
1	2	3	4	5	6	7	9	10		11	8																2
1	2	3	4	5	6	7	9	10		11	8																3
1	2	3	4	5	6	7		10		11	8	9															4
1	2	3	4	5	6	7		10		11	8	9															5
1	2	3	4	5	6	7		10		11	8	9															6
1	2	3		5	6	7	10			11	8	9	4														7
1	2	3	4		6	7	8		10	11		9	5														8
1	2		4	5	6	7		10		11	8	9		3													9
1	2	3	4	5	6	7	8	10		11		9															10
1	2	3	4	5	6		8			11	10	9			7												11
1	2	3	4	5	6		8			11	10	9				7											12
1	2	3	4	5	6		8			11	10	9				7											13
1	2	3	4	5			8			11	10	9			7		6										14
1	2	3		5				10		11		9	4		8	7		6									15
1	2			5						11	10	9	4	3	8	7		6									16
1		3		5	6			10		11	8	9	4			7			2								17
1	2	3		5	6			10		11	8	9	4			7											18
1	2	3	4	9	6					11	8	10	5			7											19
1	2	3	4	5	6					11	8	9			7					10							20
1	2	3	4	5	6			10		11	8	9				7											21
	2	3	4		6			10		11	8	9	5			7					1						22
	2	3	4	5	6					11	8	9				7					1	10					23
	2		4	5	6		8	10		11		9		3		7							1				24
	2		4	5			8			11		9	6	3								10	1	7			25
	2		4	5			8			11	10	9	6	3							1			7			26
	2		4	5			8			11	10	9	6	3									1	7			27
	2		4	5	6		8			11	10	9							3		1			7			28
	2		4	5	6		8		9	11	10								3				1	7			29
	2	3	4	5	6		8			11	10	9											1	7			30
			4	5	6			10		11		9		3					2	8			1		7		31
		3		5	6		8		9		10		4						2				1	7	11		32
		3		2			8	9		6	10		4										1	7	11	5	33
	2	3		5	6		8	9			10		4										1	7	11		34
21	30	25	26	32	27	10	20	17	4	32	27	27	14	7	5	11	1	2	5	2	4	2	9	9	4	1	
				5			10	10	3	5	3	29				1						2				1	

1	2	3	4	5	6	7		10		11	8	9															P
1	2	3	4	5	6	7	10			11	8	9															1Q
1	2	3		5	6	7	8		10	11		9	4														2Q
1	2	3	4	5	6	7		10		11	8	9															3Q
1	2	3	4	5	6	7		10		11	8	9															4Q
1	2		4	5	6	7		10		11	8	9		3													R
1	2	3	4	5	6	7		10		11	8	9															5Q
1	2	3	4	5	6	7	8	10		11		9															6Q
1	2	3	4	5	6	7	8	10		11		9															1
9	9	8	8	9	9	9	4	7	1	9	6	9	1	1													
			1			1		3	2	2	1	8															

1	2	3	4	5	6	7		8	11		10	9															2
1	2	3	4	5	6	7	8		11			9								10							3
2	2	2	2	2	2	2	1	1	2		1	2								1							
				2				2			2	1															

1923-24

Manager: Bert Pelham

1	Aug	25	(a)	Bradford	D 1-1	Quinn	8,000
2		29	(h)	Chesterfield	D 0-0		3,000
3	Sep	1	(h)	Bradford	W 1-0	Challinor	8,000
4		3	(a)	Chesterfield	L 0-1		8,000
5		8	(a)	Accrington S	D 0-0		6,000
6		12	(h)	Durham C	W 2-0	M.Reid, Mathieson	5,500
7		15	(h)	Accrington S	L 1-2	Edge	7,000
8		22	(a)	Halifax T	L 1-2	Thompson	8,000
9		29	(h)	Halifax T	W 2-0	Challinor, Kirsopp	6,000
10	Oct	6	(h)	Tranmere R	D 0-0		13,112
11		13	(a)	Tranmere R	W 2-1	Mathieson, Lyon	15,500
12		20	(h)	Grimsby T	D 0-0		8,000
13		27	(a)	Grimsby T	D 0-0		9,000
14	Nov	3	(a)	Hartlepools U	W 1-0	Jones	3,000
15		10	(h)	Hartlepools U	D 0-0		8,000
16		24	(a)	Wolves	L 1-5	Mathieson	12,000
17	Dec	1	(h)	Wolves	L 0-1		8,000
18		8	(h)	Walsall	W 1-0	Crooks	5,000
19		15	(h)	Crewe A	W 2-1	J.Reid, Mathieson	6,000
20		22	(a)	Ashington	L 0-5		4,000
21		26	(h)	Ashington	D 1-1	J.A.C.Mehaffy (pen)	6,000
22		29	(h)	Wigan Borough	W 5-0	Lyon, Quinn, Thompson, Edge, Crooks	9,000
23	Jan	1	(a)	Southport	L 0-3		6,000
24		5	(a)	Wigan Borough	L 0-1		7,000
25		12	(a)	Walsall	L 0-3		4,000
26		19	(a)	Rotherham C	L 1-3	Crooks	7,000
27		26	(h)	Rotherham C	L 1-2	Burton	5,000
28	Feb	2	(a)	Wrexham	D 0-0		6,000
29		9	(h)	Wrexham	D 0-0		6,000
30		16	(a)	Doncaster R	L 0-2		6,000
31		23	(h)	Doncaster R	W 2-0	Howard 2	6,000
32	Mar	1	(a)	Rochdale	L 2-6	Crooks 2	4,000
33		8	(h)	Rochdale	D 1-1	Howard	6,000
34		15	(h)	Southport	D 0-0		6,000
35		29	(h)	Darlington	D 1-1	Mathieson	4,000
36	Apr	5	(a)	Darlington	L 1-3	Burton	5,200
37		12	(h)	Barrow	W 5-0	Lyon 3, Burton, Crooks	4,000
38		18	(a)	Crewe A	L 0-2		7,000
39		19	(a)	Barrow	L 1-2	Burton	3,000
40		21	(a)	Durham C	L 1-2	Burton	5,000
41		26	(h)	Lincoln C	W 3-1	Howard, J.Reid, Crooks	
42	May	3	(a)	Lincoln C	L 0-1		4,000

FINAL LEAGUE POSITION: 18th in Division Three North

Appearances
Goals

FA Cup

4Q	Nov	17	(a)	Southport	D 1-1	Mathieson	6,000
R		21	(h)	Southport	L 0-1		6,000

Appearances
Goals

Appearance and goals grid (shirt numbers by player and match):

Mehaffy JAC	Mehaffy JW	Niven	Jones J	Reid M	Reid J	Challinor	Edge	Crooks	Lyon	Thompson	Quinn	Mathieson	Whitter	Burton	Critchlow	Gee	Spencer	Kirsopp	Glover	Leadbetter JH	Waddell	Robertson AH	Bryson	Hamilton	Howard	#
1		2	3	4	5	6	7	8	9	10	11															1
1		2	3	4	5	6	7	8	9		11	10														2
1		2	3	4	5	6		8	9			10	7	11												3
1		2	3	4	5	6			8	9		10	7	11												4
1		3	4			5		8	9	11	10	7			2	6										5
1		3	4			6	7		9		10		11	2			5	8								6
1		3	4	5	6	7			9		11	10		2				8								7
1		3	4	5	6	7	8	9	10	11				2												8
1		3	4	5	6	7			10		11	9						8	2							9
1		3	4	5	6	7			10		11	9						8	2							10
1		3	4	5	6	7			10		11	9						8	2							11
1		3		5	6	7			10		11	9				4		8	2							12
1		3		5	6	7			10		11	9						8	2	4						13
1		3		5	6	7			10		11	9						8	2		4					14
1		3		5	6	7	8		10		11	9							2		4					15
1			2		6	7	8				11	9					10	5	3		4					16
1				4	2	6	7	8			11	9							3			5	10			17
1			3	4	5	6	7	8			11	9							2				10			18
1			3	4	5	6	7		10		11	9						8	2							19
1			3	4	5	6	7		10		11	9						8	2							20
1			3	4	2	6	7	8		10	11	9										5				21
1			3	4	5	6	7	8	9	10	11								2							22
1			3	4	5	6	7	8	9	10	11								2							23
1			3	4	5	6		8	9	10			7	11					2							24
	1		3	4	5			8	9			10	7	11		6			2							25
1			3	4	5	6	7	8	9	10				11					2							26
1			3	4	5		7	8	9	10				11		6			2							27
1			4	5	6		8		10		11	9	7	3					2							28
1			3	4	5	6	7	8	10		11	9							2							29
1			3	4	5	6		8			11	10						7	2						9	30
1			3	4	5	6		8			11	10						7	2						9	31
1			3	4	5	6		8			11	10						7	2						9	32
	1		3	4	5	6	7	8				10		11					2						9	33
	1		3	4	5	6		8			11	10						7	2						9	34
1			3	4	5	6				10		8	7	11					2						9	35
1			3	4	5	6		8			10		7	11					2						9	36
	1		3	4	5	6		8			10		7	11					2						9	37
1			3	4	5	6		8	9		10		7	11					2							38
1			3	4	5	6		8	9		10		7	11					2							39
1			3	4	5	6		8			10		7	11					2						9	40
	1		3	4	5	6	7	8			11	10							2						9	41
1			3	4	5	6	7	8			11	10							2						9	42
37	5	4	39	38	39	40	26	32	28	6	30	35	11	15	5	4	3	14	32	1	3	2	2	1	10	
1			1	1	2	2	2	7	5	2	2	5		5				5							4	

Mehaffy JAC	Mehaffy JW	Niven	Jones J	Reid M	Reid J	Challinor	Edge	Crooks	Lyon	Thompson	Quinn	Mathieson	Whitter	Burton	Critchlow	Gee	Spencer	Kirsopp	Glover	Leadbetter JH	Waddell	Robertson AH	Bryson	Hamilton	Howard	
1			3	4	5	6	7		10		11	9						8	2							4Q
1			3	4	5	6	7		10		11	9						8	2							R
2			2	2	2	2	2			2		2	2					2	2							
												1														

1924-25

Manager: Bert Pelham

1	Aug	30	(h)	Bradford	D	0-0		9,000
2	Sep	3	(a)	Darlington	L	1-3	Kelly	5,000
3		6	(a)	Wrexham	D	0-0		8,000
4		13	(h)	Rotherham C	W	3-1	Wilcox, Kelly, Carney (pen)	5,000
5		17	(h)	Rochdale	W	5-0	Kelly, Wilcox 3, Mathieson	6,000
6		20	(a)	Chesterfield	L	0-3		8,361
7		27	(h)	Accrington S	W	4-0	Wilcox 2, Burton, Kelly	
8	Oct	4	(a)	Halifax T	W	2-1	Whitter, Wilcox	10,000
9		11	(h)	Lincoln C	W	4-1	Mathieson, Wilcox, Kelly 2	
10		18	(h)	Grimsby T	W	3-2	Wilcox 2, Mathieson	6,000
11		25	(a)	Barrow	D	1-1	J.Reid	4,000
12	Nov	1	(h)	Nelson	W	5-0	Kelly, Mathieson 2, Wilcox 2	
13		8	(a)	Ashington	D	1-1	Mathieson	3,500
14		22	(a)	Doncaster R	L	0-1		7,000
15	Dec	6	(a)	Crewe A	L	0-1		6,000
16		10	(h)	Durham C	W	4-0	Mathieson, Wilcox, Kelly 2	
17		13	(h)	Wigan Borough	W	3-0	Wilcox 2, Mathieson	
18		20	(a)	Walsall	L	1-2	Wilcox (pen)	
19		26	(h)	Tranmere R	W	1-0	Mathieson	15,000
20		27	(a)	Bradford	L	2-5	Wilcox 2	5,000
21	Jan	1	(a)	Tranmere R	W	3-1	Wilcox 2 (1 pen), Kelly	
22		3	(h)	Wrexham	W	2-1	Whitter, Wilcox (pen)	
23		10	(h)	Southport	D	1-1	Wilcox	6,000
24		17	(a)	Rotherham C	L	1-2	Wilcox	7,000
25		24	(h)	Chesterfield	W	2-1	Wilcox, Mathieson	
26	Feb	7	(h)	Halifax T	W	3-1	Hird 2, Whitter	
27		14	(a)	Lincoln C	L	0-2		8,000
28		21	(a)	Grimsby T	W	3-2	Kelly 2, Mathieson	
29		28	(h)	Barrow	W	3-0	Wilcox 3	
30	Mar	7	(a)	Nelson	L	0-5		5,000
31		14	(h)	Ashington	D	4-4	Wilcox 3 (1 pen), Mathieson	
32		21	(a)	Southport	L	0-2		5,750
33		28	(h)	Doncaster R	L	0-2		
34	Apr	4	(a)	Durham C	D	0-0		2,000
35		10	(h)	Hartlepools U	W	2-0	Wade, Wilcox	6,000
36		11	(h)	Crewe A	W	3-0	Mathieson 2, Wade	
37		13	(a)	Hartlepools U	W	2-0	Wilcox, Mathieson	3,000
38		14	(a)	Rochdale	L	0-2		2,000
39		18	(a)	Wigan Borough	W	1-0	Wade	6,000
40		25	(h)	Walsall	W	3-2	Whitter, Wilcox 2	6,000
41		27	(a)	Accrington S	W	1-0	Mathieson (pen)	1,000
42	May	2	(h)	Darlington	W	1-0	Wilcox	

FINAL LEAGUE POSITION: 3rd in Division Three North

Appearances
Goals

FA Cup

4Q	Nov	15	(h)	Stalybridge C	W	3-0	Kelly 2, Whitter
5Q		29	(h)	Accrington S	D	0-0	
R	Dec	1	(a)	Accrington S	L	2-3	Wilcox 2

Appearances
Goals

Appearances and shirt-numbers grid (shirt number worn by each player in each match):

Mehaffy JAC	Niven	Jones	Reid M	Reid J	Collins	Lacey	Hird	Wilcox	Kelly	Carney	Walker	Gee	Mathieson	Whitter	Burton	Critchlow	Spencer	McCrae	Denwood	Robertson	Gutteridge	Crooks	Wade	Gaffney	#
1	2	3	4	5	6	7	8	9	10	11															1
1	2		4	5	6	7	8	9	10	11	3														2
1	2		4	5	6	7	8	9	10	11	3														3
1	2		4	5		7		9	10	11	3	6	8												4
1	2		4	5				9	10	11	3	6	8	7											5
1	2		4	5				9	10	11	3	6	8	7											6
1	2		4	5				9	10		3	6	8	7	11										7
1			4		6	11		9	10		2		8	7		3	5								8
1			4	5	6	11		9	10		2		8	7		3									9
1			4	5	6	11		9	10		2		8	7		3									10
1		3	4	5	6			9	10	11	2		8	7											11
1		3	4	5	6			9	10	11	2		8	7											12
1		3	4	5				9	10	11	2		8	7				6							13
1		3	4	5				9	10	11	2		8	7				6							14
1	2	3	4	5	6			9	10	11			8	7											15
1	2	3	4	5				9	10	11		6	8	7											16
1	2	3	4	5				9	10	11		6	8	7											17
1	2	3	4	5				9	10	11		6	8	7											18
1	2	3	4	5				9	10	11		6	8	7											19
1	2	3	4					9	10	11		6	8	7			5								20
1	2	3	4	5				9	8	11		6	10	7											21
1	2	3	4	5				9	10	11		6	8	7											22
1	2	3	4					9	10	11		6	8	7			5								23
1	2	3	4	5				9	10	11		6	8	7											24
1	2		4				8	9		11	3	6	10	7			5								25
1		3	4	5			8	9	10	11	2	6		7											26
1	2	3	4				8	9	10	11		6		7			5								27
1	2	3	4					9	10	11		6	8	7				5							28
1	2	3	4					9	10	11		6	8	7				5							29
1	2	3	4					9	10			6	8	7				5	11						30
1	2		4					9	10			6	8	7		3	5		11						31
1	2	3	4		6			9	10				8	7					11	5					32
1	2	3	4					9				6	8	7						11	5	10			33
1	2	3	4					9		11		6	8	7							5	10			34
1	2	3	4					9	10	11		6	8	7										5	35
1	2	3	4					9		11		6	10	7									8	5	36
1	2	3	4					9		11		6	10	7		5							8		37
1	2	3	4					9		11		6	10	7									8	5	38
1	2	3	4					9		11		6	10	7									8	5	39
1	2	3	4					9		11		6	10	7									8	5	40
1	2	3	4				8	9		11		6	10	7										5	41
1		3	4					9			2	6	10	7						11			8	5	42
42	33	31	41	22	11	7	7	42	32	33	16	30	37	38	1	5	5	6	5	1	2	1	7	7	
			1		2			35	12	1			16	4	1						3				
1		3	4	5				9	10	11	2		8	7				6							4Q
1		3	4	5	6			9	10	11	2		8	7											5Q
1		3	4	5	6			9	10	11	2		8	7											R
3		3	3	3	2			3	3	3	3		3	3				1							
								2	2					1											

1925-26

Manager: Bert Pelham

1	Aug	29	(a)	Barrow	W	3-2	Sayer 2, Whitter	5,519
2	Sep	2	(h)	Wrexham	D	2-2	Mathieson, Booth	7,444
3		5	(h)	Ashington	D	1-1	Kelly	6,251
4		9	(a)	Wrexham	W	2-1	Whitter, Sayer	7,437
5		12	(a)	Wigan Borough	L	1-3	Kelly	11,863
6		19	(h)	Tranmere R	W	3-2	M.Reid, Sayer, Gaffney	7,235
7		24	(a)	Doncaster R	L	0-2		3,518
8		26	(h)	Crewe A	L	2-3	Mathieson, J.Reid	5,086
9	Oct	3	(a)	Lincoln C	L	1-3	Mathieson	7,124
10		10	(h)	Southport	W	1-0	Wade	7,032
11		17	(a)	Walsall	L	1-3	Whitter	2,386
12		24	(h)	Chesterfield	L	1-2	Sayer	4,799
13		31	(a)	Hartlepools U	L	1-6	Mathieson (pen)	4,956
14	Nov	7	(h)	Rochdale	W	3-0	Kelly, J.Reid, Dunne	2,142
15		14	(a)	Rotherham U	L	0-1		4,526
16		21	(h)	Halifax T	W	2-1	Dunne, Mathieson	4,086
17	Dec	4	(h)	Durham C	L	1-2	Mathieson	3,010
18		16	(a)	Bradford	L	0-1		4,895
19		19	(h)	Grimsby T	L	1-4	Mathieson	4,101
20		26	(h)	Nelson	D	0-0		6,973
21	Jan	1	(h)	Doncaster R	W	2-1	Kelly, Whitter	3,019
22		2	(h)	Barrow	W	2-1	Broad 2	4,187
23		16	(a)	Ashington	D	1-1	Kelly	3,799
24		20	(a)	Accrington S	W	2-0	Dunne 2 (1 pen)	2,352
25		23	(h)	Wigan Borough	W	4-2	Kelly, Dunne, Whitter, Gee (pen)	4,693
26	Feb	6	(a)	Crewe A	L	1-4	Gee (pen)	4,441
27		13	(h)	Lincoln C	W	5-0	Mathieson 2, Dunne, Duggins 2	4,793
28		20	(a)	Southport	L	2-3	Hird, Wade	4,683
29		27	(h)	Walsall	W	3-2	Duggins, Wade, Mathieson	3,897
30	Mar	6	(a)	Chesterfield	L	0-3		4,873
31		13	(h)	Hartlepools U	W	3-2	Gaffney, Whitter, Gee (pen)	4,198
32		20	(a)	Rochdale	L	1-2	Copitch	6,794
33		27	(h)	Rotherham U	W	5-1	Morrison, Gee (pen), Gaffney, Carney, Wade	3,889
34	Apr	2	(h)	Coventry C	W	5-1	Mathieson, Whitter 2, Morrison 2	5,720
35		3	(a)	Halifax T	L	0-1		6,394
36		5	(a)	Nelson	D	1-1	J.Reid	5,858
37		6	(a)	Coventry C	D	0-0		5,479
38		10	(h)	Accrington S	W	4-1	Whitter, Mathieson, Carney, Broad	4,136
39		12	(a)	Tranmere R	W	1-0	Gee (pen)	12,012
40		17	(a)	Durham C	D	0-0		1,687
41		24	(h)	Bradford	D	1-1	Wade	6,368
42	May	1	(a)	Grimsby T	L	0-1		14,548

FINAL LEAGUE POSITION: 12th in Division Three North

Appearances

Goals

FA Cup

1	Nov	28	(h)	Barrow	W	2-0	Dunne, Whitter	5,005
2	Dec	12	(h)	Darlington	W	2-0	Kelly 2	7,397
3	Jan	9	(h)	Sheffield W	W	2-1	Gee (pen), Broad	10,376
4		30	(a)	Notts C	L	0-2		18,944

Appearances

Goals

212

Football appearance / line-up grid (shirt numbers per match).

Mehaffy JAC	Worrall	Jones	Reid M	Reid J	Booth	Whitter	Mathieson A	Sayer	Kelly	Duggins	Gaffney	Gee	Hird	Foulkes	Wilson	Wade	Hannah	McMurray	Morrison	Dunne	Livingstone	Broad	Copitch	Carney	No.
1	2	3	4	5	6	7	8	9	10	11															1
1	2	3	4	5	6	7	8	9	10	11															2
1	2	3	4		6	7	8	9	10	11	5														3
1	2	3	4		6	7	8	9	10	11	5														4
1	2	3	4		6	7	10	9	8	11	5														5
1	2	3	4			7		9	10	11	5	6	8												6
1	2		4	5		7		9	10	11	3	6	8												7
	2	3	4	5		7	10	9	8	11		6		1											8
	2	3	4	5	6		10	8						1	7	9	11								9
1	2	3	4	5	6		10	8							7	9	11								10
1	2	3	4	5	6	7	10	8								9	11								11
1	2		4	5	6	7	10	9	8						11			3							12
1	2	3	4	5	6		10	7					8		11	9									13
1	2	3	4	5		7	10		8						11				6	9					14
	2	3	4	5		7	10		8					1	11				6	9					15
1	2	3	4	5		7	10		8						11				6	9					16
1	2	3	4	5		7	8								11				6	9	10				17
1	2	3	4	5		7	10		8						11				6		9				18
1	2	3	4	5		7	10		8						11				6		9				19
1	2	3	4	5		7	10		8						11				6		9				20
1	2	3	4	5		7			8						11				6	9	10				21
1	2	3		5	4	7			8						11				6	10	9				22
1	2	3		5	6	7			8	11									4	10	9				23
1	2	3		5		7			8	11		6							4	9	10				24
1	2	3		5		7	10		8	11		6							4	9					25
1	2	3		5		7			4	10		6			11					8	9				26
1	2	3		5		7	10		8	11		6							4	9					27
1	2	3		5		7	10			11		6				8	9		4						28
1	2	3		5		7	10			11		6				8	9		4						29
1	2	3		5		7	10					6							4	9		8		11	30
1	2	3		5		7	10				9	6							4				8	11	31
1	2	3		5		7	10				9	6							4				8	11	32
1	2	3		5		7	10				9	6							4			8		11	33
1	2	3		5		7	10				9	6							4			8		11	34
1	2	3		5		7	10				9	6							4			8		11	35
1	2	3		5		7	10				9	6							4			8		11	36
1	2	3		5		7	10				9	6							4			8		11	37
1	2	3		5		7	10					6							4	9		8		11	38
1	2	3		5		7	10					6							4	9		8		11	39
1	2	3		5		7	10					6							4	9		8		11	40
1	2	3		5		7	10					6							4	9		8		11	41
1	2	3		5		7	10					6	8						4	9				11	42
39	42	40	21	38	12	39	35	12	23	13	12	23	6	3	12	16	6	1	28	8	6	11	3	13	
	1	3	1	9	12	5	6	3	3	5	1				5				3	6		3	1	2	

Mehaffy JAC	Worrall	Jones	Reid M	Reid J	Booth	Whitter	Mathieson A	Sayer	Kelly	Duggins	Gaffney	Gee	Hird	Foulkes	Wilson	Wade	Hannah	McMurray	Morrison	Dunne	Livingstone	Broad	Copitch	Carney	No.
1	2	3	4	5		7	10		8						11				6	9					1
1	2	3	4	5		7	10		8						11				6	9					2
1	2	3		5		7	10		8			6			11				4	9					3
1	2	3		5		7	10		8	11		6							4	9					4
4	4	4	2	4		4	4		4	1		2			3				4	2	2				
				1			2			1									1	1					

1926-27

Manager: Bert Pelham

1	Aug	28	(h)	Ashington	W	4-0	Williams 3, Wade	6,146
2		30	(a)	Bradford	D	1-1	Williams	10,560
3	Sep	4	(a)	Tranmere R	L	1-4	Williams	16,047
4		8	(h)	Bradford	W	3-1	Williams, Gee (pen), A.Mathieson	4,397
5		11	(a)	Wrexham	D	2-2	Williams, J.Reid	9,269
6		15	(a)	Nelson	L	0-2		5,244
7		18	(h)	Wigan Borough	W	3-1	Williams 3	5,530
8		25	(a)	Doncaster R	D	2-2	Whitter, Williams	4,260
9	Oct	2	(h)	Stoke C	W	5-0	Williams 2, A.Mathieson, Whitter, Lyner	9,715
10		9	(a)	Rotherham U	D	0-0		3,624
11		16	(h)	Southport	W	4-1	Williams 3, Wade	6,853
12		23	(a)	Rochdale	D	1-1	Wade	6,751
13		30	(h)	Durham C	W	3-1	Williams, Whitter, A.Mathieson	5,975
14	Nov	6	(a)	Accrington S	W	3-2	Hawksworth, Williams 2	3,301
15		13	(h)	Lincoln C	D	1-1	Whitter	5,690
16		20	(a)	Halifax T	D	2-2	Williams 2	5,581
17	Dec	4	(a)	Crewe A	L	2-3	Williams, Whitter	4,767
18		11	(h)	Hartlepools U	W	2-1	Whitter, Wade	4,319
19		18	(a)	Stockport C	L	0-1		7,406
20		25	(a)	Chesterfield	L	1-3	Wade	7,751
21		27	(h)	Chesterfield	W	1-0	Williams	8,409
22	Jan	8	(h)	Barrow	W	3-1	Whitter 2, Williams	3,728
23		15	(a)	Ashington	W	3-2	Williams 2, Wade	3,291
24		22	(h)	Tranmere R	D	0-0		8,597
25		29	(h)	Wrexham	W	2-1	Whitter, A.Mathieson	5,691
26	Feb	5	(a)	Wigan Borough	L	2-3	Worrall, Williams	4,025
27		12	(h)	Doncaster R	L	0-2		3,677
28		19	(a)	Stoke C	D	1-1	Williams	12,378
29		26	(h)	Rotherham U	W	3-0	Shelton, Williams 2	4,298
30	Mar	5	(a)	Southport	L	2-7	Williams, Shelton	3,153
31		12	(h)	Rochdale	L	1-2	Worrall (pen)	4,442
32		19	(a)	Durham C	D	2-2	Hawksworth, Wade	1,457
33		26	(h)	Accrington S	L	0-1		1,760
34	Apr	2	(a)	Lincoln C	L	1-4	Williams	4,874
35		9	(h)	Halifax T	L	0-3		2,446
36		15	(h)	Walsall	W	3-1	Wade 2, Whitter	4,329
37		18	(a)	Walsall	W	1-0	J.Mathieson	4,010
38		23	(h)	Crewe A	W	3-0	Wade 2, Whitter	2,923
39		27	(h)	Nelson	W	7-2	Wade 2, Williams 2, Shelton, Whitter, J.Mathieson	3,104
40		30	(a)	Hartlepools U	L	0-4		1,983
41	May	2	(a)	Barrow	W	3-0	J.Mathieson, J.Reid, Gee	1,100
42		7	(h)	Stockport C	L	1-2	Whitter	4,650

FINAL LEAGUE POSITION: 10th in Division Three North

Appearances

Goals

FA Cup

1	Nov	27	(a)	Wrexham	D	1-1	Williams	11,009
R	Dec	1	(h)	Wrexham	D	2-2†	Whitter, Worrall (pen)	6,641
2R		6	(n*)	Wrexham	L	1-3	Hawksworth	10,973

*Played at Anfield, Liverpool. †After extra-time

Appearances

Goals

Football team line-up / appearances grid (player positions by match).

Mehaffy	Worrall	Jones	Morrison	Reid J	Gee	Whitter	Wade	Williams	Mathieson A	Shelton	Reid M	Lyner	Foulkes	Hawksworth	Mathieson J	Beattie	Murray	Savage	Higgins	
1	2	3	4	5	6	7	8	9	10	11										1
1	2	3	4	5	6	7	8	9	10	11										2
1	2	3	4	5	6	7	8	9	10	11										3
1	2	3		5	6	7	8	9	10	11	4									4
1	2	3		5	6	7	8	9	10	11	4									5
1	2	3	8	5	6	7		9	10		4	11								6
1	2	3	8	5	6	7		9	10		4	11								7
	2	3	4	5	6	7	8	9	10	11			1							8
1	2	3	4	5	6	7	8	9	10			11								9
1	2	3	4	5	6	7	8	9	10			11								10
1	2	3	4	5	6	7	8	9	10			11								11
1	2	3	4	5	6	7	8	9	10			11								12
1	2	3	4	5	6	7		9	8			11		10						13
1	2	3	4	5	6	7		9				11		10	8					14
1	2	3	4	5	6	7		9				11		10	8					15
1	2	3	4	5	6	7		9	8			11		10						16
	2	3	4	5	6	7		9	8			11	1	10						17
1	2	3	4	5	6	7	8	9				11		10						18
1	2	3	4	5	6	7	8	9				11		10						19
1	2	3	4	5	6	7	8	9				11		10						20
	2	3	4	5	6	7	8	9				11	1	10						21
1	2	3	4	5	6	7	8	9				11		10						22
1	2	3		5		7	8	9				11		10	4	6				23
1	2			5		7	8	9				11		10	4	6	3			24
1	2			5		7	8	9	10			11			4	6	3			25
1	2	3		5	10	7	8	9		11					4	6				26
1	2	3		5		7		9		11				10	8	4	6			27
1	2	3		5		8		9	10	11	4	7		6						28
1	2	3		5		8		9	10	11	4	7		6						29
1	2	3		5		7	8	9	10	11	4						6			30
1	2	3		5		7		9	10	11	4	8					6			31
1	2	3	6			7	8	9		11				10	4	5				32
1	2	3			6	7	8	9		11				10	4	5				33
1	2		6		5	7	8	9	10	11					4	3				34
1	2			5	6	7	8	9		11	4			10		3				35
1	2	4		5		7	8	9		11				10		3	6			36
1	2	4		5		7	8	9		11				10		3	6			37
1	2	4		5		7	8	9		11				10		3	6			38
1	2	4	5			7	8	9		11				10		3	6			39
1	2	4	5			7	8	9		11				10		3	6			40
1	2	4	5	10		7		9		11				8		3	6			41
1	2	4	5			7	8	9		11				10		3	6			42
39	42	31	29	36	30	42	31	41	21	24	9	21	3	17	11	8	7	11	9	
	2		2	2	13	13	34	4	3			1			2	3				

Mehaffy	Worrall	Jones	Morrison	Reid J	Gee	Whitter	Wade	Williams	Mathieson A	Shelton	Reid M	Lyner	Foulkes	Hawksworth	Mathieson J	Beattie	Murray	Savage	Higgins	
1	2	3	4	5	6	7		9	8			11		10						1
1	2	3	4	5	6	7		9	8			11		10						R
1	2	3	4	5	6	7		9	8			11		10						2R
3	3	3	3	3	3	3		3	3			3		3						
1			1		1							1								

215

1927-28

Manager: Bert Pelham

#	Month	Date		Opponent	Result	Scorers	Attendance
1	Aug	27	(a)	Darlington	L 0-3		6,961
2		31	(h)	Doncaster R	W 3-1	Hoddinott, Laycock, J.Reid	5,715
3	Sep	3	(h)	Ashington	W 6-0	Laycock 2, Williams 3, Whitter	5,489
4		5	(a)	Doncaster R	L 1-5	Williams	5,435
5		10	(a)	Crewe A	D 1-1	Laycock	4,655
6		17	(h)	Halifax T	W 3-1	Hoddinott, Dickie, Harley	5,700
7		24	(a)	Bradford C	L 1-3	Laycock	11,701
8	Oct	1	(h)	Tranmere R	L 0-1		9,228
9		8	(h)	Lincoln C	L 2-3	Hoddinott 2 (1 pen)	4,667
10		15	(a)	Hartlepools U	D 3-3	Harley 2, Hoddinott	4,243
11		22	(a)	Nelson	W 3-0	Harley, Dickie, Wade	2,698
12	Nov	5	(a)	Stockport C	D 0-0		6,382
13		12	(h)	Rochdale	W 2-1	Harley 2	4,409
14		19	(a)	Rotherham U	D 0-0		4,135
15	Dec	3	(a)	Durham C	L 1-2	Dickie	1,447
16		17	(a)	Chesterfield	W 3-2	Harley, Whitter, Wade	1,984
17		24	(h)	Bradford	L 1-2	Harley	2,589
18		26	(a)	Accrington S	L 1-2	Harley	5,644
19		27	(h)	Accrington S	W 3-1	Laycock 2, Whitter	5,384
20		31	(h)	Darlington	D 0-0		1,829
21	Jan	7	(a)	Ashington	L 2-3	Dickie, Whitter	1,619
22		21	(h)	Crewe A	W 5-1	Laycock 2, Hoddinott, Harley 2	4,039
23	Feb	4	(h)	Bradford C	D 1-1	Whitter	2,939
24		11	(a)	Tranmere R	L 0-4		6,664
25		15	(h)	Southport	L 0-1		2,871
26		18	(a)	Lincoln C	W 2-1	Laycock, Lightbody	5,375
27		25	(h)	Hartlepools U	W 2-1	Laycock, Roberts	2,861
28	Mar	3	(h)	Nelson	W 4-0	Roberts 2, Laycock, Dickie	4,290
29		7	(h)	Wrexham	D 0-0		3,020
30		10	(a)	Barrow	L 1-2	Dickie	6,232
31		17	(h)	Stockport C	D 0-0		4,876
32		24	(a)	Rochdale	D 0-0		2,404
33		31	(h)	Rotherham U	D 1-1	Sanderson	3,240
34	Apr	6	(a)	Wigan Borough	D 2-2	Whitter 2	4,858
35		7	(a)	Wrexham	W 2-0	Harley, Roberts	4,296
36		9	(h)	Wigan Borough	W 2-1	Harley, Dickie	4,128
37		14	(h)	Durham C	W 4-0	Dickie, Roberts 3	2,710
38		18	(h)	Barrow	D 3-3	Roberts, Wade, Dickie	1,515
39		21	(a)	Southport	L 2-4	Roberts, Dickie	2,139
40		23	(a)	Halifax T	D 1-1	Laycock	1,761
41		28	(h)	Chesterfield	D 3-3	Harley, Dickie (pen), Roberts	2,702
42	May	5	(a)	Bradford	L 1-2	Laycock	9,538

FINAL LEAGUE POSITION: 10th in Division Three North

Appearances
Goals

FA Cup

#	Month	Date		Opponent	Result	Scorers	Attendance
1	Nov	26	(a)	Shildon	W 3-1	Whitter, Harley 2	4,500
2	Dec	10	(h)	Rhyl A	W 7-2	Lewis, Dixon (og), Reid, Harley 4	8,227
3	Jan	14	(h)	Corinthians	W 2-1	Whitter 2	9,256
4		28	(a)	Port Vale	L 0-3		10,513

Appearances
Goals

216

Appearances and goalscorers grid.

Mehaffy	Carr	Howson	Sanderson	Reid J	McKenna	Whitter	Laycock	Williams	Hoddinott	Dickie	McDonald	Beattie	Smedley	Morrison	Harley	Lewis	Wade	Flood LTB	Lightbody	Roberts	No.
1	2	3	4	5	6	7	8	9	10	11											1
1	2		4	5	6	7	8	9	10	11	3										2
1	3		4	5	6	7	8	9	10	11	2										3
1	3			5	6	7	8	9	10	11	2	4									4
1	3			5		7	8	9	10	11	2	4		6							5
1	3			5		7	8		10	11	2	4		6	9						6
1	3			5		7	8		10	11	2	4		6	9						7
1	3			5		7	8		10	11	2			6	9	4					8
1	3	2	8	5		7			10	11				6	9	4					9
1	3			5		7			10	11	2			6	9	4	8				10
1	3			5		7			10	11	2			6	9	4	8				11
1	3			5		7			10	11	2			6	9	4	8				12
1	3			5		7			10	1	2			6	9	4	8				13
1	3	2		5		7			10	11				6	9	4	8				14
1	3			5		7			10	11	2			6	9	4	8				15
1	3			5		7			10	11	2			6	4	9	8				16
1	3			5		7	8		10	11	2			6	4	9					17
1	3		8	5		7	10			11	2			6	4	9					18
1	3		8	5		7	10			11	2			6	4	9					19
1	3		8	5		7	10			11	2			6	4	9					20
1	3			5		7	10		8	11	2			6	9	4					21
1	3			5		7	10		8	11	2			6	9	4					22
1	3		8	5		7	9		10	11	2			6	4						23
	3		8	5		7	9		10	11	2			6	4			1			24
1	3			5		7	8		10	11	2			6	9	4					25
1	3			5		7	8			11	2			6	4	10				9	26
1	3			5		7	10			11	2			6	4		8			9	27
1	3			5		7	10			11	2			6	4		8			9	28
1	3			5		7	10			11	2			6	4		8			9	29
1	3			5		7	10			11	2			6	4		8			9	30
1	2					7	10			11	3	4		6		5	8			9	31
1	2					7	10			11	3	4		6		5				9	32
1	2		8			7	10			11	3	4		6		5				9	33
1	2		8			7				11	3	4		6	10	5				9	34
1	2			5		7				11	3	4		6	10		8			9	35
1	3			5		7				11	2	4		6	10		8			9	36
1	2					7				11	3		5	6	4	10	8			9	37
1	2					7				11	3		5	6	4	10	8			9	38
	2					7	8			11	3		5	6	4	10		1		9	39
1	3					7	8			11	2		5	6	4	10				9	40
1	3					7	8			11	2		5	6	4	10				9	41
1	3					7	8			11	2			6	4	10	5			9	42
40	34	11	11	32	4	42	28	5	23	42	39	15	16	34	27	22	18	2	1	16	
		1	1			7	14	4	6	11				14		3			1	10	

Mehaffy	Carr	Howson	Sanderson	Reid J	McKenna	Whitter	Laycock	Williams	Hoddinott	Dickie	McDonald	Beattie	Smedley	Morrison	Harley	Lewis	Wade	Flood LTB	Lightbody	Roberts	No.
1	3			5		7			10	11	2			6	9	4	8				1
1	3			5		7			10	11	2			6	9	4	8				2
1	3			5		7	10		8	11	2			6	9	4					3
1	3			5		7	10		8	11	2			6	9	4					4
4	4			4		4	2		4	4	4		1	3	4	4	2				
														6	1						

1 own-goal

1928-29

Manager: Bert Pelham

1	Aug	25	(h)	Barrow	L 1-3	Kirk	4,037
2	Sep	1	(a)	Doncaster R	W 2-1	Dickie, Cowper	8,595
3		8	(h)	Ashington	W 3-2	Dickie (pen), Reid, Parker	2,821
4		10	(h)	Chesterfield	L 2-3	Kirk 2	3,553
5		15	(a)	South Shields	W 2-0	Kirk, Parker	5,533
6		22	(h)	Nelson	L 0-1		4,882
7		29	(a)	Darlington	L 1-3	Iddon	5,021
8	Oct	6	(h)	Southport	W 3-1	Parker, Whewell, Kirk	4,731
9		13	(a)	Rochdale	L 2-4	Whewell, Cowper	5,096
10		20	(a)	Tranmere R	W 3-1	Cowper 2, Whewell	10,641
11		27	(h)	Stockport C	W 4-1	Whewell 3, Dickie	6,051
12	Nov	3	(a)	Halifax T	D 1-1	Cowper	5,725
13		10	(h)	Lincoln C	W 6-1	Parker 2, Kirk 2, Cowper 2	4,387
14		17	(a)	Bradford C	L 2-5	Cowper, Dickie	14,812
15	Dec	1	(a)	Hartlepools U	L 2-5	Whewell, Cowper	1,843
16		12	(h)	Carlisle U	W 1-0	Whewell	2,061
17		15	(a)	Rotherham U	L 1-3	Cowper	3,620
18		22	(h)	Wigan Borough	D 2-2	Kirk, Davidson	2,616
19		25	(a)	Crewe A	L 0-3		5,951
20		26	(h)	Crewe A	L 2-3	Cowper, McDonald (pen)	5,281
21		29	(a)	Barrow	D 0-0		4,282
22	Jan	1	(a)	Chesterfield	W 2-0	Iddon, Davidson	6,448
23		5	(h)	Doncaster R	D 1-1	Cowper	3,800
24		19	(a)	Ashington	D 1-1	Davidson	1,344
25		26	(h)	South Shields	W 1-0	Whewell	3,400
26	Feb	2	(a)	Nelson	L 0-3		3,168
27		6	(h)	Accrington S	W 2-1	Lewis, Parker	1,535
28		9	(h)	Darlington	W 1-0	Davidson	3,712
29		16	(a)	Southport	D 0-0		2,732
30		23	(h)	Rochdale	W 6-1	Wadsworth 2, Parker, Cowper 2, Kirk	2,946
31	Mar	2	(h)	Tranmere R	L 1-2	Whewell	9,292
32		9	(a)	Stockport C	L 1-2	Parker	12,844
33		16	(h)	Halifax T	W 1-0	McDonald (pen)	2,959
34		23	(a)	Lincoln C	L 0-4		4,033
35		29	(h)	Wrexham	W 2-0	Whewell, Davidson	8,667
36		30	(h)	Bradford C	L 0-3		8,772
37	Apr	1	(a)	Wrexham	D 1-1	Cowper	7,637
38		6	(a)	Accrington S	L 1-3	Whewell	3,645
39		13	(h)	Hartlepools U	L 1-3	Davidson	2,832
40		20	(a)	Carlisle U	L 1-2	Whewell	5,441
41		27	(h)	Rotherham U	D 0-0		2,239
42	May	4	(a)	Wigan Borough	D 1-1	Cowper	4,372

FINAL LEAGUE POSITION: 14th in Division Three North

Appearances
Goals

FA Cup

1	Nov	24	(a)	Darlington	L 0-3		5,023

Appearances
Goals

218

Mehaffy	McDonald	Carr	Lewis	Chambers	Morrison	Iddon	Parker	Reid T	Kirk	Dickie	Higgins	Cowper	Beattie	Smedley	Whewell	Davidson	Flood LTB	Wadsworth	Curr R	Wall A	
1	2	3	4	5	6	7	8	9	10	11											1
1	2	3	4		6		8	9	10	11	5	7									2
1	2	3	4		6		8	9	10	11	5	7									3
1	2	3	4		6		8	9	10	11	5	7									4
1	2	3		4			8	9	10	11		7	5	6							5
1	2	3		4	8	9			10	11		7	5	6							6
1	2	3		4	8	9			10	11		7	5	6							7
1	2	3	5	4		8			10	11		7		6	9						8
1	2	3		4		8			10	11		7	5	6	9						9
1	2	3		5		8			10	11		7	4	6	9						10
1	2	3	4	5		8			10	11		7		6	9						11
1	2	3	4	5		8			10	11		7		6	9						12
1	2	3	4	5		8			10	11		7		6	9						13
1	2	3	4	5		8			10	11		7		6	9						14
1	2	3	4	5		8			10			7		6	9	11					15
	2	3	4	5	9	8						7		6	10	11	1				16
	2	3	4	5		8						7	10	6	9	11	1				17
	2	3	4	5	7	8		10						6	9	11	1				18
	2	3	4	5		8		10				7		6	9	11	1				19
	2	3	4	5		8		10				7		6	9	11	1				20
	2	3	4	5	9	8						7		6	10	11	1				21
	2	3	4	5	9	8		10				7				11	1				22
	3		8	4	9	2		10				7		6		11	1	5			23
	2	3	9	4				10				7		6	8	11	1	5			24
	3		8	4		9						7		6	10	11	1	5	2		25
	3		8	4	9	10						7		6		11	1	5	2		26
	3		8	4	9			10				7		6		11	1	5	2		27
	3		8	4	9			10				7		6		11	1	5	2		28
	3			4	9			8				7		6	10	11	1	5	2		29
	3			4	9			8				7		6	10	11	1	5	2		30
	3			4	9			8				7		6	10	11	1	5	2		31
	3	2	8	4				10				7		6	9	11	1	5			32
	2	3	8	4				10				7		6	9	11	1	5			33
1	3	2	8	4				10				7		6	9	11		5			34
1	3	2	8	4				10				7		6	9	11		5			35
1	3		8	4				10				7		6	9			5	2		36
1	3		8	4				10				7		6	9			5	2	11	37
1	3		8	4				10				7		6	9	11		5	2		38
1	3		7	4					10			8		6	9	11		5	2		39
	3			4	9	8						7		6	10	11	1	5	2		40
	3	9	4		8							7		6	10	11	1	5	2		41
	3		8	4				10				7		6	9	11	1	5	2		42
21	42	28	33	1	42	11	38	5	27	14	3	40	6	38	30	27	21	20	14	1	
	2	1	1		2	8	1	9	4			16		13	6			2			

Mehaffy	McDonald	Carr	Lewis	Chambers	Morrison	Iddon	Parker	Reid T	Kirk	Dickie	Higgins	Cowper	Beattie	Smedley	Whewell	Davidson	Flood LTB	Wadsworth	Curr R	Wall A	
1	2	3	4	5			8		10	11		7		6	9						1
1	1	1	1	1			1		1	1		1		1	1						

1929-30

Manager: Bert Pelham

1	Aug	31	(a)	Barrow	L 0-3		8,644
2	Sep	2	(h)	Port Vale	L 0-1		4,833
3		7	(h)	Wrexham	W 2-1	Pither, Taylor	5,970
4		9	(a)	Port Vale	L 1-5	Templeman	8,260
5		14	(a)	Wigan Borough	L 0-5		7,180
6		18	(a)	York C	L 0-3		5,422
7		21	(h)	Carlisle U	W 2-1	Cowper, Pither	3,865
8		28	(a)	Nelson	L 1-2	Pither	3,458
9	Oct	5	(h)	Southport	L 1-3	Roscoe	3,498
10		12	(a)	Crewe A	W 3-2	Johnson 3	5,716
11		19	(a)	Halifax T	L 0-4		2,756
12		26	(h)	Rotherham U	D 2-2	Page, McDonald	3,051
13	Nov	2	(a)	Rochdale	L 0-5		3,136
14		9	(h)	South Shields	W 4-1	Roscoe 2, Kelly 2	3,112
15		16	(a)	Accrington S	L 0-5		4,121
16		23	(h)	Darlington	L 1-3	Brown (og)	3,446
17	Dec	7	(h)	Doncaster R	W 1-0	Roscoe	1,785
18		21	(h)	Lincoln C	L 1-4	Johnson (pen)	2,582
19		25	(a)	Tranmere R	L 1-3	Smedley	6,155
20		26	(h)	Tranmere R	W 3-0	Johnson, Taylor, Williamson	9,289
21		28	(h)	Barrow	W 5-0	Oakes, Taylor 3, Johnson	1,839
22	Jan	1	(h)	York C	D 1-1	Roscoe	5,440
23		4	(a)	Wrexham	L 1-2	Johnson	4,258
24		11	(a)	Hartlepools U	D 1-1	Taylor	3,472
25		18	(a)	Wigan Borough	W 5-0	Taylor 2, Johnson 3 (1 pen)	3,685
26		25	(a)	Carlisle U	D 2-2	Taylor, Oakes	3,960
27	Feb	1	(h)	Nelson	W 2-1	Johnson, Oakes	3,906
28		8	(a)	Southport	L 1-2	Oakes	3,370
29		15	(h)	Crewe A	W 3-1	Cowper, Taylor, Oakes	4,275
30		22	(h)	Halifax T	W 4-0	Johnson, Oakes, Smedley, Wadsworth	4,338
31	Mar	1	(a)	Rotherham U	D 2-2	Oakes, Johnson	4,024
32		8	(h)	Rochdale	W 2-0	Oakes, Taylor	4,160
33		15	(a)	South Shields	W 2-1	Taylor 2	2,068
34		22	(h)	Accrington S	W 5-0	Johnson 3, Taylor 2	4,129
35		29	(a)	Darlington	W 2-1	Pither, Taylor	3,705
36	Apr	5	(h)	Hartlepools U	D 0-0		4,415
37		7	(a)	Chesterfield	L 0-1		2,794
38		12	(a)	Doncaster R	D 1-1	Pither	4,502
39		18	(h)	Stockport C	W 3-2	Cowper, Taylor 2	11,370
40		19	(h)	Chesterfield	D 1-1	Taylor	3,469
41		26	(a)	Lincoln C	L 3-5	Johnson (pen), Taylor 2	3,431
42	May	3	(a)	Stockport C	L 0-2		4,140

FINAL LEAGUE POSITION: 13th in Division Three North

Appearances
Goals

FA Cup

1	Nov	30	(h)	Lancaster T	W 4-1	Taylor 2, Johnson, Roscoe	4,500
2	Dec	14	(a)	Doncaster R	L 0-1		6,545

Appearances
Goals

220

Flood LTB	Curr R	McDonald	Lewis	Wadsworth	Smedley	Cowper	Page	Reid T	Oakes	Pither	Carr	Taylor J	Templeman	Curr W	Johnson	Roscoe	Maher	Kelly	Campbell	Higgins	Davidson	Morrison	Ward H	Robinson	Williamson	
1	2	3	4	5	6	7	8	9	10	11																1
1		2	4	5	6	7	8	9		11	3		10													2
1		2	4	5	6	7	8			11	3	9	10													3
1		2	5		6	7	8			11	3	9	10	4												4
1		2	4	5	6	7	8			11	3	9	10													5
1		2			6	4			10	11	5	9			8	7									3	6
1		2		5	6	7			10	11	3	8		4	9											7
1		2		5	6	7	10			11	3	8		4	9											8
1		2	4	5	6		8			11	3	9			10	7										9
1		2	4	5	6	7			10	11	3	9			8											10
		2	4	5	6	7			10	11	3	9			8		1									11
1		2		5	6	7	10			11	3			4	9			8								12
	2	3			6	7				11	5	9		4	10		1	8								13
	2	3	4		6	7				11	5				10	9	1	8								14
	2	3	4		6	7					5				10	9	1	8								15
	2	3			6	7			10	11	5				9			8		1	4					16
		2	4	5	6				10	11	3	9				7		8	1							17
		2	4	5	6	7			10	11	3	9						8	1							18
		2	4	5	6				10	11	3	9				7		8	1							19
		2	4	5	6				10	11	3				8	7			1			9				20
		2	4	5	6				10	11	3	9			8	7			1							21
		2	4	5	6				10	11	3	9			8	7			1							22
	2		4	5	6				10	11	3	9			8	7			1							23
		2	4	5	6				10	11	3	9			8	7			1							24
		2		5	6				10	11	3	9			8	7			1		4					25
		2	4	5	6				10	11	3	9			8	7			1							26
		2	4	5	6				10	11	3	9			8	7			1							27
		2	4	5	6	7			10	11	3	9			8				1							28
		2		5	6	7			10	11	3	9			8				1		4					29
		2		5	6	7			10	11	3	9			8				1		4					30
		2		5	6	7			10	11	3	9			8				1		4					31
		2	4	5	6				10	11	3	9			8				1			7				32
		2	4	5	6	7			10	11	3	9			8				1				1			33
		2	4	5	6	7			10	11	3	9			8				1							34
		2	4	5	6	7			10	11	3	9			8				1							35
		2	4	5	6	7			10	11	3	9			8				1							36
		2	4	5		7			10	11	3	9			8				1			6				37
		2	4	5		7			10	11	3	9			8				1			6				38
		2	4	5	6	7			10	11	3	9			8				1							39
		2	4	5	6	7			10		3	9			8				1			11				40
		2		5	6	7			10		3	9			8				1		4	11				41
		2		5	6	7			10		3	9			8				1		4	11				42
11	6	41	30	35	40	31	8	2	26	37	41	35	4	5	36	16	4	8	26	1	7	9	1	1	1	
	1		1	2	3	1			8	5	21	1			17	5			2						1	

1 own-goal

Flood LTB	Curr R	McDonald	Lewis	Wadsworth	Smedley	Cowper	Page	Reid T	Oakes	Pither	Carr	Taylor J	Templeman	Curr W	Johnson	Roscoe	Maher	Kelly	Campbell	Higgins	Davidson	Morrison	Ward H	Robinson	Williamson	
		2	4	5	6						3	10			9	7		8	1	11						1
		2	4	5	6	8				11	3	10			9	7			1							2
		2	2	2	2	1				1	2	2			2	2		1	2	1						
												2			1	1										

1930-31

Manager: Bert Pelham until April 1931

#	Month	Date		Opponent	Result		Scorers	Attendance
1	Aug	30	(h)	Lincoln C	W	2-1	Oakes, Johnson	4,963
2	Sep	1	(a)	Stockport C	L	0-2		7,985
3		6	(a)	Hartlepools U	L	1-4	Oakes	4,224
4		8	(a)	Gateshead	L	0-4		5,396
5		13	(h)	Wigan Borough	L	0-2		3,317
6		15	(h)	Gateshead	D	0-0		2,488
7		20	(a)	Nelson	D	2-2	Oakes 2	2,585
8		27	(h)	Darlington	L	1-5	Waites	3,466
9	Oct	4	(a)	Halifax T	L	0-1		5,944
10		11	(h)	Tranmere R	L	1-3	Waites	10,054
11		18	(a)	Carlisle U	L	0-2		5,748
12		25	(h)	Wrexham	D	1-1	Smedley	3,502
13	Nov	1	(a)	Rotherham U	L	0-2		6,135
14		8	(h)	Chesterfield	W	3-1	Oakes, Whewell 2	3,198
15		15	(a)	Barrow	L	1-4	Morrison	4,756
16		22	(h)	Southport	L	1-2	Hough	2,635
17	Dec	6	(h)	Rochdale	W	2-1	Stevens 2	2,369
18		17	(a)	Crewe A	W	3-1	Lewis, Waites, Pither	1,140
19		20	(h)	York C	W	5-3	Pither, Lewis, Johnson 3	2,223
20		25	(a)	Doncaster R	D	0-0		3,717
21		26	(h)	Doncaster R	W	2-1	Stevens, Johnson	4,389
22		27	(a)	Lincoln C	L	0-4		8,418
23	Jan	1	(h)	Stockport C	L	0-2		4,720
24		3	(h)	Hartlepools U	W	1-0	Oakes	2,872
25		10	(a)	Accrington S	L	0-3		1,843
26		17	(a)	Wigan Borough	D	1-1	Pither	3,896
27		24	(h)	Nelson	W	2-0	Stevens 2	2,227
28		31	(a)	Darlington	L	1-3	Matthews	1,453
29	Feb	7	(h)	Halifax T	W	3-0	Oakes, Stevens, Johnson	2,845
30		14	(a)	Tranmere R	L	2-3	Pither, Stevens	9,154
31		21	(h)	Carlisle U	W	2-0	Stevens, Waites	2,740
32		28	(a)	Wrexham	L	1-2	Stevens	3,466
33	Mar	7	(h)	Rotherham U	W	3-1	Stevens, Waites 2	1,742
34		14	(a)	Chesterfield	L	0-1		4,786
35		21	(h)	Barrow	W	3-1	Whewell 2, Pither	2,527
36		28	(a)	Southport	L	0-3		2,430
37	Apr	3	(h)	Hull C	D	1-1	Whewell	4,524
38		4	(h)	Accrington S	D	0-0		2,323
39		6	(a)	Hull C	L	0-3		5,881
40		11	(a)	Rochdale	L	0-2		1,855
41		18	(h)	Crewe A	W	3-0	Stevens 3	1,879
42		25	(a)	York C	L	1-4	Lewis	1,735

FINAL LEAGUE POSITION: 19th in Division Three North

Appearances
Goals

FA Cup

1	Nov	29	(a)	Carlisle U	L	1-3	Pither	9,300

Appearances
Goals

Campbell	McDonald	Carr	Lewis	Reid J	Smedley	Waites	Johnson	Taylor	Oakes	Pither	Dixon	Curr R	Pollock	Whewell	Morrison	Greatrex	Matthews	Hough	Baker	Stevens	Templeman	Curr W	#
1	2	3	4	5	6	7	8	9	10	11													1
1	2	3	4		6	7	8	9	10	11	5												2
1	2	3	4	5	6	7	8	9	10	11													3
1	2	3	4	5	6	7	8	9	10	11													4
1		3		5	6	7	8		10	11		2	4	9									5
		3			6	7	8		10	11	5	2		9	4	1							6
1	2	3		5	6	7	8	9	10	11				4									7
1	2	3		5	6	7	8	9	10	11				4									8
		3		5	6	7	8	9	10	11		2		4	1								9
1		3			6	7	8		10	11		2	9	4		5							10
1	2	3			6	7	8		10	11			9	4		5							11
1	2	3			6	7	8		10	11			9	4		5							12
1	2	3	4		6	7		9	10	11				8		5							13
	2	3	4		6	7			10	11				9		1	5	8					14
	2	3			6	7			10	11				9	4	1	5	8					15
1	2	3			6	7			10	11				9	4		5	8					16
1	2	3			6	7			10	11					4		5	8	9				17
	2	3	9		6	7	8		10	11			4			1	5						18
	2	3	9		6	7	8		10	11			4			1	5						19
	2	3			6	7	8		10	11					4	1	5		9				20
	2	3			6	7	8		10	11			4			1	5		9				21
	2	3			6	7	8		10	11			4			1	5		9				22
		3	7		6		8		10	11		2			4	1	5		9				23
	2	3			6	7	8		10	11					4	1	5		9				24
	2	3			6	7	8		10	11					4	1	5		9				25
1	2	3			6		8			11				10	4		5		9	7			26
1	2	3			6		8			11				10			5	4	9	7			27
1	2	3			6		8			11				10			5	4	9	7			28
1	2	3			6		8		10	11					4		5		9	7			29
1	2	3			6	7	8			11				10	4		5		9				30
1	2	3			6	7	8		10	11					4		5		9				31
1	2	3			6	7	8		10	11							5	4	9				32
1	2	3			6	7	8		10	11							5	4	9				33
1	2	3	4		6	7	8			11				10			5		9				34
	2	3	9		6	7	8			11				10	4	1	5						35
1	2	3	9		6	7	8			11			4	10	5								36
1	2	3	9		6	7	8			11				10	4		5						37
1	2	3			6	7	8			11				10	4		5				9		38
1	2	3			6	7	8			11			5		4						10	9	39
1	2	3			6	7			10	11			5		4				9		8		40
1	2	3			6	7			10	11		8	4				5		9				41
1	2	3	8		6	7			10	11					4		5		9				42
29	38	41	14	7	42	37	38	8	28	42	2	5	11	16	26	13	30	4	4	19	5	3	
	3		1			6	6		7	5				5	1		1	1		13			

Campbell	McDonald	Carr	Lewis	Reid J	Smedley	Waites	Johnson	Taylor	Oakes	Pither	Dixon	Curr R	Pollock	Whewell	Morrison	Greatrex	Matthews	Hough	Baker	Stevens	Templeman	Curr W	#
1	2	3			6				10		7		4	9			5			8		11	1
1	1	1			1				1		1		1	1			1			1		1	
										1													

1931-32

Manager: No paid official this season

1	Aug	29	(h)	Gateshead	L 1-3	McCosh	4,134
2		31	(a)	Halifax T	D 0-0		6,008
3	Sep	5	(a)	Tranmere R	L 1-5	Smedley	6,904
4		9	(h)	Walsall	L 0-1		2,308
5		12	(a)	Barrow	L 1-4	Duff	7,992
6		14	(a)	Walsall	L 0-3		2,112
7		19	(h)	Hull C	L 1-2	McCosh	3,023
8		26	(a)	Lincoln C	L 0-3		7,335
9	Oct	3	(h)	Chester	L 0-1		5,105
10		10	(a)	Hartlepools U	L 0-1		5,094
11		17	(h)	York C	L 0-2		2,836
12		26	(a)	Southport	L 0-1		3,550
13		31	(h)	Doncaster R	W 1-0	Smedley (pen)	2,381
14	Nov	7	(a)	Rochdale	L 2-3	Rawsthorne 2	1,888
15		14	(h)	Crewe A	L 0-1		1,443
16		21	(a)	Carlisle U	D 0-0		3,577
17	Dec	5	(a)	Accrington S	L 1-4	Stevens	3,124
18		19	(a)	Rotherham U	D 2-2	Twell, Parle	2,240
19		26	(h)	Darlington	D 0-0		2,661
20		30	(h)	Stockport C	W 2-1	Smedley (pen), Stevens	1,741
21	Jan	1	(a)	Darlington	L 0-3		4,048
22		2	(a)	Gateshead	L 0-4		8,111
23		9	(h)	Wrexham	D 1-1	Stevens	2,094
24		16	(h)	Tranmere R	D 1-1	Smedley (pen)	7,277
25		23	(h)	Barrow	L 0-3		4,036
26		30	(a)	Hull C	L 1-4	Stevens	5,916
27	Feb	6	(h)	Lincoln C	W 2-1	Stevens 2	2,768
28		13	(a)	Chester	L 0-2		6,294
29		20	(h)	Hartlepools U	D 1-1	Stevens	2,524
30		27	(a)	York C	L 0-4		3,169
31	Mar	5	(h)	Southport	W 3-1	Liggins, Parle, Stevens	2,874
32		12	(a)	Doncaster R	L 1-2	Stevens	2,808
33		19	(h)	Rochdale	D 1-1	Stevens	2,362
34		26	(a)	Crewe A	L 2-3	Stevens, Ratcliffe	4,195
35	Apr	2	(h)	Carlisle U	W 4-1	Stevens 4	2,455
36		9	(a)	Wrexham	L 1-2	Stevens	2,122
37		16	(h)	Accrington S	W 2-1	Liggins, Parle	2,334
38		23	(a)	Stockport C	L 1-3	Stevens	2,270
39		30	(h)	Rotherham U	W 3-1	Stevens 2, Miller	1,923
40	May	7	(h)	Halifax T	W 2-0	Liggins, Stevens	1,974

FINAL LEAGUE POSITION: 20th in Division Three North

Appearances
Goals

FA Cup

1	Nov	28	(h)	York C	W 3-1	Johnson (og), Stevens 2	3,367
2	Dec	12	(h)	Hull C	L 0-4		4,500

Appearances
Goals

Walker	Clement	Carr	Pollock	Matthews	Smedley	Parle	McCosh	Stevens	Miller	Henderson	Curr R	Jenkins EJ	Duff	Davies GI	Twell	Carter H	Lindsay	Dorrans	Ratcliffe	Rawsthorne J	Spencer	Liggins AG	Whelan GF	Lewis	No.
1	2	3	4	5	6	7	8	9	10	11															1
1	2		4	5	6	7	8		10	11	3	9													2
1	2		4	5	6	7	8	9	10	11	3														3
1	2		4	5	6		8	9	10		3			7	11										4
1	2	3		5	6		8	4	10					7	11	9									5
1	2	3		5	6		8		10					7	11	9			4						6
1	2	3		5	6	7	8		10						11	9	4								7
1	2	3	4	5	6	7	8		10						11	9									8
1	2	3		5	6			9	10		7				11		8								9
1	2	3		5	6			9	10		7				11		8	4							10
1	2	3		5	6	7			10						11		8	4		9					11
1	2	3			6	7	8		10						11				5	9	4				12
1	2				6	7	8		10		3				11				5	9	4				13
1	2	3	4		6	7			10	11							8		5	9					14
1	2	3	4		6	7			10	11							8		5	9					15
1	2	3	4		6	7			10	11							8		5	9					16
1	2	3	4		6	7		9	10	11							8		5						17
1	2	3	4		6	7		9	10	11							8		5						18
1	2	3	4		6	7		9	10	11							8		5						19
1	2	3	4		6		8	9		11									5	10	7				20
1	2	3	4		6	7		9		11									5	10					21
1	2	3			6	7			10	11									5	9	4				22
1	2	3	4		6			9	10	11									5		7				23
1	2	3			6		8	9	10							4			5			7	11		24
1	2	3			6		8	9	10							4			5			7	11		25
1	2				6		8	9	10		3					4			5			7	11		26
1	2	3			6		8	9	10										5		4	7	11		27
1	2	3			6		8	9	10										5		4	7	11		28
1	2	3			6		8	9	10										5		4	7	11		29
1	2	3			6		8	9	10	11									5			7		4	30
1	2	3			6		8	9	10	11									5			7		4	31
1	2	3			6		8	9	10	11									5			7		4	32
1	2	3			6		8	9	10	11									5			7		4	33
1	2	3			6		8	9	10	11									5			7		4	34
1	2	3			6		8	9	10	11									5			7		4	35
1	2	3			6		8	9	10	11									5		7	7		4	36
1	2	3			6		8	9	10	11									5			7		4	37
1	2	3			6		8	9	10	11									5		7	7		4	38
1	2	3			6		8	9	10	11									5			7		4	39
1	2	3			6		8	9	10	11									5			7		4	40
40	40	35	15	11	40	34	24	35	34	11	8	1	4	3	11	4	7	3	31	9	8	15	6	11	
			4	3	2	20	1				1		1						1	2		3			

Walker	Clement	Carr	Pollock	Matthews	Smedley	Parle	McCosh	Stevens	Miller	Henderson	Curr R	Jenkins EJ	Duff	Davies GI	Twell	Carter H	Lindsay	Dorrans	Ratcliffe	Rawsthorne J	Spencer	Liggins AG	Whelan GF	Lewis	No.
1	2	3	4		6	7		9	10	11							8		5						1
1	2	3	4		6	7		9	10	11							8		5						2
2	2	2	2		2	2		2	2	2							2		2						
						2																			

I own-goal

1932-33

Manager: Bill Sawyer from 21 March 1933

1	Aug	27	(a)	Rotherham U	L 0-1		4,941
2		31	(h)	Mansfield T	W 1-0	Quayle	3,331
3	Sep	3	(h)	Accrington S	D 2-2	Quayle, Miller	3,803
4		5	(a)	Mansfield T	L 0-5		4,636
5		10	(a)	Tranmere R	W 3-2	Miller 2, Amery	7,433
6		17	(a)	Chester	L 0-3		9,655
7		24	(h)	Barrow	L 1-2	Kitching	4,183
8	Oct	1	(a)	Carlisle U	W 3-1	Dickie, Amery, Liggins	5,054
9		8	(h)	York C	L 0-1		2,840
10		15	(a)	Crewe A	L 0-4		4,724
11		22	(h)	Halifax T	L 0-3		2,578
12		29	(a)	Hartlepools U	L 2-3	Miller, Kitching	1,916
13	Nov	5	(h)	Barnsley	L 3-5	Kitching, Liggins 2	3,143
14		12	(a)	Hull C	L 0-5		6,792
15		19	(h)	Doncaster R	D 4-4	Shaw 2, Amery 2	2,472
16	Dec	3	(h)	Stockport C	D 1-1	Smedley	2,261
17		10	(a)	Barnsley	W 2-1	Shaw, Miller	3,353
18		17	(h)	Walsall	D 2-2	Miller, Parle	2,465
19		24	(a)	Wrexham	L 0-5		3,714
20		26	(h)	Rochdale	L 0-3		3,738
21		27	(a)	Rochdale	L 0-1		6,055
22		31	(h)	Rotherham U	W 5-2	Ratcliffe 2, Parle, Dickie, Major	1,855
23	Jan	2	(a)	Gateshead	L 0-2		3,001
24		7	(a)	Accrington S	L 4-5	Stevens 2, Parle, Dickie	2,958
25		18	(a)	Darlington	L 1-2	Stevens	1,642
26		21	(h)	Tranmere R	D 1-1	Liggins	4,885
27	Feb	4	(a)	Barrow	L 1-2	Miller	2,893
28		8	(h)	Chester	W 3-1	Smedley, Dickie (pen), Liggins	3,384
29		11	(h)	Carlisle U	W 2-0	Miller, Amery	2,780
30		18	(a)	York C	L 0-3		2,683
31		25	(h)	Crewe A	L 1-2	Lowndes	1,955
32	Mar	4	(a)	Halifax T	D 3-3	Liggins, Miller 2	3,864
33		11	(h)	Hartlepools U	W 5-2	Lowndes 3, Liggins, Miller	3,055
34		25	(h)	Hull C	W 1-0	Lowndes	4,377
35	Apr	1	(a)	Doncaster R	L 0-2		4,287
36		8	(h)	Darlington	W 7-1	Miller 2, Lowndes 4, Liggins	3,032
37		14	(a)	Southport	D 1-1	Parle	4,634
38		15	(a)	Stockport C	D 1-1	Ratcliffe	6,041
39		17	(h)	Southport	W 2-1	Lowndes, Parle	4,890
40		22	(h)	Gateshead	D 1-1	Parle	3,559
41		29	(a)	Walsall	D 0-0		4,056
42	May	6	(h)	Wrexham	L 0-2		4,053

FINAL LEAGUE POSITION: 21st in Division Three North   Appearances

Goals

FA Cup

1	Nov	26	(a)	Tranmere R	L 0-3		8,000

Appearances

Goals

Greatrex	Clement	Carr	Robb	Ratcliffe	Smedley	Barley	Kitching	Quayle	Parle	Miller	Liggins	Amery	Ball	Bradshaw	Dickie	Grice	Carter	Shaw	Major	Bower	Stevens JN	Egan	Lowndes	No.
1	2	3	4	5	6	7	8	9	10	11														1
1	2	3	4	5	6	7	8	9	10		11													2
1	2	3	4	5	6	7	8	9		11		10												3
1	2	3	4	5	6	7		9		11		10	8											4
1	2	3	4	5	6		8	9		11	7	10												5
1	2	3	4	5	6	11	8	9			7	10												6
	2	3	4	5	6		8	9			7	10		1	11									7
	2	3	4	5	6		8	9			7	10		1	11									8
	2	3	4	5	6		8	9			7	10		1	11									9
	2	3	4	5	6		8		9		7	10		1	11									10
	2	3	4	5	6				9	10	7	8		1	11									11
1	2	3	4	5	6		8		10	11	7					9								12
1	2	4		3	6		8		10	11	7					9	5							13
	2	3	4	5	6		8			11	7	10		1		9								14
	2	3	4	5	6		8			11	7	10		1				9						15
	2	3	4	5	6		8			11	7	10		1				9						16
	2	3	4	5	6		8			11	7	10		1				9						17
	2	3	4		6				8	11	7	10		1				9	5					18
1	2	3	4	5	6				8	11	7	10						9						19
	2	3	4	5	6				8	11	7	10		1				9						20
		3	4	9	6				8	10	7			1	11				5	2				21
		3	4	9	6				8	10	7			1	11				5	2				22
		3	4	9	6				8	10	7			1	11				5	2				23
		3	4	5					8	10	7			1	11				6	2	9			24
	2	3	6	5	4				8	10	7			1	11						9			25
	2	3	6	5	4				8	10	7			1	11						9			26
	2	3	6	5	4			9	8	10	7			1	11									27
	2	3	6	5	4			9	8	10	7			1	11									28
	2	3	6	5	4				8	11	7	9		1	10									29
	2	3	6	5	4				8	10	7	9		1	11									30
	2		6	5	4				8	10	7			1	11							3	9	31
	2	3	6		4				8	10	7			1	11				5				9	32
	2	3	6		4				8	10	7			1	11				5				9	33
	2	3	6		4				8	10	7	5		1	11								9	34
	2		6		4				8	10	7	5		1	11				3				9	35
	2	3		6	4				8	10	7	5		1	11								9	36
	2	3		6	4				8	10	7	5		1	11								9	37
	2	3		6	4				8	10	7	5		1	11								9	38
	2	3		6	4				8	10	7	5		1	11								9	39
1	2	3		6	4				8	10	7	5			11								9	40
1	2	3		6	4				8	10	7	5			11								9	41
1	2	3		6	4				8	10	7	5			11								9	42
12	38	40	34	37	41	5	16	11	31	35	39	27	1	30	27	3	1	6	8	4	3	1	12	
		3	2		3	2	6	13	8	5					4			3	1		3		10	

Greatrex	Clement	Carr	Robb	Ratcliffe	Smedley	Barley	Kitching	Quayle	Parle	Miller	Liggins	Amery	Ball	Bradshaw	Dickie	Grice	Carter	Shaw	Major	Bower	Stevens JN	Egan	Lowndes	No.
	2	3	4	5	6		8			11	7	10		1				9						1
	1	1	1	1	1		1			1	1	1		1				1						

1933-34

Manager: Bill Sawyer

#		Date		Opponent	Result	Scorers	Att.
1	Aug	26	(a)	Doncaster R	L 0-1		6,033
2		30	(h)	Walsall	W 2-0	Liggins, McPherson	4,658
3	Sep	2	(h)	Barrow	D 2-2	Davis, Pegg	5,308
4		4	(a)	Walsall	L 1-2	Davis	6,407
5		9	(a)	Carlisle U	W 2-1	Miller, Pegg	5,679
6		16	(h)	Stockport C	W 2-1	Taylor (og), Pegg	5,265
7		23	(a)	Halifax T	D 1-1	Davis	9,890
8		30	(h)	Crewe A	W 2-1	Davis, McPherson	5,062
9	Oct	7	(a)	Tranmere R	L 0-1		10,491
10		14	(a)	Rotherham U	D 2-2	Pegg, Davis	3,297
11		21	(h)	Rochdale	L 0-2		4,450
12		28	(a)	Chesterfield	L 0-4		8,866
13	Nov	4	(h)	Accrington S	L 0-3		3,535
14		11	(a)	Gateshead	L 0-6		3,810
15		18	(h)	Darlington	W 3-2	Allen, Barley, Pegg	2,850
16	Dec	2	(h)	Wrexham	L 0-1		3,705
17		16	(h)	Mansfield T	W 5-1	Davis 3, Smedley, McPherson	2,101
18		23	(a)	Barnsley	L 0-2		4,111
19		25	(a)	Chester	D 0-0		8,970
20		26	(h)	Chester	L 0-2		6,153
21		30	(h)	Doncaster R	D 2-2	Barley 2	2,033
22	Jan	6	(a)	Barrow	D 3-3	Kitching 2, Miller	2,707
23		13	(a)	Southport	L 0-4		2,728
24		20	(h)	Carlisle U	W 2-1	Davis, Barley (pen)	2,634
25		27	(a)	Stockport C	L 1-5	Kitching	9,448
26	Feb	3	(h)	Halifax T	W 3-0	Amery 2, Davis	2,568
27		10	(a)	Crewe A	L 2-6	Davis, Liggins	3,553
28		14	(a)	Hartlepools U	L 1-2	Allen	1,441
29		17	(h)	Tranmere R	W 1-0	Davis	5,533
30		24	(h)	Rotherham U	W 3-1	Miller 2, Pegg	2,929
31	Mar	3	(a)	Rochdale	D 1-1	Davis	2,534
32		10	(h)	Chesterfield	D 0-0		4,958
33		17	(a)	Accrington S	L 0-8		1,429
34		24	(h)	Gateshead	W 3-1	Davis 2, Pegg	2,598
35		30	(a)	York C	L 1-2	Davis	5,026
36		31	(a)	Darlington	L 0-1		4,244
37	Apr	2	(h)	York C	W 2-1	Davis, Amery	3,441
38		7	(h)	Southport	W 5-2	Allen 3, Amery, Davis	3,102
39		14	(a)	Wrexham	L 4-5	Pegg, Davis, Allen 2	2,936
40		21	(h)	Hartlepools U	W 4-1	Davis 4	2,878
41		28	(a)	Mansfield T	L 2-5	Allen, Davis	2,472
42	May	5	(h)	Barnsley	L 0-1		8,508

FINAL LEAGUE POSITION: 15th in Division Three North

Appearances
Goals

FA Cup

1	Nov	25	(h)	Mansfield T	D 0-0		4,289
R		29	(a)	Mansfield T	W 4-3	Barley 3, Pegg	6,300
2	Dec	9	(a)	Queen's Park R	D 1-1	Barley (pen)	12,000
R		13	(h)	Queen's Park R	L 0-4		5,062

Appearances
Goals

Division Three North Cup

1	Jan	3	(a)	Wrexham	L 1-11	Miller	2,600

Appearances
Goals

228

Appearances and goals grid (shirt number worn by each player per match; blank = did not play).

Bradshaw	Kerr	Carr	Smedley	Amery	Butler	Barley	McPherson	Davis	Miller	Pegg	Liggins	Bower	Ratcliffe	Rice	Major	Lowndes	Woods	Allen	Kitching	Flood	No.
1	2	3	4	5		7	8	9	10	11							6				1
1	2	3	4	5	6		8	9	10	11	7										2
1	2	3	4	5	6		8	9	10	11	7										3
1	2	3	4	5	6		8	9	10	11	7										4
1		3	4	5	6		8	9	10	11	7	2									5
1	2	3	4	5	6		8	9	10	11	7										6
1	2	3	4	5	6		8	9	10	11	7										7
1	2	3	4	5	6		8	9	10	11	7										8
1	2	3	6	5	4		8	9	10	11	7										9
1		3	4		6		8	9	10	11	7	2			5						10
1		3	4		6	7	8	9	10	11		2			5						11
1		3	4	5	6	7	8	9	10	11		2									12
1		3	4	5	10	7	8	9		11		2		6							13
1	2	3	4			6	7	8		10	11				5	9					14
1	2	3	4			6	7	8			11				5	10			9		15
1		3	4			7	5	9	10	11	8	2			6						16
1		3	4	5	6	7	8	9	10	11		2									17
1		3	4	5	6	7	8	9	10	11		2									18
1		3	4	5	6	7	8		10	11		2	9								19
1		3	4	5	6	7	8		10	11		2	9								20
1		3	4	5	6	7	8		10	11		2	9								21
1		3	4	5	8	7	6		10	11		2						9			22
1		3	4	10		7	6	8		11		2			5			9			23
1		3				7	6	8	10	11		2	4		5			9			24
1		3	4		10	7	6	8		11		2			5			9			25
1		3			10	6	9	8	11	7		2			5			4			26
1		3		5	10	6	9	8	11	7		2						4			27
1		3		5	8	6	9	10	11	7		2						4			28
1		3			8	6	9	10	11	7		2			5			4			29
1		3			8	6	9	10	11	7		2			5			4			30
1		3			8	6	9	10	11	7		2			5			4			31
1		3	4		8	6	9	10	11	7		2			5						32
1		3	4		8	6	9	10	11			2			5			7			33
		3	4	5	8	6	9	10	11			2						7		1	34
		3	4	5	8	6	9	10	11			2						7		1	35
		3	4	10	8	6	9		11			2			5			7		1	36
		3	4	10	8	6	9		11			2			5			7		1	37
1		3	4	5	10	6	9		11	7		2						8			38
1		3	4		10	6	9		11	7		2			5			8			39
1		3	4		10	6	9		11	7		2			5			8			40
1		3	4		10	6	9		11	7		2			5			8			41
1		3	4	5	10	6	9		11	7		2						8			42
38	10	42	33	29	37	16	42	35	33	41	22	19	21	1	13	1	1	20	4	4	
		1	4			4	3	24	4	8	2							8	3		

1 own-goal

Bradshaw	Kerr	Carr	Smedley	Amery	Butler	Barley	McPherson	Davis	Miller	Pegg	Liggins	Bower	Ratcliffe	Rice	Major	Lowndes	Woods	Allen	Kitching	Flood	No.
1	2	3	4		6	7	8			11					5			9	10		1
1	2	3	4			7	8	9	10	11					5			6			R
1			4		6	7	5	9	10		11	3	2					8			2
1			4		6	7	5	9	10		11	3	2					8			2R
4	2	2	4		3	4	4	3	3	2	2	2	4					1	4		
					4			4			3	3									

Bradshaw	Kerr	Carr	Smedley	Amery	Butler	Barley	McPherson	Davis	Miller	Pegg	Liggins	Bower	Ratcliffe	Rice	Major	Lowndes	Woods	Allen	Kitching	Flood	No.
1			6	4	5	11		10		7	3	2		9		8					1
1		1	1	1	1		1	1	1	1		1		1		1					
								1													

1934-35

Manager: Bill Sawyer

#	Month	Date		Opponent	Result	Scorers	Attendance
1	Aug	25	(a)	Accrington S	W 3-1	Davis, Brown, Miller	4,249
2		29	(h)	Crewe A	D 1-1	Miller	5,468
3	Sep	1	(h)	Darlington	L 0-1		4,134
4		3	(a)	Crewe A	W 3-2	McCrae, Davis, Kenyon	4,879
5		8	(a)	York C	L 0-1		4,217
6		15	(h)	Tranmere R	L 0-1		9,411
7		22	(h)	Chester	L 0-2		5,249
8		29	(a)	Southport	L 1-2	Davis	2,579
9	Oct	6	(h)	Doncaster R	D 1-1	Davis	2,040
10		13	(a)	Hartlepools U	D 2-2	Davis, Allen	3,208
11		20	(a)	Wrexham	L 0-3		4,695
12		27	(h)	Halifax T	D 0-0		3,323
13	Nov	3	(a)	Rotherham U	W 2-1	Kenyon, Davis	6,491
14		10	(h)	Walsall	D 2-2	L.Carr, Brown	3,154
15		17	(a)	Chesterfield	L 0-1		4,649
16	Dec	1	(a)	Barrow	W 2-1	Allen, Kenyon	3,246
17		15	(a)	Rochdale	L 1-3	Allen	3,095
18		22	(h)	Lincoln C	L 0-2		2,852
19		25	(a)	Gateshead	L 1-2	Davis	2,130
20		26	(h)	Gateshead	W 3-0	Davis 3	4,047
21		29	(h)	Accrington S	W 2-1	Kitching, Davis	2,815
22	Jan	5	(a)	Darlington	L 0-1		4,503
23		12	(h)	Wrexham	D 0-0		2,705
24		16	(h)	Mansfield T	W 2-1	Beckett, Lawrence	2,075
25		19	(h)	York C	W 4-2	Salmon, Davis 2, Lawrence	2,948
26		26	(a)	Tranmere R	W 1-0	Allen	12,316
27	Feb	2	(a)	Chester	L 4-5	Beckett 2, Davis, Allen	6,608
28		9	(h)	Southport	D 0-0		3,583
29		16	(a)	Doncaster R	L 1-7	Davis	7,339
30		23	(h)	Hartlepools U	L 1-4	Smedley	2,428
31		27	(h)	Carlisle U	W 5-1	Davis 4, Allen	852
32	Mar	9	(a)	Halifax T	L 2-6	Miller, Davis	4,673
33		16	(h)	Rotherham U	W 3-2	Davis, Allen 2	2,834
34		23	(a)	Walsall	L 1-5	Allen	2,563
35		30	(h)	Chesterfield	W 3-1	Allen, Davis, Smedley (pen)	2,652
36	Apr	6	(a)	Mansfield T	L 1-2	Davis	3,152
37		13	(h)	Barrow	W 3-1	Lawrence, Davis 2	2,643
38		19	(h)	Stockport C	L 1-2	L.Carr (pen)	5,460
39		20	(a)	Carlisle U	L 1-4	Davis	2,674
40		22	(a)	Stockport C	D 1-1	Miller	6,887
41		27	(h)	Rochdale	W 1-0	Worthy (og)	1,875
42	May	4	(a)	Lincoln C	L 0-1		3,128

FINAL LEAGUE POSITION: 16th in Division Three North

Appearances
Goals

FA Cup

#	Month	Date		Opponent	Result	Scorers	Attendance
1	Nov	24	(a)	Southport	D 1-1	L.Carr (pen)	4,880
R		28	(h)	Southport	D 1-1*	Allen	3,757
2R	Dec	3	(n†)	Southport	W 2-1	Kenyon, Butler	4,702
2		8	(a)	York C	L 0-1		6,039

*After extra-time. †Played at Goodison Park, Liverpool.

Appearances
Goals

Division Three North Cup

#	Month	Date		Opponent	Result	Scorers	Attendance
1	Jan	1	(h)	Crewe A	L 1-2	Butler	1,225

Appearances
Goals

Appearances and goals grid (player columns left to right: Bradshaw, Ratcliffe, Carr L, Smedley, Amery, McPherson L, Brown, Davis, McCrae, Butler, Miller, Kenyon, Allen, Kitching, Salmon, Carr AG, Beckett, Tarrant, Lawrence, Milligan, Bird, Bower, McPherson PC; match number at right).

Bradshaw	Ratcliffe	Carr L	Smedley	Amery	McPherson L	Brown	Davis	McCrae	Butler	Miller	Kenyon	Allen	Kitching	Salmon	Carr AG	Beckett	Tarrant	Lawrence	Milligan	Bird	Bower	McPherson PC	No.
1	2	3	4	5	6	7	8	9	10	11													1
1	2	3	4	5	6	7	8	9	10	11													2
1	2	3	4	5	6		8	9		11	7	10											3
1	2	3	4	5	6		8	9		11	7	10											4
1	2	3	4	5	6		8	9		11	7	10											5
1	2	3		5	6	7	8	9		10	11	4											6
1	2	3		5	6		10	9		11	7	4	8										7
1	2	3		5	8		9	11	6	10	7	4											8
1	2	3		5		7	8	9	6	11		4										10	9
1	2	3		5		7	8	9	6	11		4										10	10
1	2	3		5		7	8	9	6	11		4										10	11
1	2	3		5		7	9		6	10		4		8								11	12
1	2	3		5		7	9		6	10	11	4		8									13
1	2	3		5		7	9		6	10	11	4		8									14
1	5	2		3		7	9		6	10	11	4		8									15
	5	2	6	3		7	9			4	10	11	8		1								16
	5	2	6	3			9			4	10	7	8		1	11							17
	5	2	6	3		7	8			4	10				1	11	9						18
	5	2	6	3		7	9				10		8	4	1	11							19
	2	3	6	5		7	9			4	10		8		1	11							20
	2	3	6	5			9			4	10	7	8		1	11							21
	2	3	6	5			9			4	10		8		1	11		7					22
	2	3	6	5			9			4	10		8		1	11		7					23
	2	3	6				9		8	10				4	1	11		7	5				24
	2	3	6				9		8	10				4	1	11		7	5				25
	2	3	6				9			10		8		4	1	11		7	5				26
	2	3	6				9			10	7	8		4	1	11			5				27
	2	3	6				9			10		8		4		11		7	5	1			28
	2	3	6				9				10	8		4		11		7	5	1			29
	2		6				9			10		8		4		11		7	5	1	3		30
	2	3	6	5			9			10	11	8						7	4	1			31
	3	2	6	5			9		8	10				4		11		7		1			32
	2	3	4	5	8		9		6	11		10						7		1			33
	2	3	4	5	8		9		6	11		10						7		1			34
	2	3	4	5	8		9		6	11		10						7		1			35
	2	3	4	5			9		6	10		8				11		7		1			36
	2	3		5			9		6	10		8		4		11		7		1			37
	2	3		5			9		6	10		8		4		11		7		1			38
	2	3		5			9		6	10		8		4		11		7		1			39
	2	3	4	5			9		6	10		8				11		7		1			40
	2	3	6	5			9			10		8		4		11		7		1			41
	2	3	6	5			9			10		8		4		11		7		1			42
15	**42**	**41**	**29**	**35**	**11**	**11**	**42**	**11**	**32**	**38**	**13**	**31**	**8**	**20**	**12**	**22**	**1**	**20**	**8**	**15**	**1**	**4**	
Goals	2	2				2	26	1		4	3	10	1	1		3		3					

1 own-goal

Bradshaw	Ratcliffe	Carr L	Smedley	Amery	McPherson L	Brown	Davis	McCrae	Butler	Miller	Kenyon	Allen	Kitching	Salmon	Carr AG	Beckett	Tarrant	Lawrence	Milligan	Bird	Bower	McPherson PC	No.
	5	2	6	3		7	9		8	10	11			4	1								1
	5	2	6	3		7	9		8	10	11	4			1								R
	5	2	6	3		7	9		8	4	10	11			1								2R
	5	2	6	3		7	9		8	4	10	11			1								2
	4	**4**	**4**	**4**		**4**	**4**		**4**	**4**	**4**	**3**		**1**	**4**								
Goals							1		1	1	1												

Bradshaw	Ratcliffe	Carr L	Smedley	Amery	McPherson L	Brown	Davis	McCrae	Butler	Miller	Kenyon	Allen	Kitching	Salmon	Carr AG	Beckett	Tarrant	Lawrence	Milligan	Bird	Bower	McPherson PC	No.
	2	3	6	5		7	9			4	10		8		1	11							1
	1	**1**	**1**	**1**		**1**	**1**			**1**	**1**		**1**		**1**	**1**							
Goals							1																

231

1935-36

Manager: Bill Sawyer

1	Aug	31	(h)	Tranmere R	D	0-0	11,603
2	Sep	2	(a)	Barrow	L	0-3	4,298
3		7	(a)	Chesterfield	L	1-3 Lawrence	5,826
4		11	(h)	Barrow	L	2-3 Griffiths, Lawrence	3,546
5		14	(h)	Stockport C	W	2-0 Elliot, Salmon	4,969
6		18	(a)	York C	L	0-2	3,271
7		21	(a)	Crewe A	L	1-5 Griffiths	3,738
8		28	(h)	Accrington S	L	2-3 Brown 2	3,409
9	Oct	5	(a)	Southport	L	1-2 Search	2,774
10		12	(h)	Chester	D	3-3 Griffiths, Beedles (pen), Search	5,065
11		19	(h)	Gateshead	W	1-0 Search	2,173
12		26	(a)	Darlington	L	1-4 Johnson	3,898
13	Nov	2	(h)	Halifax T	L	1-4 Johnson	3,006
14		9	(a)	Oldham A	L	0-6	6,775
15		16	(h)	Wrexham	L	0-4	3,028
16		23	(a)	Rotherham U	L	0-5	6,230
17	Dec	7	(a)	Hartlepools U	L	1-4 Ainsworth	3,249
18		14	(h)	Carlisle U	W	3-0 Johnson 3	1,719
19		21	(a)	Walsall	W	2-1 Johnson, Lawton	5,445
20		26	(a)	Lincoln C	L	0-2	5,185
21		28	(a)	Tranmere R	L	1-3 Brock	13,529
22	Jan	1	(h)	Lincoln C	L	0-5	4,319
23		4	(h)	Chesterfield	L	1-2 Beckett	3,216
24		11	(h)	Mansfield T	W	1-0 Westcott	2,208
25		18	(a)	Stockport C	D	1-1 Westcott	5,226
26		25	(h)	Crewe A	W	3-1 Lawrence 2, Lawton	2,069
27	Feb	1	(a)	Accrington S	L	2-5 Westcott 2	3,645
28		8	(h)	Southport	W	2-1 Westcott 2	2,264
29		15	(a)	Chester	L	2-8 Lawton 2	4,860
30		22	(a)	Gateshead	L	1-3 Brock	2,846
31		29	(h)	Oldham A	L	1-3 Westcott	1,490
32	Mar	7	(a)	Halifax T	L	0-3	3,374
33		14	(h)	Darlington	D	1-1 Westcott	2,076
34		21	(a)	Wrexham	L	0-3	2,531
35		28	(h)	Rotherham U	W	3-0 Westcott 2, Brown	2,092
36	Apr	4	(a)	Mansfield T	L	0-2	3,220
37		10	(h)	Rochdale	W	2-0 Ainsworth 2	3,299
38		11	(h)	Hartlepools U	D	0-0	2,187
39		13	(a)	Rochdale	L	0-1	4,124
40		18	(a)	Carlisle U	L	0-3	3,592
41		25	(h)	Walsall	D	1-1 Brock (pen)	1,451
42	May	2	(h)	York C	L	0-2	1,675

FINAL LEAGUE POSITION: 22nd in Division Three North

Appearances
Goals

FA Cup

1	Nov	30	(h)	Workington	L	1-3 Lawrence	4,000

Appearances
Goals

Division Three North Cup

1	Nov	5	(a)	Southport	L	0-2	600

Appearances
Goals

Dense player-appearance grid. Column headers (left to right), then match rows 1–42, totals, and two sub-tables.

#	Bird	Beedles	Amery	Salmon	Hoggan	Baxter	Brown	Kitching	Griffiths	Lawrence	Elliot	Johnson	Burke	McMullan	Brock	Temple	Ainsworth	Greenhalgh	Search	Lloyd	Milligan	Rose	Beckett	Lumberg	Lawton	Westcott	Richardson	Wright	Morley	Ingham
1	1	2	3	4	5	6	7	8	9	10	11																			
2	1	2	3	4	5	6	7		9	10	11	8																		
3	1	2	3	4	5	6			9	8	7	11	10																	
4		2	3	5	4		8	9	7	11		10	1	6																
5		2	3	10	5	4		9	7	11				6	1		8													
6		2	3	10	5	4		9	7	11				6	1		8													
7		2	3	10	5	4		9	7	11				6	1		8													
8		2	3	4	5		7		9	10	11			6	1		8													
9		2	3		5				10	7	11			6	1		8	4	9											
10		2	3		5				10	7	11			6	1		8	4	9											
11		2	3		5				10	7	11		1	6			8	4	9											
12		2	3		5				10	7	11	9	1	6			8	4												
13		2	3		5				10	7	11	9	1	6			8	4												
14		2	5					7				1					8	4	9	3	6	10	11							
15		2	5					7				1					8	4	9		6		10	11	3					
16		2	5							10	7	11	1				8	4	9	6				3						
17		10				4				7	11	9	1	6			8	2		3	5									
18			3		5					7	11	9		6	1		8	2			4				10					
19			3		5	4				7	11	9		6	1		8	2							10					
20			3		5	4				7	11	9		6	1		8	2							10					
21			3		5	4				7	11	9		6	1		8	2							10					
22		4	3		5					7	11	9		6	1		8	2							10					
23			3		5	4				7		9		6	1		8	2						11	10					
24			3		5	4				7	11			6	1		8	2							10	9				
25			3		2	4				7	11			6	1		8	5							10	9				
26			3		5	4				7	11			6	1		8	2							10	9				
27			3			4				7	11			6	1		8	2		5					10	9				
28		3		4	5					7	11			6	1		8	2							10	9				
29		3		4	5					7	11			6	1		8	2							10	9				
30	1			5		7	4				11			6			8	2							10	9	3			
31	1			5		8	7				11			6		10		2								9	3	4		
32	1			5		8	7				11			6		10		2								9	3	4		
33	1			5		7					11			6		10		2								9	3	4	8	
34	1			5		7					11			6		10		2								9	3	4	8	
35	1			5		8	7				11			6		10		2								9	3	4		
36	1	10		5		7					11			6			8	2								9	3	4		
37	1			5		7			10		11			6			8	2								9	3	4		
38	1			5		7					11			6			8	2							10	9	3	4		
39	1			5		7					11			6			8	2							10	9	3	4		
40	1			5		7					11			6			8	2							10	9	3	4		
41	1			5		7					11			6			8	2							10	9	3	4		
42	1			5		7	9							6			8	2							10		3	4		11
Total	16	19	26	10	38	11	16	11	15	31	38	10	2	8	36	18	38	33	6	5	4	2	3	2	18	18	13	12	2	1
	1		1			3		3	4	1	6				3		3		3						1	4	10			

Sub-table 1:

Bird	Beedles	Amery	Salmon	Hoggan	Baxter	Brown	Kitching	Griffiths	Lawrence	Elliot	Johnson	Burke	McMullan	Brock	Temple	Ainsworth	Greenhalgh	Search	Lloyd	Milligan										#
	2	3							7	11		1	6			8	4	9	10	5										1
	1	1							1	1		1	1			1	1	1	1	1										
									1																					

Sub-table 2:

Bird	Beedles	Amery	Salmon	Hoggan	Baxter	Brown	Kitching	Griffiths	Lawrence	Elliot	Johnson	Burke	McMullan	Brock	Temple	Ainsworth	Greenhalgh	Search	Lloyd	Milligan										#
	2	3							7	11	9	1	6			8	4		5	10										1
	1	1							1	1	1	1	1			1	1		1	1										

1936-37

Manager: Bill Sawyer

1	Aug	29	(a)	Oldham A	L	1-3	Mustard	4,741
2	Sep	2	(h)	Port Vale	W	2-0	Ainsworth 2	4,522
3		5	(h)	Accrington S	D	1-1	Shiels	4,711
4		7	(a)	Port Vale	L	1-3	Gunn (og)	6,096
5		12	(a)	Lincoln C	L	0-1		5,647
6		16	(h)	Wrexham	W	1-0	Ainsworth	4,455
7		19	(h)	Tranmere R	L	1-2	Fogg	9,579
8		26	(h)	Hull C	D	1-1	Leonard	4,319
9	Oct	3	(a)	Gateshead	D	1-1	Watters	2,951
10		10	(h)	Darlington	W	2-0	Mustard, Watters	3,775
11		17	(a)	Halifax T	D	0-0		5,174
12		24	(h)	Mansfield T	D	0-0		4,722
13		31	(a)	Crewe A	W	2-0	Griffiths, Brock	3,651
14	Nov	7	(h)	Chester	W	1-0	Griffiths	8,435
15		14	(a)	Rochdale	L	0-4		3,356
16		21	(h)	Barrow	D	1-1	Griffiths	4,014
17	Dec	5	(h)	Carlisle U	D	1-1	Griffiths	2,353
18		19	(h)	Southport	W	3-1	Shiels, Foulkes 2	3,703
19		25	(h)	Stockport C	D	1-1	Foulkes	5,618
20		26	(h)	Oldham A	L	0-2		7,036
21		28	(a)	Stockport C	L	1-3	Leonard	5,368
22	Jan	1	(a)	Wrexham	L	1-4	Ainsworth	2,435
23		2	(a)	Accrington S	L	0-5		2,897
24		9	(h)	Lincoln C	L	1-2	Hullett	3,635
25		23	(a)	Tranmere R	L	2-3	Shiels, Hullett	6,493
26		30	(a)	Hull C	L	1-4	Ainsworth	2,928
27	Feb	6	(h)	Gateshead	D	1-1	Hullett	2,941
28		13	(a)	Darlington	W	2-1	Hullett 2	3,515
29		20	(h)	Halifax T	D	1-1	Mustard	2,677
30		27	(a)	Mansfield T	W	3-2	Hullett 2, Ainsworth	3,229
31	Mar	6	(h)	Crewe A	W	1-0	Bulloch	3,125
32		13	(a)	Chester	L	1-4	Ainsworth	5,755
33		20	(h)	Rochdale	W	5-1	Ainsworth 3, Mustard, Hullett	2,929
34		26	(h)	Rotherham U	W	4-0	Ainsworth, Bulloch, Roberts 2	4,420
35		27	(a)	Barrow	L	1-2	Roberts	5,718
36		29	(a)	Rotherham U	L	0-3		4,148
37	Apr	3	(h)	York C	W	4-1	Greenhalgh 2, Roberts, Shiels	3,487
38		10	(a)	Carlisle U	D	1-1	Greenhalgh	5,246
39		17	(h)	Hartlepools U	W	4-0	Greenhalgh 2, Shields 2	1,865
40		21	(a)	York C	L	1-2	Greenhalgh	3,313
41		24	(a)	Southport	L	0-3		4,375
42		28	(a)	Hartlepools U	L	0-5		2,870

FINAL LEAGUE POSITION: 15th in Division Three North

Appearances
Goals

FA Cup

1	Nov	28	(a)	Lincoln C	D	1-1	Griffiths	6,899
R	Dec	2	(h)	Lincoln C	L	2-3*	Mustard (pen), Watters	5,077

*After extra-time, score at 90 mins 2-2.

Appearances
Goals

Division Three North Cup

1	Oct	21	(a)	Wrexham	W	1-0	Leonard	1,382
†3	Mar	10	(a)	Chester	L	2-9	Hullett, Ainsworth	

†New Brighton had a bye in the second round

Appearances
Goals

Hawthorn	Greenhalgh	Richardson	Wright	Vaughton	Brock	Mustard	Ainsworth	Watters	Shiels	Watkins	Fogg	Lawrence	Bulloch	Leonard	Roberts	Griffiths	Foulkes	Ingham	Hullett	Lynch	
1	2	3	4	5	6	7	8	9	10	11											1
1	2	3	4	5	6	11	10	8	9		7										2
1	2	3	4	5	6	11	10	8	9		7										3
1	2	3	4	5	6	11	10	8	9		7										4
1	2	3	4	5	6	7	10	8	9			11									5
1	2	3	4	5	6	7	10	8	9			11									6
1	2	3	4	5	6	7	10	8			9	11									7
1	2	3			6	7	8		11		4		5	9	10						8
1	2	3			6	7	10	8	11		4		5	9							9
1		3		2	6	7	10	8	11		4		5	9							10
1		3		2	6	7	10	8	11		4		5	9							11
1		3		2	6	7	10	8	11		4		5	9							12
1		3		2	6	7	10	8	11		4		5			9					13
1		3		2	6	7	10	8	11		4		5			9					14
1		3		2	6	7	10	8	11		4		5			9					15
1		3		2	6	7	10	8	11		4		5			9					16
1		3		2	6	7	10	8	11		4		5			9					17
1	3			2	6	7	10		11		4		5			9	8				18
1	3			2	6		10		7	11	4		5			9	8				19
1	3			2	6	7	10		11		4		5			9	8				20
1	3		4	2	6	7	10		11				5	9			8				21
1	3		4	2	6	7	10		11				5	9			8				22
1	2	3	4	5	6	7	10									9	8	11			23
1	2	3	4	5	6	7	10					11					8		9		24
1	2	3	8	5	6	7	10		11		4								9		25
1		3	4	2	6	7	8		11		5				10				9		26
1		3	4	2	6	7	10		11		5						8		9		27
1		3	4	2	6	7		8	11				5		10				9		28
1		3	4	2	6	7		8	11				5		10				9		29
1		3	4	2	6	7	8		11				5		10				9		30
1		3	6	2		7	8		11		4		5		10				9		31
1		3	4	2		7	8		11		6		5		10				9		32
1		3	4	2		7	8		11		6		5		10				9		33
1		3	4	2		7	8		11		6		5		10				9		34
1		3	4	2		7	8		11		6		5		10				9		35
1		3	4	2		7	8		11		6		5		10				9		36
1	9	3	4	2		7	8		11		6		5		10						37
1	9	3	4	2		7	8		11		6		5		10						38
1	9	3	4	2		7	8		11		6		5		10						39
1	9	3	4	2		7	8		11		6		5		10						40
1	9	3	4	2		7	8		11		6		5		10						41
1	9	3	4	2		7	8		11		6		5		10						42
42	23	37	29	40	30	41	40	19	39	1	32	4	30	8	16	9	8	1	13		
	6				1	4	11	2	6		1		2	2	4	4	3		8		

1 own-goal

Hawthorn	Greenhalgh	Richardson	Wright	Vaughton	Brock	Mustard	Ainsworth	Watters	Shiels	Watkins	Fogg	Lawrence	Bulloch	Leonard	Roberts	Griffiths	Foulkes	Ingham	Hullett	Lynch	
1		3		2	6	7	10	8	11		4		5			9					1
1		3		2	6	7	10	8	11		4		5			9					R
2		2		2	2	2	2	2	2		2		2			2					
						1		1								1					

Hawthorn	Greenhalgh	Richardson	Wright	Vaughton	Brock	Mustard	Ainsworth	Watters	Shiels	Watkins	Fogg	Lawrence	Bulloch	Leonard	Roberts	Griffiths	Foulkes	Ingham	Hullett	Lynch	
1		3	4	2	6	7	10	8	11				5	9							1
1			4	2		7	8		11		6		5		10				9	3	3
2		1	2	2	1	2	2	1	2		1		2	1	1				1	1	
						1								1							

1937-38

Manager: Bill Sawyer

1	Aug	28	(h)	Barrow	W 2-1 Roberts, Montgomery	4,172
2	Sep	1	(a)	Crewe A	L 0-1	4,216
3		4	(a)	Wrexham	W 1-0 Greenhalgh (pen)	5,993
4		8	(h)	Crewe A	W 4-0 Mustard, Roberts, Shiels, Montgomery	4,655
5		11	(h)	Hartlepools U	W 4-1 Proctor (og), Montgomery 2, Ainsworth	5,419
6		13	(a)	Port Vale	L 2-3 Mustard (pen), Greenhalgh	4,257
7		18	(a)	Lincoln C	L 1-4 Ainsworth	8,935
8		25	(h)	Hull C	D 0-0	5,792
9	Oct	2	(a)	Tranmere R	L 2-5 Montgomery, Roberts	12,983
10		9	(a)	Gateshead	L 1-3 Roberts	10,713
11		16	(h)	Halifax T	W 2-0 Montgomery 2	4,092
12		23	(a)	Carlisle U	D 1-1 Roberts	3,911
13		30	(h)	Accrington S	W 2-1 Mustard, Montgomery	3,179
14	Nov	6	(a)	Chester	W 2-1 Ainsworth, Roberts	6,924
15		13	(h)	Rotherham U	L 2-3 Montgomery, Ainsworth	4,495
16		20	(a)	Rochdale	L 1-2 Mustard (pen)	5,295
17	Dec	4	(a)	Southport	D 0-0	3,264
18		18	(a)	York C	L 1-3 Montgomery	4,235
19	Jan	1	(a)	Barrow	L 0-3	4,888
20		12	(h)	Doncaster R	L 1-2 Ainsworth	2,460
21		15	(h)	Wrexham	D 1-1 Ainsworth	2,078
22		29	(h)	Lincoln C	L 0-1	2,898
23	Feb	2	(a)	Hartlepools U	L 0-1	1,911
24		5	(a)	Hull C	D 1-1 Wood	9,337
25		12	(h)	Tranmere R	L 0-1	12,005
26		19	(h)	Gateshead	W 4-1 Ainsworth, Conroy (og), Montgomery 2	4,262
27		26	(a)	Halifax T	L 0-2	4,551
28	Mar	5	(h)	Carlisle U	W 5-1 Montgomery 2, Mustard 2 (1 pen), Wood	4,075
29		12	(a)	Accrington S	L 1-3 Montgomery	3,710
30		19	(h)	Chester	W 4-0 Ainsworth 2, Montgomery 2	4,629
31		26	(a)	Rotherham U	W 2-1 Montgomery, Wood	9,179
32	Apr	2	(h)	Rochdale	W 2-0 Wood, Shiels	3,419
33		9	(a)	Doncaster R	L 0-3	9,169
34		11	(h)	Bradford C	D 1-1 Montgomery	2,868
35		15	(h)	Darlington	W 3-0 Wood, Mustard, Montgomery	4,974
36		16	(h)	Southport	D 2-2 Wood 2	4,436
37		18	(a)	Darlington	L 0-1	5,321
38		23	(a)	Bradford C	L 0-3	4,544
39		25	(a)	Oldham A	L 1-2 Roberts	7,447
40		30	(h)	York C	W 2-1 Montgomery 2	2,775
41	May	4	(h)	Oldham A	W 1-0 Montgomery	2,735
42		7	(h)	Port Vale	D 1-1 Montgomery	3,259

FINAL LEAGUE POSITION: 13th in Division Three North

Appearances
Goals

FA Cup

1	Nov	27	(h)	Workington	W 5-0 Montgomery 4, Mustard	5,287
2	Dec	15	(a)	Crewe A*	D 2-2 Wright, Montgomery	3,922
R		20	(h)	Crewe A	W 4-1 Ainsworth, Gilchrist (og), Smith, Montgomery	4,221
3	Jan	8	(h)	Plymouth A	W 1-0 Mustard (pen)	10,757
4		22	(h)	Tottenham H	D 0-0	13,029
R		26	(a)	Tottenham H	L 2-5 Hitchens (og), Bulloch	36,004

*Original game on 11 December was abandoned after 84 minutes (fog), when Crewe were leading 1-0.

Appearances
Goals

Division Three North Cup

1	Sep	22	(h)	Wrexham	W 2-0 Montgomery 2	2,000
2	Feb	9	(a)	Chester	L 0-5	1,600

Appearances
Goals

Hawthorn	Vaughton	Greenhalgh	Wright	Bulloch	Fogg	Mustard	Ainsworth	Montgomery	Roberts	Shiels	White A	Richardson	Millar	Small	Johnson	Buxton	Smith	Foulkes	Wood	Morris	No.
1	2	3	4	5	6	7	8	9	10	11											1
1	2	3	4	5	6	7	8	9	10	11											2
1	2	3	4	5	6		7	9	10	11	8										3
1	2	3	4	5	6	7	8	9	10	11											4
1	2	3	4	5	6	7	8	9	10	11											5
1	2	3	4	5	6	7	8	9	10	11											6
1	2	3	4	5	6	7	8		10	11		9									7
1	2	3	4	5	6	7	8	9	10	11											8
1	2	3	4	5	6	7	8	9	10	11											9
1	2	3	4	5	6	7	8	9	10	11											10
1	2	3	4	5	6	7	8	9	10				11								11
1	2	3	4	5	6		8	9	10	11				7							12
1	2	3	4	5	6	11	8	9	10					7							13
1	2	3	4	5	6	11	8	9	10					7							14
1	2	3	4	5		11	8	9	10					7	6						15
1	2	3	4			11		9	10					7	6	5	8				16
1	2	3	4	5		11		9	10					7	6		8				17
1	2	3	4		6	11		9						7		5	10	8			18
1	2	3	4	5	6	11	8	9						7		10					19
1	2	3	4	5	6	11	10	9						7			8				20
1	2	3	4		6	11	8	9						7		5	10				21
1	2				6	11	8	9				3		7	4	5	10				22
1	2		4			6	7	8	9				3		5	10	11				23
1	2		4			6	7		9	10			3		5		11	8			24
1	2		4			6		8		10		3	7	11	5		9				25
1	2		4			6	11	8	9				3	7		5			10		26
1	2		4			6	11	8	9	10			3	7		5					27
1	2		4			6	7	8	9		11	3				5			10		28
1	2		4			6	7	8	9		11	3				5			10		29
1	2		4			6	7	8	9		11					5			10	3	30
1	2		4			6	7	8	9		11					5			10	3	31
1	2		4			6	7	8	9		11					5			10	3	32
1	2		4			6	7	8	9		11					5			10	3	33
1	2		4			6		8	9		11	7				5			10	3	34
1	2		4			6	7	8	9			11				5			10	3	35
1	2		4			6	7		9			11		5	8				10	3	36
1	2		4			6			9	8		7				5		11	10	3	37
1	2		4			6	7		9	8						5		11	10	3	38
1	2		4			6	7		9	10						5		11	8	3	39
1	2		4			6	7		9	10						5		11	8	3	40
1	2					7	8	9						6	5			11	10	3	41
1	2		4			6	7	8	9							5		11	10	3	42
42	42	21	41	18	38	37	33	40	24	18	1	9	1	18	6	23	8	10	19	13	
		2				7	9	24	7	2						7					

2 own-goals

Hawthorn	Vaughton	Greenhalgh	Wright	Bulloch	Fogg	Mustard	Ainsworth	Montgomery	Roberts	Shiels	White A	Richardson	Millar	Small	Johnson	Buxton	Smith	Foulkes	Wood	Morris	No.
1		3	4	5		11	8	9	10					7	6	2					1
1	2	3	4	5	6	11	8	9						7		10					2
1	2	3	4	5	6	11	8	9						7		10					R
1	2	3	4	5	6	11	8	9						7		10					3
1	2	3	4	5	6	11	8	9						7		10					4
1	2	3	4	5	6	11	8	9						7		10					R
6	5	6	6	6	5	6	6	6	6	1				6	1	1	5				
		1	1			2	1	6									1				

2 own-goals

Hawthorn	Vaughton	Greenhalgh	Wright	Bulloch	Fogg	Mustard	Ainsworth	Montgomery	Roberts	Shiels	White A	Richardson	Millar	Small	Johnson	Buxton	Smith	Foulkes	Wood	Morris	No.
1	2	3	4	5	6	7	8	9	10	11											1
1	2		4		6	11	7	9	10			3			5		8				2
2	2	1	2	1	2	2	2	2	2	1		1			1		1				
								2													

1938-39

Manager: Bill Sawyer

1	Aug	27	(h)	Stockport C	D 0-0	5,782
2		31	(a)	Chester	W 3-1 Wood, Montgomery, Ainsworth	6,306
3	Sep	3	(a)	Accrington S	W 2-1 Montgomery 2	4,348
4		7	(h)	Lincoln C	W 3-2 Stein, Ainsworth, Wood	6,009
5		10	(h)	Barnsley	L 1-2 Ainsworth	7,574
6		12	(a)	Lincoln C	D 0-0	4,159
7		17	(a)	Oldham A	L 0-1	10,399
8		24	(h)	Halifax T	W 1-0 Frost	5,375
9	Oct	1	(a)	Wrexham	W 2-1 Frost 2	5,414
10		8	(a)	Barrow	L 0-3	5,596
11		15	(h)	York C	W 3-2 Frost, Stein, Ainsworth	5,177
12		22	(a)	Rochdale	L 0-2	7,292
13		29	(h)	Rotherham U	W 3-0 Frost, Ainsworth, Stein	5,126
14	Nov	5	(a)	Doncaster R	L 1-4 Wood	12,279
15		12	(h)	Southport	D 1-1 Stamps	7,755
16		19	(a)	Crewe A	L 1-7 Frost	5,626
17	Dec	3	(a)	Darlington	L 0-3	3,396
18		10	(h)	Carlisle U	L 2-3 Ainsworth, Bulloch	3,991
19		17	(a)	Gateshead	W 3-0 Frost, Ainsworth, Small	2,469
20		24	(a)	Stockport C	D 1-1 Frost	6,537
21		26	(a)	Hull C	L 0-3	8,053
22		27	(h)	Hull C	W 6-1 Blyth (og), Frost 3, Ainsworth 2	5,966
23		31	(h)	Accrington S	W 4-1 Stamps 2, Allmark, Frost	4,779
24	Jan	14	(a)	Barnsley	D 1-1 Stamps	11,342
25		18	(h)	Hartlepools U	W 5-2 Frost 2, Stamps, Ainsworth, Stein	1,453
26		21	(h)	Oldham A	L 0-1	3,658
27		28	(a)	Halifax T	L 1-3 Allmark	4,090
28	Feb	4	(h)	Wrexham	L 2-3 Frost, Ainsworth	4,207
29		11	(h)	Barrow	W 2-0 Ainsworth, Frost	4,480
30		18	(a)	York C	L 0-2	4,935
31		25	(h)	Rochdale	W 3-1 Wood, Frost 2	3,296
32	Mar	4	(a)	Rotherham U	D 0-0	4,620
33		11	(h)	Doncaster R	L 3-6 Montgomery 2, Ainsworth	2,925
34		18	(a)	Southport	D 1-1 Smith	3,605
35		25	(h)	Crewe A	L 1-2 Ainsworth	3,657
36	Apr	1	(a)	Carlisle U	D 1-1 Ainsworth	3,998
37		7	(h)	Bradford C	W 2-1 Montgomery, Ainsworth	5,480
38		8	(h)	Darlington	W 3-0 Montgomery, Smith, Small	2,746
39		10	(a)	Bradford C	D 3-3 Smith, Montgomery, Stein	4,745
40		15	(a)	Hartlepools U	L 2-3 Montgomery, Turner	1,554
41		22	(h)	Gateshead	L 0-1	2,725
42		29	(h)	Chester	L 1-3 Montgomery	2,553

FINAL LEAGUE POSITION: 16th in Division Three North

Appearances
Goals

FA Cup

1	Nov	26	(a)	Doncaster R	L 2-4 Stamps, Allmark	11,006

Appearances
Goals

Division Three North Cup

2	Mar	8	(a)	Wrexham	D 1-1 Montgomery	400
R		22	(h)	Wrexham	W 4-3* Ainsworth, Smith, Mathias (og), Stein	903
SF	Apr	19	(h)	Accrington S	D 0-0	2,000
R		26	(a)	Accrington S	L 0-2	1,400

*After extra-time, score at 90 minutes 3-3.

Appearances
Goals

238

Season appearance and goalscoring grid (shirt numbers shown per match).

Hawthorn	Vaughton	Topping	Wright	Bulloch	Turner	Small	Ainsworth	Montgomery	Wood	Stein	Gale	Buxton	Frost	Stamps	Kirkman	Allmark	Richardson	Hughes	Smith	Johnson	Haydon	Duff	Broadhurst	Morris	
1	2	3	4	5	6	7	8	9	10	11															1
	2	3	4	5	6	7	8	9	10	11	1														2
	2	3	4	5	6	7	8	9	10	11	1														3
	2	3	4	5	6	7	8	9	10	11	1														4
	2	3	4	5	6	7	8	9	10	11	1														5
1	2		4	5	6	7	8	9	10	11		3													6
1	2		4	5	6	7	8	9	10	11		3													7
1	2		4	5	6	7	8		10	11		3	9												8
1	2		4	5	6	7	8		10	11		3	9												9
1	2		4	5	6	7	8		10	11		3	9												10
1	2		4	5	6	7	8		10	11		3	9												11
1	2		4	5	6	7	8		10	11		3	9												12
1	2		4	5	6	7	8		10	11		3	9												13
1	2		4	5	6	7	8	9	10	11		3													14
	2		4	5	6	7	8			11	1	3	9	10											15
	2		4	5		7	8			11	1	3	9	10	6										16
	2		4	5			8			11	1	3	9	10	6	7									17
	2		4	5	6	7	8			11	1	3	9	10											18
	2		4	5	6	7	8			11	1	3	9	10											19
	2		4	5	6	7	8			11	1	3	9	10											20
	2		4	5	6	7	8				1	3	9	10				11							21
	2		4	5	6	7	8				1	3	9	10				11							22
	2		4	5	6		8				1	3	9	10		7		11							23
	2		4		6		8			11	1	3	9	10		5	7								24
	2		4				8			11	1	3	9	10		5	7	6							25
	2		4				8			11	1	3	9	10		5		6	7						26
	2		4		6		8			11	1	3	9			7	5	10							27
	2		4		6	7	8		10	11	1		9				3	5							28
1			4	2	6	7	8		10	11		3	9				5								29
1			4		6	7	8		10	11		2	9				3	5							30
1			4	2	6	7	8		10	11		3	9				5								31
1			4	2	6		8	9	10	11		3				7	5								32
1			4	2	6		8	9	10	7		3					5		11						33
1			4	2	6		8			7		3				9	5	10	11						34
1			4	2	6		8			7		3					5	10	11	9					35
1			4		6	7	8	9	10	11		2					5						3		36
1			4	2	6	7	8	9	10	11		3					5								37
1			4	2	6	7		9	10	11		3					5	8							38
1			4	2	6	7		9	10	11		3					5	8							39
1			4		6	7		9	10	11		3				2	5	8							40
1			4	5	6	7	8	9	10	11		3					2								41
1			4	5	6	7	8	9	10	11		3					2								42
24	28	5	42	34	38	32	39	17	27	39	18	31	23	12	2	5	13	17	8	2	1	3	1	1	
			1	1	2	16	10	4	5				18	5		2		3							

1 own-goal

Hawthorn	Vaughton	Topping	Wright	Bulloch	Turner	Small	Ainsworth	Montgomery	Wood	Stein	Gale	Buxton	Frost	Stamps	Kirkman	Allmark	Richardson	Hughes	Smith	Johnson	Haydon	Duff	Broadhurst	Morris	
	2		4	5			8			11	1	3	9	10	6	7									1
	1		1	1			1			1	1	1	1	1	1	1									
													1		1										

Hawthorn	Vaughton	Topping	Wright	Bulloch	Turner	Small	Ainsworth	Montgomery	Wood	Stein	Gale	Buxton	Frost	Stamps	Kirkman	Allmark	Richardson	Hughes	Smith	Johnson	Haydon	Duff	Broadhurst	Morris	
1			4	5	6		8	9	10	7		3					2		11						2
1			4		6		8			7		2					3	5	10	11	9				R
1			4	5		7	8	9	10			3					2		6	11					SF
1			4	5	6	7	8	9	10	11		3					2								R
4			4	3	3	2	4	3	3	3		4					4	1	1	1		3	1		
													1												

1 own-goal

1939-40

Manager: Bill Sawyer

1	Aug	26	(a)	Wrexham	L 0-2		5,607
2		30	(h)	Bradford C	W 2-1	Dodd, Main	3,655
3	Sep	2	(h)	Doncaster R	W 4-2	Dodd 2, Ainsworth, Bulloch (pen)	3,441

Above matches were played in the abortive Division Three North

Appearances
Goals

Regional League Western Division

4	Oct	21	(a)	Wrexham	L 4-6	Small, Ainsworth, Waring 2	3,088
5		28	(h)	Everton	L 0-1		5,790
6	Nov	11	(a)	Stoke C	L 1-4	Frost	2,000
7		18	(h)	Stockport C	W 4-2	Frost, Hanson, Wright, Waring	2,170
8		25	(h)	Manchester C	L 1-3	Hanson	2,781
9	Dec	2	(a)	Chester	D 1-1	Waring	1,500
10		9	(h)	Crewe A	W 6-1	Frost 2, Hanson 2 (1 pen), Malam, Waring	702
11		23	(a)	Liverpool	L 2-6	Hanson 2	2,000
12	Jan	6	(h)	Port Vale	D 2-2	Waring 2	1,299
13		20	(a)	Tranmere R	W 4-2	Hanson (pen), Frost 2, Wright	1,000
14	Feb	10	(h)	Wrexham	W 4-1	Frost 3, Hanson	1,366
15		24	(a)	Everton	L 0-3		3,595
16	Mar	9	(h)	Stoke C	W 3-1	Waring 3	1,357
17		16	(a)	Stockport C	L 1-4	Malam	3,000
18		22	(h)	Tranmere R	W 5-2	Waring 2, Frost 2, Small	5,430
19		23	(a)	Manchester C	W 3-2	Frost 3	5,900
20		30	(h)	Chester	W 4-2	Frost, Malam 3	2,997
21	Apr	6	(a)	Crewe A	W 4-0	Frost, Waring, Small, Davies	2,000
22	May	6	(a)	Manchester U	L 0-6		1,000
23		13	(a)	Port Vale	L 0-3		1,000
24		18	(h)	Manchester U	W 6-0	Waring, Frost 2, Hanson 3	1,800
25	Jun	1	(h)	Liverpool	D 0-0		2,035

FINAL LEAGUE POSITION: 7th in Regional League Western Division

Appearances
Goals

League War Cup

P	Apr	13	(h)	Crewe A	W 2-1	Malam, Frost (pen)	3,765
1		20	(h)	Stoke C	L 1-4	Frost (pen)	5,289
		27	(a)	Stoke C	L 1-2	Frost	4,000

Appearances
Goals

Hawthorn	Bulloch	Buxton	Wright	Hughes S	Turner	Main	Ainsworth	Montgomery	Dodd	Stein J	Richardson	Smith W	Ratcliffe	Davies J	Small	Waring	Frost	Steen AW	Eastham	Hanson	Murphy	Rawcliffe	Malam	Stevens JN	Chedgzoy	Newcomb	Anderson	Morris	Davis E	Tompkin	Smith CJ	Mottram W	No.
1	2	3	4	5	6	7	8	9	10	11																							1
1	2		4	5	6	7	8		9	11	3	10																					2
1	2		4	5	6	7	8		9	11	3	10																					3
3	3	1	3	3	3	3	3	1	3	3	2	2																					
1					1	1			3																								
1		3	4	5		10							2	6	7	8	9	11															4
1		3		5		10							2	6	7	8	9		4	11													5
1		3		5									2	6	7	8	9			11	4	10											6
1		3	4	5	7								2	6		8	9			11			10										7
1		3	4	5	7								2	6		8	9			11			10										8
1		3	4	5									2	6	7	8	9			11			10										9
1		3	4	5									2	6		8	9			11			10	7									10
1		3	4	5									2	6	7	10	9			11			8										11
1		3	4	5									2	6		10	9			11			8			7							12
1		3	4	5									2	6	7	10	9			11			8										13
1		3		5									2	6	7	10	9			11	4		8										14
1		3		5									2		7	10	9			11	4		8		6								15
1		3		5									2	4	7	10	9			11	6		8										16
1		3		5									2	4	7	10	9			11	6		8										17
1		3		5	7								2	4		10	9			11	6		8										18
1		3		5	7								2	4		10	9			11	6		8										19
1		3		5									2	4		10	9			11	6		8				7						20
1		3		5									2	4		10	9			11	6		8				7						21
1				5												10	9		7	11	6		8					3	4		2		22
1		3		5									2			10	9			11	6		8						4			7	23
1		3		5									2		7	8	9			11	6		10						4				24
1				5									2		7	8	9			11	6		10					3	4				25
22		20	8	22	4	2							21	17	12	22	22	1	2	21	13	1	19	1	1	1	2	2	4		1	1	
		2		1										1	3	14	18			11			5										
1		3	4	5	7								2	6	11	10	9						8										P
1		3	4	5	7								2	6	11	10	9						8										1
1		3		5									2	6	7	10	9						8						4	11			
3		3	2	3	2								3	3	3	3	3						3						1	1			
																	3						1										

1940-41

Manager: John Bebbington

1	Aug	31	(h)	Tranmere R	D	4-4	Dellow, Waring 2, Hanson	1,000
2	Sep	7	(a)	Tranmere R	L	1-5	Hanson (pen)	1,000
3		14	(a)	Manchester C	L	2-5	Waring 2	3,000
4		21	(a)	Wrexham	L	0-5		1,400
5		28	(h)	Southport	W	5-3	Frost 2, Hanson 2, Malam	750
6	Oct	12	(h)	Crewe A	W	6-2	Malam 2, Waring 2, Frost, Cope (og)	880
7		19	(a)	Crewe A	W	3-2	Frost 3	700
8		26	(h)	Wrexham	W	6-2	Hanson 4 (2 pens), Frost 2	963
9	Nov	2	(a)	Wrexham	L	2-4	Hanson, Waring	520
10		9	(a)	Southport	W	5-2	Hanson 3, Frost, Malam	487
11		16	(h)	Tranmere R	W	10-1	Malam 4, Hanson, Frost, Waring 3 (1 pen), Dellow	1,450
12		23	(h)	Chester	W	4-2	Waring 2, Hanson, Frost	1,100
13		30	(a)	Everton	L	1-2	Malam	1,000
14	Dec	7	(a)	Chester	L	2-6	Dellow, Frost	500
15		14	(a)	Liverpool	L	4-6	Hanson, Frost 2, Waring	1,000
16		25	(a)	Southport	W	4-2	Waring 2, Hanson, Frost	1,000
17	Jan	4	(a)	Wrexham	W	5-3	Frost 2 (1 pen), Hanson, Waring, Malam	860
18		11	(h)	Wrexham	W	6-1	Waring, Hanson, Malam 2, Dellow	800
19	Feb	1	(a)	Chester	L	1-7	Malam	400
20		8	(h)	Chester	W	2-0	Dellow, Mallam	750
21	Mar	22	(a)	Southport	W	6-2	Frost 3, Waring 2, Hanson	300
22		29	(a)	Tranmere R	W	5-3	Frost 3, W.B.Price (og), Waring	1,000
23	Apr	5	(a)	Chester	L	3-7	Howarth (og), Hanson, Malam	300
24		12	(h)	Crewe A	W	5-0	Waring 2, Chedgzoy 3	500
25		19	(a)	Crewe A	W	5-2	Waring 2, Frost 3	300
26		26	(h)	Everton	L	0-4		1,500

FINAL LEAGUE POSITION: 13th in North Regional League   Appearances

Matches 17-20 inclusive also counted as Lancashire Cup ties   Goals

League Cup

	Feb	15	(h)	Wrexham	W	2-1	Malam, Hanson	1,000
		22	(a)	Wrexham	W	8-5	Waring 2, Hanson 2, Frost 3, Dellow	1,358
	Mar	1	(a)	Tranmere R	W	3-0	Hanson 2, Frost	3,800
		8	(h)	Tranmere R	L	0-4		1,850

Appearances

Goals

Football appearances and goalscorers grid. Players (columns, left to right): Hawthorn, Bower, Morris, Rawcliffe H, Hughes S, Davis E, Dellow, Waring, Frost, Malam, Hanson, Cook S, Longdon, Surgey, Chedgzoy, Burnett, Buxton, Griffiths, Lambert, Anderson EW, Sloan, Price, Kiernan, Dooley, Cartwright, Hill M, Brown V, Gregson, Waller, Jones D, Lowe, Major, Roberts, Banks E, Ashurst, Kelsall, Ratcliffe, Anderson J, Rawcliffe F, Doyle T.

Hawthorn	Bower	Morris	Rawcliffe H	Hughes S	Davis E	Dellow	Waring	Frost	Malam	Hanson	Cook S	Longdon	Surgey	Chedgzoy	Burnett	Buxton	Griffiths	Lambert	Anderson EW	Sloan	Price	Kiernan	Dooley	Cartwright	Hill M	Brown V	Gregson	Waller	Jones D	Lowe	Major	Roberts	Banks E	Ashurst	Kelsall	Ratcliffe	Anderson J	Rawcliffe F	Doyle T	#
1	2	3	4	5	6	7	8	9	10	11																														1
1	2	3	4	5	6	7	8	9	10	11																														2
1		3			5	6	7	8	9	10	11	2	4																											3
1		3			5	6	7	8	9	10	11		4	2																										4
1		3	4	5	6	7	8	9	10	11		2																												5
1		3			5	6	7	8	9	10	11	2	4																											6
1		3			5	6	7	8	9	10	11	2	4																											7
1		3			5	6	7	8	9	10	11	2	4																											8
1		3			5	6	7	8	9	10	11	2	4																											9
1		3			5	6	7	8	9	10	11	2																										4		10
1		3				6	7	8	9	10	11	2	5																									4		11
1		3				6	7	8	9	10	11	2	5																									4		12
1		3				6	7	8	9	10	11	2	5																									4		13
1		3				6	7	8	9	10	11	2	5																									4		14
1		3				6	7	8	9	10	11	2	5	4																									15
1		3				6	7	8	9	10	11	2	4																								5			16
		3				6	7	8	9	10	11		4		1	2	5																							17
		3				6	7	8	9	10	11	2	5	4	1																									18
						6	7	8	9	10	11	2	4		1		5	3																						19
						6	7	8	9	10		2	4	5	1				3	11																				20
							8	9	10	11				7	1							2	3	4	5	6														21
							8	9	10	11				7	1								3	4		6	2	5												22
							8	9	10	11				7	1											6	5	3	4								2			23
							8	9	10	11				7	1							2				6	5		3									4		24
		3					8	9	10					7	1											6	5			2	4	11								25
							8	9	10	11				7	1											6	5			3			2	4						26
16	2	19	3	10	20	20	26	26	26	24	15	17	1	9	10	1	2	1	2	1	1	2	2	1	6	1	5	1	1	3	1	1	1	1	1	1	1	5	1	
						5	24	26	15	21				3																										

3 own-goals

Hawthorn	Bower	Morris	Rawcliffe H	Hughes S	Davis E	Dellow	Waring	Frost	Malam	Hanson	Cook S	Longdon	Surgey	Chedgzoy	Burnett	Buxton	Griffiths	Lambert	Anderson EW	Sloan	Price	Kiernan	Dooley	Cartwright	Hill M	Brown V	Gregson	Waller	Jones D	Lowe	Major	Roberts	Banks E	Ashurst	Kelsall	Ratcliffe	Anderson J	Rawcliffe F	Doyle T
						6	7	8	9	10	11	2		5	1											3										4			
							7	8	9	10	11		2	4	1							3		5	6														
							7	8	9	10	11		2	4	1							3		5	6														
							7	8	9	10	11	2	4		1							3		5	6														
						1	4	4	4	4	4	2	3	3	4							3		3	4											1			
							1	2	4	1	5																												

1941-42

Manager: John Bebbington

1	Aug	30	(a)	Manchester U	L 1-13	Frost	2,000
2	Sep	6	(h)	Manchester U	D 3-3	Waring, Malam (pen), Frost	1,500
3		13	(h)	Tranmere R	W 2-1	Malam, Frost	2,500
4		20	(a)	Tranmere R	D 1-1	Waring	4,100
5		27	(a)	Liverpool	L 2-7	Malam, Eden	5,000
6	Oct	4	(h)	Liverpool	D 5-5	Frost 2, Malam 2 (1 pen), Waring	3,000
7		11	(h)	Wrexham	D 2-2	Waring 2	1,000
8		18	(a)	Wrexham	D 2-2	Frost 2	700
9		25	(a)	Manchester C	D 2-2	Malam, Waring	2,000
10	Nov	1	(h)	Manchester C	W 3-2	Frost, Pilling, Dellow	1,500
11		8	(h)	Stoke C	L 3-5	Waring 2, Frost	2,000
12		15	(a)	Stoke C	L 0-4		1,500
13		22	(h)	Stockport C	W 6-3	Waring 2, Dellow, Malam 2, Pilling	500
14		29	(a)	Stockport C	L 1-7	Brand	1,000
15	Dec	6	(a)	Everton	L 0-4		2,577
16		13	(h)	Everton	L 1-5	Waring	2,000
17		20	(h)	Chester	W 4-3	Malam, Waring 3	1,000
18		25	(a)	Chester	L 1-6	Malam	3,000

FINAL LEAGUE POSITION: 30th in Football League Northern Section (First Competition)   Appearances
Goals

Second Competition

19	Dec	27	(a)	Southport	L 1-2	Malam	2,000
20	Jan	3	(h)	Southport	W 4-3	Waring 2, Frost 2	1,000
21		10	(a)	Bury	L 5-10	Waring, Frost, Malam 2 (1 pen), Dellow	1,310
22		17	(h)	Bury	L 0-6		1,000
23		31	(h)	Blackburn R	L 0-5		1,000
24	Feb	7	(a)	Tranmere R	W 2-0	Dellow, Frost	2,000
25		14	(h)	Tranmere R	W 3-1	Waring 2, Malam	1,000
26		21	(h)	Chester	W 2-1	Waring 2	1,000
27		28	(a)	Chester	L 0-5		2,500
28	Mar	7	(a)	Blackburn R	L 1-5	Dellow	1,000
29	Apr	4	(a)	Tranmere R	W 5-0	Caffrey 2, H.Lamb (og), Malam, Frost	1,500

FINAL LEAGUE POSITION: 36th in Football League Northern Section (Second Competition)   Appearances
Goals

In the Second Competition, matches 21 to 28 inclusive were also in the League Cup Qualifying Competition.

Football appearances and goals grid (shirt numbers worn by each player per match).

Burnett	Lowe	Gregson	Brand	Chedgzoy	Pilling	Dellow	Waring	Frost	Malam	Vose J	Eden	Campbell C	Parker WD	Hill	Adams	Hughes S	Leyfield	Redwood	Davis E	Woods	Castle	Caffrey J	Fenton W	Parker H	Bennett JR	No.
1	2	3	4	5	6	7	8	9	10													11				1
1	2	3	4	5	6	7	8	9	10	11																2
1	2	3	4	5	6	7	8	9	10	11																3
1	2	3	4	5	6	7	8	9	10		11															4
	2	3	4	5	6	7	8	9	10		11												1			5
	2	3	4	5	6	7	8	9	10		11	1														6
	2		4	5	6	7	8	9	10		11		3										1			7
		3	7	5	6		8	9	10		11		2	4										1		8
		3		5	6	7	8	9	10		11		2	4										1		9
		3		5	6	7	8	9	10		11		2	4										1		10
		3	11	5	6	7	8	9	10				2	4	1											11
		3		5	6	7	8	9	10		11		2	4	1											12
		3	11		6	7	8	9	10				2	4	1	5										13
		3	5	11	6	7	8	9	10				2	4	1											14
		3	5		6	7	8	9	10				2	4	1		11									15
			5		6	7	8	9	10				3	4	1		11	2								16
		3	5		6	7	8	9	10					4	1		11							2		17
		3			6	7	8	9	10					4	1	5	11							2		18
4	13	14	11	12	18	17	18	18	18	2	8	1	10	11	8	2	4	1				1	2	5		
			1		2	2	14	9	10		1															

Burnett	Lowe	Gregson	Brand	Chedgzoy	Pilling	Dellow	Waring	Frost	Malam	Vose J	Eden	Campbell C	Parker WD	Hill	Adams	Hughes S	Leyfield	Redwood	Davis E	Woods	Castle	Caffrey J	Fenton W	Parker H	Bennett JR	No.
		3			6	7	8	9	10					4	1	5	11							2		19
		3	5		6	7	8	9	10					4	1		11							2		20
		3		11	6	7	8	9	10					5	1				4					2		21
		3		11	6	7	8	9	10						1	5			4					2		22
		3	5		11	7	8	9	10					6					4	1				2		23
		3			6	7	8	9	10					4		5					1	11		2		24
		3	5	6		7	8	9	10					4							1	11		2		25
		3	5		6	7	8	9	10					4							1	11		2		26
		3			6	7	8	9	10					4		5					1	11		2		27
		3	5		6	7	8	9	10					4						1		11		2		28
		3	4		6	7		9	10					8		5				1		11		2		29
		10	6	4		10	11	10	11				10	4	5	2			3	2	5	6		11		
							3	7	5					5									2			

1 own-goal

1946-47

Manager: Neil McBain

1	Aug	31	(a)	Wrexham	L 2-3	Buist, Pendergast	10,024
2	Sep	4	(h)	Bradford C	D 0-0		6,126
3		7	(h)	Doncaster R	L 2-5	Buist (pen), Forsyth	10,242
4		9	(a)	Bradford C	L 1-2	Pendergast	9,614
5		14	(a)	Rochdale	D 2-2	McGeachie, Kilshaw	5,612
6		21	(h)	Tranmere R	W 2-1	Wells, McLellan	14,291
7		28	(h)	Halifax T	D 1-1	Pendergast	9,798
8	Oct	5	(a)	Carlisle U	L 2-3	McLellan, McGeachie	10,118
9		12	(h)	Accrington S	W 4-0	McLellan Pendergast, Pritchard, Buist	6,450
10		19	(a)	Darlington	L 0-4		6,922
11		26	(h)	Hull C	L 1-5	Buist (pen)	5,005
12	Nov	2	(a)	Gateshead	L 0-3		4,264
13		9	(h)	Hartlepools U	W 2-1	Pritchard, Pendergast	4,857
14		16	(a)	Crewe A	L 0-3		7,133
15		23	(h)	Lincoln C	W 4-2	Shirley 2, Pendergast, McGeachie	4,017
16	Dec	14	(a)	Chester	L 1-2	Pendergast	5,942
17		25	(a)	Oldham A	D 2-2	A.Ainsworth 2	10,804
18		26	(h)	Oldham A	W 4-0	Pendergast 3, A.Ainsworth	6,898
19	Jan	1	(h)	Stockport C	W 1-0	McLellan	5,298
20		4	(a)	Doncaster R	D 0-0		14,482
21		11	(a)	Southport	L 0-2		4,196
22		18	(h)	Rochdale	L 1-2	Wells	5,130
23		25	(a)	Tranmere R	D 3-3	Pendergast 2, A.Ainsworth	13,580
24	Feb	1	(a)	Halifax T	W 1-0	A.Ainsworth	3,842
25	Mar	8	(h)	Gateshead	L 2-3	Pendergast, Buist	4,252
26		15	(a)	Hartlepools U	L 0-3		5,874
27		22	(h)	Crewe A	W 4-0	Shirley, A.Ainsworth, Pritchard, Forsyth	4,581
28		29	(a)	Lincoln C	L 1-5	A.Ainsworth	5,058
29	Apr	4	(h)	Barrow	L 0-1		6,628
30		5	(h)	Southport	W 1-0	Pendergast	3,291
31		7	(a)	Barrow	W 1-0	Pritchard (pen)	6,963
32		12	(a)	Rotherham U	L 0-3		11,558
33		19	(h)	Chester	L 0-3		7,006
34		26	(a)	York C	W 2-1	Forsyth, A.Ainsworth	4,448
35	May	3	(a)	Stockport C	L 0-2		5,610
36		10	(a)	Accrington S	L 1-3	Hitchen (pen)	2,406
37		17	(h)	York C	L 0-3		4,223
38		24	(h)	Darlington	W 4-1	Buist, Paterson 2, McGeachie	3,485
39		26	(h)	Carlisle U	D 2-2	Paterson, J.Ainsworth	4,561
40		31	(h)	Wrexham	W 1-0	Paterson	4,615
41	Jun	7	(a)	Hull C	D 1-1	Paterson	9,802
42		14	(h)	Rotherham U	W 1-0	Paterson	3,426

FINAL LEAGUE POSITION: 18th in Division Three North

Appearances
Goals

FA Cup

1	Nov	30	(a)	Hull C	D 0-0		21,895
R	Dec	4	(h)	Hull C	L 1-2*	Wells	7,688

*After extra-time, score at 90 minutes 1-1.

Appearances
Goals

246

Corbett	Topping	Richardson	McGeachie	Hill	Paterson	Buist	Wells	Pendergast	Ainsworth A	Forsyth	Pritchard	Long	Kilshaw	McLellan	Clewlow	Hitchen	Shirley	McBain	Evans N	Birkett	Ainsworth J	
1	2	3	4	5	6	7	8	9	10	11												1
1	2	3	4	5	6	7		9	8			10	11									2
1	2	3	4	5	6	7		9	8	11		10										3
1	2	3	4	5	6	7	8	9		11	10											4
1	2	3	4	5	6		8	9		11		10	7									5
1	2	3	4	5	6		8	9			11	10	7									6
1	2	3	4	5	6		8	9			11	10	7									7
1	2	3	4	5	6	7		9		11	10			8								8
1	2	3	4	5	6	7		9		11	8			10								9
1	2	3		5	6	7		9		11			8	10	4							10
1	2	3	4	8	6	7		9		11				10		5						11
1	2	3	4	5	6	7		9		11			8	10								12
1	2	3	4	5	6		8	9		11	10			7								13
1	2	3	4	5	6		8	9		11	10			7								14
1	2	3	4	5	6		8	9	10	11							7					15
1	2	3	4		6		8	9	10	11						5	7					16
1	2	3		4	6			9	10	11				8		5	7					17
1	2	3		4	6			9	10	11				8		5	7					18
1	2	3		4	6			9	8	11				10		5	7					19
1	2	3		4	6			9	8	11				10		5	7					20
1	2	3		4	6		8	9		11				10		5	7					21
1	2	3	4		6		8	9		11				10		5	7					22
1	2	3	4		6	7	8	9		11				10		5						23
1	2	3	4		6	7	8	9		11				10		5						24
1	2	3	4		6	7	8	9		11				10		5						25
	2	3	4	8	6			9		11				10		5		1	7			26
1	2	3	4		6			9	8	11	10					5	7					27
1	2	3	4		6			9	8	11				10		5	7					28
1	2	3	4		6			9	8	11	10					5	7					29
1	2	3	4		6			9	8	11	10					5	7					30
1	2	3	4	6	10			9	8	11						5	7					31
1	2	3	4	6	10	11		9	8							5	7					32
1	2	3		4	6			9	8	11	10					5	7					33
1	2	3		4	6			9	8	11	10					5	7					34
1	2	3		4	6	11	10	8	9							5	7					35
1	2	3		4	6	11	10	8	9							5	7					36
1	2	3		4	6	11	10	8	9							5				7		37
1	2	3	4	6	10	7	8			11						5					9	38
1	2	3	4	6	10	7	8			11						5					9	39
1	2	3	4	6	10	7	8	9		11						5						40
1	2	3	4	6	10	7				11				8		5					9	41
1	2	3	4	6	10	7				11				8		5					9	42
41	42	42	31	36	39	21	20	35	20	32	17	2	8	22	1	28	18	1	1	1	4	—
			4		6	6	2	14	8	3	4		1	4		1	3				1	—

Corbett	Topping	Richardson	McGeachie	Hill	Paterson	Buist	Wells	Pendergast	Ainsworth A	Forsyth	Pritchard	Long	Kilshaw	McLellan	Clewlow	Hitchen	Shirley	McBain	Evans N	Birkett	Ainsworth J	
1	2	3	4		6		8	9	10	11						5	7					1
1	2	3	4		6		8	9	10	11						5	7					R
2	2	2	2		2		2	2	2	2						2	2					
								1														

When manager Neil McBain turned out in goals in Match 26 he became the oldest player ever to appear in a Football League game, at 51 years and four months.

1947-48

Manager: Neil McBain until February 1948

1	Aug	23	(h)	Bradford C	L 0-2	6,616
2		30	(a)	Barrow	D 1-1 Pendergast	6,121
3	Sep	3	(h)	Accrington S	L 0-1	4,458
4		6	(h)	Wrexham	D 1-1 Paterson	6,819
5		10	(a)	Lincoln C	W 2-1 Wells, Pendergast	10,092
6		13	(a)	Halifax T	W 2-1 Pendergast 2	8,057
7		20	(h)	Rochdale	D 0-0	7,135
8		27	(a)	Tranmere R	L 0-1	17,359
9		30	(a)	Accrington S	L 3-5 Pendergast 3	8,385
10	Oct	4	(a)	Southport	L 0-4	9,170
11		11	(h)	Oldham A	D 2-2 McLean, Hitchen	5,890
12		18	(a)	York C	L 1-3 Pritchard	8,218
13		25	(h)	Mansfield T	D 2-2 Wells, Pritchard	5,540
14	Nov	1	(a)	Chester	L 2-4 Pritchard 2	7,733
15		8	(h)	Crewe A	L 1-2 Pendergast	5,494
16		15	(a)	Carlisle U	L 1-2 McLean	11,829
17		22	(h)	Rotherham U	L 1-2 Pendergast	5,231
18	Dec	6	(h)	Gateshead	L 1-2 A.Ainsworth	4,025
19		20	(a)	Bradford C	D 1-1 Paterson	7,481
20		25	(a)	Stockport C	W 2-1 J.Ainsworth, McLellan	11,816
21		27	(h)	Stockport C	W 1-0 Paterson	5,884
22	Jan	1	(h)	Lincoln C	L 0-1	3,321
23		3	(h)	Barrow	D 1-1 Paterson	4,858
24		10	(a)	Hartlepools U	L 0-1	6,927
25		17	(a)	Wrexham	D 0-0	10,157
26		24	(a)	Darlington	L 1-3 Pendergast	5,167
27		31	(h)	Halifax T	W 1-0 J.Ainsworth	3,958
28	Feb	7	(a)	Rochdale	L 0-1	4,496
29		14	(h)	Tranmere R	L 0-2	10,934
30		21	(h)	Southport	D 2-2 Forsyth, McLellan	3,512
31		28	(a)	Oldham A	L 0-3	10,009
32	Mar	6	(h)	York C	W 2-1 Brindle, Pendergast	4,614
33		13	(a)	Mansfield T	L 0-5	10,886
34		20	(h)	Chester	L 0-1	4,806
35		26	(h)	Hull C	W 1-0 Pendergast	7,591
36		27	(a)	Crewe A	L 0-4	4,735
37		29	(a)	Hull C	L 0-3	21,860
38	Apr	3	(h)	Carlisle U	L 1-3 McLellan	3,935
39		10	(a)	Rotherham U	L 1-6 Selkirk (og)	13,669
40		17	(h)	Hartlepools U	L 1-2 Brindle	2,810
41		24	(a)	Gateshead	L 1-3 Rainford	2,923
42	May	1	(h)	Darlington	W 2-1 Earl, Brindle	2,377

FINAL LEAGUE POSITION: 22nd in Division Three North

Appearances
Goals

FA Cup

1	Nov	29	(h)	Marine	W 4-0 McGeachie, A.Ainsworth, Hope, Pendergast	8,990
2	Dec	13	(a)	Bristol R	L 0-4	10,723

Appearances
Goals

248

Corbett	Topping	Richardson	McGeachie	Hitchen	Hill	Broughton	Pendergast	Ainsworth J	Paterson	Forsyth	Birkett	McLean	Wells	Mackie	Hope	Ainsworth A	McLellan	Pritchard	Baines	Daniels	Hounslea	Redfern	Brindle	Rainford	Earl	
1	2	3	4	5	6	7	8	9	10	11																1
1	2	3	4	5	6	7	8	9	10	11																2
1	2	3	4	5	6		8	9	10	11	7															3
1	2	3	4	5	6			9	10	11		7	8													4
1	2		4	5	6			9	10	11			8	3	7											5
1	2		4	5	6			9	10	11		7	8	3												6
1	2	3	4	5	6			9	10	11		7				8										7
1	2	3	4	5	6			9		11		7	8				10									8
1	2	3	4	5	6			9		11			8		7		10									9
1	2	3	4	5	6			9	10			7	8					11								10
1	2	3	4	5	6			9				7	8				10	11								11
1		3	4	5					9	6		7	8			2	10	11								12
1	2	3	4	5					9	6		7	8				10	11								13
1	2	3	4	5					9	6		7	8				10	11								14
1	2	3	4	5					9	6		7	8				10	11								15
1	2	3		5	6				9	4		7	8				11	10								16
1	2	3	4	5	6				9			7	8				11	10								17
	2	3	4	5	6				9			11	8		7	10				1						18
		3	4	5	6			9	8	11						7	10			1	2					19
		3	4	5	6			9	8	11						7	10			1	2					20
		3	4	5	6			9	8	11						7	10			1	2					21
		3	4	5	6			9	8	11						7	10			1	2					22
		3		5	6			9	8	11						7	10			1	2	4				23
		3	4	5	6			9	8	11						7	10			1	2					24
		3		5	6			9	8	11						7	10			1	2	4				25
		3		5	6			9	10	11		8				7				1	2	4				26
		3		5	6	10		9		11		8				7				1	2	4				27
		3		5	4	10		9		6	11					7				1	2	8				28
		3		5	4	10		9		6	11	7								1	2	8				29
		3	4	5	6			9		11	7					8	10			1	2					30
		3	4	5	6			9		11	7					8	10			1	2					31
		3	4	5	6			9		11	7						10			1	2		8			32
		3	4	5	6	10	9			11	7									1	2		8			33
	2	3	4	5	6					11					8		7			1				9	10	34
	2	3	4	5	6			9		11										1		7	8		10	35
	2	3	4	5	6			9		11										1		7	8		10	36
	2	3	4	5	6					11	9				7					1			8		10	37
	2	3	4	5	6			9									11			1		7	8		10	38
	2	3	4	5	6			9		11							8			1		7			10	39
	2	3		5	6					11						4				1		7	8	9	10	40
		3		5	6					11						4				1	2	7	8	9	10	41
	2	3		5	6					11			9			4				1		7	8		10	42
17	25	40	32	42	37	4	34	10	28	32	7	12	16	2	19	8	12	8	2	25	16	13	9	3	9	
			1				12	2	4	1		2	2				1	3	4			3	1	1		

1 own-goal

Corbett	Topping	Richardson	McGeachie	Hitchen	Hill	Broughton	Pendergast	Ainsworth J	Paterson	Forsyth	Birkett	McLean	Wells	Mackie	Hope	Ainsworth A	McLellan	Pritchard	Baines	Daniels	Hounslea	Redfern	Brindle	Rainford	Earl	
	2	3	4	5	6			9			11		8		7	10				1						1
	2	3	4	5	6			9	8	10	11		7							1						2
	2	2	2	2	2			2	1	1	2		1		2	1				2						
				1				1							1	1										

1948-49

Manager: Jack Atkinson

1	Aug	21	(a)	Gateshead	L 0-3	6,100
2		25	(h)	Carlisle U	W 2-0 Lyon 2	7,178
3		28	(h)	Hartlepools U	D 1-1 S.Roberts	9,093
4	Sep	2	(a)	Carlisle U	D 2-2 McTaff, Lyon	13,216
5		4	(a)	Darlington	W 2-0 McClure, Lyon	12,186
6		8	(h)	Stockport C	L 0-2	9,238
7		11	(h)	Rochdale	L 1-2 Lyon	8,385
8		15	(a)	Stockport C	L 0-1	9,525
9		18	(a)	Tranmere R	W 1-0 S.Roberts	16,336
10		25	(a)	Chester	L 0-2	8,546
11	Oct	2	(h)	Southport	L 0-1	8,497
12		9	(h)	Oldham A	L 0-1	5,925
13		16	(a)	Accrington S	L 1-5 S.Roberts	5,800
14		23	(h)	Rotherham U	L 0-1	7,052
15		30	(a)	Hull C	L 1-4 Lyon	31,039
16	Nov	6	(h)	Doncaster R	L 0-1	6,030
17		13	(a)	Bradford C	D 1-1 Russell (pen)	9,390
18		20	(h)	Halifax T	W 2-0 Lyon, Eaves	5,607
19	Dec	4	(h)	Mansfield T	W 1-0 Carter	5,900
20		25	(h)	York C	W 3-1 McClure 2, S.Roberts	4,772
21		26	(a)	York C	L 1-2 Carter	10,870
22	Jan	1	(a)	Hartlepools U	L 1-3 Taylor	7,891
23		15	(h)	Darlington	W 1-0 Taylor	3,454
24		22	(a)	Rochdale	D 1-1 Taylor	5,867
25		29	(a)	Wrexham	L 1-2 S.Roberts	9,500
26	Feb	5	(h)	Tranmere R	W 2-1 McClure, Carter	11,990
27		12	(a)	Mansfield T	L 0-2	9,187
28		19	(h)	Chester	D 1-1 Taylor	8,672
29		26	(a)	Southport	W 1-0 Taylor	6,321
30	Mar	5	(a)	Oldham A	L 2-4 McTaff, McClure	8,378
31		12	(h)	Accrington S	L 1-3 S.Roberts	5,296
32		19	(a)	Rotherham U	D 1-1 McPeake (pen)	9,380
33		26	(h)	Hull C	D 0-0	8,650
34	Apr	2	(a)	Doncaster R	L 1-2 Taylor	9,463
35		9	(h)	Bradford C	W 1-0 Eaves	4,999
36		15	(a)	Crewe A	L 1-2 Carter	6,256
37		16	(a)	Halifax T	W 2-0 Taylor, S.Roberts	8,928
38		18	(h)	Crewe A	W 2-1 S.Roberts, Eaves	7,101
39		23	(h)	Wrexham	W 2-0 Taylor, McClure	6,300
40		27	(h)	Barrow	W 3-1 Taylor, Carter 2	4,911
41		30	(a)	Barrow	L 1-2 Taylor	3,671
42	May	4	(h)	Gateshead	D 2-2 McPeake, Carter	5,032

FINAL LEAGUE POSITION: 17th in Division Three North

Appearances
Goals

FA Cup

1	Nov	27	(h)	Carlisle U	W 1-0 Lyon	10,000
2	Dec	11	(a)	Bradford C	D 0-0*	18,330
R		18	(h)	Bradford C	W 1-0 Lyon	7,000
3	Jan	8	(a)	Sheffield U	L 2-5 Carter, Latham (og)	28,097

*No extra-time possible (poor light)

Appearances
Goals

Grimley	Carr	Richardson	McTaff	Atkinson	McPeake	Taylor	Lyon	Roberts S	Russell	McClure	Hope	Wells	Galbraith	Redfern	Roberts PL	Carter	Eaves E	Bowman	Bannerman	Daniels	#
1	2	3	4	5	6	7	8	9	10	11											1
1		3	4	5	6	7	8	9	10	11	2										2
1		3	4	5	6	7	8	9	10	11	2										3
1		3	4	5	6	7	8	9	10	11	2										4
1		3	4	5	6	7	8	9	10	11	2										5
1		3	4	5	6	7	8	9	10	11	2										6
1		3	4	5	6		8	9	10	11	2	7									7
1		4		6		10	9	8	11	5	2		3	7							8
1		4		6	7	10	9	8	11	5	2		3								9
1		4		6	7	10	9	8	11	5	2		3								10
1		4		6	7	10	9	8	11	5	2		3								11
1		6	5		7	8		10	11	4	2		3	9							12
1		4		6	7	8	9		11	5	2		3	10							13
1		4		6	7	8	9	10	11	5	2		3								14
1		4	5	6	7	8	9	10	11		2		3								15
1		4	5	6	7	9		10			2		3		8	11					16
1		4	5	6	7	8	9	10			2		3			11					17
1		4	5	6	7	8		10			2		3			11	9				18
1		4	5	6		8	9	10	11		2		3			7					19
1		4		6	7	8	9		11	5	2		3			10					20
1		3	4	5	6	7	8	9	11	2						10					21
1		3		5	6	7	8	9	10	2			4			11					22
1		3		5	6	7	4	9	8	11						10	2				23
1		3		5	6	7	4	9	8	11						10	2				24
1		3		5	6		8	9	10	11			4			2	7				25
1		3		5	6	7	4	9	8	11						10	2				26
1		3		5	6	7	4	9	8	11						10	2				27
1		4	5	6	7	8	9		11	2			3			10					28
1		4	5	6	7	8	9		11	2			3			10					29
1		4		6	7	8	9		11	2			3			10	5				30
1		4		6	7	8	9		11	2			3			10	5				31
1		4	5	10	6	7	8		11				3			9		2			32
1		4	5	6	7	8		11					3			10	2	9			33
1		4		6	7	8		11		5			3			10	2	9			34
1		4	5	6	7	8		11					3			10	2	9			35
		4	5	10	6	7	8		11				3			9		2	1		36
		4		7	6		8	11		5			3			10	2	9		1	37
		4		7	6		8	11		5			3			10	2	9		1	38
1		4	5	10	6	7	8		11				3			9		2			39
1		4	5		6	7	8	11					3			10	2	9			40
1		4		7	6	8		11		5			3			10	2	9			41
1		4	5	6	7	8		11					3			10	2	9			42
39	1	39	36	29	37	38	36	34	24	37	19	1	28	3	3	25	11	18	1	3	
		2		2	10	7	8	1	6							7	3				

Grimley	Carr	Richardson	McTaff	Atkinson	McPeake	Taylor	Lyon	Roberts S	Russell	McClure	Hope	Wells	Galbraith	Redfern	Roberts PL	Carter	Eaves E	Bowman	Bannerman	Daniels	#
1		2	4	5	6	7	8	9	10				3			11					1
1		2	4	5	6	7	8		9	11			3			10					2
1		2	4	5	6	7	8	9		11			3			10					R
1		3		5	6	7	4	9	8	11				2		10					3
4		4	3	4	4	4	4	3	3	3			3	1		4					
					2											1					

I own-goal

1949-50

Manager: Jack Atkinson

#	Month	Date		Opponent		Score	Scorers	Attendance
1	Aug	20	(h)	Darlington	W	1-0	Shepherd	8,111
2		22	(a)	Hartlepools U	L	0-2		9,738
3		27	(a)	Tranmere R	L	1-2	Carter	14,093
4		31	(h)	Hartlepools U	W	1-0	Roberts	6,225
5	Sep	3	(a)	Halifax T	L	0-3		8,503
6		7	(h)	Stockport C	L	1-3	Yates	6,305
7		10	(h)	Rochdale	L	0-4		5,986
8		14	(a)	Stockport C	W	2-0	McClure, Roberts	10,108
9		17	(a)	Bradford C	L	1-2	Carter (pen)	12,146
10		24	(h)	Chester	D	3-3	Yates 2, Carter	6,417
11	Oct	1	(a)	Southport	W	2-0	Jones, Yates	8,761
12		8	(h)	Crewe A	L	0-2		7,433
13		15	(a)	Barrow	D	1-1	Roberts	6,306
14		22	(h)	Lincoln C	W	1-0	Shepherd	5,626
15		29	(a)	Rotherham U	L	0-3		10,492
16	Nov	5	(h)	Carlisle U	W	3-2	Yates 3	4,978
17		12	(a)	Mansfield T	D	2-2	Yates 2	11,419
18		19	(h)	Accrington S	W	3-0	Roberts 3	4,661
19	Dec	3	(h)	Oldham A	D	0-0		2,753
20		17	(a)	Darlington	L	1-3	Carter	3,823
21		24	(h)	Tranmere R	D	0-0		9,245
22		26	(h)	Doncaster R	D	2-2	Shepherd, Yates	7,698
23		27	(a)	Doncaster R	D	0-0		23,381
24		31	(h)	Halifax T	D	1-1	Carter	4,729
25	Jan	14	(a)	Rochdale	L	0-4		9,300
26		21	(h)	Bradford C	W	1-0	Shepherd	3,903
27		28	(a)	Wrexham	D	2-2	McTaff, Roberts	6,740
28	Feb	4	(a)	Chester	L	0-2		5,953
29		11	(a)	York C	L	1-2	Jones	5,257
30		18	(h)	Southport	W	1-0	Jones	5,583
31		25	(a)	Accrington S	L	0-3		3,969
32	Mar	4	(h)	Wrexham	W	3-1	Roberts, Shepherd, Carter	4,500
33		11	(a)	Lincoln C	W	2-1	Shepherd 2	10,160
34		18	(h)	Rotherham U	L	0-3		4,229
35		25	(a)	Carlisle U	D	0-0		8,451
36	Apr	1	(h)	Mansfield T	L	1-2	Yates	4,122
37		7	(h)	Gateshead	L	0-1		6,095
38		8	(a)	Crewe A	W	2-1	Roberts 2	7,624
39		10	(a)	Gateshead	L	1-2	Jones	9,172
40		15	(h)	Barrow	W	2-0	Roberts, Yates	3,495
41		22	(a)	Oldham A	L	0-3		11,179
42	May	6	(h)	York C	W	3-1	Yates, Roberts, Shepherd	2,512

FINAL LEAGUE POSITION: 14th in Division Three North

Appearances
Goals

FA Cup

#	Month	Date		Opponent		Score	Scorers	Attendance
1	Nov	26	(a)	Doncaster R	L	1-5	Carter	13,287

Appearances
Goals

252

Football appearance / line-up grid. Column headers (left to right) are player surnames; the right-hand column is the match number. Totals are given at the foot of the grid.

Grimley	Barton	Galbraith	McTaff	Lees	McPeake	Shepherd	Jones	Yates	Carter	McClure	Atkinson	Richardson	Taylor	Roberts	Williams RF	Eaves E	Redfern	Mortimer	Stirland	Hope	Bannerman	Fitzpatrick PP	
1	2	3	4	5	6	7	8	9	10	11													1
1	2	3	4	5	6	7	8	9	10	11													2
1		3	4	2	6	7	8	9	10	11	5												3
1		3	4	5	6		8	9	11			2	7	10									4
1		3	4	5	6	9	8		11			2	7	10									5
	2	3	4	5	6			9	10	11			7	8	1								6
1	2	3	4	5	6				11	10			7	8		9							7
1	2	3	4	5				9	11	10			7	8			6						8
1	2	3	4	5				9	10	11			7	8			6						9
1	2	3	4	5				9	10	11			7	8			6						10
1		3	4	2	6	11	8	9	10		5		7										11
1		3	4	2	6	11	8	9	10		5		7										12
1	2	3	4			7	8	9	11		5			10			6						13
1	2	3	4			7	8	9	11		5			10			6						14
1	2	3	4			7	8	9	11		5			10			6						15
1	6	3	4	2			8	9	11		5		7	10									16
1	6	3	4	2			8	9	11		5		7	10									17
1	6	3	4	2			8	9	11		5		7	10									18
1	2	3	4	5	6		8	9	11				7	10									19
1	2	3	4	5	6		8	9	11				7	10									20
1	6	3	4	2			8	9	11		5		7	10									21
1	6	3	4	2		11	8	9	10		5		7										22
1	6	3	4	2			8	9	11		5		7	10									23
1	2	3	4	5	6	11	7	9	10					8									24
1	6	3		2	11	7	8	9			5			10				4					25
1	2	3	4			11	8	9	10		5			7					6				26
1	2	3	4			11	8	9	10		5			7					6				27
1	2	3	4			11	8	9	10		5			7					6				28
1	2	3				11	8	9	10		5			7				4	6				29
1	2	3	4			11	8	9	10		5			7					6				30
1		3	4	2		11	8		10		5			9					6	7			31
1		3	4	2		11	8	9	10		5			7					6				32
1	2	3	4			11	8	9	10		5			7					6				33
1	2	3	4			11	8	9	10		5			7					6				34
1	2	3	4				8	9	10					7					6	5	11		35
1	2	3	4				8	9	10					7					6	5	11		36
1	2	3	4				8	9	10		5			7					6		11		37
1	6	3	4	5			8	9	11					10					2	7			38
1	6		4	5			8	9	11			3		10					2	7			39
1	6	3	4	5			8	9	11					10				2		7			40
1	6	3		5			8		11					9		4		2			7	10	41
1	6	3	4			7	8	9	11					10				2		5			42
41	35	41	39	28	13	22	37	38	41	8	23	3	17	35	1	2	6	4	14	5	8	1	
			1				8	4	13	6	1			12									

Grimley	Barton	Galbraith	McTaff	Lees	McPeake	Shepherd	Jones	Yates	Carter	McClure	Atkinson	Richardson	Taylor	Roberts	Williams RF	Eaves E	Redfern	Mortimer	Stirland	Hope	Bannerman	Fitzpatrick PP	
1	6	3	4	2			8	9	11		5		7	10									1
1	1	1	1	1			1	1	1		1		1	1									
									1														

1950-51

Manager: Walter Galbraith

1	Aug	19	(a)	Halifax T	W 2-0	Carter, Roberts	7,680
2		22	(h)	Southport	W 1-0	Jones	8,114
3		26	(h)	Hartlepools U	W 1-0	Jones	6,079
4		29	(a)	Southport	W 1-0	Bannerman	8,938
5	Sep	2	(a)	Gateshead	L 0-4		14,037
6		5	(h)	Darlington	D 2-2	Musgrave, Carter	6,536
7		9	(h)	Crewe A	L 0-2		6,582
8		13	(a)	Darlington	L 3-5	Roberts 2 (1 pen), Musgrave	6,278
9		16	(h)	Tranmere R	D 1-1	Yates	8,847
10		23	(a)	Bradford C	L 0-3		14,395
11		30	(h)	Rochdale	L 1-5	Carter	4,852
12	Oct	7	(h)	Rotherham U	L 2-4	Bannerman, Carter	4,419
13		14	(a)	Mansfield T	L 0-4		10,464
14		21	(h)	York C	D 0-0		3,839
15		28	(a)	Barrow	D 1-1	Forbes (og)	5,683
16	Nov	4	(h)	Accrington S	D 1-1	Bannerman	3,455
17		11	(a)	Carlisle U	L 0-1		12,629
18		18	(h)	Scunthorpe U	L 1-2	Roberts	3,060
19	Dec	2	(h)	Oldham A	W 2-0	Shepherd 2	3,280
20		16	(h)	Halifax T	W 1-0	Carter	2,124
21		23	(a)	Hartlepools U	W 1-0	Roberts	4,520
22		25	(h)	Stockport C	W 1-0	Carter	4,153
23		26	(a)	Stockport C	L 0-4		12,588
24	Jan	6	(h)	Lincoln C	L 0-1		2,256
25		13	(a)	Crewe A	L 0-2		4,629
26		20	(a)	Tranmere R	L 3-4	McDonald (og), L J Saunders 2	12,253
27		27	(a)	Lincoln C	L 0-3		11,332
28	Feb	3	(h)	Bradford C	L 0-6		3,590
29		10	(h)	Shrewsbury T	D 0-0		3,827
30		17	(a)	Rochdale	L 0-1		3,689
31		24	(a)	Rotherham U	L 0-5		13,386
32	Mar	3	(h)	Mansfield T	L 0-1		3,347
33		10	(a)	York C	L 0-2		6,386
34		17	(h)	Barrow	L 1-2	Galbraith	1,922
35		24	(a)	Accrington S	D 1-1	Jones	3,495
36		31	(h)	Carlisle U	L 0-1		2,668
37	Apr	4	(h)	Gateshead	L 0-1		2,273
38		7	(a)	Scunthorpe U	L 0-6		8,588
39		11	(a)	Bradford	L 1-2	Finlay	5,227
40		14	(h)	Wrexham	W 3-0	Jones 3	2,563
41		18	(a)	Wrexham	W 1-0	Finlay	4,924
42		21	(a)	Oldham A	L 1-3	Ball (og)	9,827
43		25	(a)	Chester	L 1-3	Jones	3,535
44		28	(h)	Bradford	D 3-3	Barton, Heggie 2	2,450
45	May	2	(h)	Chester	W 1-0	Heggie	2,421
46		5	(a)	Shrewsbury T	L 2-4	Heggie 2	7,320

FINAL LEAGUE POSITION: 24th in Division Three North

Appearances
Goals

FA Cup

1	Nov	25	(a)	Port Vale	L 2-3	Carter 2	9,100

Appearances
Goals

254

Grimley	Lamont	Galbraith	Stirland	Lees	Barton L	Bannerman	Jones J	Roberts	Carter	Alldis	Musgrave	Shepherd	Yates	McTaff	Friel	Jones JA	Mortimer	Richardson	Saunders LJ	Turner AS	Finlay	Heggie	Guild	Cochrane	Eaves	
1	2	3	4	5	6	7	8	9	10	11																1
1	2	3	4	5	6	7	8	9	10	11																2
1	2	3	4	5	6	7	8	9	10	11																3
1	2	3	4	5	6	7	8	9	10	11																4
1	2	3	4	5		7	8	9	10	6	11															5
1	2	3	4	5	6		8	9	10		11	7														6
1	2	3	4	5	6		8	7	10		11		9													7
1	2			5	3	7	6	8			11		9	4	10											8
	2	3		5		7		8		6	11		9	4	10	1										9
	2	3		5		7		8		6	11		9	4	10	1										10
	2	3	6	5		7	8	9	10		11			4		1										11
	2	3	6	5		7	8	9	10		11			4		1										12
1		3		5	6	7	8		10		11		9	4				2								13
1		3	6	5		9	8	7	10		11			4				2								14
1		3	6	5		9	8	7	10		11			4				2								15
1		3		5	6	9	8	7	10		11			4				2								16
1		3		5	6	9	8	7	10		11			4				2								17
1		3	4	5	6	9	8	7	10		11							2								18
		3	6	5			8	9	10		11	7		4		1		2								19
		3	6	5			8	9	10		11	7		4		1		2								20
		3	6	5			8	9	10		11	7		4		1		2								21
		3	6	5			8	9	10		11	7		4		1		2								22
		3	6	5		7	8	9			11			4		1		2						10		23
		6	5	2			8	9	10		11	7		4		1		3								24
		3	6	5		7	8	9	10		11			4		1		2								25
		3	6	5		7	8		10		11			4		1		2	9							26
	3		6	5		7	8		10		11			4		1		2	9							27
	3		6	5			8	7	10	4	11					1		2	9							28
		6	5	2	7	8			10		11			4		1		3	9							29
	3	6	5	2	7	8			10		11			4		1					9					30
		3	4	5	6	9	8		10	11		7				1		2								31
	2	3	4	5	6	9	8		10		11						1				7					32
	3	10	5	4			8	9			11					1					7	2	6			33
	3	6	5			9	8		10		11					1					7	2	4			34
	5	3	6	2			8		10		11			4		1				9	7					35
		3	6	5	2		8		10		11			4		1				9	7					36
		3		5	2		8		10	6	11			4		1				9	7					37
		3	6	5	2	7					11	9		4		1				8					10	38
	2	3	6	5	4		8		10		11					1					7	9				39
	2	3	6	5	4		8		10		11					1					7	9				40
	2	3	6	5	4		8		10		11					1					7	9				41
	2	3	6	5	4		8		10		11					1					7	9				42
	2	3	6	5	4		8		10		11					1					7	9				43
	2	3	6	5	4		8				11					1					7	9		10		44
	2	3	6	5	4		8		10		11					1					7	9				45
	2	3		5	6		8		10	4	11					1					7	9				46
14	27	40	37	44	29	26	40	34	39	12	35	8	5	25	3	32	1	17	4	4	15	10	2	2	1	
	1		1	3	7	5	6		2	2	1					2					2	5				

3 own-goals

Grimley	Lamont	Galbraith	Stirland	Lees	Barton L	Bannerman	Jones J	Roberts	Carter	Alldis	Musgrave	Shepherd	Yates	McTaff	Friel	Jones JA	Mortimer	Richardson	Saunders LJ	Turner AS	Finlay	Heggie	Guild	Cochrane	Eaves	
1		3	6	5			8	9	10	11		7		4				2								1
1		1	1	1			1	1	1	1		1		1				1								
								2																		

SUBSCRIBERS

1. The Metropolitan Borough of Wirral
2. The Football League
3. The Football Association
4. Garth Dykes
5. Ann E.Whitchelo
6. Marjorie Litt
7. Alex Wilson (in Memoriam)
8. J A Harris
9. Raymond Shaw
10. John A Pitts
11. A N Other
12. Paul Gilligan
13. Ian Farrell
14. K P Wood
15. John Lathan
16. Derek Hyde
17. Harry Kay
18. Brendan Bates
19. Dave Parine
20. Roberto J Gamble
21. Don Hales
22. David Earnshaw
23. Errick Peterson
24. Peter Lunn
25. R K Shoesmith
26. Douglas Lamming
27. Harald Löhr
28. David A Howgate
29. B H Standish
30. Moira & Frederick Furness
31. Duncan Watt
32. Gilbert Upton
33. D T Bryant
34. L Burgess
35. Sports Marketing (Australia)
36. Brian H Hobbs
37. Ian Willott
38. Chris Minchin
39. Gordon Small
40. David Downs
41. Angus W Rodger
42. Colin Cameron
43. Michael Tubb
44. Michael Cheadle
45. Paul H Bannister
46. Julian Mann
47. Donald Ashwood
48. J Ringrose
49. Douglas Bidgood
50. David J Godfrey
51. Lars-Olof Wendler
52. John Treleven
53. J Mulrennan
54. P Marks
55. David Keats
56. J D M Whitaker
57. Tony Sheldon
58. David Marsh
59. Kevin C Wyatt
60. Jim Lakin
61. Paul Vibert
62. Christer Svensson
63. Richard D N Wells
64. Barry Watson
65. Keith Coburn
66. Roger Hudson
67. W D Phillips
68. Maurice Curtin
69. Roger Wash
70. Gilbert Monnereau
71. Diamant Yosef
72. Geir Juva
73. Richard Quinn
74. Harry Thompson
75. Fred Lee
76. Mark Fowler
77. George Bordessa
78. Philip Scoble
79. J Gardiner
80. Tony Musker
81. Trond Isaksen
82. Malcolm Barber
83. M F Tuohey
84. Raymond A Kelly
85. I Watts
86. T D Culshaw
87. Alan Davies
88. Brian J Tuohey
89. John van den Elsen
90. Jeffrey J Page
91. J S Pyke
92. C J Morton
93. Terry Frost
94. Gary James — 'The Blue'
95. David Gregg
96. Karen Jones
97. Dave Harrison
98. L A Zammit
99. Gerald Henry Voas
100. Stephen Chaloner
101. Brian Tabner
102. Stephen Charles Handley
103. David Coulson
104. Alan F Lynch
105. Mike Jackman
106. George Humphreys
107. Theodore Mantzouranis
108. Paul Jones
109. F Beale
110. Paul Jerome
111. B R Phillips
112. Dave Hillam
113. Alan Wheatley
114. B R Butler
115. Eric Heesom
116. Michael Joyce
117. Jon Robinson
118. Mike Purkiss
119. Andrew Anderson
120. Stanley A Robinson
121. Alan Hindley
122. Jim Walker
123. M R Pearce
124. Geoffrey Wright
125. Tony Bluff
126. Filippo Rossi
127. Dave Green
128. Mervyn Powell
129. David S Allen
130. Richard Stocken
131. Norman Green
132. A N Davis
133. David Pease
134. Peter Pickup
135. Andrew Whittle
136. Walter Harby
137. J Buitenga
138. Gerald Hill
139. Kostas Fotopoulos
140. Tasos Botsis
141. Ian Griffiths
142. Surapot Saengchote
143. Peter Overton
144. Geoff Allman
145. S P Tomlin
146. A H Atkins
147. A Young
148. M Swart
149. P W Stevenson
150. Q C M Olsthoorn
151. Guy Lovelady
152. G D Painter
153. Tonny Otten
154. R G Woolman
155. R W Lane
156. Simons Martin
157. David Lumb
158. Mario Sirriani
159. David Helliwell
160. Graham P Oglesby
161. Alison Whitchelo
162. Peter Windle
163. Ted Redfern
164. Michael Swaffield
165. Better Sox Ltd
166. Harry & Paul Gee
167. Jonathan Hall
168. J F Burrell
169. Terry Porter
170. Matt McPeake
171. Andrew William Costain
172. Richard Albert Parry
173. David Crawford
174. John Hagan
175. N Whitehead
176. Mr & Mrs David Ross
177. G C Clayton
178. Ernest Longden
179. Paul Gale
180. David Philip O'Reilly
181. Billy Dobbs
182. Frank Hilton
183. Kenneth John Hilton
184. Robert Nelson
185. William Ryan
186. John W Farrant
187. John Hill
188. Noël E Smith
189. Peter Ridgway
190. James Innes
191. Raymond Hughes
192. Paul Frank Davies
193. Jeremy B Brewer
194. A Foster
195. T R Jones
196. F Stott
197. Robert Alfred Hughes
198. R V Calmels
199. Robert M Pickstone
200. George Kenneth Carroll
201. Carl Stonall
202. M O'Brien
203. M O'Brien
204. M O'Brien
205. Tom Sault
206. Ian Runham
207. Hugh G Lloyd
208. George A Higham
209. Esa Kautonen
210. E A Carr
211. W Mark Lloyd
212. Michael R Patterson
213. N S Evison
214. E J Gates
215. Ronald Finney
216. William J Gibson
217. Tony Jones
218. David Jeffrey Bartley
219. T McKee
220. Ted Wilson
221. C R Scammell
222. David Lawrence Kellner
223. W P Colebourne
224. T A Smith
225. J M Johnson
226. J W Irvine
227. Mark Vaos
228. Ken Edgar
229. Adam J Huby
230. C Davies
231. Basil A Thomson
232. Eric Davies
233. P S Basnett
234. J A Evans
235. E M Briggs